TOMORROW'S TIDE

Malcolm Ross

PIATKUS

First published in Great Britain in 1996 by
Judy Piatkus (Publishers) Ltd of
5 Windmill Street, London W1

ISBN 0 – 7499 – 0326-0

Typeset by the author using Spellbinder™ DTP
Glyphix™ Times fonts and a
Hewlett-Packard™ Laserjet 4MPlus printer

Printed and bound in Great Britain by
Mackays of Chatham PLC, Chatham, Kent

for

Oscar Lafferty

facile princeps

Contents

Part One

Helston Workhouse

Growing up in Godolphin

1 SHE HEARD laughter, a baby's laugh, from beyond the hedge somewhere. It was small and gurgly — the way babies laugh to themselves when they're all alone with a joke not even another baby could share. When grown-ups are around they laugh quite differently. Jennifer, being so much older than her brothers and sisters, knew every kind of baby's laugh there was. She stopped and listened, right there at the bend in the lane where the stream passed through the cundard under the road. Sometimes a bantam hen could make a noise like that, enough to deceive you until you listened hard.

The stream gurgled. The baby laughed again. And this time there was no doubting it. That was a baby's laugh if ever she heard one — and she'd heard plenty, having two brothers and two sisters, all younger. In fact, the laugh she had just heard could easily have come from her latest little brother, Colin — except that she'd seen Mrs Harvey tuck him up in his bassinet, not ten minutes ago.

She moved swiftly and quietly along the hedge, a dozen paces or so to the bend in the road. There a narrow, leafy lane meandered up to the crown of Godolphin Hill. TRESPASSERS WILL BE PROSECUTED at the end. Right at the start of this lane a pair of gates gave access to the fields that flanked it on each side. To the left was a single sty with a grumpy old boar who could break a child's leg off with a single chomp of his jaws. And gobble it down in three more. She could hear him now, fast asleep in the sun, sighing with boredom every now and then.

In the field to the right, where the baby's laugh had come from, were four empty sties. Because Willy Meagor said there was no money in pigs this year, but Daddy said he was too lazy. Anyway, the sties were empty — except, it now seemed, for this laughing baby.

It laughed again, a laugh that ended in a hiccup and then turned to crying. Jennifer peeped through the bars of the gate, waiting to see would the mother tend to it. She was an authority on all kinds of crying, too. This wasn't the full-throated howl that compelled immediate attendance. It was more of an experimental sort of cry, as if to say, 'Do I really feel like doing this? Well, let's give it a try and see if anything happens.'

When nothing happened, it began laughing again. Daddy said all babies were slightly mad. No one would tolerate grown-ups who behaved like them.

She looked around the field, a long, narrow triangle of grazed meadow that flanked the road as far as the spring, which gushed out of the hillside back near the village. She could see every part of it except the insides of the sties and the bit of field that lay immediately beyond. If there was such a thing as a mother there, she must be lying down inside a sty or behind the far wall.

"I say!" Jennifer called out. Then, "Hallo — anyone there?"

The baby was briefly silent and then began babbling, "Blullum-blala-bloem ..." It must be in the farthermost sty. Or just outside, in the shadow of the wall.

Lucky there were no sows there. Even a sow could eat a baby. Sometimes they ate their own babies. And Mary Foster said once in a whisper that Cathy Carney got rid of her baby that way.

The sudden thought that some other delinquent mother might have left this baby here for the identical purpose filled Jennifer with alarm.

"No!" she cried aloud and, heedless of what animals might or might not be at liberty in the field, she scaled the gate and leaped down on the other side, skirts flying.

The baby was not in any of the sties but was lying in the grass, neatly swaddled, in the shade of the farthermost wall. Its clothes were clean and of good quality. It was chubby, well fed and cared for, and had a bonny colour to its cheeks. It fixed its eyes upon her and, aiming a single bent finger more or less in her direction, burst into laughter.

"D'you need changing?" she asked hopefully.

It didn't, fortunately; but, in ascertaining the fact, she also discovered that *it* was a he.

"Which way did your mammy go?" she asked next.

He crooked his finger still further and swung his arm away to his right, toward the top of the hill. The movement attracted his attention and his eyes followed his hand all the way down to the grass.

I've ceased to exist now, Jennifer thought. Daddy said it took a baby a long time to learn that things went on being there even when it wasn't actually looking at them. It must be wonderful to discover something exciting, then look away, forget it, then look back — and discover it all over again. Daddy also said that a philosopher called Berkeley proved that babies were right — things *did* stop existing when there was no one to observe them.

The baby was watching his own hand opening and closing like a sea anemone. With his ear to the ground like that he also appeared to be listening intently.

"You won't hear any miners working down there any more, little man," she told him.

She could only just recall it herself when, at the age of three or four, Mrs Harvey had made her put her ear to the scratching stone in Josie Mollard's field, near Carleen, just before the appointed hour for dynamiting down in the stopes. That was very loud, of course, but she'd also heard them drilling down there. The ring of hammer on steel was like fairy music. It was eery to look around the wide, smiling fields and to think of men standing up in vast caverns down there, underneath hundreds of feet of rock. Now it was all silent, however, and those same men had vanished over the seas and far away.

"Where's your mammy?" she asked.

He sought the face that made the voice, discovered it all over again, and laughed afresh.

"Aren't you bonny!" She held out a finger for him to grab.

His grip was intense. His stare became fixed. He shivered slightly.

She realized he was doing a pu-pu in his nappy. Moments later her nostrils confirmed her guess. "Oh dear!" she sighed happily and lifted his skirts to unpin him. "Hallo, what's this?"

The nappy was held by a curious sort of brooch — a penny that someone had soldered onto a common or garden brooch pin. She undid it and, though curious to inspect it, slipped it instead into her pinafore pocket. First things first.

The pu-pu was quite hard, wrinkled like a sheep's. It had not marked the nappy at all.

"No more?" she asked.

He kicked his legs vigorously, relishing their sudden freedom.

"No wee-wee? Wee-wee-wee-wee?" She touched his floppy little tail to encourage him.

He just went on kicking, and grinning to show little nacreous teeth emerging from their gums.

"Don't go away," she said. "Jenny's coming back."

She carried the nappy to the hedge and threw the stool over into the lane. It had already attracted a small swarm of bluebottles and horseflies. She wiped the cloth perfunctorily in the grass and returned to find a horsefly busy feeding on the baby's calf. With the rolled-up nappy she swatted it to the ground and then crushed it with the toe of her boot.

He started to cry but stopped again when she gripped both his ankles in her left hand and lifted his botty to slip the nappy beneath him again. His calm eyes watched her.

"What's your name?" she asked. "You're old enough to have a name, I'm sure. Tommy? Charley? George? No, you can't possibly call a *baby* George. All Georges have red faces and beards. Frank? Frankie?" As she uttered each name she watched him for signs of recognition — in vain, as it turned out.

"I shall call you Moses, then," she said at last. "That's an honour, you know. Moses was just a little foundling, too. And now he's got a whole book in the Bible, all to himself. So all you need do, if you want to follow suit, is find a people to lead, and get some other people to chase you …"

The little joke was veering toward blasphemy, she realized. "Never mind," she said. "Let's get this nappy pinned up, eh? I'll bet you're much more interested in that. I wish I had some talcum, that's all."

She held his legs down to stop his kicking. The corners of his mouth dropped menacingly. To distract him she put her lips to his tummy and blew a raspberry on the taut drumskin of his belly. A deep, gurgling laugh rewarded her. She did it again. The laughter rose in pitch and took on overtones of a delighted scream.

"This will end in tears," she warned herself, and did it again.

More screaming laughter.

Surreptitiously she gathered the three corners of the nappy together and fished the brooch from her pinny pocket. She paused while she examined it more closely. Perhaps there was a name engraved on it somewhere. Someone told her once that you could go to gaol for defacing the coin of the realm like this. You could do it to foreign coinage, of course, but not to His Imperial Majesty's money.

Or *Her* Imperial Majesty's in this case. The penny was one from the reign of the late Queen Victoria — not the very late one, though, where she looked like the Rock of Gibraltar, but the early one, where she had her hair in a bun, and ribbons, like a girl going out to a ball. It said 1854.

There was no name engraved on it, nor on the brooch part of the pin.

She secured the three corners of the nappy and just got in another raspberry before he could cry again.

"Where *is* your mammy?" she asked anxiously over his renewed laughter. "You're a very careless little boy, Moses, to have gone and lost her like this. You know that? Yes you are! Yes you are!"

To distract him from the raspberry game she plucked a stalk of grass, the one she called 'tickly brown caterpillar,' and brushed it deftly over his lips and under his chin.

"The babies that people leave in fields, you know, aren't chubby, bonny little things like you — with your lovely clothes and all. They're little piggy-widdens at death's door. Which way did your mammy go? Did you see her?"

Moses sneezed and began to cry at last, this time in earnest.

She picked him up and, rocking him like one of her dolls, carried him off into the shade of an oak tree that grew out of the hedge a little way uphill from the sties.

"It's the sun in your eyes, isn't it. Now you'll feel better."

She rocked him steadily and sang *Hush-a-bye baby on the treetop* … until his crying stopped. Moments later he was fast asleep.

Such trusting natures they had! How did he know she wouldn't just drop him and run away? How did he know she'd sooner die than do such a thing? But *why* would she sooner die than do that? How long since she discovered him lying there? Ten minutes? Fifteen? What mysterious forces now compelled her to care for him — and allowed him to fall asleep so trustingly in her arms?

Pondering these mysteries she sauntered up and down in the shade of the hedge, putting her own body between his eyes and the sun where the shade was sparse and telling him by telepathy how right he was to trust her so utterly.

"If your mother doesn't return," she told him, "I'll take you home and bring you up myself. I'm sure one more won't make any difference. We get a new one every three years, anyway, so all it means is that you're a little early."

The sound of her voice, babbling on and on, seemed to soothe him as much as her lullaby. Nothing disturbed his slumber except for an occasional extra-deep breath, which he exhaled with that lovely, shivery sigh which babies make, each one of which was a new Cupid's arrow to her heart. By the time they had strolled to the top of the field and back down again to the gate, Jennifer was as in love with Moses as any young girl of fourteen could be.

2 GORONWY OWEN, about to kill a greenfly with a little jab of the Flit spray, was distracted by a movement beyond the leaf on which it was preying. Her eyes refocused and the white blur resolved itself into the figure of her eldest daughter, Jennifer, sauntering up the lane toward her. She was carrying Crotchety Ann, her biggest doll. A weary vexation filled her. How many times had she told the girl *not* to take that doll — any of her dolls — out into the fields, not even on a dry, sunny day like

this? But especially not Crotchety Ann. Her Aunt Myfanwy would have an apoplexy if she saw it. "A hundred and twenty-three hours of work I put into that doll ..." She could just hear her going on.

She poked the spray-gun into the gap among the leaves and drew the whole branch aside. "How many times have I told you ..." she began. Then the words dwindled away — or, rather, turned into: "What on *earth* is that you're holding?"

"I couldn't just leave him there, Mummy." Jennifer, halted for a moment by her surprise, now hastened forward, eager to show off her little trophy. "He was lying there all alone. No one to look after him. No mother, not anywhere. I looked. I called ..."

"Whoa!" her mother called out. "Stop where you are — don't you take another pace."

The girl went on explaining what she had done while Goronwy crouched low and forced her way through the snowberry thicket that formed a hedge with the lane at that point in her garden. By the time she emerged, Jennifer was holding Moses tilted up for her to inspect. "Isn't he sweet?" she said hopefully.

Goronwy surveyed him with distaste. "No," she said, "not really. Now start again from the beginning. You say you *found* him?"

Jennifer started to explain.

"By the empty sties?" her mother interrupted. "But ... I mean ... one simply doesn't *find* babies — especially not well-cared-for babies like that — one doesn't just find them lying about in fields with no one around. You only need to take one look at it to know ..."

"Him."

"... to know it — he's no foundling. There must have been a mother somewhere near by."

"Well, there wasn't, honestly. We looked and looked — everywhere. Didn't we, Moses?"

"How d'you know his name if ... oh, I see!" Goronwy sighed. "Well, you're not the pharaoh's daughter, Jennifer — let me assure you of that! Little Moses is going straight back where he came from."

Her daughter stared at her, aghast. "We can't just leave him to die of exposure, like the Spartans."

She had done the Spartans in school last term.

"Aargh!" Goronwy choked off a scream of frustration and peeled away her gardening gloves, which she laid like crossed heraldic gauntlets on the spray-gun at the foot of the hedge. "The first perfect gardening day for weeks — and you have to go and find a baby of all things!"

"I didn't set *out* to find a baby, honestly. But what could I do? I couldn't just walk on and leave him ..."

"There *must* have been a mother there. You just didn't look."

"I did. I did! We looked and called. And hunted for tracks in the grass and everything — didn't we, Moses?"

"She could be drunk. Or she could have had a fit. Or a stroke. Or she might be diabetic ..."

"Come and see for yourself. There is honestly no one there — honestly and really and truly."

Goronwy gazed reluctantly at the spray-gun, at the clear blue heavens, at her garden, full of fluttering green leaves, all under threat from greenfly, blackfly, whitefly ... flies of every hue and all the more insidious for being invisible from where she stood. "Oh ... botheration!" she exclaimed. "You'd better leave the baby here for Mrs Harvey to tend."

Jennifer clutched Moses more tightly to her but said nothing.

"No, I suppose not," her mother concluded with another sigh. "The mother's bound to be there. Going frantic with worry, no doubt. Very well, then. Let's get it over with. Oh, you are a *pest!*"

Half an hour later, having searched along every foot of hedgerow in all the fields around the empty sties, she was forced to concede that her daughter had been right all along. Moses — and now she conceded, too, that the name was apt — had, indeed, been abandoned where Jennifer had found him. If the mother had just laid him there to obey a call of nature, she'd hardly have gone more than ten paces away, to the shelter of the nearest hedge, or just into one of the empty sties. So, if she were lying unconscious somewhere, it would certainly be near by. The only other kind of involuntary absence would be if someone had come along and carried her off. But in broad daylight? Not half a mile from a busy village like Godolphin — and less than a mile from the even busier village of Carleen — and no road that did not pass through one or other of them? It was more likely that she'd grown wings and flown.

So the most believable conclusion by far was that the mother had, indeed, abandoned the baby there and quietly gone her ways.

Or pitched herself down the nearest mineshaft.

This dire thought set Goronwy's mind off on a new trail. Where was the nearest shaft, anyway?

She turned and stared west, toward Poladras. There were some out there, she remembered. They'd be nearest. But there was too much thorn and furze between them and the road. There must be easier ones, even if they were a little farther away. Up at Balwest? Or Deepwork? Or

Great Wheal Vor? They'd all be accessible across the fields at the end of the lane that ran up the hill from the sties. And she'd pass no houses on the way — whereas, if she took the other lane outside Carleen, she'd have to pass a couple of dozen cottages and hovels, where people would surely have seen her, spoken to her, and later remembered her.

A feeling of doomed certainty was stealing over Goronwy, the more she considered all the possibilities. But she said nothing to Jennifer, of course. Later, when they'd dealt with the problem of the baby, she'd send her husband up the lane to look for tracks. The lower part was too dry but there was a stretch about half-way up where it was always muddy.

She smiled at her daughter and said, "Your mother owes you a profound apology, darling — only you must agree that it is a preposterous-sounding tale — a well-clothed baby just lying abandoned in a field like that, and no mother in sight."

They turned their faces homeward. "What d'you think has become of her?" Jennifer asked.

"Shall I take him, dear? Your arms must be dropping off by now."

The girl clutched the baby more tightly to her breast.

"Please?" Goronwy insisted. She knew she had to wean her daughter from her treasure trove before she started getting absurd ideas of keeping it.

Reluctantly Jennifer yielded, but she stayed close to her mother's side as they started for home, patting and rearranging the baby's clothes from time to time. "I wonder what happened to his mother?" she repeated as they set off.

"Who knows?" Goronwy replied vaguely. "A woman must be in a dreadful state of mind to abandon such a bonny baby as this. He's certainly been loved and cared for until now. Perhaps she wasn't married and couldn't face the disgrace of it any longer."

She smiled to see how embarrassed Jennifer was at this suggestion. "You're getting to be a big girl now, dear," she went on gently. "It's high time you knew such things. We don't talk about them often, not openly, but they happen. And they're much more common than you might think. Just don't ever let it happen to you, that's all."

"How?" Jennifer swallowed heavily and wondered why her heart was racing so.

"All in good time. I'll tell you all in good time — I promise. For the moment, just be warned by this little drama. Perhaps this little creature's mama couldn't face the disgrace a moment longer, and so she decided to run away and start a new life somewhere where nobody knew her shameful secret. Perhaps she waited there at the corner until she saw you coming. And you'd be ideal, too, because a grown woman would just pick the baby up and go looking at once for its mother. But a girl your age would be much more likely to sit down and play with it and only slowly begin to wonder where its mama was — which, indeed, was exactly was happened, wasn't it! So she left the baby there and hid herself just long enough to be sure you'd noticed it and then, while you got all excited and broody about it, she slipped off to begin her new life … somewhere else."

"I'd have seen her," the girl protested; then, hearing how unconvincing she sounded, added, "I'm sure."

"Not if she'd gone quietly up the lane and then across the fields at the top. You'd have to be standing on the brow of Trigonning Hill to see anyone up there. I expect that's what she did. I'm sure if we'd gone right up the lane just now, we should have seen her footprints in that bit where it's always muddy. In fact, I think I'll ask your father to go and see if I'm right, later today, when he's finished his round."

Jennifer considered this theory, which, coming as it did from her mother, carried more conviction than it would if she had thought it up herself. She decided that that must be what had happened. Anyway, she'd never think up a more likely tale by herself. "It must be awful for her," she said at last. "To be so miserable that your only way out is to give up such a lovely little fellow."

"Mmm." Goronwy wondered whether it would be overdoing things if she were to repeat her warning on the perils of conceiving out of wedlock … and decided it would be. In any case, her daughter's next words seized all her attention.

"Still … it's an ill wind and all that."

"Oh?" her mother asked sharply.

"Yes. Her sad loss is our happy gain."

"Oh … no!" Goronwy said in a long-drawn-out laugh — not, however, of a humorous kind, more the kind that promises implacable opposition. "Put any such thought completely out of your mind."

"What then?" Jennifer was devastated. "We can't just" — she looked back over her shoulder, to the bend by the sties, which was just passing out of view — "put him back there."

"No, not that, either," her mother said. "What usually happens to orphans, dear? Think!"

"But he's not an orphan."

"As good as. Or 'as bad as' would be more appropriate in the circumstances, I suppose."

"But he's got *us*. Oh, can't we keep him? Please?" When she used that particular wheedling tone it showed she already knew she was on the losing side. "Ple-e-ease?" she repeated.

Goronwy was careful not to crow. "It'll be best for him, darling, and as for us, don't you think we have quite enough mouths to feed already?"

Jennifer *was* growing up, though, her mother now realized. As little as a month ago she'd have accepted this as final. Not now, however. "Oh please," she repeated. "I'll look after him. I'll do everything. And he can share *my* food and I'll wash him and mend his clothes and ..." Her voice trailed off as, with each new promise, she saw her mother's face set more firmly in rejection. "You're horrid!" she cried, stamping her foot and halting in the middle of the road.

Goronwy did not even falter. "Come on, dear," she replied mildly. "It'll be a nine-day wonder. You can feed him and change him and then we'll take him down to PC Riddick."

3 THE RESCUE of the infant Moses was, as Goronwy had predicted, something of a nine-day wonder. They carried him home, fed him some pap, bathed him, put him in a clean nappy, and then Martha Walker, the housemaid, took him in her arms and boarded the horse bus to Helston. There she carried him to the orphanage attached to the workhouse up in Meneage Street. On her return, Goronwy asked her if all had gone well and she replied that yes, indeed, it had all gone very well. And that was that. Jennifer moped about the place for a day or two, getting on her mother's nerves until, in desperation, she promised to take her daughter in to see how Moses was getting on — "Not now but later, dear. In a few months' time, when he's had a chance to settle in."

But when 'later' came around, that autumn of 1910, Jennifer felt an odd reluctance to take up the offer — a compound of guilt and growing up. A few months may pass in the twinkling of an eye to a grown woman with five young children and a doctor's household to manage, but to a girl of fourteen they can be an eternity; and the events of early summer, seen from the perspective of mid-autumn, might as well have happened in another life, or in a dream.

One day, toward the end of September — just over three months after Moses had been delivered to the orphanage — all the Owen children were taken to Helston for the annual new-shoes ritual. For Hector, who was nine, Flora, six, and June, three, it was, in fact, a semi-annual ritual, for they had already outgrown the shoes that had been new in the spring. And Colin, who would be a year old that very week, was to have his first soft-leather lace-ups. Goronwy wanted to buy them all 'with plenty of room for growth' and pack them with bits of bath sponge but Bevis wouldn't allow that. He said it invited foot sores and diseases and he had many examples from his practice to prove it. So new, well-fitting shoes it had to be.

As a kind of test, when they were all proudly wearing their new shoes, Goronwy led them up Meneage Street to a tearoom almost opposite the orphanage. They took a window seat and she arranged them such that Jennifer was facing the street. Not a word was said − not about Moses and the orphanage, anyway. Toward the end of their tea a short crocodile of young orphan boys emerged and marched down to the centre of town, probably to get their fortnightly 'convict's crop' from the barber.

"A penny a nob," Goronwy murmured, keeping a sidelong watch for her daughter's response.

No emotion showed on Jennifer's face but she watched the little file go by with profound dismay. *That's what I condemned him to,* she told herself. But when she wondered what else she might have done, the conscience that condemned her so loudly fell to silence.

She considered asking her mother to honour her promise there and then. It would be so easy just to cross the road. And, what with all the family being there, too, they needn't stay more than a minute or so. But the thought of entering that cheerless building and staring, even for a minute, at a fifteen-month-old baby, and realizing that in another ten years or so he'd be just one more shaven-headed nobody in that crocodile … was one to shrivel the soul. And so, knowing she would never see him again, she nonetheless promised herself never to forget him − despite the days, and even weeks, during which she had blithely forgotten him during the past three months alone.

If he had gone to one of the *nice* orphanages she had read about, like the Bluecoats or the Haberdashers colleges, formed by rich tradesmen to look after their own, it would be so different. She could have visited him there with pleasure, knowing he'd have a future as bright as any. But as for those poor little lads in that crocodile … you only had to look in their eyes to know they were already among the defeated and the downtrodden. They weren't starved or riddled with skin complaints like the orphans in *Oliver Twist,* but the same despondency stared out in their baffled gaze. Her guilt was a poor substitute for the pleasure she might otherwise have felt, but, since she had to feel an emotion of *some* kind, guilt it must be.

Goronwy, now watching her eldest daughter openly, divined something of these silent conflicts in her soul and, fleetingly, regretted she had not done the outrageous and impossible thing and simply kept little Moses. It was not the first time such feelings overcame her, either. During the previous months she had probably remembered the foundling more often than had Jennifer. He was quite the bonniest baby she had ever seen — with the cuckoo's ability to charm any mother away from her own, less charismatic brood. Of course it would have been difficult to keep him, both legally and practically — to say nothing of the social consequences — but it would have been possible. One more mouth to feed among the dozen or so who who daily supped at various tables in her household would hardly have broken the bank. She knew she had done the sensible, practical thing but had it been the truly Christian one? Every sermon she had since heard on the subject of charity and on the difficulty of leading a righteous life had left her conscience decidedly uneasy, too.

That evening, after she had tucked the younger ones up in bed, she went back to the drawing room, where Jennifer was carefully taking some of that summer's flowers out of the press and laying them in fresh tissue. Later, on many a long winter evening, she'd paste them with even greater care into her herbarium. As the eldest child she was allowed to stay up half an hour later than the others.

Bevis was playing chess up at Godolphin Hall, as he did every Wednesday evening from September to May. In summer they played badminton and Goronwy went up there, too.

"We forgot to go and see how little Moses is getting along this afternoon," she said casually as she seated herself at the piano.

"Mmm ..." Jennifer, with much licking of her lips, carefully slid her ivory spatula between a fine specimen of the sea mayweed and the tissue paper against which it had been pressed and dried.

"That's kept its yellow very well." Goronwy opened the lid and flexed her fingers.

"Mary Tyler paints hers with water colour — paints the actual dried flowers, I mean. But they never look right." She screwed the used tissue into a ball and dropped it in the waste basket.

"Nature is far more subtle than we imagine — as your father often says." She sorted idly among Brahms, Chopin, Liszt ... "D'you know what sea mayweed calls itself on Sundays?"

Jennifer smiled and nodded. Her mother always called them 'Sunday' names and 'weekday' names. *"Triplospermum maritima,"* she said proudly, and she wrote it with a very soft pencil on the new bit of tissue before laying it gently in her box file.

Goronwy started on a slow Chopin prelude from memory and, when that failed her, improvised something in the same style. "Did it cross your mind when we were having tea — about going to see how Moses is getting on?" she asked.

Jennifer did not answer directly. Instead she said, "I could have suggested to Martha to adopt him herself. I just didn't think of it. After all, she was getting married soon after. She and ... what was his name?"

"Billy Tregear?"

"Yes. She and Mister Tregear could have had a ready-made family."

"Well, dear ... people rather like to do that sort of thing for themselves." It fascinated Goronwy that the girl had said *"I* could have suggested ..." Not we. So the guilt she felt was hers and hers alone. Her mother had decided to send Moses to the orphanage but the guilt for that decision was still hers. How could one reach such thoughts and pull them out by the roots?

Or snip them off and press them safely away in some moral or emotional herbarium? Perhaps even recolour them with a few deft touches here and there!

"We could have kept him, couldn't we." Jennifer's light, almost inconsequential manner did not deceive Goronwy. She could sense that the girl was holding her breath for an answer. Denials of every kind rose to her lips but all she actually replied was, "Yes ..." in a rather guarded, wary tone.

Jennifer dropped her tweezers in her surprise. She stared at her mother while her hands fumbled automatically for them.

Goronwy stopped playing briefly. "I did think of it, you know," she added. "It may have seemed like an outright rejection to you, but that's only because you were being so insistent. I did actually consider it, though — Lord help us!"

"And why didn't you ... or we ...?"

Goronwy resumed her gentle improvisation. "He was too close in age to Colin. You know how boys fight. Think of poor Mrs Caughtrey and her twins! We'd have had no peace. It'll be bad enough with Colin and Hector one day — and there's all of nine years between them. And then think of Moses, growing up knowing he's not *really* one of us ... and Colin, too, either resenting it when we appear to favour Moses or feeling superior when we don't. Why should we saddle our own little boy with such an extra burden?"

Jennifer set down her work and went to stand beside her mother. She laid a hand on her shoulder so as not to interrupt her playing. "I didn't know," she said.

"You thought I had a heart of stone."

"No!" The girl chuckled at the exaggeration though she was, in fact, close to tears.

"The thing *I* don't know," Goronwy went on, "is, was I right? What d'you think, darling?"

The lump in Jennifer's throat was now too big for her to talk around. She leaned her head against her mother's, relishing the warm earth-smell that rose out of her bodice, and swallowed heavily. Tears trembled in the cisterns of her eyes but she managed to sniff them back.

Goronwy, in whose right ear the sniffs were deafening, winced but said nothing. She slipped her arm around her girl and went on playing the bass alone. "Come on," she murmured. "Play something with your right hand and I'll follow."

4 As THE YEAR turned, the name of baby Moses was less and less mentioned in the Owen household. It was not so much that Jennifer forgot him but, as with any growing girl, there were so many other claims upon her attention.

When her herbarium was within four pages of being filled she lost interest in wild flowers. But then she discovered an even more intense fascination for wild birds. After a year she could name any garden visitor at a hundred paces and identify most of them by their song. By then, though, her interest in birds was waning, too. In its place was an even more absorbing curiosity about young men — not, to be sure, the youths of her own age (God forbid!) but *real* young men, old enough to joust at Cornish wrestling.

Women were never seen at a big, set-piece wrestling match. That was serious business — man's business — where immortal reputations were made and lost. But there were lighter-hearted bouts among mere ordinary mortals; they formed the climax of almost every local festival and pageant, no matter what other attractions each might hold. Jennifer and her school chums became ardent if faithless followers of whichever lesser champion carried the day. And, of course, mere practice bouts of an evening on some bit of common land were open to all onlookers, some being no more than horseplay.

The sight of manly young muscles rippling under weather-tanned skin — muscles grown and hardened at the plough, at the hauling-in of nets, or at drilling through the deep, unyielding granite of some still-working mine — was enough to set Jennifer's heart racing and to stretch her every sinew with the strangest tension. She desperately wanted to talk about it with someone. Indeed, the words were on the tip of her tongue more than once when she was turning her mother's music and they came to the end of a piece. But her very desperation kindled an equal and opposite shyness and, in the end, it was left to Sally Pask to break the silence among them. She was then rising seventeen; Jennifer had just turned sixteen but was sure she looked much older.

"Hasn't he got lovely curly hair," Sally murmured one day.

It was a hot, hazy summer afternoon during their school holidays in 1912 and they were on that patch of common called the Flow, watching the Carleen — Godolphin wrestlers practising for next Saturday's match with Nancegollan. "It simply isn't fair."

She was doubly right, Jennifer thought, for in its colour, too, it certainly wasn't fair, either. In fact, it was dark chestnut with the gold of the sun caught in its myriad tight little curls. She had not been able to lift her eyes from him ever since he had taken the field. He must be new to the district, she decided, for she had never seen him before.

He was about nineteen, tall and loose-limbed, broad in the chest but tapering to a wasplike waist that any woman would envy. His chin was like a pair of knuckles; his cheekbones were high and wide; his dark eyes seemed to smoulder in the depths beneath his beetling brows; and as for his lips … the two girls nearly died when he turned and smiled at them between holds, for he had the most perfect cupid's bow imaginable. Crown him with golden laurel, stand him in the Tuscan sun, and any painter in search of a model for the young Adonis or the young Bacchus would seek no more.

"He smiled at me!" Sally whispered ecstatically.

Jennifer, who knew he had really smiled at *her,* said magnanimously, "He smiled at *us,* actually. Who is he? I don't remember seeing him before. Do you?"

An older girl near by — old enough to be more amused than annoyed at their interest — said, "That's Barry Moore, that is. Champion feller. Don't 'ee know 'un?"

The two youngsters shook their heads, slightly in awe of the speaker, whom they knew vaguely to be one of several daughters of a farmer over Goldsithney way. Although both of them were socially superior to her and could, in other circumstances have taken quite a high tone in any conversation, they knew by instinct that here, on this afternoon, they were planting their first, hesitant footsteps onto a field where higher social standing could be more hindrance than help.

"Does he live in Carleen, then?" Jennifer asked hopefully, adding, "You're Jessie Penhaligon, aren't you?"

"Florence," the girl replied. "Jessie's older'n me. And you'm Jennifer Owen, the doctor's daughter over to Godolphin. But you?" She glanced at Sally, who said, "Sally Pask. My father is agent to the Duke of Leeds's estate. Does Barry Moore live in Carleen now?"

Flossie looked them over slowly, calmly, to show them both that she didn't consider either of them a threat. "Like to meet him after?" she suggested casually.

The offer was not as generous as the two younger girls believed it to be. Flossie's father would scalp her if he knew she was here admiring Barry Moore instead of helping old Mrs Tehidy whitewash her privy. So it occurred to her that if *three* girls were seen talking to him after, it would be less gossip-worthy than a solo tête-à-tête; the ripples might expire before they travelled the half-dozen miles between Carleen and home. And if two of those young females offered no real challenge, from her point of view, so much the better.

"Yes, please," Jennifer said in a feeble voice she hardly recognized.

"He do live over to Ludgvan," Flossie said. "He's only stoppin' here in Carleen along of his cousin. That's him rasslin' with 'n, now. You know Gerald Body, up Townshend, do 'ee?"

They nodded. Everyone within ten miles of Townshend knew Gerald Body, tomorrow's champion, they said. Townshend, which, despite the 'h,' is called 'Towns-end,' was the next village beyond Godolphin on the road to St Ives.

"Well, his father married Marion Moore, Barry's aunty. That's how he's here, see? They're cutting hay to carry next week."

The two girls were only half listening; genealogy is to Cornish conversation what the weather is to the English. Neither could take her eyes off the young god who was, at that moment, taking a new grip in the hope of tripping his cousin and pinning him to the sward. Her eyes followed theirs and, almost involuntarily, she said, "Don't 'ee love the way his hair do curl at his collar?"

Jennifer was thinking, at that very moment, how pleasant it would be to touch her lips to his neck, just at the point where the curls danced in the afternoon sun. And to run her fingertips over the muscles at the top of his arms. And to rest the tip of her nose in the little cavities between his collarbones and the strings of his neck. And … well, she could have gone on all day like that.

But a long-drawn-out, barely voiced "Yes!" was all she spoke.

"And his eyes …" Sally added boldly.

"What about them?" an amused Flossie prompted.

"He reminds me of Heathcliff."

"No!" Jennifer was stung into exclaiming. "Heathcliff had cruel eyes."

"But that was after the world had wronged him. I'll bet he had eyes just like Barry Moore's when he was young."

"Who's this-here Heathcliff then?" Flossie asked. A girl should keep a weather eye out for all the likely lads.

The two young ones, who would normally have mocked her ignorance, knew they durst not now, not if they wished to retain the slightest chance of meeting this new god of the wrestling field. "Someone in an old book we read," Sally said dismissively.

"In *Peg's Weekly*." Jennifer corrected her, thinking that even 'an old book' sounded too superior. *Peg's Weekly* would be what servant maids called 'a book.'

It is a rare thing for three young females to hold any length of conversation without looking at one another — or giving only the most fleeting glance. Old Ma Bucket, who ran the village shop, had her eye on them from across the impromptu ring. She nudged her sister and said, "They three maids are some interested in rasslin' all of a sudden!"

"Maids!" the other replied scornfully, for she and her sister could converse only by contradicting each other. "Two on 'em aren't nothin' but l'il giglets."

"They'm maids today, I tell 'ee," came the reply.

"And ruin'd tomorrow, I shouldn't wonder."

They fell to silence in happy contemplation of that dread fate.

"Good hitch!" came a cry from one of the waiting contestants.

The long, tense play for a fall had come to an end with Gerald Body, tomorrow's champion, going down beneath his cousin Barry's 'flying mare' and giving him a fair back — both pins and shoulders. The three who were acting as sticklers agreed — it was a very fair back, indeed. They consoled Gerald with the thought that none but a Moore could best a Moore and the two cousins rose wearily to their feet and struggled out of their loose canvas jackets, for which the next eager contestants were waiting with outstretched hands.

"Can we go over now?" Jennifer whispered to Flossie.

"Certainly not!" She was horrified at the suggestion. "And stop gawping at 'n so," she added. "Both on 'ee. He do know we seen 'n. If us do stop looking now, that'll hurt 'n in his pride and he'll come to we — which is the right and proper way 'bout. Look here — tell me now, did 'ee ever see the likes o' this?"

She turned her back on the wrestlers and held out an empty hand.

"What?" Sally asked.

"Pretend, can't 'ee? Look at 'n closely, then laugh." She threw back her head and let out a most fetching silvery peal.

The two youngsters took pattern from her and joined in, proud at how convincing it sounded. The fact that it was genuinely funny to laugh at nothing, as part of some clever, feminine ruse, helped, of course.

Sally glanced sidelong toward the young men and was rewarded with a barrage of curious stares.

"Don't 'ee gawp, I said!" Flossie screamed under her breath. "We've forgotten they exist. Look — see what I got in the other hand!"

The laughter was even louder. Then Jennifer told a risqué story about three worms crossing the road — mammy, daddy, and baby — who were almost run over by a cart. "And when it had gone by, Baby Worm counted them and said, 'One, two, three, four — we're all safe and well.' What had happened?"

Of course, when it was established that the cart *hadn't* cut one of them in two, the next likely explanation was that Mother Worm had been (whisper it) *expecting a happy event*. But both Flossie and Sally were much too embarrassed to say so. Thus, when Jennifer explained that Baby Worm hadn't learned to count properly yet, they laughed and laughed and laughed.

Moments later all these convolutions were rewarded with the simple, unoriginal question, "Does your mother know you're coming out tonight?" from Gerald Body, who was now standing immediately behind Flossie.

Daring to peek out of the corner of an eye, Jennifer saw that Barry Moore was a pace or so behind him. Her heart dropped a beat and then raced double to catch up.

Flossie didn't turn round. "Did someone speak?" she asked the other two in a couldn't-care-less tone.

Taking cue from her, as ever, Jennifer stammered that she wasn't sure. Sally, more daring, said she thought it could have been Harry Goldsworthy's donkey braying down at Scott's, by the bottom end of the Flow.

"Wit as well as beauty, forsooth!" Barry exclaimed. "We're out of our league here, cousin. Let us return where we're welcome."

They drifted back toward the wrestlers again.

Jennifer was about to cry out and call them back but one glance from Flossie silenced her. "Let 'em go," she said firmly. "They've bitten. Let 'em run out some line and us'll play 'em pretty-like."

Now she turned round and watched the next pair of wrestlers, who were patiently playing and feinting for a fall.

"You may look upon them every now and then," she advised her pupils, as they had now become. "Just put on a little high-quarter smile — like so." Her lips parted in something that was more sneer than smile. " 'S if to say we just knowed they'd fall back defeated at the first little puff o' wind."

The two young men clearly did not like it. After the first of these treatments they developed an intense interest in what was, in fact, a rather mediocre bout between a pair who had wrestled each other since childhood, knew every trick, and were more bent on not giving a fair back than on actually gaining one.

Eventually that very dullness forced them to look at the girls again; and again that chill, triumphal barrage repelled them.

"That's 'nuff, now," Flossie told the youngsters. "Keep an eye on the rasslin' till they look again. This time they'll come back."

To Jennifer it was like magic. The young men did exactly as the all-knowing Flossie predicted. Without looking directly at them she saw them gazing at her (and the other two, of course) across the impromptu ring. With superhuman effort she managed to keep her eyes on the wrestling. Then the young men turned to each other, canvassing courage and daring themselves to return.

This time they sidled slowly around among the scattered crowd, pausing often to appraise the contest, as if they could see in it what others could not. (Which was probably the case, by the by, for nothing is more tedious to the ignorant outsider than a bout of Cornish wrestling between two skilled and perfectly matched contenders.) Eventually, however, they arrived within easy conversational distance of their goal. There, Gerald pretended to recognize Flossie for the first time — almost as if he had not known of her presence until that moment.

"Why, if it isn't Miss Flossie Penhaligon," he said pleasantly.

"Florence, if you don't mind, Mister Body," she replied, but her smile was all encouragement now.

"Gerald," he said. "I don't believe you've met my cousin, Barry Moore — the luckiest wrestler in the whole of West Penwith this afternoon. May I present him to you? Miss Florence Penhaligon."

"He means I'm lucky not to have done him an injury, Miss Penhaligon." Barry smiled as he took her hand.

Watching her, Jennifer wondered how she didn't fall down in a faint. Her own heart was beating so fast it was more of a flutter than a pulse. And her head felt light and the whole world seemed to be wobbling.

"Gusson, you couldn't hurt he!" Flossie sneered jocularly. "You know what they do say — 'Country born, country bred — strong in th'arm, weak in th' head.'"

He smiled ruefully. "That would apply to me, too, I fear," he said. "I saw you in chapel last Sunday and I was hoping we'd meet before I go."

"Go?" Jennifer blurted out in her disappointment.

He smiled at her, at her alone, and said, "Yes, I go all the way to Ludgvan, Miss ...?"

"Jenny Owen," Flossie said.

"Jennifer, if you please," Jennifer said, amazed that her hand was obeying her and not shivering and weaving all over the place.

"A back!" Gerald laughed. "A fair back, Miss *Florence!*"

Flossie looked daggers at Jennifer — not that the girl noticed. She was transfixed by those dark, piercing eyes in which ... yes, there *was* a hint of Heathcliffian cruelty, too. She hardly felt his hand grasp hers, which seemed miles away.

"And won't you present me to your friend?" Barry asked.

"Oh yes," she replied, still in a daze. "Miss Sally Pask. Mister Barry Moore."

"Sally's not short for anything," Sally said pertly as she reached out and shook his hand.

"I imagine that's true," he replied, meeting her eye.

"Not short for cheek, anyway," Flossie grumbled.

"I think I helped your father with some land-surveying last holidays," Barry said. "Give him my regards."

"My father tended your little brother in the spring," Jennifer interrupted. "With the whooping cough."

Barry laughed. "Why, give him my regards, too, then!"

"Are you going to the Band of Hope dance tonight, Miss Penhaligon?" Gerald asked.

"I might," she replied warily.

"Well, we might see you there then," was the reply as they prepared to move off.

"Might you save me a dance if you do go?" Barry asked.

"I might," she said again, this time without a trace of wariness.

Later, as the two younger girls walked back to Godolphin, Jennifer broke their silence with a cry of, "It's not fair!"

"I said that at the very beginning," Sally pointed out.

"I mean by the time *we're* old enough to go to dances there won't be anyone like that to save a dance for. Only spotty Harry Johns and pests like Graham Smart with his big, flapping ears."

They pondered their dreadful fate in silence awhile and then Sally said, "Actually ... come to think of it ..."

"What?"

"When we're nineteen, he'll only be twenty-two."

Jennifer halted, dazed again — but this time with all the possibilities opened up by the new persepctive.

"Lots of girls marry at nineteen but not many men marry at twenty-two," Sally went on. "Twenty-*nine* is more like it. Boo-hoo!" She burst into pretend tears. "It's not that we're too young for *him* — he's already too young for *us!*"

5 JENNIFER WAS to enjoy no second encounter with her new idol, Barry Moore. He went back home as soon as the haymaking came to an end in the fields that Gerald Body's father rented in Carleen. But she met him almost hourly in her daytime dreams, relishing the turmoil the merest thought of him could stir within her. It was love, to be sure. The purest, noblest, deepest, and yet highest love that a woman might feel. One day they would meet again, and in far more romantic circumstances — on a misty crag above some rock-embosomed tarn in a faraway land, for instance — and neither of them would show the slightest surprise, for each would know it was decreed by Fate since the beginning of time. And they would peer deep into each other's eyes, and a little, knowing smile would play about their lips, and he would take her in his arms and press those smiling lips together, and then an overwhelming passion would seize them, and ... well, an overwhelming passion would seize them. That was that.

At first it was a torment never to see him — to know he was so close, breathing the same air, treading the same turf — but always just missing him. Down every lane, as she walked, she would think up some plausible reason why he might be just around the next bend, and then she'd hurry forward, eager to prove herself right. Once she even went to Ludgvan, where Flossie Penhaligon had said he lived.

That was when her mother took her over to Penzance to buy some new dress material and ribbons and things. As they bowled along the back lane between Goldsithney and Marazion, she begged her mother to make a little detour across the marshes between Marazion Hill and that village so dear to all her dreams. "Milly Edwards says you can't see Saint Michael's Mount from Ludgvan," she explained. "And I say you can. So can we go and see, please?"

Her mother was already suspicious of her daughter's condition (else why should the girl take such care to hide *Love Letters of an English Lady* behind *The Linnæan Plant System* behind the shoes behind the bonnets in her wardrobe!). So she replied, airily, "We hardly need *go* to Ludgvan to prove what all the world knows already, my dear. It's barely a mile inland across a great, open, marshy valley. How could the Mount *not* be visible from there?"

Jennifer cursed herself for choosing something so cut-and-dried. All the same, when they reached the top of Marazion Hill, her mother turned the gig aside down the byroad that led to the current centre of the universe. But the light of that universe was not there — or, if it was, it had chosen to shine indoors for the ninety-odd seconds it took them to pass through the place.

Perhaps he was in Penzance itself today, she thought at once, for she could tolerate all of love's pains but the pain of hopelessness. As it had been with the empty lanes of her own parish, so it was now with the crowded pavements of Penzance. Along Market Jew Street, Causeway Head, Church Street ... and all the other roads in town, each bend promised to reveal the magic of his presence, and broke that promise, and renewed it once more at every new turn, sustaining a hope that no number of disappointments could ever quench.

Love Letters of an English Lady was both an inspiration and a let down to Jennifer. At first it delighted her to discover that one could write in ordinary words about this wonderful new experience called love. The great poets were all very well in their way but their language was too high-flown and their thoughts too refined for everyday sentiment. So, when the anonymous Lady wrote to her unnamed lover, 'I awoke with your name on my lips this morning,' it seemed so much more powerful than Troilus 'sighing his heart toward the Syrian tents, where Cressid lay that night' — or something along those lines, which they studied at school. After a time, though, the Lady's very coyness in refusing to name either herself or her darling robbed the printed page of its power to move her. For, out of all the myriad words in all the languages of the world, what single one has the greatest power when a person is in love? Surely the name of the one most beloved!

To stand alone in the garden on a balmy summer's eve, in that bewitching moment of the late twilight when things lose their colour and begin to move subtly, as if some night-magic were gently stirring them, when night-perfumed flowers lay their heady spice upon the senses … to close her fluttering eyelids and breathe deep draughts of that giddy perfume and murmur, "Barry! Oh my Barry! My dearest, sweetest, darling Barry!" over and over until the words lost their meaning — or, rather, while their meaning coalesced with her senses, agitating and inflaming them until she felt the whole world liberated, intoxicated, all about her — that was an experience all her own.

Surely no others had ever felt *precisely* as she now felt about Barry. They had come close, of course, or there would be no love poetry at all, and no one would write, publish, or buy such books as the *Love Letters of an English Lady.* But surely none of them had scaled the final peaks, back into this Eden.

As the weeks turned to months, and the months stretched to a year and beyond, the real Barry Moore was slowly replaced by an even more exciting Barry of her imagination. His chestnut hair was even glossier and more tightly curled; his eyes darker, more brightly gleaming, more filled with love and tenderness … so much so that, in the end, the sudden reappearance of the man himself — in the manner she so often daydreamed over — would have been something of an anticlimax.

When this pleasing phantasm had quite replaced her memory of the real young man, she had, in effect, fallen out of love with him as completely as she had earlier fallen into it. She was bright enough, and by this time self-aware enough, too, to realize what had happened; and yet she remained faithful to her by-now-imaginary lover for reasons she could not so easily pin down. It kept that awkward, challenging world of *other* young men — real young men — at a distance. And for that reason alone it was worth her fidelity, for it allowed her to experiment with all sorts of dangerous and explosive feelings, but in the safety and silence of her mind. And that was as far as she wished to pursue her self-examination, for the moment, anyway.

The outbreak of war in 1914 jolted her life out of these pleasant grooves. She was eighteen by then and had just left school. As if that were not unsettling enough, there came the news that Barry Moore and his cousin Gerald had enlisted in the Duke of Cornwall's Light Infantry as soon as the rolls were opened. That was the real Barry Moore, of course, and he was now in danger of a real death in Belgium or Germany or Turkey ... or wherever this war was to be fought. True, the papers promised it would soon be over and that the 'boys' would all be home again for Christmas, but even so that left four long months — more than a hundred days, or two thousand four hundred hours — during any one of which a sniper's bullet could finish his life and turn hers from a paradise into a living hell. Indeed, a bullet could do its fell work in less than a second ... but she wasn't going to torture herself by working out how many seconds of hazard there are in a hundred days.

Instead she bought a 1914 calendar, which she thought she would get cheap, because they usually started selling them off in July; but they were still at full price because, of course, everybody else was doing the same. At the end of each day in which no news of his death had reached Cornwall, she pencilled the word *Safe!* against its date and replaced the thing in its secret place in her wardrobe. *Love Letters of an English Lady* had long since been sneaked out to a jumble sale.

By the time she heard of his enlistment he was under canvas on Salisbury Plain, learning to bivouac, to entrench, to mount picquets and sorties, to enfilade, to reconnoitre ... and a host of other things — things she had never so much as heard of before but which were now the staple of everyone's daily conversation. When news came that he was to be given a commission, she was filled with pride — until she overheard the vicar's wife saying that her sister had heard a colonel of the regiment telling a colleague that a junior officer in the front line had a life expectancy of about five minutes during an actual battle. After that, she began writing the word *Safe!* in ink. And at the end of each week she added two more exclamation marks.

The war did not end at Christmas but Barry, back in England for training in gunnery liaison, was allowed home on two days' leave. Jennifer did not get to hear of it until he had rejoined his unit. In fact, she might never have heard of it at all if he hadn't taken a camera with him the previous autumn. The *Penzance Chronicle* organized an exhibition of his work, which included sketches and watercolours as well as photographs. They reproduced some of them in the *Chronicle* and the article gave credit for the photographic printing to Mrs Jim Collett of Collett & Trevarton, who were *the* photographers in Penzance, with branches in Redruth and St Ives. It added that many readers would recall her outstanding paintings of local scenes at the last Newlyn exhibition, under her professional name, Christobel Moore. 'She is, in fact, the gallant subaltern's aunt,' it concluded.

At dinner that evening Jennifer said, "It's absolutely ages since I had a portrait taken, Mummy. And the last one was frightful. Don't you think we ought to get a new one sometime?"

"Ten months doesn't seem like 'absolutely ages' to me, dear. Nor to my housekeeping allowance, I'm sure."

"But it was awful." She exaggerated her distaste. "I was all spots and my complexion was sallow and ..."

"You still are and it still is."

"But I know how to disguise it so much better now. Can't we take a better one? Please? I hate it when Daddy shows ..."

"Well, I am going to Falmouth the Saturday after next and I suppose we could just about ..."

"No — Penzance!" Jennifer insisted. "Collett and Trevarton are so much better than Stanton."

Her mother suppressed a smile. She actually had no intention of going to Falmouth; she had simply confirmed her suspicion that her enigmatic eldest daughter, so passionate in her nature and yet so uninterested in any young man of their acquaintance, had some private reason for going to Penzance and only to Penzance. Whether or not it also had to do with Collett & Trevarton was still an open question.

"We could go to Falmouth by way of Redruth," she went on. "If you insist on Collet and Trevarton, they have a studio there, too."

"But Mrs Collett isn't there — you know, Christobel Moore, the lady artist. I particularly want to ask her one or two things about painting. Two birds with one stone, you know."

Her mother, who had also read that article, was beginning to see the pattern. "Very well, darling," she said. "Penzance it shall be."

6 THAT CHRISTMAS of 1914 marked a watershed in people's attitudes to the war. In the days when the authorities were saying it would all be over by then, the populace saw it as a brief but glorious flourish — a *Boy's Own* escapade. With a few deft punches Tommy Atkins would tap the claret of the barbarian Hun and put him firmly in his place. Young men, who had been starved of easy adventure for the past two generations (that is, adventure within a ferry-boat ride of Blighty's shores), could not wait to get to the front and help plucky little Belgium to put the kibosh on the Kaiser. And their even younger brothers feared it would all be over by the time they were legally qualified to enlist; so they lied about their

age and marched off to Flanders' fields in patriotic ecstasy. Spirits were high. The songs were gaily belligerent. Everyone wanted a bash at the Boche before it was too late.

But when Christmas came and the end seemed farther off than ever, a new, much grimmer mood set in. The Allies lost at Mons and fell back to the Marne. The French government fled from Paris. Attempts to drive the Hun back at the Aisne, and in Picardy, and at Artois all failed. Plucky little Belgium fell and was plucked. The enemy took Lille and massed in huge numbers for an assault on Ypres — or 'Wipers,' as everyone called it. By then people's expectations had changed so much that merely to repulse these attacks had to be counted as a victory. By then, too, there were over 200 miles of trenches (400 if you counted those on the other side of no-man's-land), stretching westward from Verdun almost to Paris, then north to Wipers and the Channel coast near Ostend. Soldier stared out at soldier, appalled by the dawning realization that each was about to be asked the impossible.

Little of that pessimism had percolated back home as yet; but even in Cornwall, as far from the front as you could get on the Channel coast, everyone knew that what had started as a sprint had turned into a marathon. The consequence could be summed up in a single word: *knitting*. 'Our Boys' now faced the full rigours of a European winter. They needed scarves, balaclava helmets, mittens, socks, and warm unmentionables. The shops were filled with khaki wool, black wool, gray wool — all the colours acceptable to a military high command that had been taught by the Boer how dangerous it was to dress in red, white, and blue in the sight (and sights) of snipers.

Jennifer had more than 'done her bit.' Since October, when the knitting movement first took hold, she had spent all her pocket-money on wool and needles. By the early winter of 1915 she had completed two pairs of socks, several mittens, and a scarf. She was not sure if officers wore balaclavas, and in any case she did not like to think of Barry's gorgeous locks all crushed and hidden in such uncomely headgear. The bobbles on the scarf had taken longest — especially the one inside which she had hidden a tiny piece of silk bearing the words: *With ALL my love — J* in fifteen different colours, one for each letter, including the dash, and all so tiny that she had risked her sight to do it. Even the little mice in *The Tailor of Gloucester* could not have stitched it finer.

On the day she went into Penzance to get a new portrait taken, she carefully wrapped these comforts in some tissue paper left over from her herbarium days. She'd give them to Mrs Collett, desiring her to make sure they were passed on to her nephew. She pondered a long time over what public message — if any — to include and, at last, settled for her father's card with her own name handwritten below his, plus the simple message: 'Good Luck!' diagonally across the corner. No one could make too much of that, surely? Yet Barry himself might find his thoughts turned in her direction — just a little … perhaps?

The gig was filled with rags, paper, glass jamjars, and bits of old iron — all carefully hoarded for the salvage depôt in Penzance. It was easy enough for Jennifer to hide her own little package among them. The depôt was beyond Collett & Trevarton's studios in Market Jew Street, so all she'd have to do was distract her mother while she retrieved it.

Why she wanted to keep it such a secret — especially from her own mother — she could not say … except that it was an easy way to reassure herself that she was nineteen now, not sixteen. And every self-respecting nineteen year old should, she felt, have acquired one or two secrets, especially from her own mother.

As soon as they set off, Goronwy said, "It'll probably be *Mrs* Collett who'll take your portrait. I hear that her husband has gone on some business to the War Office in London. Of course, they don't put things like that in the papers now."

"She's a good artist with pencil and brush," Jennifer said. "I suppose it's easier for a good artist to be a photographer than for a good photographer to be an artist."

A squall of rain blew up out of nowhere and they had to make a hasty job of raising the hood. And, of course, the rain stopped the moment they succeeded. The sun came out again. The road gave off wisps of steam. Daffodils and paperwhites nodded in a gentle southerly breeze.

Jennifer sighed contentedly. Her mother, mistaking her tone, asked her what was wrong. Rather than admit the simple truth, she answered with an acceptable sentiment: "It's hard to believe that, only a few hundred miles away, all those men, hundreds of thousands of them, are trying to slaughter each other for … what?"

When she was half way through this rather trite little speech the profound truth behind it gripped her. The broken-backed ending to her question masked a lump in her throat. Tears prickled behind her eyelids, a compound of rage at the world of high politics and fear for its victims — for one in particular.

Goronwy, having noticed the girl's concern for one of the parcels in the back, took a gamble and said, "Oh, bother! We've left your knitted comforts behind. The salvage people accept them, too, you know."

Jennifer, glad to be back on safe domestic ground and seeing that further concealment was pointless, replied, "Actually, I've parcelled them up for the Colletts. They must have *someone* at the front — such a large family. And I thought they might not charge us so much for the portrait, then. Not that I'd put it quite so bluntly, mind."

Her mother laughed and patted her arm. "You'll do," she said. Then, conversational again, she added, "Talking of large families — you know Mrs Collett's own story, I suppose?"

"She was an orphan? Daddy told me that once."

Goronwy nodded. "She must have been about your age when her parents died."

"And Daddy also said she was a good example of what people can achieve if they really set their mind to it, because she started from practically nothing."

Her father had said those words in order to comfort her at the time Moses went into the Helston orphanage; she hadn't thought about Moses for … well, she couldn't remember the last time. Ages.

"In a way she started with less than nothing," Goronwy went on. "I mean, she had to overcome her parents' reputation — a father who drank himself to death and a mother who was … flighty, to say the least."

"Flighty?" Jennifer wondered what sort of behaviour the word might cover in this case.

"Almost literally. I mean, she took flight at the first chance she got. She was born with a silver spoon in her mouth, as they say, and yet she eloped with the coachman. She was a Trevarton, of Trevarton's Mills, the flour people. Her youngest brother is the same Mark Trevarton who's Jim Collett's partner."

"So he's Mrs Collett's uncle! I always thought they were cousins. They look the same age."

In fact, Jennifer was still at that age where the grown-up world was simply divided into old people (over 25) and really old people (actually gray-haired and wrinkled).

"I think they are," her mother responded. "You know how families get out of step between the generations. You yourself have an aunt in Australia who's only twelve — by Grandad's second marriage."

They never talked about Grandad's second marriage; indeed, they hardly ever talked about the man himself. It surprised Jennifer to hear it come out so casually now. "I wonder if we'll ever meet?" she mused. "And what'll I tell her? 'You'd better show your elderly niece a little respect, young'un!'" She giggled.

"I was telling you about Christobel Collett," Goronwy went on. "Or Crissy Moore, as she then was. The coachman — her father — his name was Barry Moore."

Jennifer gave a start.

Goronwy turned away to hide her smile. Little bits of a half-finished jigsaw puzzle were falling into place.

Jennifer's mind was racing now. So *her* Barry Moore was the grandson of another Barry Moore — the coachman to the great Trevarton family. Now she wanted to know all about him — the elopement, the romance, the orphaned family ... everything.

Unfortunately, at that point they were drawing nigh the gate of Penhaligon's farm at Goldsithney, and who should be standing there but Flossie Penhaligon. Gone was the pert, confident young woman Jennifer knew; the poor creature had a face on her as long as a wet Sunday.

"G'win Penzance are 'ee, missiz?" she asked wearily, with little hope in her voice.

"We are, as a matter of fact," Goronwy said. "Miss Florence Penhaligon, isn't it? May we offer you a lift?" To Jennifer she said, "Move over, dear. Make room."

"I'll go in the back," Flossie said, climbing in rather gingerly over the wheel. The hood had fallen flat again by now.

Jennifer darted a hand ahead of her and rescued the precious parcel. "The rest is just salvage," she explained.

"Unwanted cast-offs, eh," Flossie said gloomily. "Ah well!"

Goronwy laughed. "Are you feeling a bit of an unwanted cast-off yourself today, Miss Penhaligon? We all get days like that."

"I daresay," Flossie replied.

"Cheer up! It never lasts long."

"I'm going to have my portrait taken," Jennifer explained. "At Collett and Trevarton's."

"Oh ah?" Flossie seemed quite put out at the news.

"I was telling my daughter something of Mrs Collett's extraordinary history," Goronwy remarked, and quickly summarized what had been said so far.

Flossie's somewhat prickly attitude gave way to fervent interest. Jennifer wondered if the Penhaligons were related to the Colletts, or perhaps the Trevartons; Flossie was certainly paying more attention than you'd expect from a merely casual listener. She hoped her mother wouldn't say anything too derogatory, for — Cornwall being Cornwall — it would certainly get back to the ears of the victim.

"Crissy were th'oldest, were she?" Flossie asked.

"The eldest, yes. Or no, come to think of it. I rather think her sister ... forgotten her name ... the one who married Henry Body, who farms at Townshend ..."

"Marian," Flossie said. "Marian Body."

"That's right. Marian was the eldest. You know the family then? All the ins and outs of this tale?"

Jennifer recalled the wrestling bout on the Flow between Gerald Body and Barry Moore. She winked at Flossie, who grinned back.

"I did know Gerald Body, backalong," the young woman admitted — in a tone that made further questions unnecessary.

"Ah," was all Goronwy said.

"And the boys, missiz," Flossie said. "They orpheling brothers — what become o' they? There's Ole Tom Moore, I do know. He do farm over Ludgvan." She winked at Jennifer.

Goronwy, dividing her attention between the horse and the potholes in the road, missed these silent messages, but Jennifer knew that Flossie was showing she understood the meaning of that earlier wink. She was also showing a rather sick-making interest in the Moores of Ludgvan — that is, her inquiry was so casual-sounding that it could only be a camouflage (to use a suddenly popular word) for something rather heartfelt.

"I remember Tom Moore!" Goronwy said, in such a significant tone that the other two could only stare at her in amazement. She stared back at them and then said, "For heaven's sake — he's two years *younger* than me! I mean I remember his reputation." She lowered her voice and added, " 'Ludgvan Bull,' they called him. No girl was safe. And, I'm sorry to say," — she smiled knowingly at her daughter — "the son is the same. A buck-rabbit with a bicycle, as they say."

By now Jennifer realized that her mother's suspicions about Barry Moore were roused to the point of confirmation. She therefore expected those knowing eyes to go on dwelling in hers and she prepared herself not to flinch. Instead, to her surprise, her mother's gaze strayed onward to rest on Flossie Penhaligon. That knowing smile had not been one of challenge but of complicity — as if to say, 'Watch Miss Penhaligon now, dear, and I think you'll see something interesting.'

Jennifer followed her mother's gaze and, indeed, saw that Flossie's lips had vanished to a thin, livid line and that the rims of her nostrils were pale and quivering. These signs of bottled-up anger lasted only a moment. The young woman drew a deep breath and visibly braced herself. "So I heard tell, missiz," was all she said.

Goronwy turned back to negotiate a narrow portion of the road. To her daughter she said, "Don't be embarrassed by my frankness, darling. You're of an age when you should know such things."

"Mother!" Jennifer was purple with embarrassment. But that was temporary. The shattering effect of the revelation she had just witnessed was more lasting.

After that, however, Goronwy steered the conversation toward safer topics — how Willy Stour was up for drunk-in-charge again, and poor Mrs Stour and those sweet children. And how Arthur Hinks had forgotten to unlock the vestry at Godolphin church for the first service last Sunday, and *he* wouldn't last long. And the vicar had left his own keys in the trousers his wife had taken to Mrs Bodilly for letting out. Yes, and wasn't *he* getting fat!

And so the rest of the journey passed in amicable mood while they set the world to rights and thanked heavens they were not as stupid, venial, or self-righteous others were.

As they drove up Market Jew, a little way short of Collett & Trevarton's studios, Flossie said, "This-yur'll do for I, missiz. And I'll thank 'ee both for a very pleasant journey."

When they had let her off, Goronwy murmured to Jennifer, "Don't look back, darling. Just fish the little vanity mirror out of my bag."

"Why are we driving past the studios?"

"Just do as I say. We've got fifteen minutes before your appointment. Now pretend to fuss with your bonnet or something while you tell me if I'm wrong. I'll bet all of Lombard Street to a china orange that young Miss Penhaligon goes straight into Collett and Trevarton."

Fortunately there was a traffic jam ahead. A dray had locked wheels with a hansom, so Jennifer had an unjolted view of the road behind. After a few moments she gave a whispered whistle of amazement and said, "How did you know?"

"I think I even know what she's about to say," her mother replied grimly. "A little gentle blackmail that will end with the words, 'So how may we avoid a paternity summons against your nephew Barry, Mrs Collett — and all the public scandal that would bring?' Something to that effect, anyway."

Jennifer did not risk any sort of reply. She knew that, whatever she said, it would come out sounding scornful. Barry was *not* like that — not a chip off the old block. He was an officer and a gentleman.

7 IT AMAZED Jennifer to see how even a little background knowledge about a person could completely change your attitude to him or her. In this case it was a her — Mrs Collett, to be precise. Jennifer couldn't recall a time when she had *not* known Mrs Collett, for all the Owen children had been taken to the Penzance photographers at least once a year, almost from the day of their birth. The woman was a fixture in the landscape of her childhood and adolescence; but in that she was no different from, say, the blacksmith, the postman, or the hurdy-gurdy player on the promenade in summer. She was one of those people who existed merely because *every* community had blacksmiths, postmen … and people who managed photographers' studios.

True, Mrs Collett was slightly different in that she was also an artist, which made her somewhat more prominent in Jennifer's picture of the world. Even so, she had never thought of her as anything more than a kindly old woman of about forty — her mother's sort of age — with blonde hair that was enviably curly, shrewd eyes, an engaging smile, and a brisk, no-nonsense manner. But, watching her now as she placed the camera and told the assistant how to set the lighting, Jennifer could not help thinking back over the extraordinary tale her mother had told her on the way into Penzance that morning.

She tried to imagine this woman as she must have been at around her own age — or a bit younger — seventeen or so — orphaned suddenly and left without a penny. And with half a dozen brothers and sisters, too. But it was impossible — just as she could not imagine her own mother at that age, not even with the help of the family album. The past was like a country on the other side of the world. Australia. Full of people you heard about but never met. Like Grandad and his second wife and their never-to-be-encountered family.

I know things about you that you'd never imagine! Jennifer tried telling herself as she watched Mrs Collett move securely and confidently about the studio, her little kingdom. But the sentiment fell rather flat, because the most important thing she knew about the woman was that she knew next to nothing; her mother's revelations had barely scratched the surface of a life that, she felt sure, was ten thousand times more interesting than her own — past, present, or future. She was never going to *do* anything or *be* anything. She was already quite sure of that. She was just going to marry someone — not even someone exciting like Barry Moore

— and manage a household and bring up a family ... and learn to think of contentment as if it were happiness.

The utter unknowability of other people depressed her. There must be someone, somewhere in this great wide teeming world, *someone* whose soul was a natural twin to her own. A person she could love and live with and get to know through and through, just as he would get to know her. But what chance of finding him when she hardly ever went anywhere or did anything or met anyone?

Crissy Collett waited until the mechanical elements of the portrait were completed to her satisfaction before she set about relaxing Jennifer with some light conversation. The poor girl was a bundle of nerves. All sorts of people trooped through these studios in the course of a year — the pompous, the nervous, the reluctant, the bored; and they came in every mood as well — frosty, jovial, impatient, flirtatious ... she could deal with them all. But middle-class girls on the verge of womanhood were a breed apart, and utterly unknowable as far she was concerned. Moods and contradictions were the very fabric of their lives. They could sulk their way into happiness and laugh on the brink of tears. She should know, for she had two of her own — one of eighteen and the other coming up to sixteen. And Susan Trevarton, Mark's wife, had gone through it, too; her eldest girl was twenty-two and settling down now, thank heavens. But she had another of fifteen coming along.

Idleness was the problem, poor things. They had nothing important to do and eighteen hours a day to do it in. She herself had never had the luxury of time in which to indulge all those so-called 'adolescent difficulties.' Her childhood had ended around the age of five. After that it was always, "Get some work into your hands, maid!" She had taught at dame school until her parents died — and helped her mother with laundering and mending in the evenings. Then, for a few months, she had been her own grandmother's lady's maid at Fenton Lodge in Falmouth, before she married Jim Collett and they went into the photographic business in partnership with Mark Trevarton. She and Susan often talked about it, for Susan had been an upstairs maid at Fenton Lodge, too. They passed many a happy moment shaking their heads at the unfathomable ways of the strange, middle-class misses they had both somehow reared.

So, with more resignation than confidence, she braced herself to jollying up Miss Jennifer Owen, to put her in the sort of mood that would lead to a portrait worth the thirty shillings her parents would be paying. Jennifer, however, gave her an opening she would never have dreamed of trying.

"How did you learn to do all this, Mrs Collett?" she asked admiringly.

Crissy glanced at the clock and saw that she had plenty of time in hand; her midday appointment had come out with a cold sore that morning and had cancelled. The chance to enlighten this empty-headed young miss was too good to turn down. "I learned it the way anyone learns to do anything worthwhile, Miss Owen," she replied. "Look, listen, and reason it out. Come my side of the lens for a moment — change places with me. Go on, it doesn't matter about the pose. We can soon get you back where you belong."

Intrigued, Jennifer obeyed, gingerly stepping over the invisible line between artist and sitter.

Crissy told her to pull the black cloth over her head and look at the ground-glass plate at the back of the camera. Under the cloth the smell of old macassar oil repelled Jennifer slightly but her nose grew used to it as swiftly as her eyes accustomed themselves to the dark. And then what a beautiful little upside-down wonderland appeared on the screen before her! A perfectly dainty scene that she would have called sharply crystalline had it not also been a world in motion. There was an upside-down Mrs Collett mounting the dais … turning to face her … taking her seat …

Jennifer cocked her head to one side and turned the scene into a world-on-edge.

"No," Crissy called out. "Stand upright. Accept it as an upside-down view. Forget I'm a person. Think of everything you see on the plate as a mere object. Part of a composition."

Jennifer obeyed.

"You can make me out, I hope?" Crissy waved.

The girl laughed. "Of course."

"You see this light shining down my left cheek — or right cheek as it will appear to be?"

"Yes."

"I'm going to ask Arthur to turn it on and off. Watch what happens to my head. Off. On. Off. On … see?"

Jennifer giggled in fascination. "It goes all flat. Well … not flat but … I don't know."

"Dull? Turn it off again, Arthur."

"Yes. It goes all dull."

"Well, we'll leave it off and also turn off the spotlight on the background — please, Arthur? What d'you think about it now?"

"I say!" Jennifer was amazed.

"Still dull?"

"No — dark and dramatic. It's the sort of picture you'd take of ... Hamlet doing his soliloquy or something." She came out from under the black cloth and gazed directly at Mrs Collett, not wide-eyed but with hooded lids, just as she had seen the woman herself doing earlier.

Crissy saw it and approved. She realized she had found rather a quick learner in young Miss Owen.

"Can I try something?" Jennifer asked hesitantly.

"By all means, my dear. What?"

Jennifer looked at a spare lamp lying on the floor. "Could that be made to shine on you from down there?"

"Why?"

"There was a picture I saw in *The Studio* last year. It was of a girl leaning on a balcony and smiling down at her lover, with bright sunlight reflecting up off the marble below."

Crissy remembered it. "Alma Tadema," she said and gave the assistant a nod.

Arthur turned the lamp on at full power. Jennifer gave a cry of mock horror. "You look like a ghost!" she exclaimed.

As if to support the opinion Arthur made a screeching sound that set her teeth on edge. She turned to ask him not to but then saw he was, in fact, sliding a knob on some piece of electrical apparatus. Looking again at Mrs Collett she saw that the light was now only half as strong as before, and the effect was getting much closer to the one she sought.

"Stop!" she cried when it was perfect. And then she just stood there, hands pressed together, biting her lip in amazement. "The things you can do!" she marvelled.

"We can even make Liberal politicians seem almost human," Crissy assured her.

Jennifer chuckled dutifully but was still overcome with astonishment at the transformation she had just witnessed. The muted lighting now achieved what her imagination had earlier failed at: Now she *could* imagine Mrs Collett as a girl of around her own age. The way the light bathed beneath her chin and gently modelled her upper lip was *so* appealing. And those observant, artist's eyes twinkled with a merriment that was almost mischievous.

"Change places again," Crissy said. "We'll expose a couple of plates of you lit like this — not for your parents, just for you. Your own lighting."

"It won't ..." Jennifer hesitated. She was going to say she hoped it wouldn't make her look like a baby in the cradle — that is, take as many years off her as it had off Mrs Collett.

"Come on." The woman smiled as if she knew exactly what Jennifer had been thinking. "Don't look at the camera. Look over there. Pretend you're daydreaming — thinking of something very pleasant but denied to you just at this moment. Happy-wistful is what we're after here."

Jennifer thought of Barry.

"That's it!" Crissy pressed the shutter release. Teasingly she added, "I envy the young man!"

Jennifer almost blurted it all out, then and there. The pink that flushed her ears and cheeks told Crissy she had hit the mark. "Now think of the happiest day you ever knew — or hour, if a day's too long."

For some strange reason Jennifer thought of the time when she had found baby Moses in that field — something that had not even crossed her mind for months.

"Splendid!" Crissy said. "You know, Miss Owen, you have the sort of face that cameras love. It's more than just the face, actually. It's expression and mood and … everything. We've often talked about it here and never been able to pin it down. But there are some people who just *click* on film, and I rather think you're one of them."

"Another useless accomplishment!" Jennifer said jovially.

"Not at all, my dear. It could be very profitable — especially in films for the bioscope. Still — you'll probably never need to turn your hand to anything so sordid as a paid career. Or turn your face, rather. Would it be awful of me to ask what that happy memory was? Don't tell me if you'd rather not."

Eagerly Jennifer told her all about the finding of little Moses. For some reason it had a powerful effect on Mrs Collett, whose response was quite unlike that of other women to whom she had, from time to time, told the same story in the past. They had made the expected, sentimental cries of 'Bless my soul!' and 'Aaah, love the little mite!' But Mrs Collett showed an extraordinary interest in the exact date of the incident, the probable age of the baby, the clothes he had been wearing … and, especially, the bun-penny brooch that had been used to pin his swaddling.

"Was it like this?" she asked, doing a rapid sketch on a scrap of paper.

The hair prickled on Jennifer's neck. "Exactly like that," she said. "It wasn't shop-bought. It was sort of home made …"

"By my husband, I believe," Mrs Collett murmured.

"Do you know who the baby was, then?" Jennifer asked, her heart pounding madly beneath her ribs.

The woman smiled sadly and shook her head. "No — but that brooch was stolen from this house five or six years ago. We think we know who did it — a friend of ours, in fact. She may be a little ... you know." She tapped her temple. "Inclined to walk off with little trinkets."

"You couldn't tell me who?" Jennifer asked hesitantly. "No, of course not. Forgive my asking."

"I couldn't," Crissy agreed apologetically. "Besides, I don't think it'd lead you to the real mother — if that's what you were hoping. She doesn't keep the things she takes. There was one item she took from a shop, an old-fashioned bodice hook for which she had no earthly use ... I saw her myself, leaving it on a garden wall down on Causeway Head. She probably did the same with the brooch. She might even have left it on *our* wall, hoping we'd find it — which we never did, alas. Oh dear!" She gave a sympathetic sigh. "To come so close to getting an answer and then have the door slam in your face! I'm so sorry."

"Ah well ..." Jennifer shrugged with resignation. "I haven't thought about the little mite for months, so I can't say it's a burning ambition to find out what his story was. I know where *he* is — in the Helston Union orphanage — but what of it?"

"One of life's little mysteries," Crissy said comfortingly. "We'd better get on with the proper portraits."

And for the next twenty minutes she worked away like the professional she was, exposing half a dozen plates, which was twice as many as she usually took. She wanted plenty to show her husband, Jim, when he returned next week. She hated waste, and if Miss Owen was as good a model as she suspected, it would be a dreadful waste, in her opinion.

When it was all over and Arthur had vanished into the darkroom with the plates, and the bill was safely entered in the ledger, Jennifer took the packet for Barry from her copious shopping bag. "We have no one in the forces," she explained, licking her lips and clearing her throat nervously. "So I, that is, *we* wondered, my mother and I, if *you* did. Or do, rather. It's just some knitting I've done. Not very good, I'm afraid ..." Her unconvincing monologue petered out.

Mrs Collett stared at her uncertainly.

"Someone told me you have a nephew?" Jennifer suggested. "An officer, they said?"

The woman shook her head and said, "Oh dear! The someone, I suppose, would be Miss Florence Penhaligon?"

Jennifer stared at the floor. "No, I knew already. I fibbed. I saw him once in Carleen, wrestling with Gerald Body."

"And fell head-over-heels, no doubt — or hook-line-and-sinker, more probably. Don't tell me! The coincidence with Miss Penhaligon seemed too great — she was here not an hour ago, and I know she lives out your way. I thought you might have given her a lift."

Jennifer confessed, too, that they had. "And … did she talk about … about your nephew Barry?" she asked daringly.

"That's her business, I'm afraid, my dear. But I'll tell you this … though I don't know. Sometimes warning girls your age *against* doing something is the one sure way to get them to do it — though it never seems to work with keeping bedrooms tidy, somehow."

"I do want these little comforts to go to Barry," Jennifer put in before the sentiment would sound like disobedience — for she'd have had to be both blind and deaf not to realize that Mrs Collett was about to warn her off her 'dangerous' nephew. "I did them for him."

"Then I'll say nothing. And I promise you they'll go in the very next parcel." Crissy took the lovingly wrapped bundle from the girl.

At that moment an excited Arthur returned from the darkroom with a still-damp contact print in his hand. He passed it to his mistress with a *so-there!* gesture. She stared at it a moment in expressionless silence and then passed it on to Jennifer with a "What did I tell you!"

The girl stared at it in amazement. It was one of the poses using 'her' lighting, with the lamp casting a gentle underglow. It hadn't taken twenty years off her but it had given her an ethereally innocent quality she would never have linked with the everyday self who stared back so uncomfortably from every looking glass she dared to consult. It was *so* unlike her, indeed, that she could inspect it quite impersonally — and see, without a trace of vanity, that 'she,' that creature who existed solely on photographic film, was something quite special.

"Listen," Crissy added when she saw that the girl had taken the point. "My husband will return from London next week. May I ask your mother to allow you to come back one afternoon? Wednesday would be a good day. You and Kodak film belong together in the most extraordinary way. I must look out your old negatives and see if we've missed it in the past or if it's something that has just … come out of nowhere. What I'd like to do is discover where this rare quality of yours is weakest and where it's most strong. You wouldn't mind, would you?"

Mind! Jennifer's heart dropped a beat. It was just about the most exciting thing that had ever happened to her. All the same, some native caution made her add, "I wouldn't be required to … you know …" She went pink again with embarrassment.

Crissy laughed and patted her on the arm. "Certainly not! Bare shoulders in an evening gown, perhaps, but that's all."

"And you'll see that parcel goes off to Lieutenant Moore — soon?"

The smile left Mrs Collett's face. "If you insist. I'll post it this very afternoon. Is there a note inside to say it's from you?" In a gesture remembered from childhood she crossed her fingers behind her back and added, "I shan't peek."

"Just my father's card — and I've written my own name underneath."

"Is that all?"

Jennifer crossed her fingers behind her back and said, "Just that."

When Goronwy came to collect her daughter, Crissy showed her the contact print and repeated her suggestion, which the other was intrigued enough to accept. She also kept the print, to show her husband and justify the decision.

Later, just after lunch, when Crissy was assembling the latest parcel for Barry out in Flanders, she took up another of the contacts that Arthur had made. "This is the last thing on earth you deserve, young man," she murmured. "Especially after Clemmy Bowden and the Hotchkiss girl — and now the young Miss Penhaligon. However ..." She slipped the print in among the comforts Jennifer Owen had knitted and then tied the parcel up before she could have second thoughts about it.

"You must be mad," she told herself on the way back from the post office, when it was too late to undo the act.

8 AT LUNCHTIME on the Friday of that same week Jennifer's father came home with the grave news that Florence Penhaligon had been found drowned at the foot of Tremearne cliffs in Breage parish. There would be an inquest, of course, but, from the quantity of fresh soil found on the beach around her, it was fairly obvious that she had been walking along a part of the headland that had given way beneath her. Quite why she had been there at all was a mystery, for the cliffs along that part of Mount's Bay between Porthleven and Trewarvas Head were notoriously unstable. Every year some portion or other collapsed beneath the weight of an unfortunate cow or sheep. The odd visitor also — and quite literally — fell victim to them; but local people, who knew of their fickle nature, usually steered well clear of them.

Jennifer cried herself to sleep that night. Not that she and Flossie had been close; indeed, she hadn't even liked the girl all that much. Perhaps if their acquaintance had not been renewed so recently, she might not have taken it so to heart. But ... to think that the young woman who had climbed so gratefully into the back of the gig, just three or four days earlier, and who had winked at her behind her mother's back over their memories of that evening in Carleen ... to think that they would never meet again was almost unbearable. And never to hear her laugh again. And never know what it was between her and Barry Moore — if, indeed, there had been anything at all. Never!

All that living and growing up, the tears, the laughter, the learning in school, the catechism, the poetry, the multiplication tables ... and all the friendships she'd formed, the secrets she had shared with her friends ... the dances, the kisses — everything that goes to make up a life ... all wiped out, just like that! What had it been *for?* Where was the point in it, if all that preparation was going to end with a bit of rotten clifftop giving way beneath you one February afternoon and ... *pfft!* — out you went like a snuffed candle?

"Gathered unto God," the preacher said at the funeral the following Tuesday, after the coroner had released the body. The phrase was meant to sound comforting but it did nothing to explain away the pointlessness of it all for Jennifer. She was in a sombre mood when she caught the bus to Penzance the following day, to keep her appointment with the Colletts.

Normally she would have sat at the back, as far from the clatter of the horses' hooves as possible, so as to enjoy 'a bit chat' with whoever was next to her. But today she took the seat immediately behind the driver, where conversation was all-nigh impossible, and there she sank into her own brooding thoughts.

They were not about Flossie, though. The high emotions aroused by the funeral had done their work and, for the moment, her heart and mind were numb. Instead, her thoughts wandered back to her conversation with Mrs Collett last week — especially to the moment when she had told her about finding the infant Moses.

And now, for the first time, she was struck by an oddity in the woman's response to the story. Mrs C had made such a fuss about that bun-penny brooch — how her husband had made it and how that kleptomaniac friend had walked off with it, and so on. Jennifer had gone away from their meeting thinking *it* was the item that had awakened her interest in the first place. But now, thinking back over the entire conversation, she recalled that her mention of the brooch had come toward the end, whereas the story had agitated the older woman almost from the beginning. All those other details she had asked for — about the date and the clothes and the colour of the baby's hair and all that — she had been interested in those things even before the brooch was mentioned.

Jennifer began to suspect that Mrs Collett had gone on and on about the brooch as a distraction — realizing that her earlier interest in the clothes, etcetera, had been a bit of a give-away. Something she had said about the baby early on had pricked the woman's interest. Some little detail must have told the woman: 'It's *that* baby!'

What detail, though? Hard as she tried she could not recall her words so minutely.

And what baby? That was much more to the point. A baby born sometime in 1909 was of significance to Mrs Collett. No doubt about it.

She felt as if her mind was on the edge of a whirlpool, and she was staring down into the mouth of its vortex. She tried to reassure herself that she'd never get sucked into it — even though she knew it was inevitable if she so much as dipped a toe into those waters.

You're to stop thinking about it this very minute, she told herself. *Leave well alone. No good can come of it.*

Her stubborn will thumbed its nose at her good sense and she let the thought drag her into the race: *Barry! It has something to do with Barry. Could the baby have been his?*

Back in 1909 Barry Moore would have been seventeen. *Work it out!* she told herself scornfully — and felt very mature to be thinking such thoughts at all.

Her mind leaped to another part of their conversation in the studio that day — where she had mentioned Barry's name and Mrs Collett had jumped to the conclusion that it was Flossie who had been speaking about him on their way into Penzance that same morning. Now why should she have assumed that? Unless Flossie's conversation with her, Mrs Collett had, indeed, been all to do with Barry himself.

But why should Flossie have gone to Penzance to talk to Mrs Collett about her nephew?

Jennifer froze rigid as the thoughts came crowding in all at once: Flossie climbing so gingerly into the gig, quite unlike her usual agile self; Flossie's unwontedly gloomy mood; Flossie's agitation when her mother spoke of 'a buck rabbit on a bicycle.' And now Flossie lying dead in the Methodist burial ground at Godolphin! Were *two* lives cut short by that accident at Tremearne last week? she wondered.

And, more shocking still, had it truly been an accident at all?

She began to feel sick.

There was a place at eastern Praa Sands where the 'cliffs' were only twelve feet high, though otherwise identical to the hundred-and-fifty-foot ones along the rest of the coast. Often in her younger years she and

her friends had stood upon them and jumped until the edge gave way —
screaming and laughing as they plunged with it to the sands below. She
was sure that Flossie had been among the most avid players of that game
— until the day came when a big lump gave way under Mary Liggett and
the sand nearly suffocated her and all the children were forbidden to play
it ever again.

Jennifer took off a glove and passed a hand over her brow, surprised to
find it beaded with cold perspiration. She should never have slipped into
this mood of dismal speculation. The trouble with such thoughts is that,
once you put them into words, they go on in your mind no matter how
hard you want to stop. And if they are questions, they demand an answer.

At least, they do if they're questions about people and life and love and
death. And so they went on ringing in Jennifer's mind, no matter how
hard she tried to think of other, happier things, all the way to Penzance:

Had Flossie Penhaligon been carrying Barry Moore's child when she
died?

Had she come to Penzance last week of a purpose to speak with
Barry's aunt about it — and been sent off with a flea in her ear?

Had she brooded on it for two or three days and then decided to end it
all — but in a way that people would accept as an accident?

Why *had* she been walking all alone on those particular cliffs that
Thursday evening — when all the world knew how dangerous they were?

And then there was the infant Moses — had he been another love child
of the Moores, sired by the son of the Ludgvan Bull? Like father, like son,
like grandson ...

And how was she going to look Mrs Collett in the face when all these
suspicions were whirling around in her mind?

She hesitated so long outside the studio — across the street, in fact,
staring at the display in the draper's window there — that Mrs Collett
came out and called her over. "Did you forget the time and imagine you'd
arrived too early?" she asked.

"No ..." Jennifer replied hesitantly, then was annoyed with herself for
not accepting such an easy excuse.

"Nervous, eh?" Mrs Collett took her arm. "There's absolutely no
need, you know. Mister Collett has looked at the photos I took of you last
week and he agrees. You have that indefinable don't-know-what which
makes some people blossom on film. A lucky few. Why, my dear, you're
shaking like a leaf!"

"Could I have a drink of water, please?" Jennifer played for time,
hoping her racing heart would slow down in the meanwhile.

"Better than that — I'll make us a nice cup of tea. You look as if you need it. Why, you must have frozen half to death, standing out there in the street. The kettle's just boiling."

She took Jennifer through to the back, where customers never went. The front offices were all opulent and gaudy, because the patrons expected it like that; but the back was grand in a much less pretentious manner — all in dark mahogany and simple brass furnishings. Watching the woman as she turned down the gas and busied herself over the teapot, Jennifer realized that if she had any kind of a conscience over Flossie Penhaligon, it was well under control. Before she could stop herself she said, "I'm amazed I didn't catch cold yesterday, actually."

"How?" Mrs Collett asked.

She framed herself and replied, "At Florence Penhaligon's funeral."

"Oh yes, poor girl." She spoke unemphatically and hardly paused in her preparations. "I heard. She was here only last week, you know. Well, of course you do! I forgot. You brought her in, didn't you."

"We picked her up on our way, yes."

The older woman paused then and, staring Jennifer straight in the eye, said, "Tell me — what did you make of her?"

"Make of her?" she echoed. Her pulse was racing once again.

"Yes. Did her mood strike you as at all odd? What did she talk about — if I may make so bold?"

Jennifer realized that if she said nothing now, she'd be kicking herself for weeks. All this panic and nothing to show for it! So, very hesitantly, as if she expected Mrs C to explode with anger, she answered, "As a matter of fact, we spoke about your nephew, Barry Moore."

Mrs Collett, having heated the pot, was now measuring the tea into it. Jennifer, watching closely for her response to this news, saw that it came as no surprise. But she said, "Goodness gracious!" very convincingly. She stared doubtfully at Jennifer for a moment or so, as if uncertain whether or not to speak her mind, and then slipped the cosy over the pot, saying, "We'll let that draw a moment. By the way, talking of my nephew, I sent your parcel off."

While Jennifer was saying her thank yous the woman added, "I hope you don't mind, but I included one of those pictures of you — a nice one. A visiting card is so impersonal. And it's no use pretending that life in the trenches observes all the niceties of tea at the vicarage, is it! I see by your blushes that you don't mind in the least. But you've no cause for embarrassment, you know. There's nothing at all amiss in ... well, in a *miss* taking a certain definite interest in a *mister!* The world would cease to turn if we didn't." She carried the pot over to where Jennifer was sitting. "Do you know my nephew at all well?"

It crossed the girl's mind to say, 'Only by reputation.' Instead she replied: "I have met him." After a pause she added, "From time to time ..." To avoid telling a lie she assured herself she meant the words as the start of a new sentence, one she failed to complete. It was not her fault if Mrs Collett took it as one complete sentence. She went on to describe the first (and, indeed, only) occasion, that June evening on the Flow before the war.

While she spoke Mrs Collett went over to a drawer, rummaged through it, and returned at last with a ten-by-eight of Barry and Gerald; they were wrestling in the garden at Ludgvan, with St Michael's Mount on the horizon. Jennifer stared at it and felt her innards fall away inside her. He was so beautiful! And strong and rugged and ... well, just so unlike any other man in all the world!

"Keep it," Mrs Collett said. "We still have the negative. Then you'll have a picture of him and he'll have one of you. I think the tea will be ready by now."

A short while later Mr Collett finished his session with a customer and came back to join them. He was a still-handsome old fellow in his mid-forties, with slightly thinning dark hair and a kindly twinkle in his eyes. Jennifer prepared for some gentle, well-intentioned teasing. All old men of that age seemed to want to tease her, as if they did not know what else to do. It was very boring, but then, life was full of boring things, so what was one more?

But Mr Collett was an exception to that rule. After a few polite questions about her parents and things like that he started talking about the camera and the strange, almost mystical quality of the images it paints in fine dots of silver halide on white paper. He spoke to her without condescension, too, as if she were in the same trade as himself. He showed her the pictures his wife had taken the previous week, properly printed this time, with all sorts of tricks used during the exposure so as to bring out the finer points of the negative — softening a harsh contour, burnishing the lustrous gleam on her long, dark hair, adding to the sparkle in her eyes ...

If the rushed contacts Jennifer had seen last week were impersonal enough for her to be able to view them dispassionately, these were so far removed from anything that had ever stared back at her from a looking glass that she hardly connected them with herself at all. She just stared at them with amazement.

"Well?" he asked, a little disappointed by her coolness.

"Photography certainly is an *art,* isn't it!" she replied.

Mrs Collett laughed. "She's a professional, Jim, even before she's had time to become an amateuse!"

The word *professional* stirred something in Jennifer. It hinted at an exciting life beyond the bounds she had always assumed would limit her own adult choices. All through the sessions that followed, the thought kept coming back to her: *I could be someone.* It gave her a new strength, without which she might have wilted under the tedium of just standing there, holding the pose, while the Colletts fiddled endlessly with the lighting, the camera position, the *f*-stop (whatever that was), and the length of the exposure.

Then they had a rushed lunch at the buffet down at the railway station, which was half way between their studio in Market Jew and their home, a house called Devoran, above Chyandour Cliff. Mr Collett said he wanted to make a few more trials of her with a slightly different camera that he always kept at home.

This turned out to be a cinematograph camera and Jennifer had to do simple things like walk toward it, smile, nod her head graciously, laugh, look at herself in a glass, and so on. At first she was excruciatingly self-conscious about doing such things when there was no other reason for them than that a man was peering at her through the lens of a camera and cranking a handle on its side. But he kept up such a jolly stream of conversation that she soon forgot the machine — or, rather, that there was anything artificial in the situation — and then it all went swimmingly.

Encouraged by this, Mr Collett changed the film and set her some harder assignments. He told her to look up toward a lighted window and pray for a dying child. She prayed for Barry to be brought safely through this war. Next she had to read a letter from a loved one far away. She imagined it was from Barry. The result, they said, was incredible. Then she was a poor field servant receiving notice to quit the humble family cottage; she was to plead with the bailiff sent to execute the warrant. She imagined Barry was to be shot at dawn and she pleaded with his commanding officer to spare him.

And she felt the most awful fraud when a rather shaken pair of Colletts told her they thought she and the camera were just made for each other. *"Any* camera," Mr Collett said. "Still or motion-picture. You're like that!" And he held up crossed fingers.

Yes, Jennifer thought. *Cross fingers — and hope I'm never found out!*

9 IT NEVER occurred to Jennifer that she might get a letter back from Barry Moore. Perhaps, if she had posted the parcel directly to him, she might have had such hopes; but the most she expected was a note from Mrs Collett to say her nephew had written to say how grateful he was and would she please pass it on? So there were no long weeks of agonized waiting. The first she knew of it was when her father dropped a sheet of paper on the dinner table one evening and said, "What is the meaning of this, young lady?"

His tone was kindly but she always grew wary when he called her 'young lady.' It had not led to friendly exchanges in the past. Her younger brother, Hector, who had just turned fourteen and gone into long trousers — and was therefore allowed to the dinner table *en famille* — licked his lips and craned forward with interest. He, too, smelled battle on the wind.

She reached for the paper but her father trapped it with a finger. "It's addressed to you from a Lieutenant Moore."

"Addressed to *me?*" she echoed in horror. "You mean to tell me you opened one of *my* letters?"

"Now, now, Jennifer!" Goronwy was surprised at their daughter's outburst. Jennifer had always been the most tractable of children. "Your father is quite right …"

"Right?" she exclaimed, cutting her mother off. "You have no right to open my correspondence."

Her father smiled tolerantly — which was the worst sort of smile of all, for it suggested she was not important enough to take seriously. "For as long as you are still a minor and live in this house under our protection, we shall naturally scrutinize all your correspondence. No dutiful parent could do otherwise."

She stared at him, too shocked for words. Hector had never seen his sister so furious. Her face was all white and the way her nostrils flared would remind you of a winded horse. He held his knife and fork like the grips of a racing bicycle.

"Hector, manners!" Goronwy said. "You'll scratch the polish."

He laid the cutlery down, his eyes still riveted on his sister.

Their father went on: "And by *all* your correspondence I naturally mean both incoming and outgoing. *If* we permit you to reply to this letter, we shall expect to see what you write. And you needn't look so shocked. I don't know any other parents who would not insist on a similar condition — and I'm sure you don't, either."

A possible future flashed through Jennifer's mind, in the way that drowning men are supposed to see the whole of their lives sketched out in their final seconds. It did not come in connected words and phrases, in the way she later confided it to her diary, but rather in whole chunks, instantly comprehensible — great stepping stones over which her mental feet could fly. She'd leave home this very night and try the 'brilliant career' the Colletts were pressing her to consider. Practical matters hardly featured here — like where she'd stay, what she'd live on until the projected fortune materialized, and so on. It was a blurred vision of lights and clicking shutters and make-up. And it ended with a rewarding fantasy in which her parents begged her forgiveness, saying she was right and they had been wrong.

The impulse to make that grand gesture struggled with the more cautious elements in her character, which, even as this brief daydream flashed its rainbow arc across her mind, told her she was surely old enough by now to distinguish such dreams from actual, sensible plans. *If you really want it,* she told herself, *you can, indeed, turn this idle fancy into a proper enterprise — but not on the spur of the moment like this. Play clever and play for time!*

"You will be very sorry for this," she said quietly. Then, looking her mother in the eye, she added, "Both of you."

"Go to your room this minute!" her father said. But when, to his surprise, she rose quite calmly to obey him, he went on, "Unless, of course, you are willing to apologize."

Goronwy was surprised, too — less at Jennifer's response than at her own. Partly she was as offended by the girl's disgraceful behaviour as Bevis was; but partly, too, she felt a certain thrill at her anger and rebellion. She was not so old that she had forgotten her own fury when her parents had belittled her, in much the same way as she and Bevis were now belittling Jennifer — treating her like a child still, telling her, in effect, that her emotional incompetence would land her in trouble unless she was watched night and day by wiser guardians.

"Your letter, darling," she said, hoping to distract both combatants from their head-on collision. "Don't you wish to read it?"

Her husband, panicking slightly at the thought that his daughter might now leave the table without submitting to his authority, said, "If you leave this table without apologizing, I shall put this letter on the fire at once. And don't imagine I won't!"

Jennifer walked calmly to the door — amazed that, even inside herself, she felt quite as calm as she now appeared.

"Jennifer!" Goronwy called out in anguish.

She opened the door and turned to face them. Icily she said, "I would not read that letter now if you magnified it a thousand times and pasted it across the sky. You have polluted it by your prying." And she closed the door soundlessly behind her.

Now it was Bevis Owen's turn to sit in flabbergasted silence. He glanced at Goronwy for support — only to find her expression conveying, as clearly as an expression may convey anything, the thought: 'That was not the wisest threat you've ever issued, dear!' She said nothing to that effect, of course, because of the boy, but he had no doubt she'd elaborate upon it later.

Which she did.

"Never back that girl into a corner again," she said as he undid the top hook of her bodice at the back.

A skilled finger ploughed on down, popping buttons as it went. His fingernails raked gently up and down her spine. She luxuriated in the sensation but said, "Not tonight, dear. I'm too upset by this business."

His hand fell away. "Was I so wrong?" he asked. "Can we possibly allow her to receive letters — unopened — from *that* young man? I'd never sleep a wink."

"*That* young man?" She echoed his emphasis. "What do we know about him? Why d'you say it like that?"

In the looking glass she saw him wrestling with what seemed like a number of replies but in the end he said nothing.

"Bevis?" she prompted him.

"I shouldn't really tell anyone," he replied, turning away to begin undressing. "Hippocratic oath and all that." After a pause he added, "Still … it's our daughter."

"Is this also about Barry Moore? And would it have anything to do with the Penhaligon girl?"

He turned and stared at her, trousers at half-mast. "Good God!" he exclaimed. "Is it all over the parish?'"

She shook her head but said nothing.

He raced into his pyjamas and then came over to brush out her hair.

"Just my nasty suspicious mind," she said with a sigh. "When we gave the girl a lift into Penzance that day — the moment I clapped eyes on her — I said to myself, 'You're *enceinte,* my lass.' The bloom on her skin and the colour in her cheeks. It's unmistakable, isn't it. And then, funnily enough, we'd already been talking, Jennifer and I, about Mrs Collett, who was a Moore, as you know — well, not so funnily, perhaps, since we were, after all, going to see her about Jennifer's portrait ... Anyway, where was I? Oh yes. We were talking about the Moores, and Tom Moore of Ludgvan, and his reputation ..."

"You spoke about *that* to two unmarried girls?" He stopped his brushing and stared at her in dismay.

"Someone has to warn them such things are possible. I particularly wanted to warn Jennifer about young Master Barry, for whom she's had a soft spot ever since I can remember."

"Delicately, of course? I mean, you warned her delicately?"

"I said he's a buck rabbit on a bicycle."

Bevis could not help laughing, though he was also shocked.

"Anyway," Goronwy continued, "you could have cut the air with a knife. Young Miss Penhaligon was very frosty after that. And then, when her first port of call proved to be Collett and Trevarton — and I knew *Mister* Collett was away — well, two and two made four. So" — she took his hand long enough to kiss it briefly — "I don't think you'll be breaking any Hippocratic oath if you just fail to deny that Flossie Penhaligon was in that same condition when she fell off the cliff and drowned. Did you do a post-mortem?"

"I didn't cut her open. It wasn't really necessary."

Goronwy shivered. "The poor thing!"

"And yet what sort of life would she have had if she'd lived on and brazened it out? Old Penhaligon would have turfed her out on her ear. And the fact that she didn't go back to Mrs Collett shows what sort of reception she got there." He laid the brush down and went to his side of the bed, where he pushed his hot-water bottle over to join hers. "It is an indictment of us and our society that Miss Penhaligon's decision to end it all was the best and most reasonable one she could make."

Goronwy put on her nightie and then slipped out of her underwear. "You said nothing at the inquest."

"I wasn't asked. I was very carefully *not* asked. We've all got to go on living together. Why uncover a truth that's harmful to tell and pointless to know?"

She climbed into bed and relished the touch of the hot-water bottles, which were still hot enough to scald. Her frozen feet thrust them this way and that, making impolite gurgling sounds beneath the blankets. Soon they yielded enough of their warmth to the sheets to become touchable in themselves. Then she lay back, one foot firmly plunged into each blubbery mass, and said, "D'you really think it's an indictment of us — what you said just now?"

"Don't you?" he countered.

"Then why are we making such a fuss when Jennifer gets a rather charming and entirely proper thank-you letter from young Mister Moore?"

"Oh, surely we can criticize society and its hypocrisy while admitting at the same time that it's too powerful for us to resist?"

Goronwy thought this over and then said, "Shouldn't we try telling Jennifer that? Why can't we say, 'Look, darling, we think this is stupid, too. But it's the way society expects people to behave, so there's not much we can do about it except to play along.' I think she'd find that much more acceptable than … well, what you tried to do this evening. You didn't burn that letter, I hope?"

He chuckled. "No. I left it on the table as if I'd forgotten it. In fact, I *did* forget it. I just stopped myself going back when I finally remembered."

"Why?"

"I expect she'll creep down at dead of night tonight, to cut herself a slice of leftovers, and so she'll read it — and then she'll go on telling us she never-never-never wants to read the thing because we've polluted it!"

"Ah yes." Goronwy smiled at the ceiling. "She has your stubbornness, all right. I hope she also has your shrewdness." She reached her lips toward him for a goodnight kiss.

He snuffed the candle. The moon was waxing but only four days old. It had set hours ago, leaving the world to almost total darkness.

"I wasn't very shrewd tonight," he said ruefully.

After a pause she replied, "That depends on what you were trying to do. If you were simply trying to stop her from having anything more to do with Mister Moore, then yes, you weren't at all shrewd. But is that what you really wanted?"

He sighed. "I suppose not."

"What then?"

"I suppose I wanted to put so many obstacles in her way that — if she really wished to continue her correspondence with the fellow, well then, she'd jolly well have to work for it. We're not going to strew her path with rose petals."

There was an even longer pause before Goronwy said, "The trouble is, we'll never know if she has inherited your shrewdness, Bevis, unless she somehow gets the chance to test it."

"And what if she comes a cropper?"

"Quite."

10 WHEN ALL was silent in the house, Jennifer got dressed and tiptoed downstairs clutching her boots in her hand. She wasn't actually going to run away, she told herself, only practising, to see how easy it would be if a midnight flit became really necessary. She felt so humiliated by her father's treatment of her at dinner that she simply had to make some kind of defiant gesture, and a practice absconding seemed as good as anything else she might try. She'd go as far as the blacksmith's. Or, perhaps, to the corner where the pigsties were — where she found Moses that time. On a moonless night like this she ought to manage it without being seen.

Inside the house it was so dark she could only feel her way down the stairs. She counted carefully so as to avoid the seventh and the third treads, which creaked. Near the bottom she froze in terror, thinking that someone had just struck a match in the dining room. But then, when no other sound followed, she peered cautiously round the door jamb and saw that the fire, which her father had banked down with slack for the night, had sprouted a little flare of bright yellow gas. If you came in by daylight, you wouldn't even notice it, but now, after hours of velvet darkness, it was like a naphtha flare in a fairground. And by its light she spotted the piece of paper on the dining-room table.

It couldn't be the offending letter, of course, and yet — on the slimmest chance that it might be — she had to see for herself.

My dear Miss Owen, it began.

She folded it to her breast, closed her eyes, and fought for breath.

My dear Miss Owen!

My *dear* Miss Owen!

For those few words alone she'd have knitted her fingers down to stumps for him. What other verbal riches were there in the rest of this treasured page? She wanted to read it all in one quick sweep of the eye. Or she wanted to take it upstairs and lock it away and read just one new sentence each day — to really-really-really savour it. Her beating heart was all over the place.

She knelt on the hearthrug and, with trembling fingers, turned the page toward the flare. Almost immediately it died and she was in darkness once again. She stifled a cry of frustration and returned to the stairs, where she made an equally cautious way back to her bedroom. There, with greater stoicism than she knew she possessed, she laid the letter face down while she lit the candle and got undressed again before creeping back between her sheets. Then, with just her head and fingers out in the cold, and with the light shining through the paper, she read the letter at last. The writing was tiny, unnaturally so, as if he had been constrained to fit it all on one side of the paper. Perhaps that was the case, she thought, for if the censor cut out anything, you didn't want him cutting out what was on the back as well. It read:

My dear Miss Owen,
I cannot even begin to say how grateful I was to receive the scarf and mittens you gave my aunt to send. I have known some cold nights in Cornwall, or so I thought before coming here, but an arctic wind sweeping out of Russia and across Europe has no sea to moderate its bite. I doubt you have ever been blessed more warmly than I blessed you on opening that parcel. Nor could you be thought of more warmly than I think of you each day as I put on my mittens and scarf and hose. Without the mittens, my fingers would not obey me to write this letter!

I don't know whether <u>you</u> have any fingers left after what must have been a marathon of knitting, but a balaclava helmet would be an enormous boon. (My head is not as big as this brusque hint must make it seem. I take a 7¼ in hats.) Also a <u>very loose-knitted</u> vest of string. The Canadians here wear them under their shirts and they swear by them. The loose mesh traps air, they say, which is the secret of keeping warm. You may tell by this how obsessed we have become with keeping warm.

You may not know it but my aunt included a photograph of you, which I now carry in my pay-and-record book in my breast pocket. I think I had better say no more about that, except, perhaps, to add that it is a grave offence for any soldier to be without his "P-and-R" day or night. And that the pocket in question is the one on my left, nearest to you may guess what.

Don't think me impertinent but your photograph makes me ask whether you were that extremely pretty young girl I met in Carleen once, three or four years ago, when I let my cousin, Gerald Body, beat me in a wrestling practice — or did he let me beat him? You would have been with Florence Penhaligon and someone else. I don't remember whom. If so, I'm delighted to have renewed our acquaintance. It is something I have often wished for.

Oh dear! An attack is expected. The sky is full of star shells and we must stand to. Will you ask your parents if we may correspond? A sympathetic ear back home is as warming to the spirit as are knitted comforts to our extremities.

Believe me your grateful friend,

Barry Moore

Jennifer wasn't exactly crying but there were tears on her cheeks as she finished the letter. Of course, she read it again at once, and then again, and yet again — by which time she was, indeed, crying. The minutely perfect words dissolved and swam before her eyes. It was so utterly beautiful — probably the most beautiful letter ever written in any language. *The Love Letters of an English Lady* paled in comparison.

A knot of panic twisted inside her: How was she *ever* going to be able to reply? Her words would be dross beside his pure gold. He'd see at once what a tawdry, threadbare mind she had; then he'd either patronize her or stop writing altogether.

What could she tell him about? What exciting things ever happened to her? There were no star shells in her sky. Today I helped my mother; we turned out one of the attic rooms. Today I helped my mother again; we made jam. Today we dug an extra patch for the potatoes and turnips, because of the War Effort ... we sold flags in the street for the nursing auxiliaries ... we went to church and prayed for victory ...

It made her yawn even to think of it.

But what if her life changed? What if she could say she was playing the part of a heroic young nurse, on a film 'lot' (or 'set' or whatever they called it), which looked exactly like Wipers or Mons, and he could show her photo round, just casually letting it drop that she was the star of *The New Nightingale* or some such motion picture ... wouldn't that just be something to brag about!

She fell asleep soon after that, hoping her pleasant fantasy would melt into her dreams. But instead she found herself standing on a foreshore looking at monstrous waves, higher and more violent than any she had ever seen, all boiling with white foam, hurling themselves against her, one after another. Yet somehow, although they were only a few dozen yards away, and taller than a cathedral spire, they never quite touched her.

When she woke up the following morning she didn't know whether to take it as a sign that she would pass unscathed through whatever threats life had in immediate store for her, or did it mean that all life's excitement and hurly-burly would forever pass her by and that she would never be more than a passive spectator at that exciting and turbulent feast?

She waited until she heard her father leave — not wanting to meet him until she'd had a chance to speak with her mother — and only then rose to wash and dress. She hid the letter in her diary (not the one her mother would sneak in and read but the one she kept under the loose floorboard) before she went downstairs.

"Sorry I'm late," she said, helping herself to porridge. "I didn't sleep very well."

"I don't suppose you did," Goronwy replied warily.

Jennifer touched the corner where the letter had lain the previous night. "Gone," she murmured.

Her mother suppressed a smile and said, "He's a man of his word. You should know that by now."

Jennifer ate in silence, her face impassive.

The telephone rang. Her mother went to answer it. When she came back she said, "An epidemic of influenza is all we need!"

"D'you want me to run up those new curtains today?"

"Good idea."

"Only I need more bias binding in that case. I think I saw some exactly the right shade in Mrs Treloar's in Market Jew. I could pop in on the bus. I'll get another eight ounces of wool, too. Is there anything you want?"

Goronwy sighed. How were they ever going to be able to communicate when the girl was all spines inside and all alabaster on the surface? "I can't spare the time today, dear," she said. "Next week, perhaps."

"It hardly takes two of us to carry a packet of bias binding and eight balls of wool!"

"You know what I mean, darling."

"No I don't."

"I mean that when I was your age the very idea of going unchaperoned into a town like Penzance was unthinkable."

"Perhaps that was because all the young men they were guarding you against weren't hundreds of miles away, freezing to death in the trenches. Distant soldiers are our chaperons now!"

"There are plenty left in civilian clothes," Goronwy said heavily.

"I'll carry a bag of white feathers for them. Anyway, Queen Victoria's been dead more than ten years now. There are girls my age actually nursing young soldiers out in France, hundreds of miles from families and chaperons and things."

Her mother laughed at this fancy. "They're chaperoned, my dear — believe you me." When her daughter made no reply she added, "Is that what you'd like to do? Become a nurse and go over to France?"

Still she said nothing. It was a trick, of course, to see if she'd leap at the chance to get close to Barry.

"Or work here in England?" her mother went on. "They're crying out for nurses here, too. Would you like that?"

Jennifer stared at her in amazement. This was no trick. She really meant it. "Could I?" she asked with bated breath.

"We'd have to ask your father but I'm sure he'd be delighted. You could train at the Royal Cornwall and come home weekends."

Jennifer's heart turned a somersault. The Royal Cornwall was just half a mile from the Colletts. Barry could write there and she could pick up his letters and leave her own and no one would be any the wiser.

"I've got to do *something,*" she said. "We've all got to do our bit now. Do they have application forms or anything like that? I could pick them up this morning when I go in."

"We'll have to ask your father first," Goronwy warned her. "And you, young lady, have a fence to mend with him before that."

11 PEOPLE WERE already talking about 'the old days.' They meant 'before the war,' which was not yet one year old. Already it seemed a lifetime away. In the early months, when everyone felt sure it would be short and swift, with just sufficient casualties to make heroes of the survivors, people felt no obligation to change their habits or ways of thinking. But when they came to realize what perils the nation faced, nothing was sacred that stood in the way of salvation. Munitions factories that would have taken months to build last year were now completed in weeks. Ordnance factories turned out a week's supplies in a single day. And hospitals that had never trained a single nurse now started regular courses for volunteer nursing auxiliaries — and proved every bit as good at the game as those who had been playing it a century and more. The Royal Cornwall was one such institution.

In Jennifer's case it helped, naturally, that her father was not only 'in the trade' himself but actually had one weekly session in its theatres. True, it was only in general and intestinal surgery — nothing that required a suture finer than tennis-racket catgut — but at least he knew which lapels to buttonhole and whose ears to bend to get his daughter into a course that had already been running for three weeks. She joined it on the last Monday in March, in the week when the awful news from the Dardanelles was just beginning to sink in.

She never actually 'mended the fence' with her father. He seemed to take her desire to become a nurse — to join the family business, so to speak — as an apology and submission, all in one. The letter was never mentioned again. She did not reproach him for 'burning it'; nor did he accuse her of taking it against his authority. By the standards of her childhood it was a messy ending — a loose thread over which either of them might trip at some unguarded moment in the future. But she was beginning to understand that grown-up life was full of such pitfalls — contests that were never quite settled, because even the apparent winner realized he would lose more than he gained by it. Grown-ups who could not tolerate such messiness, in a spirit of live-and-let-live, ended up facing each other in muddy trenches, fighting to the death.

Life at the hospital was oddly familiar. At first she thought it was simply that she had called there so many times when family visits to Penzance happened to coincide with her father's days in theatre; but then she realized that every girls'-school yarn she had ever read had prepared her for this new life — give or take a few years on the ages of the pupils.

There was the 'dorm,' with its curtained cubicles; and 'refec,' where they ate their meals (one could hardly say 'dined'); and the 'blues,' or ablutions, where they shone themselves up like pippins each morning for inspection by — yes — a real live matron. She was called Matron, in hushed, deferential tones, to her face and the Dragon, in hushed, fearful ones, behind her back. To complete the similarities with school, there was even a rack of hockey sticks, with which, on Tuesday, Thursday, and Saturday afternoons, they mopped up most of the energy that might otherwise have gone into climbing in and out of windows and sneaking off to dances.

The Dragon, Miss Prudence Hall, was a short, stocky woman in her late fifties. Her curly chestnut hair was always imprisoned beneath an immaculately starched cap. As she strode down corridors and into wards, theatres, or classroom, she carried a roving battlefield with her. Her pale green eyes never rested. They quartered the scene like a pair of marauding falcons and God help the nurse with a stray curl of hair showing, a stocking seam twisted, or a hastily tucked-in bed corner on her ward. Her voice was like a sergeant major's and the envelope of air for at least six inches outside her body seemed charged with some especially dangerous form of static electricity. Nurses swore that, when she stood near them, the hair on their scalps — and even the light downy fur on their arms — would stiffen in response to that electrical power and their very skin would tingle at it.

In fact, she exercised this power entirely by force of her personality; only rarely did she hand down an actual punishment, and, like a well-lobbed grenade, it was always designed to produce instant surrender rather than massive casualties. In the first week of the auxiliaries' course, for instance, she had noticed Rosalind Collett, Jim and Crissy's nineteen-year-old daughter, crossing the parking space behind the hospital; and, to her horror, the girl was *still drawing on her gloves!*

She threw up the window and bawled, "Miss Collett!" The words rolled across the open space. The girl froze like one caught in no-man's-land by unexpected sniper fire. "Come to my office this instant!"

She slammed the window down with such force that the sash weights thumped in protest inside their cases. She paused long enough to be sure of the girl's compliance and then, radiating volts, swept like a stately galleon in full sail to her room. She'd had her eye on the Collett girl from the start. They were a respectable and prosperous family nowadays but Mrs Collett was a Moore, and the Moores had always been a thorn in the flesh of authority. She recalled her colleague, Mrs Rodgers of the Sutton Orphanage in Plymouth, speaking of a time when she and her husband had had charge of the two youngest Moore boys. And young Miss Moore, no older then than her daughter Rosalind was now, had come storming in like a tigress and more or less kidnapped them out of the orphanage.

Miss Hall had seen at once that the daughter was from the same pugnacious bloodline. She would have picked her as the example-that-made-other-examples-unnecessary even had she known nothing of the family's history. Tall, well built, lean and restless, the girl seemed to be on the lookout for slights and injuries all the time. Even the frizziness of her golden hair was somehow aggressive. It infuriated the matron that the auxiliaries wore such skimpy little bonnets. It was to distinguish them from fully trained nurses, of course, but it meant she couldn't insist that the girls tuck every last wisp of hair out of sight — shaving their necks, if need be, as she shaved her own each week.

There was a knock at the door.

"Come!" she called out.

Miss Collett opened the door and stood at the threshold. Her face was a mask, neither fearful nor defiant.

"Right in!" the matron had to say.

She walked in and closed the door behind her as if she were alone in the room; her gestures conveyed as little as her face.

Oh, yes, Miss Hall thought grimly. *You're the one I must squash from the very beginning.*

"What on earth do you think you were doing just now, young lady?" she snapped.

Rosalind stared at her in genuine bewilderment. She glanced at the window and said, "Crossing the yard, Matron."

"And?"

"Are we not allowed to cross that yard? If so, please accept ..."

"Never mind all that, Miss. What else were you doing?"

"Nothing, Matron. Just crossing the yard. I didn't know it was forbidden. If so, I'm very ..."

"It's *not* forbidden. If it were, I should have told you so. But there are certain acts I do not expect to have to forbid to any genteel young lady, and you, Miss Collett, were engaged in one of them. I ask you again — what was it?"

Rosalind thought hard and came up with, "Was I humming a tune? I think I was. I'm most dreadfully sorry, but I didn't ..."

"You were *not* humming a tune, either. At least, if you were, it was quite inaudible to me. No! You were *drawing on your gloves!* Out there in public — for any passing Tom, Dick, or Harry to see! What sort of behaviour is that for a young lady?"

"Well, we only have one hour free, Matron, so I was hurrying as fast ..."

"Nothing can excuse such a dreadful lapse in decorum. Would you do such a thing at home?"

"Yes, of course." The hussy actually grinned!

"Well, you shall not do such things here. I shall not tolerate the slightest lapse from ladylike standards. You will put your gloves on completely in the privacy of your own cubicle. Is that clear?"

"Perfectly, Matron." Still she smiled! "And I'm very grateful to you for pointing it out to me. It won't happen again."

"Indeed it won't! And I shall do more than simply 'point it out.' It's quite clear you have only the haziest notion of how a lady comports herself. You are gated for a week and you'll ..."

"Oh, Matron! That's not fair. I *have* to see my father today because ..."

"How dare you tell me what's fair and what's not. I am *never* unfair. Strict, yes — as you shall soon learn if you continue to oppose me! Now, as I was about to say: During this coming week, while you are gated, you will not sit around just twiddling your thumbs. Instead you will read a little manual titled *Don't,* which you will find in the nurses' library. It is an excellent little compendium of errors and solecisms in speech and behaviour. At the end of the week I shall ask you a number of questions based upon its counsel. If you cannot answer them satisfactorily, you will be gated for a further week — and so on until your answers *are* satisfactory. Do I make myself clear?"

"Yes, Matron."

At last — at long last — the girl averted her eyes.

"And if any of your friends imagine I shall be less strict with them, you may do them the kindness of informing them it is not so."

"Yes, Matron."

"Cut along now."

"Beastly cow!" Rosalind murmured very quietly as she walked away up the corridor, stripping off her gloves as she went. The Dragon had said nothing about taking gloves *off* in public.

She did Jennifer the favour of warning her as soon as she joined the course, telling her the tale of the gloves with several rich embellishments. "The thing is," she said, "about not putting one's gloves on in public, I remember my mother telling me it was something *her* mother told her about how strict etiquette was when *she* was a girl — which would have been the sixties of the last century or something. I'd quite believe it if the Dragon turned out to have been born back then. I don't believe she was ever our age."

"What was in that book she made you read?" Jennifer asked.

"Don't? Oh, it's packed with useful advice like don't take off your cap to fan your teacup with. Don't write 'has' when you mean 'as.' Don't bump into people when walking down the street. Things we do all the time!"

"Of course!" Jennifer laughed. "I charge into them, full tilt if possible."

"Actually, it said in three separate places, 'Don't sit with your legs crossed. Men break this rule all the time but it isn't considered ladylike.' Can you believe it? I think women break that rule more than men, don't you? In fact, I've never heard the rule before."

"Nor I," Jennifer agreed. It was untrue, of course. Her mother was very strict about it. 'Ladies cross their bootlaces but never their boots' — that was the way her mother put it. But she thought it more important to get on good terms with Barry's cousin than to score petty social points against her.

"You're rather keen on my cousin Barry, aren't you," Rosalind said out of the blue.

"Me? Good heavens, no!" This time her laugh was patently false.

"Oh well, that's a relief." The girl pretended to believe her. "I was all set to warn you — you want to beware of him. But, if you're not interested anyway ... it doesn't matter."

12 TOWARD THE end of April the Germans launched the offensive that turned into the second Battle of Wipers; they also used poison gas for the first time. One small consequence was that Jennifer's father did not take his usual session at the hospital on the following Monday. Military hospitals in southeastern England, nearest the Channel ports, had sent out a call for doctors to volunteer to treat the first casualties of this appalling new weapon. He was away for only three days but he returned an altered man.

"A doctor has to inure himself against pain and suffering of all kinds," he said. "If he can't, he's no use to his patients. But one would have to be a monster with a heart of stone not to feel for those poor fellows. It isn't just the gas — it's everything. How our lads keep their spirits so high I cannot imagine. The newspapers tell us nothing of what's really going on. We need a new Russell to open our eyes."

Through innumerable private encounters of that kind, people at home learned of the horrors of trench warfare. Powerless to confront the enemy themselves, they took refuge in symbolic but futile revenge. Schmidt's Fine Food Emporium in Causeway Head was smashed up and looted. A gang of boys threw stones at a gypsy caravan inhabited by a retired and eccentric clergyman called Karl Lang — whose parents had, in fact, been Swedish, not German at all. And at Evans's Motor Repairs, Billy Evans himself painted over the word Bosch on all the signs that once proudly displayed it.

These great and stirring events impinged but slightly upon the tight little world of the hospital. There, the fact that Peggy Wilmot had lost a new pair of stockings was of far greater moment than the loss of twenty-five yards on the Wipers salient. Every trainee was under suspicion of having 'borrowed' them — until they turned up wrapped around a piece of wood in one of the cupboards and Peggy remembered she had been practising tourniquets with them.

Tourniquets and pressure points loomed large in the course. The art was to staunch the blood long enough for it to clot but not so long that gangrene set in. Splints came a close second — splints and bandages. Sister Morrison taught them bandaging, which she had learned in her training and then relearned properly in the Cape during the Boer War. She taught them the kind she learned in her training, where each turn of the bandage lapped its neighbour in perfect symmetry and there were no loose ends; then she showed them how to do it in an actual front-line field station, where the aim was to save lives rather than pass examinations in perfect bandaging.

No one thought these twin standards — one for show, one for real — at all extraordinary. The same outlook ruled every aspect of their lives. For instance, they had to rise at half-past five each morning and strip their beds right down to the mattress ticking. Then sheets and blankets were folded into a boxlike pile — very boxlike once the counterpane was folded to embrace the lot. Then Rosalind Collett intercepted some old hospital sheets and blankets on their way to the rag-and-bone man. She glued strips of them around some used cardboard boxes that had once held Kodak paper and were just the right size. Then, each morning, she simply stuffed her sheets and blankets any old how into a kitbag in her locker and set this fake display out upon her mattress. She won the neatest-bed competition three days running, until other girls started doing the same.

Rosalind swiftly became the leader of the group, the one to watch, the one who set the tone. The Dragon had recognized it from the beginning but had not seen that her gating of the girl for such a minor trespass would merely add to her status. Jennifer, new to communal life, thus had even more reason to seek her friendship, quite apart from her kinship with the most wonderful man in the world. Within a week they were inseparable — and certainly close enough for Jennifer to show her Barry's letter. They had adjacent beds in the dorm, so it was an easy matter to loop up the curtain between them and 'confab' in whispers until sleep overtook them.

Rosalind read it just before lights-out. Jennifer watched in an agony of suspense, for not a flicker of emotion passed across her friend's face.

Rosalind passed it back without a word, just a rather tight little smile that could mean anything.

"Well?" Jennifer pressed her.

"It's not a very *manly* letter, is it — except where he more or less *commands* you to knit him a balaclava and this vest of string. That's manly, all right. That's the Barry we all know and love!"

"I think you're beastly." Jennifer felt tears prickling behind her eyelids. "How can you say the rest isn't manly? I think it's very manly. A beautiful, sensitive, manly letter. What should he write about otherwise? Football and wrestling? He surely knows I wouldn't be interested."

"Exactly! It's just the sort of letter you or I might write if someone set us the task of writing our own dream letter from the man we love. Listen, pet! I *know* Barry. I grew up with him. I endured his barbs when he was young enough to be afraid of girls — and believe me, he knew how to score a bullseye every time. He's uncanny. He *knows* women — don't ask me how. He knows our emotions better than we do ourselves, and how to twist them for his own ends. And I fought off his advances when he grew up enough to lose his fear and replace it with ... well, the other thing."

Jennifer was shattered. "I don't believe you," she said sulkily. "You're making it up. You're just jealous."

"Ha!" Rosalind was too amused to be affronted. "You imagine he's interested in *you?* You as a person? As someone with feelings and wishes of your own? He couldn't even grasp that as an idea. You're not a person to him. No woman is. We're just skirts. You're 'a bit of fluff' — that's how he'd describe you to his chums. 'My skirt ... my little bit of fluff.' That's why it's ridiculous to talk of being jealous. I couldn't be jealous. I could have as much of dear Cousin Barry — or as little, rather — as you or any other girl going." She reached out and squeezed Jennifer's arm through the blankets. "All you need do is lie down and say yes."

Lights-out interrupted their conversation.

Safely in the dark she whispered, "Mind you, Jenny — if all you *want* is to lie down and say yes, then there's no one more reliable in all the world! Horses for courses, eh!"

Jennifer swallowed the lump in her throat and managed a dutiful little giggle. From then on they had to talk in whispers, or in a voice as close to a whisper as made no difference.

"Anyway, what did you reply?" Rosalind asked.

"I haven't yet. I wanted to send the balaclava with it. I've almost finished it, but we get so little spare time."

"What do you intend telling him?"

"I just sent a card saying he wasn't to write to me at home but he could use your house as a *poste restante,* if he liked. I don't suppose ... no, they'd have given you a letter for me if it had come, wouldn't they?"

"I'm sure."

"Does your mother share your opinion of Barry? If so, I can't think why she sent him my photo."

Now it was Rosalind who fell silent.

"Well?" Jennifer prompted.

She sighed. "You'd have to know Barry to understand. He's the most maddeningly attractive man you could hope to meet — but he's also repulsive, too. You'll see. You get fascinated by his charm — and he can turn it on like a tap. And you look into his eyes and you can *see* there's nothing there. It's all ... I don't know — he's like an automaton. You feel sorry for him because he's such an utter slave to this compulsion. He's got no choice. All the jolly things you could do and enjoy together — things other people do — listening to music, reading poetry, looking at paintings, talking about ideas, novels, books you've read — even just gossiping about this and that. He can *do* all those things, of course. He's got a tongue of silver when he wants. But to him they're all just means to an end. Of no value in themselves. They're just stepping stones to a seduction. And once you *know* that — once you know he's just switching on a technique ... I mean, it's not that your fascination turns into revulsion. You don't lose your fascination. You just feel fascinated *and* repelled at the same time." She drew breath. "Why did I start telling you this?"

"I asked about your mother's opinion."

"Oh yes. She's also fascinated-repelled, I think. Not that he's turned his seductive charm on her, of course!" She giggled at the thought. "But she's observed it in action. She *knows* what a menace he is and yet, I don't know ... it's a funny thing about women of her generation. They seem to *expect* men to be like that. She says he's 'a card' — and in a way she's proud of him at the same time as she deplores what he does." After a pause she added, "One thing I meant to say about his letter: He's pretty nonchalant about Flossie Penhaligon, isn't he! Just throwing in her name like that."

"She was still alive when he wrote."

"Ah — yes. Of course."

But something in Rosalind's tone told Jennifer that she hadn't been referring to Flossie's death. Recalling her own suspicions about Barry and the girl she said, "You know we gave Flossie a lift into Penzance that day — the same day I brought my knitted comforts in for your mother to send to Barry? She came in especially to see your mother."

"Did she tell you ..." Rosalind hesitated. Jennifer felt sure that the word she stumbled over was 'why.' The words that finally came out, however, were "... that? I mean, did she actually tell you she came to Penzance *especially?*"

"She hardly needed to. I mean, she got down in Market Jew right outside the studios and made a beeline for them." She let this sink in before she added, "Two days later she was dead."

Rosalind breathed fiercely in and out, several times. "I *hate* him!" she whispered at last.

Then Jennifer had the courage to ask it: "Was it about Barry? Did she say she was carrying his child?"

"She did tell you, then," Rosalind answered bitterly.

"No. It just crossed my mind after she died. Thinking about it, you know. Wondering if it really was an accident — and, if it wasn't, what sort of predicaments might have led her to do it."

When Rosalind made no reply, Jennifer said, "What d'you think?"

"I think you're not quite as green as you're cabbage-looking."

"I'm not cabbage-looking at all."

"Exactly! Therefore not green. I don't think you're in love with Barry at all, either. Just with some ideal man who looks like him but doesn't exist outside your mind. I think, when you meet, you'll see through him in the first five minutes."

"And then?" Jennifer asked bleakly, though she also felt rather flattered.

"Then you can decide, can't you! Whether to break off — or pay him back in his own coin. I mean, use him for *your* purposes."

"Such as?"

Rosalind gave out a sigh, more theatrical than heartfelt. "D'you need me to tell you absolutely *everything?*"

13 LATE IN THE afternoon of Tuesday, 1 June, the Dragon came into the auxiliaries' classroom and, seeking out Jennifer, said in a low, solemn voice, "Will you come with me, my dear?"

The gentle tone and the unprecedented endearment so stunned the girl that she could only sit there, wondering if she had heard properly.

"Yes," the Matron said, touching her arm. "Come on."

Still in something of a daze, Jennifer followed her out into the corridor. "What is it?" she asked.

"Grave news, I'm afraid," the woman replied. She walked slowly, matching her pace to the girl's.

Barry was dead! Jennifer just knew it. Her innards seemed to turn a full loop and then to fall away, leaving nothing but a great void. Her mind was blank but her senses were suddenly keen. Supernaturally keen. She noted minute hair-cracks in the paint that larded the brickwork of the corridor walls. The smallest unevenness in the linoleum felt like a ploughed field beneath her feet. She heard her own heartbeat as thunder inside her skull. The power of these sensations drove out all logic, so that she did not ask herself how the Dragon might have got to know of her love for Rosalind's cousin. The whole world must surely know of something so great and wonderful.

"Your mother wished to break it to you herself," Matron went on. "But it is only fair for me to warn you to prepare for ... well, the worst news you could possibly hear, I'm afraid."

That could only be Barry.

Matron had timed it well. Her hand was on the knob of the door to her room as she spoke the final words. It swung open and Jennifer saw her mother rising, arms outstretched toward her. "Oh, my dear!" she said. She was dressed all in black.

Even in her confused state Jennifer realized that was wrong. Her mother had never met Barry; she would hardly wear so much as a black armband to mark his death. Still, she had to ask, "Is it about ... Barry Moore?" as she fell into her mother's embrace.

She felt her mother's body stiffen. "Barry Moore?" The tone was both affronted and bewildered. "No! Good heavens! You ... you ...?" Her mother drew a sharp breath, as if to take a grip on herself. "It's your father," she said quietly.

The words had no immediate meaning. Instead of 'father' she heard 'not-Barry' and it was all that mattered. To be sure, the full significance of her mother's words penetrated a moment or so later but in that brief meanwhile she had − unforgivably − sighed with relief. Too late she tried to rescue the situation. "Daddy?" she asked in a feeble, straying voice she did not recognize as hers. The truth then overwhelmed her. "Dead? Daddy − dead? No! No-o-o-o ...!"

This was more like the response Goronwy had expected − the one she had prepared herself to cope with. Setting aside for the moment her daughter's shocking question − and reaction − she hugged her as tight as she could and said, "Yes, darling. I'm afraid it's true. Last night he was out in the ..."

"But how ... where ...?" Jennifer was fighting the hysteria that now threatened to consume her. The news was, of course, far worse than if it had been of Barry's death; she was almost prepared for *that*. In her imagination her lover had died a dozen times a day − when she scanned the lists of casualties at the Town Hall, when she completed a further row in the new woollen comforts she was knitting him in case the war went into a second winter, when she prayed for him to live. But her father was immortal − a mountain in the landscape of her life. The very possibility of his death had never seriously crossed her mind. Even now ... yes, even now, it *had* to be a mistake.

"In London," Goronwy said. "Last night. There was a zeppelin raid last night."

Now Jennifer was sobbing her eyes out. Everything inside her was aching with misery — except for one small part that was more angry than grief-stricken. No! it shouted. There was surely a mistake ... confusion with some other Owen ... millions of people in London ... one small bomb falling out of the sky ... pick him out? Ridiculous! She would never accept it.

When the aching turned to numbness, when misery itself was numb, she realized she must have been crying a long time. Her mother was patting her back and saying, "There, there!"

"What do we do now?" she asked forlornly.

"Home," her mother said, straightening up and pulling away from her. "I'll need you at home for a month or so ..." Her voice petered out. She closed her eyes and sighed. "I can't think. Every now and then my mind just goes ... empty." She smiled wanly. "Go and pack your things, darling. At least that'll make a start. I'll wait here until Matron comes back. I want another word with her before we go."

Jennifer was hardly aware of walking along the corridor — merely that its walls, floors, and ceiling were passing her. She tried to focus on little random fragments of that passing scene — a chip in the paintwork, a stain on the floor, the cord that opened and closed one of the overhead windows. *You'll never forget these tiny things,* she assured herself. *They will be burned into your memory by this unbelievable news.*

Matron must have gone back and told the class the dreadful news because Rosalind was waiting for her in the dorm, which was otherwise mercifully empty.

"Jenny, pet!" she cried, rushing to meet her and throwing her arms around her.

For a long while they just stood there, unable to express their shared sorrow in any other way, until Jennifer once again lost touch with time. The scene dissolved into swarms of black needles that flew all about her.

"If there's anything I can do," Rosalind said at last. *"Anything.* Absolutely anything. Just let me know."

Jennifer thanked her abstractedly and drifted over to her bed. "It's a dream," she said. She even managed a small, mirthless laugh. "A nightmare. I know I'm going to wake up at any moment, bathed in sweat. It's a fever. And *he'll* be there, taking my pulse ... feeling my brow ..."

She flung herself face down, full length upon the mattress, crying "Never again! I'll never feel his touch again. Never see him smile! Oh God, oh God, oh God! *Why?"*

After a respectful silence Rosalind said, "I'll pack these for you, eh?"

In less than a minute it was done. She gazed down at the now stilled and silent body of her friend and wondered if she had fallen asleep. Would it be cruel to wake her?

Jennifer resolved the dilemma by stretching out and then rolling onto her back. "I'll never see this place again, either," she murmured.

"Of course you will!" Rosalind assured her. "You *must* come back — for his sake. He was very proud of you. He told me so."

Jennifer sat up and stared at her. "You spoke to him?"

She nodded. "Or, rather, he spoke to me. He stopped me in the corridor one day — only last week, actually — and asked me how you were getting on and did the Dragon bother you too much and so on. And when I said everything was all right he said he was very proud you'd decided to take this course and do what you could for England."

"You didn't tell me."

"He asked me not to. So, you see, you've got to come back and complete the course — for his sake."

Jennifer stood up and took a grip on her case. "You won't be here then," she said gloomily.

"We'll meet up somewhere. We'll keep in touch, and one or other of us will surely wangle a posting to be together again."

Jennifer ambled awkwardly toward the door, where she turned and asked, "Aren't you coming down?"

Rosalind shook her head. "I hate goodbyes. Hey, pet, I'll tell you one bright lining to this cloud — it wasn't Barry!"

Jennifer was now as shocked as she knew her mother had been earlier.

"Go on!" the other chided. "I'll bet it crossed your mind!"

Jennifer smiled — and forced herself to go on smiling until the door was closed behind her. Then she leaned her forehead hard against the oak and said aloud, "I am awful. I'm a monster."

"We must try to be practical," Goronwy said as they mounted the gig. She patted Jennifer's knee and added, "Thank God you're here, darling. When the telegram came, I just wanted to crawl into bed and go to sleep for a month. Or a year. I wanted to wake up and find it was all over." She smiled encouragingly. "We must keep busy — and, God knows, there's enough to be done."

As they drew out of the hospital yard they passed a group of women — four or five of them supporting one who was clearly in an extremity of grief. It was a daily sight in every town and village in the land. Jennifer and her mother exchanged glances. No words were necessary. A moment later they passed the town hall, where the latest casualty lists must just have been posted. It was the first time since her coming to Penzance that Jennifer had *not* gone in to scan them through and through.

Another lapse assailed her conscience: "I never thanked Matron!" she exclaimed.

"I did," her mother assured her. "She won't have expected it, anyway. In the circumstances."

"I'll write to her."

"Yes, dear, you do that." After a pause, while they let some people with heavy luggage cross the road from the station, she said vehemently, "It's so unfair! Why us?" She glanced up at the sky. "It was the very *first* zeppelin raid on London, you know!"

If she had not said it at precisely that moment, Jennifer might not have made the connection. She looked back at the party they had let across the road. They were tired, dishevelled, and one of them, a girl in her teens, had her arm in bandages and a sling.

"Stop!" Jennifer gripped her mother's arm and then, without a further word, sprang down and ran back to the group, calling out, "Excuse me! Have you just come off the London train?"

" 'S'right, love," the eldest among the women replied — a tall, gaunt female with threadbare gloves and a huge-feathered hat in the fashion of the turn of the century.

"And do you know anything about the zeppelin raid last night?"

"*Do* we!" the smallest man of the party put in, speaking through a sad, straggly, walrus moustache. He took off his bowler hat to wipe the sweat from the band.

"They bombed our 'ouse last night," the tall woman added. "Not one brick left standing on another. Why?"

Jennifer licked her lips nervously. "Forgive my asking but it isn't mere idle curiosity. Did you ... were you ... do you know of anyone who ... who was killed in the raid?"

The youngest man of the party, a youth in his early twenties who looked as if he might be the son of the little chap in the bowler, muttered something to one of the women; she was dressed a cut above the rest. "You ask 'er," she told him.

The young fellow turned back to Jennifer and said, "Excuse me asking, miss, but would your name be Owen by any chance?" He was rather better spoken than the rest of his party.

Tears prickled once again behind her eyelids as she nodded. "It's all right," she assured him swiftly. "I've been told. He was my father. We've both been told." She added this last as her mother joined them. She had handed the horse in charge of an urchin, a short way up the road. "This is my mother," she added.

The bandaged girl came forward. "'E done that for us," she said, thrusting the bandaged arm toward them, half proudly, half in trepidation. "Doctor Owen. 'E done that."

Jennifer touched it gently, reverently almost; it was what Sister Morrison would have called a good practical job, though it would never have won a certificate. It crossed her mind to ask the girl to let them have the bandage when she was healed — the last one her father had ever touched. But then — in the same flash of thought — she realized that life was now going to be full of the last this and the last that in his life. The last pipe he smoked, the last stamp he licked, the last walking stick he ever used ... where would it end if they preserved them all?

"And did you see ... I mean, were you there when ..." Goronwy could not frame the awful question.

The young man took charge. "You lot nip on up to Aunty Edie's, else she'll think we missed that train, too."

They trooped off, all except the injured girl. Was she his sister? Jennifer wondered.

"You, too, our Ruth," he said.

As she turned to slink away Goronwy called out to her, "What did he say to you? Did he say *why* he was in the Mile End Road at that hour? Gone midnight, wasn't it?"

"Just gone," the fellow confirmed.

The girl retraced her steps a pace or two. "'E stopped the bleedin' and 'e put that yellow stuff on and 'e said, 'See 'ow that goes.' Them was 'is last words to me, mum."

"See how that goes!" Goronwy echoed the words with a bitter-sweet laugh. Bevis always said that at the end of each consultation: 'See how it goes, eh!'

Jennifer repeated her mother's question: "Did he say *why* he was there at that time of night?"

The girl nodded. "Yus, miss. 'E said as 'ow it was a stroke of luck 'e'd been visiting a pal at ..."

"Friend," the young man corrected her impatiently.

"*Colleague,* if you wannit like what 'e actually said," she answered with scorn. "'E'd been visiting a colleague at the Mile End 'Ospital. 'E said I was to go there, to casualty, and tell them as 'e was coming back. But then there was a woman screaming round the next street, so 'e went to 'elp 'er first. And that was ..."

"The next bomb fell just as he got round the corner," the man said. "I know it's little comfort but it must be *some*. He can't have suffered even *that* long." He snapped his fingers.

"And did you ... I mean, were you there?" Jennifer asked.

There was something very reassuring about him. Outwardly he was quite ordinary looking. Nothing remarkable, anyway. And he was dressed in off-the-pegs that had seen better days. Yet he possessed a sort of calm authority, a natural dignity, which made you feel you could trust him.

He shook his head. "I was working late at the labs. I didn't even know it was a raid. I just thought it was summer thunder."

"And you, Miss ... Ruth, is it?" Goronwy asked.

She shook her head. "It was all fluff and flash after the bomb fell, mum. I run back up the 'ospital to tell 'em they was needed."

A heavy dray went rumbling by, laden with quarry stone, and the urchin had a job holding their horse.

"I'd better go before he bolts on us," Goronwy said reluctantly. "Do forgive us. There's so much more I'd like to ask you, though. And perhaps we can help in some way, too — now you've lost your home? Look, here's my card."

She picked one of Bevis's but then checked herself, replaced it, and chose one of her own instead. She thought, *I'll have to get a new set printed now!* — and almost laughed aloud at the utter triviality of the notion at such a moment.

"May we come and call on you one day next week, perhaps? May I have your address?"

The man took a card from his pocket and scribbled their Penzance address on the back: 'c/o Mrs Edith Baxter, house with red door, four doors up from sweet shop, Adelaide Road.' He handed it to Jennifer with an apologetic smile, saying he didn't know the number. His name, on the printed side, was George Herbert and he was an MSCT, whatever that was. It looked impressive, anyway.

"What a chance — meeting them straight off the train!" Jennifer said as they set out for home again.

"It's nothing compared to the chance of being hit by ..." Goronwy raised her eyes to the heavens but could not complete the thought.

14 BEVIS OWEN, or as much of him as could be gathered from the rubble, was buried in the village churchyard the following week. By then his family had shed so many tears that only the most dreadful moment of all, when the coffin was lowered from sight and the first earth-to-earth thuds of cold clay fell upon its echoing lid, could draw a last few from their red-rimmed eyes. Hector, at fourteen, the man of the family, put his arm round Flora. She, for once, forgot their standing civil war and hugged the breath out of him in return. Colin, a bewildered little six year old and quite incapable of grasping the full meaning of 'never,' clung unashamedly to his mother's side and buried his face in her welcoming warmth. Jennifer clutched June to her for mutual support, not knowing which of them needed it the more. And all six of them huddled together, lost in their grief, until a restless shuffling all around them said that time, all unawares, had moved on.

Practically the whole village was there, and most of the countryside around, too, for he had been one of the most popular doctors anyone could remember. "Us'll sorely miss 'un, too!" and " 'E was some proper ol' feller, missiz!" and "There'll surely never be '*is* like agin!" were sentiments they heard over and over as friends and neighbours pressed forward to express the inexpressible and share what could never be shared. There were even some smiles amid all the solemnity — smiles for their bravery, smiles of encouragement, smiles to reinforce offers of support and comfort in the sad and lonely times to come.

In the midst of the pressing throng Colin plucked at Jennifer's dress and pointed to the sky immediately overhead, where a buzzard was wheeling. He smiled at her and she knew what he meant. Never a summer of their childhood had passed without their father coming home to announce, "The buzzard's back." It was as if the bird, too, were paying its last respects.

As it wheeled and turned and dwindled away, though, another shape filled her mind's eye: the long, sleek cylinder of a zeppelin. Such a cowardly thing! To fly higher than fighter planes could reach and, from that impregnable altitude, rain down one casual bomb after another when, even by daylight, you couldn't see your target with any certainty — it was surely the very epitome of cowardice. Indeed, the *only* certainty was that your bombs would kill and that their victims would be chosen quite at random. It might be a mother out walking her baby in its pram, an old man crippled in years ... even a doctor on an errand of mercy. How could such deaths advance the cause for which that aviator fought? How could he fly back to his mess and boast over breakfast: "Last night I murdered a mother, a pensioner, and a doctor. And all for the glory of the Fatherland!"

Her rage at the brutal casualness of her father's death swept aside her grief. She *would* go back to complete the auxiliaries' course, and she would contrive a posting to the front — as near the front as possible — and no wounded Hun the stretcher-bearers brought in would ever leave the place alive! This satisfyingly fierce resolve bore her through the rest of that doleful ceremony.

Then came the funeral tea, then the marathon of washing up, then supervising the younger ones as they bathed and got themselves off to bed, and then ... silence. It was far and away the most profound silence she had ever heard.

She realized her ear was still half-cocked, listening for those old, familiar sounds from her father's consulting room — the scrape of a chair that might herald the departure of the last patient of his evening surgery ... or his cry of 'Next!' which would mean there was at least one more to go. Or the rattle of his keys as he opened his dispensary cupboard, the strangled guttural of someone saying 'Aaah!' Or laughter as he assured one or other that they'd both live till payday. Until now she had not realized what a rich tapestry of sounds her father's profession had woven on the air of their home.

In fact, at this particular moment, the house was almost unnaturally silent. The youngsters would either be sobbing quietly or else asleep — mercifully asleep. But surely her mother should be around the place still? She listened and heard nothing, not even the ticking of the old grandfather clock in the hall. But, of course, she wouldn't hear that. Her mother had stopped it the day of his death. It still showed a moon just past full. They ought to have restarted it when they came back from the funeral, really. She went out to do so now, and then realized its next chime would be midnight, which would be long enough to wake the young ones again. She decided to leave it until the morning. Besides, she'd have to advance the moon until it showed almost nothing.

Outside, where the real, almost-nothing moon had long since set, a barn owl hooted softly. The french windows must be open, she thought crossly. Now the house would be full of midges. She went to close them before her mother found out, for she hated them being left open at night. Midges fed spiders, which frightened her.

But as she reached for the handle to close the first leaf, something stirred out there in the moonless dark.

"Who's that?" she asked softly.

"Only me, dear," Goronwy said.

Her voice sounded thin. Was she crying? Jennifer wondered, or just exhausted? "Is anything the matter?" she asked, taking a hesitant pace beyond the threshold.

"Come out here a mo," her mother replied.

"Are you all right?" She felt her way out into the blackness, step by cautious step.

"Smell that scent," Goronwy said as she drew near.

The girl took a deep breath through her nose. "Mmm!" She exhaled. "New-mown hay!"

"And the night-scented tobacco. Oh, my plants! My garden!" She began to cry.

Awkwardly, Jennifer put an arm around her mother. "Why d'you say that, Mummy?"

She took a grip of herself and, fishing a hanky from her sleeve, blew her nose heavily. "I'm afraid we have to leave this house, darling," she said in a heavy, salty sort of voice.

"Leave?" Jennifer's sense of reality began to waver once again, as it had done so many times since her father's death. "But it's our house — our home."

"I know. I know. I've been dreading having to tell you this — and God knows how we're going to make June and Colin understand, and even Hector, perhaps — but the thing is ... we have no money to speak of. Daddy had no pension, you know. It was one of the few things ..." She hesitated and then said, "He never believed he'd ... well, never mind all that now. He never earned a great deal of money, you know. And he inherited next to nothing from his parents."

"And the Scottish estate?"

Their share of 'the Scottish estate' had always been spoken of as the inheritance that would make their fortune.

"The less said about that the better!" Goronwy told her. "They made the final division last year, having traced about eight hundred residual legatees under the terms of that stupid will. Our share was a princely fourteen pounds, six shillings, and ninepence! So all we have is about two hundred pounds in savings. And this house, which is probably worth six hundred. And the practice — heaven knows what it's worth. And no income whatsoever."

It was too awful for Jennifer even to contemplate — as if her mother had just told her that the blackness immediately in front of them was, in fact, an abyss of unknown depth. She pretended it was happening to someone else, some other family. Then, by changing 'they' to 'we' as she spoke, she could just about cope with the idea. "I'll go out to work," she said. "There must be something I can do. And you can teach the piano. What's that girls' school in Penzance, out toward Heamoor? Frances Noakes, on our course, she's just come from there and she says they've lost two music teachers to the forces."

Her mother touched her arm, almost shyly.

"What?" Jennifer asked.

"You amaze me, that's all. I didn't think you'd … I mean …"

"You thought I'd go to pieces! I don't know why I'm not, actually. It's awful, isn't it."

"Let's go back indoors. I didn't mean to tell you tonight. D'you think you'll sleep now?"

"I think so. What about you?"

Goronwy sighed. "Yes, I think I will, too — now that you know. We'll work something out together. I feel sure of it now."

Jennifer took her mother's arm and they started to stroll back toward the house, where one paraffin lamp with the wick turned low shone out like a searchlight to their dark-accustomed eyes. "I can't go back to nursing, anyway," she said. "Even proper nurses hardly get paid enough to live on. For us auxiliaries it's only pin money."

"Will that be a great disappointment?" her mother asked. "I know your father set his heart on it — but then he'd have made you an allowance to top it up."

"I'll find a rich old man and trick him into marriage," she promised.

Goronwy laughed. "I just *knew* you'd find the answer to everything," she said.

It was a convenient way of closing a conversation that might otherwise have gone fruitlessly on for hours; both of them knew, however, that its proper conclusion was merely postponed.

Jennifer lay awake longer than she might otherwise have done, wondering — for the first time in months — whether she ought not now to look seriously into the Colletts' suggestion that she should become a photographers' model … and perhaps even aspire to a career in motion pictures.

Her wandering thoughts divided her in two. One half of her felt guilty at even entertaining such vainglorious — but oh-so-pleasant — thoughts at such a dreadful time. The other half tried to be practical, telling her all the old, practical, comforting things like, 'Needs must when the devil drives,' and, 'Beggars can't be choosers.'

Yet she could not deny that it was a most pleasing fantasy, and one that was especially comforting in her darkest hours — more, even, than thoughts of Barry Moore.

Part Two

George Herbert's claypits

Coming of Age in Chysauster

15 JENNIFER LIFTED the corner of the piano while her mother pulled the carpet out from underneath it. The carpet was in the sale but the piano was not, for it was to be the chief source of the family's livelihood from now on. She let it down gently on the bare floor, straightened with a theatrical groan of relief, and, massaging her back, said, "Making a decision is a bit like going up a very steep hill in an unreliable vehicle, isn't it."

Goronwy made a face at the amount of dust that rose from the carpet. "Nothing for it but to take it out and beat it, I suppose," she said wearily.

As they draped it over the line she went on: "What was that about decisions and climbing hills?"

They stood upwind — or up-zephyr, for it was a calm, cloudless July day with the temperature already soaring toward the eighties — and beat in counterpoint rhythm. Between strokes Jennifer said, "When you face the crest of the hill, the summit, you feel you'll never make it. It looks impossible. And it's the same with a decision before you take it. Like our decision to sell up here. It seemed impossible. Not even thinkable. But when you get to the hilltop the road's all downhill on the other side. Then you just take your feet off the pedals and *wheee!* — down you sail. And now we have made the decision ... don't you feel a kind of recklessness? Let it go! What does it matter?"

Her mother paused for breath and, wiping her brow on her sleeve, answered, "You're a funny one, you know. I thought you'd fight like a wildcat to keep this and spare that. This is the carpet you first learned to crawl on, and then to stand and walk on. D'you really not mind?"

Jennifer paused in her beating, too. Goronwy watched the muscles flexing in her forearm and realized how much she had grown up. It shouldn't have surprised her. After all she already knew it as a calendar-fact. But to see it as a bodily fact was somehow different. Also to find that the girl's response to this selling-up business was quite the opposite to what she had expected ... she was a bundle of surprises these days.

Jennifer stared at the carpet. "I don't remember crawling and walking," she replied. "So that doesn't mean anything to me. But see this bit of the pattern here — like those plans of fortifications in Daddy's book on the Crimean War? When I look at that, I remember your telling us the story of the three bears. 'Someone's been tasting my porridge and they've eaten it all up!' I look at this pointy bit and I can hear you saying it now.

And this swirly bit here is where the birds covered the Babes in the Wood in leaves. And where the cinder burned this hole is where Red Riding Hood said, 'What big teeth you've got!' Every square inch of this carpet, almost, has bits of your stories clinging to them. Or to it — you know what I mean?"

"Aieee!" Goronwy sighed and chuckled in the same breath. "Is that what you were doing all those times? Looking at patterns and listening? I thought you were bored to tears — as bored as I was."

This last remark took Jennifer by surprise. Her mother saw her reaction and assured her it had been so. "Tales about princesses sitting in towers doing funny things with their hair — or just sitting and weeping a lot — while the men go off and do all the exciting, challenging things — well, it's not what one would read for *preference,* is it! The most exciting thing that ever happened to any of those ladies was when someone made her sleep on nine mattresses with a dried pea under the bottom one."

"I suppose they were boring, really," the girl said. "They just didn't seem like it at the time."

"If I'd known you were genuinely interested, I'd have put more effort into it."

"Too late now!" Jennifer said with comically overdone melancholy. "Ah me!" Then, brightening: "You can still try with Colin."

Her mother's face fell. "Colin only wants stories about people fighting in trenches. It's all machine guns, snipers, star shells, and shrapnel and going 'over the top' with him."

"But it's not real to him."

"I know, but it is to me!"

"What d'you do, then?"

"We compromise. I tell him about real battles, but from history — the Trojan Wars, Cæsar's conquest of Gaul, Agincourt, and so on. It's better than Mother Goose, actually. We're doing the siege of Pendennis Castle in Falmouth at the moment — Roundheads and Cavaliers."

She laughed at a new thought and, lowering her voice, beckoned her daughter nearer. "Did you know," she murmured, "that 'roundheads' and 'cavaliers' is one of their smutty jokes at the village school? Can you guess how?"

Jennifer shook her head. "Do I dare?"

"It describes the difference between the boys who *are* circumcised and those who aren't! Poor old Miss Tanner, who has the sweetest, least sullied mind in the world — despite having taught boys of that age all these years — whenever they play team games she calls the teams 'roundheads and cavaliers,' and she hasn't the faintest idea why it always makes them snigger so!"

They both laughed heartily — and then felt rather guilty, of course, because they were still in the first months of mourning. They set about whacking the last of the dust from the carpet whose patterns still held all Jennifer's girlhood fantasies and fairy tales.

She was also not a little amazed at her mother's frankness — or, rather, at her jocularity. They had never been a prudish family. For as long as she could remember, they, the children, had always been allowed into the bathroom to watch when either of their parents took a bath. Daddy had been the most fun because he could press his back hard against the enamel and then lift it away suddenly so that the water and air would rush in with huge burping sounds that were hysterical. But, thanks to this privilege, they knew all about the differences between grown-up men and women. And not a word said.

And then, when she got her first periods — or before, in fact — Daddy had shown her his old anatomy books and explained the whole thing in completely matter-of-fact tones — so that she'd actually been looking forward to it as a mark of growing-up, instead of being taken by surprise and thinking God was punishing her for the sins of Eve, which is what silly Jane Verva thought that time.

Even so, sex and all that sort of thing had never been part of everyday conversation in the Owen household. And it certainly was not a topic you'd joke about, even in a mild, casual way like her mother's talk of 'roundheads and cavaliers'!

When the effort of beating was no longer worth the tiny amount of dust it expelled, they paused for refreshment — a glass of home-made orangeade at the picnic table under the apple tree.

Her mother looked up at the leaves and said, "I forgot the tar-oil winter wash." Smiling at Jennifer she added, "Still, that's someone else's problem now!" Cupping her hands, megaphone-like, to her mouth she called out — "D'you hear that — all you aphids, greenfly, blackfly, woolly moths, eelworm, cutworm …? You're someone else's problem now!" In a more conversational tone she concluded, "Not to mention creeping buttercup, couch, cleaver, ground elder, and hairy bittercress! We shall have the finest, cleanest, easiest, gaudiest window-boxes in all Cornwall."

She smiled again, but Jennifer knew she was close to tears. In a minor panic she played a big card, one she had been keeping for a moment of near-crisis like this. "Talking of soldiers in trenches and machine guns and shrapnel and so forth …" she said.

Goronwy sat up at once. "Yes?"

"I still feel *awful* about that day — you know what I'm talking about?"

She nodded and began to protest that it didn't matter.

But her daughter went on: "It made me realize, though ... I mean, it sounds a dreadful thing to say, but Daddy's death has ... oh dear! There must be some decent way of saying this."

There was, too. She'd thought it over so many times since then and she'd been sure she knew precisely what to say. But the opening phrases, spoken aloud for the first time, sounded so wrong that the rest simply deserted her.

"It's given you a new perspective?" her mother suggested.

Jennifer nodded. "I suppose so. It sounds so trite, though. I mean, it's made me realize how ..." She put her hands up beside her temples, imitating the blinkers of a horse harness. "I could only see one thing. I was obsessed. I only became an auxiliary volunteer, you know, because it would give me a chance, at least, of a posting to France and so be near to ... you know who! It sounds as if I'm saying that Daddy had to die in order for me to have my eyes opened. I don't mean that, but ..."

"No, of course not, darling!"

"I'd probably have seen it in time, but his dying like that has managed to do it, anyway."

"I'm sure he's happy to know that," Goronwy said, waving a hand vaguely toward Godolphin Hill — not in the direction of the graveyard. "Out there ... wherever he is."

"D'you believe he's ...?" She couldn't say that, either; it sounded so utterly idiotic.

"I'm sure he is, darling. I think there's a difference between people who die in the natural course of things — old age, and so on — and those who are 'plucked untimely' from the midst of life. Ghosts are always of people who left some unfinished business behind, aren't they — a love unconsummated, a murder unavenged — things like that. I'm sure your father is still watching over us from somewhere very near."

It was a thought that had not once occurred to Jennifer. But the idea that her life might now be invigilated by a ghostly father with the gift of all-seeing and unsleeping eyes was not one she welcomed. She thought of saying something flippant, like 'Well, if he *really* cares for us he could give us the winner of next year's Grand National, so we could get the money on at really good odds!' But she decided to save it for a more fitting occasion — if, for instance, this passing fancy of her mother's were to turn into an all-consuming obsession. Talking of which ...

"The thing is," she said, "I *know* I was a little unhinged on the subject of Lieutenant Barry Moore. I know no human being could possibly be as wonderful as my fancy made him. I know how idiotic and childish it was … and everything like that. But I still *miss* him! I mean, I miss the …" Lost for the word she hunched her shoulders and shivered. "You know that delicious feeling where you're *consumed* with loving sensations and you just want to … everything!"

Her mother smiled into her almost empty tumbler.

"I don't suppose *you* were ever that stupid!" Jennifer tried some teasing scorn.

"Little do you know!" her mother murmured, still contemplating the dregs of her drink.

"Who was it?" Jennifer pounced excitedly. "Was it someone I know?"

Her mother threw back her head and laughed again — and again hushed her voice and glanced guiltily round in case some passing neighbour should overhear their mirth. "Did nothing in my voice give me away — that time we took poor Flossie Penhaligon to Penzance? Didn't you wonder how I was so well versed in the Moores' family history?"

Jennifer stared at her, open mouthed. "Tom Moore?" she asked in a shocked whisper. "Who was two years *younger* than you!"

"But old enough!" She nodded. "So now you know!"

The girl stared off at the horizon. Pennies were falling all over the place. "That's why you warned me about 'Ludgvan Bull'! And said Barry was just like him — a buck rabbit on a bicycle …"

Goronwy laughed. "Did I say that? I'd forgotten. It's rather good, isn't it. He is a buck rabbit, too."

"Did anything happen between you — you know what I mean. Or was it all up here?" She tapped her brow. "Like it is with me. By the way, did Daddy know?"

"Daddy came along just in time to rescue me, if you must know." She tossed the last of her drink down her throat and added, "And I suppose you must. Daddy once said to me that to be a parent is to nurture an illusion that one's own life and example will one day prove of some small value to one's offspring — that they will *not* do as we did, which was to go our own sweet way, regardless! So, to answer your question, darling, anything *did* happen between us."

"Golly!" Jennifer wondered how she could put the next — rather obvious — question as delicately as possible.

"Do close your mouth, dear," Goronwy chided. "Tom may have been two years younger than me — but about two *hundred* years older in experience. He was certainly experienced enough to 'be a gentleman,' as they say — not leaving me in the same state as his son left poor Flossie."

Jennifer swallowed loudly. "But, you mean, otherwise ..."

Goronwy reached forward and tweaked her daughter's nose playfully. "Yes!" she said heavily. "Otherwise he had his fun and I had mine. So there! Don't look so shocked. I know we mothers — we respectable married women — are supposed to live in princesses' towers and comb our hair and sing and spin the livelong day — and worry about nothing more than peas under the mattress at night. Well, it's not like that."

Jennifer sat and stared into her own empty glass a long while. These revelations were too much all at once — or perhaps there was too much old lumber in her mind that had to be shifted out of the way to make room for the new.

"Penny for 'em?" Goronwy prompted her at last.

"Would you have warned me? Or would you just have said a flat *no?*"

"You mean if Barry hadn't gone off to the war? And assuming you hadn't cured yourself of your infatuation rather smartly once you'd enjoyed a bit of his actual company?"

"Yes."

"Two big ifs. Would I have warned you? Yes. Would I have flatly banned all association between you? No. Where would have been the point? It wouldn't have worked anyway, would it?"

Jennifer grinned and shook her head.

Her mother went on: "Instead, I should have told you that it's a lesson you're ready to learn. In fact, that's what I *am* telling you now. I'm also advising you to take care — in learning it — that you don't suffer too much harm."

"Why should I suffer any harm at all?"

"Ah!" Her smile was sad. "It isn't only men who must learn to withdraw in good time!"

16 IN THEIR early calculations they had forgotten the value of the practice, which turned out to be worth almost as much as the house — £600 as against the £842 17s 4d the house fetched. The contents, auctioned separately, brought in a further £250-odd. The proceeds of these various sales were put straight into War Bonds, which would yield a useful £64 a year. Goronwy gained a part-time post as music teacher at the Heamoor Girls' School — sixteen hours a week for £1 6s 8d, which

her widow's pension raised to almost £2. She placed advertisements in the *West Briton* and the *Cornishman* offering private tuition at two shillings an hour and had a satisfactory number of takers even before they moved to Penzance. Their new house was in Penare Road, not far from where the Colletts lived. The rent was a guinea a week, which was more than covered by the income from the bonds.

The biggest single expense would be Hector's fees for boarding and tuition at Truro — some £40-odd per year. Flora and June could go as day girls at Heamoor, and for reduced rates, too, since their mother was on the staff; so they posed no problem.

"Of course," Goronwy said one evening when they were working out how to balance their income and expenditure without consuming their capital, "Hector's expenses won't stop at tuition and boarding. There'll be books, clothes, train fares, and so on, too. We must budget for at least eighty pounds a year. And then there'll be Colin in a few years' time. Hector will still be at 'varsity when Colin goes to Truro. Still, we'll cross that bridge when we come to it."

"I'll be a great film actress by then," Jennifer promised.

"Oh, of course!" Her mother's expression was rather less cheerful than Jennifer had expected. "I think we shall have to hold out the begging bowl, darling," she added.

For one ridiculous moment her daughter thought she meant it literally — two ragged figures in threadbare shawls, rattling empty soup tins outside the railway station entrance.

"The Royal Medical Benevolent Fund, perhaps?" Goronwy mused. "Heaven knows we contributed enough down all the years. Never for one moment imagining that we ..."

"But it would be nice in times to come to say we did it all on our own," Jennifer pointed out. "And we could, too, if we really *really* worked hard at it. Don't you think?"

She saw that her words touched some nerve in her mother. Ever since their father's death and the discovery that he'd left them with no income to speak of, Jennifer had been struck by an odd undertone of excitement in her mother, which was barely covered by her natural grief. Indeed, as the grief began to lose its immediate intensity, that excitement seemed to grow in proportion. And it was never more evident than at times like this, when they were planning the way ahead and discovering — on paper at least — that they could manage very well, thank you.

"I'm not just a bird in a gilded cage," she said when she landed the part-time teaching post at the school.

It struck Jennifer as an odd comment, for she had never considered her mother to belong in the gilded-cage species at all. She was one of those women who practically ran the parish — sitting on every committee going, from the flower show to the Red Cross. When she pointed this out, however, her mother snorted and said, "But that wasn't actually *doing* anything, was it!"

So now, when it came to finding the money to keep Hector at Truro, her mother's willingness to 'hold out the begging bowl' — and her lukewarm response to the suggestion that they could skimp and scrape and find a way to manage — seemed doubly strange.

"At least I ought to look into the possibilities," Jennifer said. "Perhaps film acting is a bit ambitious — though you never know about such things till you try — but both the Colletts were fairly positive that I'd find work as a photographic mannequin."

"Yes, I know." Again, the tone was hardly enthusiastic. "On the other hand, I did hear that Mrs Colston-Smart is on the lookout for a companion?" Her voice rose toward the end, turning an offhand remark into a question.

"At five shillings a week pocket-money!" Jennifer sneered. "It wouldn't keep Hector in socks even — the rate he wears them out."

Her mother smiled knowingly. "Let us not forget the longer term. They have a son, Douglas, who is not only very good looking but is also Penzance's most eligible bachelor by far. He came of age this May — you must have read about the party in the papers?"

"Mummy!" Jennifer was shocked.

"All I'm saying is don't be too hasty in your dismissal, darling. The Colston-Smarts own china-clay pits and quarries all over Cornwall. Just give it some thought."

"I don't need to." She tossed her head in exasperation. "I think the whole idea is disgraceful."

"Yes, well, when your *emotions* have simmered down, perhaps you can give it some cool, calm, *reasoned* thought. And remember this: Being a companion is one of the few paid occupations open to a lady that does *not* compromise her social standing. You could hardly say the same of a photographic mannequin! You might make a great deal of money, I grant you — while your youth and beauty lasted — but you would jeopardize for *ever* your chances of a good marriage. Is it worth it?"

Jennifer rolled her eyes heavenward in frustration. "I can't believe my ears," she said. "You, of all people, telling me this!"

"Why 'me of all people'?"

"Because," she replied awkwardly.

"That's hardly an answer, dear."

"Well ..." She gestured vague circles in the air. "Look how you've been since ... I mean, not since Daddy's death, though obviously that started it off. But since you've known that you've got to be the family breadwinner."

Her mother bridled at that. "What d'you mean — how I've *been?*"

"You know how you've been."

"Jennifer, this is getting perilously close to impertinence."

"I don't think so. I don't mean it to be impertinent at all. It's just the truth — you've been ... well, you must admit it's ... what's the word? Inspired? Stimulated? Something like that. Stimulated to discover ..." She remembered her mother's exact words then: "... to discover you're no longer a bird in a gilded cage! You *can* be a breadwinner — and a pretty good one at that. But isn't that precisely what you want me to become instead — another bird in a gilded cage?"

"Not simply gilded, darling. Real, solid gold! It makes a difference."

"Oh! So the amount of money makes a difference, does it?"

Goronwy did not sense the trap. "It's the way of the world, precious."

"So if I *were* to become a successful film actress — never mind the photographic mannequin business — suppose I tried straight away in films — and made a go of it. And made more money in my own right than I'd ever get by way of allowance as Mrs Douglas Colston-Smart — that would make it all right by your definition!"

Her mother smiled wearily. "Except — as I've already explained — that you'd lose your standing in society, which is without price. I have no doubt which course your father would have insisted on."

This ultimate line in blackmail was, of course, unanswerable. The unfairness of it left Jennifer smarting in silence. Worst of all was the fact that her mother simply couldn't see it. Or wouldn't see it. She was so blinded by those ridiculous, outdated ideas.

"Social position!" she muttered scornfully.

"It's of no importance to me," Goronwy said, adroitly digging herself out of the earlier pitfall. "Besides, I'm not sure that a widow who goes out to work to support her family would necessarily forfeit *any* of her position. But an unmarried girl of *your* age, with all her prospects ahead of her, to turn down such an offer of companionship and *choose* instead to ..." She shuddered.

"You speak as if it's like becoming a ... a harlot or something!" Jennifer swallowed heavily and hoped she was not blushing as heavily as she felt she ought to.

But her mother gave a hollow laugh and said, "We don't know that, do we! It may be *very* like becoming a harlot."

"We don't know anything until we look into it. We should at least look into it."

"That's what I'm saying — if only you'd listen, darling. You should at least look into the *possibility* of becoming Mrs Colston-Smart's companion. Go and talk to her. Shall I arrange that for you?"

And so, the following day, a rather surly Jennifer donned her best summer frock, her best lace gloves (which she defiantly put on as she left the house), and a distressingly schoolgirlish straw boater, and set off up the hill to Medrose House, the ancestral home of the Colston-Smarts. The lane skirted the western edge of its demesne, turned right along the hillcrest, and led to massive gates on the northern side. As Jennifer walked down the drive she thought it must be one of the ugliest, most unwelcoming houses she had ever seen.

The original building had been Georgian, and modest enough in scale — the home of a petty squire. But it had obviously been *too* modest for that squire's wealthier Victorian descendants, who had added two fanciful wings and clad the whole structure in granite from their own quarries. Not content with that, they seemed to have instructed the masons to turn the entire building into a kind of living textbook of carving and polishing, so that every possible way of finishing the stone was finally on display. The garden walls were of random granite rubble built in eighteen-inch courses; the ground floor was of rough ashlar with polished margins; the floor above was of smooth-dressed stone with finely chased margins. And the jambs and sills of all the windows and doors were chamfered and polished to mirror-smoothness. Jennifer thought she had never seen anything so smug and conceited. Only the fact that the gardens had been maturing around it for a couple of centuries saved it from her absolute contempt. The grounds were undeniably beautiful.

She tugged at the bell pull — whose shaft, she noted with delight, was rusty. Somewhere beyond the oak-studded door a small dog yapped. No sound of footsteps followed.

Jennifer turned and surveyed the lawn. Here, on the northern side of the house, she stood in its shadow. High above and behind her, the sun poked bright shafts of dusty light through the dense foliage of two fine Cedars of Lebanon, dappling the close-cropped grass with freckles of gold. As if it had been waiting for her to notice it, a peacock turned and faced her, stamping his ground, and spreading his tail in a huge fan. The sudden eruption of colour was so brilliant it forced an involuntary cry of pleasure from her — here, of all places, where she had been quite determined to find none!

Someone cleared her throat nearby, to Jennifer's left. She turned and saw a maid, waiting diffidently. Poor thing, she thought — all in black and in this hot sun.

"Miss Owen?" she asked, drawing nearer.

"Isn't he absolutely magnificent!" she exclaimed. "Yes, I'm Miss Owen. I think I'm expected."

"Noisy devil!" the girl said. "Better'n any old alarm clock. I'm to bring you round the back, miss."

Jennifer chuckled. "The tradesmen's entrance, eh?"

"No, miss." She was shocked. "Mrs Colston-Smart's on the terrace."

"Alone?"

"Yes, miss."

As they walked around the side of the house Jennifer wondered if there was something special about black dress material that amplified human body odours. All the old women in the village who wore black — and every waitress in every teashop she'd ever visited — they all reeked like nanny goats.

Mrs Colston-Smart was not on the terrace, however. She was knocking a pair of balls solo around the croquet court. Jennifer realized she had seen her a couple of times already, being driven through Penzance in her limousine. A tall, elegant woman with bright, restless eyes. Today she was in a floral cotton dress, topped, incongruously, by an old tennis hat. "D'you play?" she asked Jennifer as soon as the introductions were over. She told the maid to bring out the tea in fifteen minutes.

Jennifer took a mallet and said, "Our court at home was more exciting than this." She didn't wish to risk anything so crass as open rudeness, but she didn't want the woman to accept her as a companion, either. "Moles," she explained.

"Ah!" Mrs Colston-Smart laughed. "I see." She waved at the two balls, which were half way round the hoops. "Take your pick. We'll just play through to the peg."

Jennifer chose the blue, whose lie was more difficult than the red's.

"Interesting," the woman said.

Jennifer, lining up her mallet for the strike, paused and queried her with a raised eyebrow.

"You pick the more difficult ball," she explained. "But is that out of deference to me or is it in the arrogant belief that you can beat me anyway? Let's see."

Jennifer realized it was going to be hard to dislike this woman. She had expected someone called Colston-Smart to be exactly what she sounded like — rich, contemptuous, snobbish, and petty minded. This mildly sardonic, slightly unconventional person just did not fit.

"You'd better play as well as you can," the woman warned her. "I shall show you no mercy when it's my turn."

Jennifer managed to put her ball through the hoop but left it awkwardly close to the metal, so her bonus shot was virtually wasted.

Mrs C-S could have put hers straight through the hoop — and, possibly through the next one with her bonus. Instead, she chose to ricochet off the metal and come to rest tight against Jennifer's. She used her bonus to roquet the girl right out of court.

Their eyes met; she smiled triumphantly and said, *"Voilà!"*

Jennifer smiled, too — the steely sort of smile that says, 'Now the gloves are off!'

Her opponent bungled the next shot, though whether by design or through overconfidence, Jennifer could not say. She got herself back into play in two and followed the woman neatly through the next hoop in one further stroke.

"Three to go," Mrs C-S said as she put herself neatly through the next hoop. "Or two, in my case."

Jennifer followed her through and brought her ball to rest, just kissing the red.

"Oh, I say — hard luck!" The woman tried to pretend they hadn't quite touched yet.

Ignoring her, Jennifer put her foot to her ball and roqueted the other off toward the end of the terrace. From there the slope of the hill did the rest of the damage.

"Well done!" Mrs C-S laughed and let her mallet fall to the ground. "I'll have to give you that one. Now — no doubt you'll be ready for tea after your *long, weary* climb?" She spoke the words with amused sarcasm.

"All of half a mile," Jennifer said.

To her astonishment the woman slipped an arm through hers and turned her toward the terrace. "Miss Owen," she said amiably. "You need not go on being so prickly, just for my benefit. It is quite clear to me that you have not the slightest desire to be my companion."

Jennifer felt pins and needles of embarrassment in her neck and scalp. "Oh dear," she stammered.

"Don't worry. I have no desire for a companion, either. It wasn't *my* idea at all."

"Oh?"

"The brigadier's away — as you probably know — and my son is working every hour God sends at the business. And the two dear sweet things got together and decided that poor lonely mumsie needs a companion. I ask you!"

She loosened her grip a little as they mounted the four steps up to the terrace. At the top she let go altogether and motioned her guest — an applicant no longer — to a chair in the shade of a huge and now rather bleached-out parasol. The maid walked out through the open french windows, bearing a large tray, laden with sandwiches and cakes.

"May I ask why you didn't simply say no to them?" Jennifer said as she took her seat.

The other laughed. "One don't 'simply say no' to the brigadier, I'm afraid — nor, indeed, to my son."

When the maid had gone she set about pouring the tea. "Milk? Sugar? Help yourself to the cucumber sandwiches," she said all in one gabble, as if shuffling it aside. Then, as she passed over Jennifer's cup, she went on, "Tell me — what would *you* do with a ghastly pile like that?" She set down the cup and waved her hand toward the house.

Actually, from this side, Jennifer thought, with the sun streaming down upon it and the garden like a well-tended jungle lapping its foundations and stretching in profusion all about — cutting out the view of those vulgar new houses down below but serving the whole of Mount's Bay in one smiling panorama — it wasn't half so awful as on the northern side. Rather beautiful, in fact.

The peacock must have heard the rattle of the cups for, accompanied by two of his harem, he now strutted proudly down the terrace, fanned out his tail, and eyed them warily for his reward.

"Well?" Mrs C-S prompted.

"Turn it into a convalescent home for wounded soldiers?" she suggested diffidently.

"Hah!" The woman clapped hands in delight.

The three peafowl fluttered several yards off in sudden alarm.

"Capital!" she went on. "D'you know, you're the first one to see it — just like that!"

"The first?" Jennifer asked. "I don't quite follow?"

"Oh, my dear! I've lost count of the number of girls I've interviewed this past month. Poor creatures! Not a real thought between them. Heaven knows what they'll do in life. One of them even suggested turning the place into an hôtel!"

"Well, come to think of it ..." Jennifer ran her eye over the place, pretending to consider the idea seriously.

But Mrs C-S just laughed. "Now, now!" she said mildly. "You don't deceive me, young lady." She popped a small triangle of cucumber sandwich into her mouth and chewed ruminatively. "Can you typewrite?" she asked suddenly.

"I'm afraid not," Jennifer admitted.

"Shorthand?"

"No."

"Well, never mind. Anyone can pick it up. For instance, I'll bet you can answer the telephone?"

Jennifer laughed and said she could just about manage that.

"You may think it funny," the other went on. "You've no idea how many girls just turn to stone the moment the bell rings." She trained her restless gaze on Jennifer, looking her shrewdly up and down. "I think you'd make a good Cerberus, too — don't you?"

"Cerberus?"

"Guard dog. Bulldog." She laughed. "Bully-dog! Anyone who can roquet as you roqueted me just now has all the makings of a useful bully. If I'm going to turn this hideous pile into a first-class convalescent home — and believe me, I *am* going to do just that — I'll need a first-class bully at my right hand. Will you think it over?"

Jennifer summoned all her courage and said, "The wages?"

Her hostess seemed surprised at first, but then she smiled and nodded. "Quite right! How much d'you want?"

"I'm having to support my family now — or to help support it, rather ..." she began.

Mrs C-S waved the words away. "That's no concern of mine."

Jennifer did not believe her; she suspected she was still being tested — and, in a roundabout way, being coached in the sort of 'bullying' that would be expected of her. "It sounds to me like a seven-day-a-week job," she said.

"Certainly."

"And no set hours in the day, either."

"It'll be a dedication. No doubt about it."

She drew a deep breath and said, "Then I think I'll need thirty shillings a week."

The woman let out a great silvery arc of laughter. "Come back," she said, "when you are prepared to be more reasonable."

17 ON HER WAY home from her meeting with Millicent Colston-Smart, Jennifer passed 'Devoran,' the Colletts' house above Chyandour Cliff. Mrs Collett, who happened to be standing at a window, gave her a wave as she went by. Jennifer waved back, and then, on an impulse, gestured to ask if she might have a word. Mrs Collett beckoned her to come in and, in fact, opened the door as she walked up the short garden path. "Welcome, stranger!" she said with a broad smile. "You've obviously heard that Rosalind's home on leave."

Before Jennifer had time to respond to this, Rosalind herself came bounding down the front steps, two at a time, and almost bowled her mother over in her eagerness to throw her arms around their visitor and hug her to bits.

When that was over she held her at arm's length and said, "How are you, pet?"

"Fine!" Jennifer assured her.

"No, really — how are you? You know ..."

"Fine, honestly." She turned to Mrs Collett. "Thank you, by the way, for your very kind letter. I'm afraid we haven't got around to answering them all yet. There were so many. We had no idea."

The woman waved away the apology. "And then having to sell up," she said sympathetically.

"That helped, actually," Jennifer replied. "Kept us busy. It'd have been awful if we'd had nothing better to do than to sit around and mope all day."

"I know what you mean, dear. I often think society is cruel to expect the bereaved to withdraw from all normal life and activity. I hear your mother is the new music teacher at Heamoor? That's splendid. Do tell her how pleased all the parents are — myself among them. That Murdoch fellow was awful."

"If he plays his bagpipes at the Germans," Rosalind put in, "the way he used to play them at us, they'll surrender in their tens of thousands."

"Why don't you two go for a walk?" her mother suggested. "But don't be long. Just go down to the harbour and back."

Rosalind took her friend's arm but still Jennifer hesitated. "I rather wanted a word with you, Mrs Collett," she said.

"Come back and have supper with us, then. It's only cold tongue and salad, I'm afraid."

"Oh, but I'd love that. I'll ask my mother on our way down. I'm sure she'll agree, though."

"About an hour, then." She turned and went back up the steps. "Oh, this heat!" she grumbled.

"Well, pet!" Rosalind exclaimed, taking her arm again and stepping out with gusto.

"Steady!" Jennifer pulled her back to a saunter. "I've already done my share of walking today. I went up to Medrose for an interview with Mrs Colston-Smart …"

"You're not going to be her companion?" Rosalind was quite shocked at the thought.

"Not a bit of it. I'll tell you the whole story later. Over supper. I want your mother to hear it too. I want her advice."

"Intriguinger and intriguinger! I can hardly wait."

"Tell me about you. You've got some leave, your mother said? Does that mean a posting?"

Rosalind nodded. "To France. My brilliant marks in bandaging have earned me a place at a field dressing station."

"Where?"

"I don't know."

"Near Barry?"

Rosalind laughed. "I don't know." She hugged Jennifer's arm tight against her. "Is that flame still burning, then?"

Jennifer sighed. "Not really. But I would like to meet him — just to see, you know."

"See what?"

"What he's really like. I mean, I'm cured of that silly infatuation but I'd still like to meet him … get to know him from scratch. You can *never* get to know anybody if you're just infatuated with him."

They had reached the corner of Penare Road. "We live down here now," Jennifer said.

Goronwy was out in their tiny front garden, painting a solution of flowers of sulphur on the roses. Jennifer introduced Rosalind and then, after the usual pleasantries, Goronwy said, "Well, darling? How did it go? Did she offer you the place?"

Jennifer shook her head but, as the anger crept into her mother's expression, she said, "Not as a companion, anyway. Or not exactly. She doesn't really want a companion, you see. That was the brigadier's idea — and her son's."

"What does she want, then?"

"A secretary-cum-bully — that's what she calls it. She offered me that, instead. She says I have the makings of a first-class bully — just because I roqueted her half way to Marazion."

Her mother relaxed and chuckled. "You have been having fun! You accepted, I presume?"

"We're both thinking it over," the girl said vaguely.

But Goronwy was not to be put off. "What is there to think over? It's not as if you're inundated with other offers."

Jennifer waved one hand awkwardly. "I asked for a slightly higher salary than she had in mind."

Her mother stared at her in amazement. "You *what?*"

Rosalind was rather surprised, too — not least at Jennifer's strangely offhanded behaviour.

"I think she'll come round to it," the girl went on. "She just needs a little time."

Goronwy's eyes narrowed. "You mean you *asked* for money? You didn't wait for her to offer it?"

"I don't think it crossed her mind at all. Just a little bit of pocket-money — exactly as I predicted."

"And may one inquire how much you asked for?"

"She'll come round to it," Jennifer assured her.

"How much?"

"Thirty shillings."

"Thirty shillings a month?" Goronwy — thinking it too modest a sum — was horrified. "You must have been out of your mind, girl! Two pounds would be ..."

"Thirty shillings a week," Jennifer said quietly.

It stopped her mother in full flight.

"And before you explode, Mummy," she continued, "I assure you she will agree in the end. She's a desperate woman."

"Ha!" Mrs Owen replied contemptuously, looking to Rosalind for support. "Did you ever hear such nonsense?"

Rosalind raised her eyebrows and shrugged helplessly, as if to say she had never known Jennifer in this frame of mind before. "Desperate in what way?" she asked.

"There is a project she desperately wishes to carry out. I may not speak of it until she has made it public but I know she has interviewed a large number of girls to be her assistant — and found them all wanting in one way or another. But she believes I am perfectly suited to it. So now she must decide whether to interview another two dozen girls in the hope of finding one who suits her just as well but who's willing to take the post at only ten bob a week — or will she cough up the extra quid and stick with me? I think she will, that's all."

Her mother touched her daughter's arm gingerly, as if she were not quite sure she was really there.

"I'll go further," Jennifer said. "I think she decided to accept me the moment I asked for thirty shillings — because she knows it will allow her to bully *me* without mercy, to get every last ounce of effort out of me. Which, of course, I'm quite prepared to give. But she'll respect me, too — much more than if she were paying me only ten bob a week. An underpaid skivvy can't stand up to the people I shall have to stand up to if her project goes ahead. All she's doing by pretending to refuse is she's seeing whether I'll cave in."

"Well, darling ..." Now there was a note of grudging admiration in her mother's voice. "I've never seen you like this before. I hope you know what you're doing. You seem to, I must say."

"May I have supper with Rosalind this evening? Mrs Collett has already invited me."

"Yes, of course, dear. Be back by ten." She gave a little laugh. "And I wonder how much longer I'll be able to lay down conditions like that!"

The two young women set off down the hill again, heading for nowhere in particular and pausing often to peer into houses and gardens where they could do so without giving offence.

"You have changed," Rosalind said admiringly.

"I didn't tell my mother the real reason," Jennifer admitted. "What I said just now, I made that up."

"You mean it wasn't true?"

"Oh, it was true enough as far as it went. But it wasn't my real reason. The real reason, the thing I want to ask your mother, is I want to know how much I might make as a photographer's model — or in films, if that'd be more. After all, she was the one who put the idea into my head in the first place. Oh God — look at that! Isn't it *sweet!*" She spoke the word with heavy sarcasm.

Some handyman had put up a little windmill in his front garden to drive an automaton on a crank lever: a British tommy who kept thrusting his bayonet into a fallen Hun, who flung up his arms at each stab. It must have been very well oiled for, even in the light breeze that came off the sea that warm August evening, it was turning about once a second in its ghastly pantomime.

"Gruesome!" Rosalind agreed.

They watched it awhile in distasteful silence. Then Rosalind repeated her earlier remark: "You really have changed, you know. Aren't you aware of it?"

She nodded. "I suppose I am."

"Is it since your father died? Tell me to mind my own ..."

"No, no — nothing like that. I've missed you, Roz. I've missed having someone to talk to. I suppose it happened this afternoon. I went up there, to Medrose, absolutely seething with annoyance at the very thought of becoming a rich old lady's companion ..."

"She's not all that old, surely?"

"She's our parents' age — old enough for me. Anyway, the moment I saw the place I began sneering at it — to myself, I mean — thinking how smug it looked, and pretentious, and ugly ..."

"And rich!"

Jennifer stopped and stared solemnly at her friend. "Exactly," she said. "I was joking."

"I wasn't. I was envious. I thought what have the Colston-Smarts ever done for mankind to be worthy of such wealth? I thought one day I'll just *show* them! And then the maid took me round to the garden side and I met Mrs Colston-Smart ... Have you ever met her?"

"She's had her portrait taken a couple of times. Not what you'd call 'meeting,' exactly. She acts like the queen of the castle."

"Well, she wasn't at all like that today. When I said she's a desperate woman I meant more than saying she's desperate to find the right girl as her secretary-cum-bully. She's desperate *not* to go on living the sort of life the brigadier and her son have been imposing on her. 'Only a bird in a solid-gold cage,' as my mother put it. She's desperate to *do* something. *Be* someone. And this war has given her the chance."

Rosalind chortled. "A bit like ..." She hesitated.

"Go on — a bit like me! I'm fully aware of that. You know how things can pass between people — intuitions, understandings, things like that — all without a word spoken? I felt it at once."

"D'you think she felt something similar in you?"

"I do. She treated me as an equal from the first go — not socially but ... I mean, she began sparring with me immediately. Challenging me, almost, and then egging me on to fight back."

They had reached Chyandour Cliff, immediately above the railway tracks just outside the terminus. For a minute or so they watched a saddle-tank engine shunting some carriages around. Then Jennifer said, "Say something. D'you think I'm being too fanciful?"

"I wasn't thinking that at all, pet," Rosalind said. "I was thinking you and she will never have an *easy* time together. Shall we go out to Penzance Green or down to the harbour?"

"The harbour. I love it when the water's almost dead calm." As they sauntered onward, Jennifer continued: "I'm not really looking for an easy time."

"What are you looking for, Jenny?"

"I don't know." She waved a hand in a hopeless gesture at the town generally and added, "More! Whatever I've had so far isn't enough. I want more than this. I want more than just having a husband and a home and a family. That's what my mother had — and just see how it all crumbled to nothing in one single night!"

"She's doing very well — or so my mother says."

"Exactly! *She's* doing very well. She's a changed woman, too. She's not my father's pensioner any more."

Rosalind received this observation in shocked silence.

"I don't mean she doesn't grieve for him," Jennifer explained hastily. "We all do. But facts are facts. She *is* the breadwinner now — and there's a certain exhilaration in proving she can do it. D'you see what I mean?"

"I suppose so."

Suddenly Jennifer halted again. This time she stared across the road, murmuring, "I'd forgotten them completely. How awful!"

"Forgotten who?" Rosalind followed her gaze and saw only an old lady in a monstrous floral hat.

"That day my mother came to the hospital — the day I left the course ..." And she went on to describe their chance meeting with the Herberts on the day after they were bombed out of London.

"Not *George* Herbert?" Rosalind asked. "It must be the same one. There couldn't be two. He was a cinema projectionist or something like that up in London."

"He gave me a card," Jennifer remembered. She fished in her purse but couldn't find it. "It had MSC ... MS ... something after his name."

"Member of the Society of Cinematograph Technicians — MSCT. That's what I said."

"How d'you know him, anyway?"

"He works for Collett and Trevarton now. He's very good, my father says. He even taught us a thing or two about lighting and lenses that we never heard of before — modern tricks, you know."

"Oh, good!" Jennifer relaxed. "He's fallen on his feet, anyway. The day they arrived, Mummy said something about trying to help them if we possibly could — and I expect she's forgotten them completely, too. What were we talking about before?"

"Grief," Rosalind replied. "Speaking of which — don't you grieve for your vanished love? Not for Barry himself, but for the love you used to feel? Don't you miss it?"

They turned the corner by the station entrance and set off down the brief slip-road to the harbour.

"Why d'you want to know?" Jennifer asked slyly.

"I'm curious, that's all. I've never felt a love like that."

"Never?"

"Never — honestly. I suppose it'll happen one day but it hasn't yet."

"You mean there's never been a man — you've never looked at a man and felt your whole body go into a spin — as if everything is all churning over inside you?"

"Nope! When I look at men ... how can I explain it? You know when you go to the zoo?"

Jennifer laughed. "Go on!"

"You know how you watch the animals and you think, *I wonder what you're going to do next, little fellow?* Well, that's how I look at men. They're like a foreign species. I always wonder what they're going to do next."

"And you don't want to touch them, and hug them, and kiss them?"

"Only out of curiosity. And you?"

"Curiosity, too, I suppose." Jennifer shrugged uncomfortably.

They had reached the harbour edge by now. There they leaned lightly on iron railings that were almost too hot to touch and gazed out over a sea as slick as oil. Upon it the bright-painted fishing boats rode at anchor, scarcely moving on their own reflections.

"More than curiosity," Jennifer admitted at last. "They're exciting and dangerous, too. Don't you feel that? Also they're malleable. D'you ever go riding? You know that feeling — here's this magnificent, powerful creature, a hundred times stronger than you and with a will of its own when it wants — and yet, if you just control it in the right way, you can bend it absolutely to your will. You can make it turn on a sixpence. Or leap fences it wouldn't even *look* at on its own. You can make it do things it never knew were possible!"

While she spoke, Rosalind watched her in horrified fascination — and she found herself hoping that this young woman's infatuation for her cousin Barry truly was over and done with. And that was not for Jennifer's sake, either, but for Barry's!

18 JENNIFER SAID nothing of her plans to Mrs Collett that evening. They ate outdoors and the whole family was there, so privacy was not possible. In any case, they were all too excited at the news of Rosalind's posting and they speculated endlessly about her prospects in France. And besides, Mrs Collett said she was going to spend most of the morrow — a Sunday — sketching among the china clay pits. Rosalind was going with her and she wondered if Jennifer would like to come along, too.

No second invitation was needed. The following morning Jennifer went to early Communion and, come nine o'clock, she was waiting at the entrance to the station, riding impatient circles on her mother's bicycle. In its capacious saddlebag nestled her own sketching materials, a packed lunch, two eccles cakes, and a bottle of ginger pop. A few minutes before the train was due to depart, the two Colletts — mother and daughter — came racing around the corner, out of breath and rather flushed.

"I say *nothing* as to the cause of our lateness," Mrs Collett remarked, darting Rosalind a significant glance.

"Then nor shall I," her daughter replied defiantly.

They stowed their bicycles in the guard's van and took their seats in the first second-class carriage they came upon, which was half way up the train. They were not, however, the last to arrive. George Herbert got his bicycle into the van just as the guard was closing the door. The man blew his whistle and waved his flag, watching with amusement as the young chap sprinted up the platform.

Rosalind, who had been leaning out of the window and tutting with annoyance every five seconds, cried out "Here, Mister Herbert! We're here!" She opened the door as he drew near. Another few seconds and the acceleration of the train would have beaten him. He grabbed the leather strap and, with one last bound, hurled himself aboard and collapsed all of a heap in the window seat. "Wretched, cheap alarm clock ..." he panted.

Then, catching sight of Jennifer, he sat up straight and, still breathless, said, "Oops, sorry! Miss Owen, isn't it?"

She nodded, feeling absurdly pleased that he remembered her name. "That's right, Mister Herbert. I didn't know you were joining us."

"Nor I, you," he replied. Then, with a smile, "Why — would it have made a difference?"

"No, no!" she assured him. "But I ought to have guessed it, anyway. I did know you were working with Collett and Trevarton." She added that to explain why they had not followed up that first meeting and her mother's implied promise of help.

"It was I who persuaded him to come along today," Rosalind put in.

She seemed miffed that his opening conversation was not with her, and it struck Jennifer that she was perhaps rather keen on him. Nothing was said. Rosalind did not even try to convey such a thought with a glance. But these things communicate nonetheless. *Keep off the grass!* Jennifer thought and resolved thenceforth to be politely cordial, no more, to the young man. The sudden decrease in the width of her smile rather puzzled him but Mrs Collett understood perfectly well what was going on and she settled back to enjoy the day in more ways than she had at first imagined she might.

And what a day! Not a cloud in the sky, and not a breath of wind to puff one along even if it decided to form itself up there in the cerulean blue. After a couple of minutes out in the sun, the combined heat of the carriage and the young man's desperate dash for the train got the better of him and, red as a boiled lobster, he begged leave to open the window, for it was not a through-corridor train.

"Take off your jacket and waistcoat instead," Rosalind urged cheekily. And she fished out the square of cloth she had brought for sitting upon and began fanning him the way they fan a boxer between rounds.

Mrs Collett caught Jennifer's eye and raised her own glance to the heavens. The girl, who had half thought of joining in, decided to follow the mother and remain a supercilious spectator. When young Herbert became aware of her attitude, however, he stopped finding Rosalind's behaviour funny. Isolated, she then had to stop — not without a reproachful glance at her friend, though.

Jennifer's heart sank as it became clear that George Herbert was more interested in her than in Rosalind — whereas she was not interested in him at all. Not in that way. At least, she didn't think so. Or no more than *any* young woman would be interested in *any* young man if he happened to be the only one in the company.

What a jolly time they'd have had if only his alarm clock had failed him utterly! And how miserable it was now going to be unless she could somehow get a few simple facts straight in his mind — but without offending him and making him feel small.

"Now would be a good time to ask my mother," Rosalind told Jennifer. "The thing we were talking about."

There it was again! If they had just been the three of them there, it would have been a warm, friendly suggestion — friend to friend. But with Herbert added in it was clearly Rosalind's wish to embarrass her by making her reveal her innermost ambitions in front of him.

"Ask me what, dear?" Mrs Collett responded, looking at Jennifer.

Rosalind replied for her. "She wants to be a ... well, you tell her, Jenny, pet. It's not my place."

Jennifer stared her out. *You surely don't want a fight?* she screamed in the silence of her own thoughts — hoping it would somehow project into Rosalind's mind. *You don't want to provoke me to it, do you?*

"Don't leave us in suspense like this," Mrs Collett complained. "One or other must say something. What is it you wish to be, Jenny? Anything to do with Mrs Colston-Smart?"

She took the proferred opening. "In a way, Mrs Collett," she replied. "That lady has certain plans — which I don't think I'm at liberty to speak of. But she thinks I would make an admirable assistant. That's her opinion, anyway."

"But not yours?" Mrs Collett put in.

"Well, I think I could *do* it — though it would certainly be a challenge. And I'd quite enjoy it, too. However, I asked for a salary of seventy-eight pounds a year ... at which ... well, you can imagine it yourself." She glanced sidelong at George Herbert, expecting to find him open-mouthed at her impudence; to her surprise he was nodding with what looked like approval. His lips were slightly pursed, too, as if to say, 'Of course — she could hardly expect to get you for less.'

As with his earlier recollection of her name, this left her feeling strangely pleased. However, aware of Rosalind's icy gaze, she pressed on: "I mean — a girl who's never done a day's paid work in her life — to ask for thirty bob a week!"

"D'you think she'll pay it, nonetheless?" Mrs Collett asked calmly.

Reluctantly Jennifer admitted that she believed she would. "Not because I think I'm so wonderful," she added, "but because she was so eager. Or seemed to be."

"Always a mistake," Mrs Collett murmured.

George chuckled and said, "Good for you, gel!" He glanced at Rosalind, expecting to recruit her laughing approval, too. Her basilisk stare surprised him. He clearly had no idea of what was going on between the two girls.

"But that's not really why I asked for so much," Jennifer admitted to Mrs Collett.

"No?"

"No. You see, I went up for that interview thinking she just wanted a companion. So my mind was full of rebellious thoughts — like, 'I'm not going to play dogsbody to some rich old woman for three farthings a week!' Because I also remembered what you and Mister Collett said, you know, about ... you know ... photography and things." She forced herself not to look in young Herbert's direction.

But Mrs Collett did it for her. "Ask him," she said with a nod in his direction. "He saw it at once, too. The moment I showed him your portrait — and those movie tests my husband made of you."

"What? Saw what?" Rosalind asked.

"The camera lens loves her," George said. "Or, to put it in everyday English, the irises of her eyes are photo-actinic, which is rare in people whose hair coloration is of a melanic hue."

Mrs Collett laughed. "You're a wag, Mister Herbert," she said. "We shall miss you when you leave."

"Leave?" If Jennifer had known she was going to speak the word in quite such a tone of disappointed surprise, she would have struggled to moderate it. But too late now.

"Didn't you know?" Rosalind said, happy to be at the right end of the goad for once. "Mister Herbert is going to be a war photographer in France. He's going to take motion pictures of battles and columns on the march and things like that for the official war archives."

Jennifer's eyes strayed to the young man while her friend was speaking. He nodded confirmation of the words. "They're forming the unit now," he said. "I join them in September — in three weeks' time."

"Ah." It was too much to take in all at once. Jennifer turned again to Mrs Collett and said, "So, anyway, that was also behind my asking for such an outrageous salary."

The woman nodded approvingly. "You did the right thing, Jenny — set a high value on yourself and the world will often follow. Mind you, if it doesn't ..." She laughed and pulled a sour face.

"Talking of people who think very highly of themselves ..." Rosalind said brightly. "And who manage to persuade *some* of the world, at least, to agree with them ... I stole this for you." And from her handbag she took a piece of card — or what looked like a piece of card. With a daring smile at her mother she handed it over to Jennifer, adding, "From our family album."

It was a photo of Barry — a recent one, too, taken in the trenches. He was wearing her mittens and the scarf she had knitted for him. She recognized the tassels. Automatically her eyes checked the one at the end, which concealed within it her embarrassing message of love. There was no sign that its threads had been teased apart, though — for which small mercy she was thankful.

Then, to her horror, she heard Rosalind explaining to George: "Poor girl, she's absolutely nuts upon him."

"Ah." There was a sorrowful dying fall in the way he spoke the single word.

Jennifer sought desperately for some way to tell him how out-of-date Rosalind was with her 'news.' But then she thought, *No — what does it matter to me what George Herbert thinks? And if it makes Roz happier to imagine she's put one over me — and therefore more agreeable to be with on what will otherwise be a long and very tedious day — so much the better!* So she merely smiled at the young fellow and said, "I'm a hopeless case, Mister Herbert — and still we have the cheek to ask for the vote!"

He laughed a little too heartily, until Rosalind told him it wasn't as funny as all that.

"So," Mrs Collett put in before the temperature could rise too far, "you'd like a salary to compare with the eighty-or-so you sought from Millicent Colston-Smart?"

"Before I say no to anything I'd like to know the size of it."

"Very wise. Well, the first thing to make clear ..." She glanced toward George Herbert and added, "Correct me if I'm wrong. The first thing to be clear about is that there is no salary, as such, attached to the business of cinema acting. You sign a contract with a film producer ..."

"... which he can break but you can't!" George put in.

"Very likely. And it will stipulate so much a day. For a small part in a four-reel drama ..." Again she turned to the young man. "What would you say? Eighteen shillings a day?"

He agreed. "While shooting lasts. Two months, say? Of course, you wouldn't work every day, or even most days, but you'd still get paid while you're retained."

"So I could earn as much in four months as I would in a whole year with Mrs Colston-Smart!" Jennifer said brightly.

"And you could be desperately out of work for the other eight," he warned. Only then did he think to add, "Not *you*, of course, but ..."

Rosalind's laugh drowned the rest; then Jennifer felt she had to laugh, too. He was right, of course; it was a prospect she had to face.

"A larger part in a two-reel comedy would pay about twice that," he added. "But it might only last a month." He smiled expansively. "Mind you, if you became a big star, you'd command a thousand pounds a picture — even more. And we'd have to write for appointments just to see you."

Jennifer squirmed in her seat with excitement at the very thought of it — not at the idea that she might spurn all her old friends but at the glittering prospect of restoring the family's fortunes, paying all her brothers' school fees — and her sisters', too, come to that. And buying a grand house like Medrose for them all to live in. No — not like Medrose, but a grand place all the same. And she wouldn't need to disappoint Millicent Colston-Smart, either. She could come down and give charity shows for the convalescents and sign her autograph on their plaster casts and so on.

Pleasant fantasies flash by even faster than pleasant hours, so Jennifer's three companions in that carriage had no idea as to the detail with which she had pursued her daydream, all in the twinkling of an eye. Much less would they have understood that, of all the delightful particulars which had flashed through her mind, the most delightful of all had been the most trivial: the notion of signing her name — her by-then-famous name — on the carapaced limbs and torsos of brave young soldier boys.

But Crissy Collett was watching her closely enough to see the brief, rapturous gleam in her expression and she knew the girl would now *have to* reach for that bright star — even though she knew how slim was her chance of success where so many others before her had seen their dreams shattered and ruined. She turned to young Herbert and said, "Why don't *you* take my husband's cine-camera and shoot some footage of her? A real pro job. See what she's made of?"

He picked up her jocular tone. "For ten per cent?" he asked, raising an eyebrow at Jennifer. "Of your first three films, that is?"

She laughed and waved a hand airily toward him, pretending she had a yard-long cigarette holder in it. "You'll have to talk to my agent about that," she said.

19 You SEE them from the train after you leave St Austell on the down line — mountainous white cones, like sugarloaves for a race of giants, scattered over the uplands to the north of the tracks. Vast as they are, however, the rest of that wide, almost treeless landscape tames them. Distance blurs their detail and bleaches out their subtle colours. So nothing of the faraway view can prepare the visitor for the moonlike fairyland that opens up on every side the moment he enters it.

Jennifer and George, neither of whom had seen anything remotely like it before, cycled in rapturous silence, struggling to take it all in. The magic was in the very earth — quite literally — in the form of massive holes in the ground, so deep and so wide that the maintenance men walking about the floor of the pit or along its farther rim were mere specks against the white. And *all* was white down there. The furze and ling that carpeted those barely fertile hills ceased abruptly at the claypit's edge — "As if you'd loaded up a pallette knife with pure lead white and just wiped it across your painting," Crissy Collett said.

"What *is* it?" Jennifer asked as they drew to a halt beside a particularly large white gash in the moor at Carpalla. "I mean what's it made of?"

"Quartz," Crissy said.

"Mouldy granite," George put in.

They looked at him to see if he were joking.

"It's true," he told them. "I went down the library and looked it up yesterday. Granite's a mixture of quartz and ... something else. I've forgotten. And if it gets the wrong side of a volcano — which most of Cornwall did millions of years ago — the rock whose name I've forgotten turns into kaolin. China clay. But the quartz crystals aren't affected. So you get this claggy white clay with lots of quartz chips in it. The book didn't say how they separate them, though. Do they wash it out? Is that what all those pipes and hoses are?"

Crissy said that if they had come on a working day, they'd be looking down at four or five teams of men, each directing a high-pressure jet of water at some part of the claypit face. "The washed-out clay flows down to the bottom of the pit and from there they pump it off like milk to big settling tanks. We'll pass some in a moment. And they scoop the quartz chips into skips, which are on little bogey wheels, and they run up those tracks to the top of the sugarloaf and tip their load out at the top. Which is how they get their shape. Up and down, up and down, all day. They don't call it a sugarloaf, actually. They call it a barrow."

Jennifer tried to picture the scene as Mrs Collett had described it but the empty vastness of the place was too powerful, its silence too seductive.

"It's not really white, is it," Rosalind said. Though she had been there before, the sense of grandeur gripped her, too, and made her forget her earlier churlishness.

"Look at that blue!" Jennifer pointed at a pool toward the farther end of the pit.

Crissy chuckled. "If you think *that's* blue, wait till you see what's beyond the ridge there. They use the same water over and over again, you see, and they store it in old, abandoned pits near by, so the colour goes on getting stronger and stronger. One of them you'd swear is pure lapis lazuli by now — it'd make Raphael's Madonna look as if she's wearing old, faded denim!"

Jennifer let out a great sigh of contentment. "We must never tell anyone about this," she said. "If people knew how beautiful it really is, they'd ... I mean, it would be spoiled. Like the Lake District. We must all agree today to keep this as our secret."

"And what about when Mummy's paintings get shown at the Royal Academy?" Rosalind asked, pretending to take her seriously.

She nodded ruefully. "You're right. We must simply make the most of it, then — enjoy it while we may."

The two girls laughed far more heartily than the pleasantry deserved, both being eager now to make up for their earlier coolness.

"You could pretend they're fantasies, Mrs Collett," George suggested. "Come to think of it, this is what South Wales would look like if coal was white instead of black!"

They laughed at that idea, too. Then Jennifer brightened. "Actually, Turner painted the Lake District quite a lot, but that didn't bring out the hordes. It was Wordsworth who wrecked the place. Perhaps we should put up a signpost at the edge of Saint Austell saying no poets past this point." After a brief silence she asked Mrs Collett if she was going to paint this particular pit today.

"No," she replied. "There's one of Treviscoe, which I've already started. It's amazing because it's almost perfectly symmetrical. And there's another at Gothers, which is the very opposite — wild and ... well, Turneresque, if you like. I'll go there after lunch. But you youngsters don't have to stay with me, you know. I'll be perfectly happy on my own."

"We'll stay together as far as Treviscoe," Rosalind suggested.

"Carpalla, Treviscoe, Gothers ... they all have such powerful names!" Jennifer mused.

"And there's Goonbarrow, and Hendra ... and Wheal Dream ..." Crissy added. "Names to dream by."

As they turned to go, one of the maintenance gang started up an empty skip, setting it to climb the long, oblique rail track up the side of the barrow. The steel hawser went *zing-zing-zing* over the rollers that kept it off the ground — a high-pitched continuo over the deep rumble of the bogey wheels.

"Ah!" Crissy held up a finger. "*That's* what's been missing — the music of the claypits!"

The road turned this way and that, making even more bends than the usual Cornish lane, which is saying something. And there was a surprise around every corner, too. Several times they saw traces of an earlier, straighter road, barred to them by a new length of stone hedge — the reason being that it now ran directly to the edge of a pit and vanished into thin air. Nothing was permanent here. At Gonnamarris half the village had been dismantled to make way for the expansion of the nearby pit. And every verge was littered with the detritus of earlier industry — iron pipes with broken flanges, steel hawsers that had frayed, and skipway rollers worn almost in two. In one place an old saddletank engine had simply been tipped off the rails and left to rust away while the furze grew back around it. The dark olive green of the leaves and the sulphur-yellow flowers made a powerful contrast with the browny-red of the corroded boiler.

George put his finger on it at last. "It's not like a landscape at all," he said. "It's more of a giant, open-air factory floor, ten miles long and ten miles wide. They don't care about the land at all, not like what a farmer cares. It's just something to be opened up and …" The word that came to mind was 'raped,' but he didn't wish to say it.

"Pillaged," Crissy suggested.

"Yes. Take what you want and move on. That's their motto."

"You don't like it?" Jennifer was surprised to think that he might not.

"Do you?" He was equally surprised that she might.

"It's magnificently singleminded," she said.

"I think they could be just a *bit* tidier," Rosalind said as if she were delivering the judgement of Solomon.

"Hear-hear," he said.

He and Rosalind smiled at their agreement and Jennifer felt a sense of relief. She had decided that she was *slightly* interested in George Herbert but not to such an extent that she'd risk losing Rosalind's friendship. (And in any case, Roz was leaving for France in a few days whereas George wasn't.)

When they reached Treviscoe, Crissy amazed them by the speed with which she unfolded her collapsible easel and set out her paints; it was all done in less than a minute. She looked at her half-finished water colour of the place, begun back in May, and decided that the August light was so different she'd have to start afresh. She drew directly on the paper with a loaded brush — needing no faint pencil sketch to guide her. The three young folk watched awhile in envious silence and then settled to their own sketching.

"Are you going to draw, too?" Jennifer asked George, rather disappointedly, for she had seen a novel in his lunch bag — *Sons and Lovers,* which her father had forbidden her to read — and she was hoping to have a peep at it. However, she did not feel she could simply ask to see it, because that would show she'd actually noticed the title. She wanted to say, 'What's the book?' and go on from there.

"I'll have a go, anyway," he replied. Then, putting on the cockney a bit, he added, "'Ave a go at anyfink, I will."

They sketched in silence for the best part of an hour. Then Crissy, having polished off two very satisfactory water colours, suggested it was time to break for lunch. "After which we'll move on to Gothers," she said.

"And Wheal Dream," Jennifer added. "I'm longing to see that. I can just imagine what it's like."

"It's small and abandoned, I'm afraid," Crissy warned her.

"Like Vesta Tilley." George laughed but she silenced him with a withering glance. "Beg pardon all round," he added, not at all contritely.

"Let's see?" Jennifer reached for his sketchbook.

But he withdrew it a token inch or two and, clutching its covers tight together, said, "I'm not one of your representational artists, you know. More of a symbolist — that's me."

"An impressionist?" Rosalind suggested. "Let's see, anyway." She, too, reached for his sketchbook.

But he still withheld it. "Not an impressionist," he insisted. "A symbolist. I look for the symbolic reality behind the obvious façade."

The two young women turned their puzzled gaze to the china claypit before them. "What symbolism is there in that?" Jennifer asked.

By way of answer he opened his sketchbook and faced its latest page toward them. What he had drawn was a curious amalgam of the landscape before them and a suggestion of a nude woman, reclining with her hands linked behind her head and one knee bent. The three conical shapes of the barrows before them made, respectively, her elbows, her right breast, and her raised knee. Her ample belly could be seen as either convex or concave; when convex it was, simply, her belly; but when concave it suggested the breadth and depth of the claypit itself. Some of the lines were finely drawn and naturalistic representations, suggesting both landscape and resting flesh; others were purely diagrammatic, embodying the underlying sweep of the land — and, somehow, the rhythms of the human figure, too.

Most of this they saw much later, when they had recovered from the initial shock. But while that shock was still upon them, they could only stare at it in horrified amazement, fully expecting an explosion of outrage from Mrs Collett, as guardian of their innocence and purity.

But no such cry came. They were even more shocked when all she did was reach forward and ask, rather quietly — almost reverently — if she might look at it more closely. She stared at it for an uncomfortably long while. Then all she said was, "Have you had any training, Mister Herbert?"

"Not really, Mrs Collett," he replied awkwardly. He obviously didn't think his sketch was worth all this attention — and yet he was also rather pleased it was getting it.

"What does that mean — not *really?*"

He pinched the end of his nose. "I mean I could never do what you do." He pointed at her sketch, now almost dry in the hot sun. "If I wanted to do that, I'd just bring out a camera. But when I look at this" — he waved a hand at the scene he'd sketched — "there's a lot of things the lens would never catch. First you can only feel them. Then, when you feel them strong enough, you start seeing them, too. I can't explain it better than that. But once I feel them there, then I can start drawing them."

"You don't need to," she told him, looking again at his sketch. "It's a revelation. It also explains why you're such a good photographer. Mister Collett and I once studied art under Roger Moynihan, you know — the academician. Photography *isn't* just a matter of opening and closing the shutter for the right length of time. It needs an artist's eye, too. And you've got it. That why you make even a passport photo look alive."

"A *passport* photo?" Jennifer was puzzled. There was no photograph in her father's passport, the only one she'd ever seen.

Crissy grinned. "Yes. All passports now have to carry a photograph. Didn't you know? *Sometimes* they pass a law that makes sense. It's been good business for us, anyway. And we — though I say it myself as shouldn't — take a pretty good passport photo."

They ate their packed lunches in the abandoned engine house at Wheal Dream, above St Dennis. The engine itself and its winding drums had been removed to somewhere more useful but all the pipes and levers were still there, rusty and precarious. After lunch Rosalind said she had a mind to walk to Roche, a couple of miles away to the north, and see the ancient fortress on the rock for which the village is named. George said he'd like that, too — no doubt assuming that Jennifer would also join the party. But she said she was feeling too lazy to walk such a huge distance. "I wish I'd brought a book," she concluded wistfully.

"Some other time, then," he said to Rosalind as he handed Jennifer his copy of *Sons and Lovers*.

"Nonsense!" Crissy told him. "If you two want to walk to Roche, you walk to Roche. But remember ..." Her gaze flickered from one to the other and they squirmed, wondering what embarrassing conditions she was about to make public. "We have to leave here by four if we don't want a mad dash for the train home," she concluded.

When they had gone she said to Jennifer, "Now you're shocked."

"No!" the girl assured her, rather too effusively.

"I expect you're always chaperoned in the company of young men."

"At dances." She didn't want to admit that the situation had never otherwise arisen.

Crissy started a new painting but it did nothing to hinder her conversation. "I see no point in it," she said. "If young people are determined to experiment with life, a whole army of chaperons isn't going to stop them. Besides, forbidding something only doubles its attraction — don't you agree?" She darted an amused glance at Jennifer, who could not help peeping at her book. "Yes, I thought so," Crissy added. "I saw you eyeing it several times this morning. I'm afraid it'll disappoint you, however. He lives outside Saint Ives, you know. His wife's German, which hasn't made them popular. We know them slightly. Would you like an introduction?"

"I'll read the book first. But thank you very much for the offer."

"Very prudent. As I say, I think it'll disappoint. He's a better painter than he is a writer. His descriptions of landscape are marvellous." After a slight hesitation she added, "Also he understands the importance of sexual desire — which brings us back to chaperons and things. He understands the beauty of it. And the power of it. He knows that it's the most important thing in most people's lives — though you could read your way through the whole of Victorian literature and never once guess the fact."

Jennifer wondered what she ought to say to this astounding assertion. "Is it?" she said at length. "The most important thing, I mean?"

"Isn't it? What made you knit your fingers to the bone last winter?"

"Oh, but that was *love!*" she protested. "Or infatuation, rather. I'm over it now, anyway."

"I'm glad to hear of it. I know he's my nephew and families should stick together and all that, but he's a disaster on two legs, that boy. Especially where infatuated young girls are concerned."

Taking a huge chance Jennifer said, "Aren't you afraid that Rosalind may be infatuated with Mister Herbert?"

The woman merely smiled. "I was being too kind," she replied. "I should have said 'infatuated *and ignorant* young girls.' Rosalind has not been brought up in ignorance. You know Zack Hosking, the boatbuilder in Newlyn? No? You should go and see his yard someday. It's a real link with the past. Anyway, my husband took some pictures of his last launching and after it was over old Zack said to him, 'You do your best by 'er, Mister Collett. You do build 'er so sound as you can and you do give 'er good balance down at the keel, but once she'm laanched on the morrow tide, she'm on 'er own.' So there you are, Jennifer. Once you're built and launched and floating on tomorrow's tide, you're on your own. That's why they call ships 'she'!"

20 JENNIFER TRIED reading for a while but found it impossible to concentrate. The things Mrs Collett had said kept coming back to her — especially the thought that her parents had done their best to rear her but now she was out on the high seas, on her own. It felt as if that particular idea had been hovering around at the back of her mind for some weeks past, waiting to be put into words. She *was* alone now — not solitary, but alone. On her own. The way a boat can be on its own in a crowded harbour. True, her mother was still there and still laying down the rules, but that was a mere convention. Love laughs at locksmiths, and a whole army of chaperons — as Mrs Collett said — couldn't stop people from experimenting with life.

After a while she gave up trying to read and, spreading her rug farther up the boulder that had been her backrest, sprawled herself on the stone and closed her eyes, taking care first to shield her face from the sun's damaging rays with her parasol.

Crissy went on sketching in silence.

But Jennifer found she could not rest, either. The same thoughts went round and round in her head, tumbling and mixing until they were just words without meaning.

"I think I'll go for a stroll myself," she said, rising to her feet. "Just once around the lake at Wheal Dream."

"That 'lake' is an abandoned pit, two hundred feet deep with sheer sides — so be careful how you fall in!"

"I shall be like Zack Hosking's boats," Jennifer replied. "I shall float."

As she went off down the path, Crissy called after her: "There's one thing you should remember, dear. It's wise to test even the best-founded boat in calm waters to start with."

Jennifer laughed. "I'll remember that."

So Mrs Collett had been thinking back over their conversation, too. But what had those thoughts been? What experiences and memories shaped them? Would she ever tell them to another — a relative stranger like herself? There must have been times in her life when she was perplexed, too — uncertain about even the most basic decisions. Wouldn't that help her to recognize it in others?

She thought of her own sister, Flora, who was eleven now and just starting to wonder about life and death and other large questions. Did she, Jennifer, remember being that age and undergoing its perplexities? Did it help her to recognize it in Flora? And, come to that, how much of her own enormous wisdom and experience had she passed on to her little sis lately!

People don't. One really is on one's own.

She tried to recall the confusions she had experienced at Flora's age. That was when she found Moses by the pigsties. No, she was fourteen then. Quite a difference. Her greatest perplexity had been to wonder *why* they couldn't just keep him. Part of her still wondered, though the rest of her understood it quite well.

Poor little Moses! He was surely a vessel launched before his time on life's sea. What had become of him, she wondered — had he even managed to stay afloat?

If she became a big film star with oodles of oof, she'd track him down and make it all up to him.

This last, childish fantasy surprised her. Not only had she not thought of Moses for months, she wasn't aware of the slightest feeling of guilt over sending him to the orphanage that day. But if no guilt, why 'make it up' to him — make *what* up?

As she breasted the ridge she felt the first stirrings of an onshore breeze, pushing inland from St Austell Bay. She stood there a moment, eyes closed, letting it play with a welcome coolness around her neck. The pleasant sensation drove out all those troublesome thoughts.

Down at the old engine house the same breeze soughed through the empty windows, shivering the dry stalks of sedge that grew on the sills. She stood at the widest of them and stared out across the man-made lake — two acres of an emerald green so brilliant it almost hurt the eyes.

She began a much pleasanter daydream. She could leave civilization behind and come up here to live, all on her own. Nobody seemed to want this old engine house. She could patch up the windows with tarpaulins and live here. She could gather berries and things ... honey from wild bees ... not locusts, probably. Grasshoppers, perhaps. Anyway, details like that could be sorted out later. Perhaps the people in the village would take pity on her and leave bowls of milk and crusts at the crossroads for her to consume at dead of night.

Then suddenly, for no particular reason, she thought of her father. Not as part of her daydream but in the here-and-now. She imagined him standing beside her, gazing out at this scene of unsurpassed beauty. And her grief, which she had believed was fast fading, struck her with a force that almost clove her in two. It swept aside all those delicate trip wires and barricades she had spent these past months building. It drowned her with all the elemental fierceness of those first days and nights, around the time of his funeral.

And yet there was a difference. It wasn't the *loss* of him that was so painful, she now realized, it was sorrow at all the things he'd never be able to share. Her mother might believe he was still hovering around them somehow but that was a comforting notion she herself could not accept. He was gone — forever gone — and it was better to face the fact. But oh, if only he *could* be here! How she would have loved to tell him of the wonders of this day — the sights, the discoveries! She longed to show him how well she was growing up. She yearned for him to stroke her hair or pat her shoulder and say, 'Well done, darling!' Her life would have so much more meaning if he were still there to share it.

"Oh, Daddy ... Daddy ... Dad-eee!" she whispered vehemently at the sun-bleached sky. "Why? *Why?*" The tears were streaming down her cheeks now and she made no attempt to wipe them away.

Suddenly there was a gush of white at the farther end of the lake. A maintenance gang must be testing one of the pumps in a working pit near by. The pipework itself was too far off to be visible from the engine house, so all she could see was this magical spouting from the farther rim, a spouting of what looked like milk, gleaming white against the scumbled greeny grey of the old pit's walls. The pump must be sucking air, too — or there was air in the pipeline — because it came out in coughs and spurts rather than in one solid jet.

A moment later the first gush hit the limpid face of the water. It happened in silence; the sound followed a full two seconds later. She watched the ripples spread in perfect circles until they reached the edges, where their rebounds made interesting patterns, like the moiré of shot silk, across the now opalescent green.

Down the centre of the lake, though, they were still perfect arcs. She watched them advancing toward her until, when they were about half way, she was distracted by a movement off to her right.

A high granite wall ran away from the engine house on that side, being a containing wall to the coal yard. It ended in a solid-stone buttress, about fifty paces away. And there she saw a figure, half in its shadow — a man, staring out, like herself, over the lake. A young man. A working man, by the look of him. At least, he was dressed in workman's clothes, all stained white with the china clay, and he wore a battered old hat at a rakish angle on his head.

"You're trespassing," he said with a smile. "Where are you from?"

He did not speak like a working man at all. But that made his smile all the more puzzling, for men of the property-owning classes did not usually accuse trespassers with a smile. Perhaps he had seen her weeping and it embarrassed him — and this was his way of pretending not to have seen it?

"Penzance, actually," she said. "I'm sorry. Do you own this ... this ..."

"Ruin?" Again that smile. "I'm afraid I do, Miss ...?"

"Owen. Jennifer Owen of Chyandour. Now you have the advantage of me, Mister ...?"

But even as she spoke she knew who he was. The name popped into her mind even as he spoke it: "Colston-Smart. Douglas Colston-Smart — also of Penzance, funnily enough. But I don't recall seeing *you* around the town, Miss Owen — and I'm sure I should if I had, if you follow? I say, do we have to shout like this? May I join you up there?"

She shrugged, trying not to show how pleased she was at the suggestion. "It's a free country, Mister Colston-Smart."

He laughed. "Thank God it's not," he said as he approached.

Her heart was racing now and her mind all a-whirl, trying to decide how much — or how little, rather — to tell him. She wondered whether he knew of his mother's real intentions for Medrose. From the way she had spoken, it would seem she had kept him in the dark. So nothing must be said now that would give her away.

And yet, Jennifer realized, she could not pretend to be a complete stranger. She still hadn't decided to take the post, even if Mrs C-S agreed to her 'outrageous' demand for thirty bob a week; but she didn't want to burn her bridges there, either. And he'd think her very sly if she did accept the position and it came out that she'd known about it even at this meeting between them.

So, taking her courage in her hands, she said, as he joined her at the unglazed window, "We've just moved to Penzance, from Carleen. But I've met your mother, Mister Colston-Smart. Only yesterday, in fact. I beat her at croquet."

He shot her an amused glance as he took out a large handkerchief, which was already liberally stained — off-white on white — with china clay, and wiped his face with it. It left him looking like a death's-head — a rather handsome death's-head, with deepset eyes of a rich hazel colour and dark, curly hair.

"Owen," he said, more to himself than to her as he tucked the kerchief away. "Now I remember. In fact, my mother mentioned you at supper last night."

"Favourably, I trust?"

"Extremely." His tone changed. "May I say how sorry I was to hear of your father's death? Such a beastly chance. I have one very fine memory of him."

"You knew him?"

He shook his head. "I could hardly claim that much. He treated me once. I grazed my leg rather nastily on some barnacles, swimming at Porthleven. Back in oh-eight, when I was fourteen."

Which made him twenty-one now, she worked out. She would have thought him a few years older — what wealth and position can do to age a person! Plus a touch of china clay.

Then she recalled the incident herself, for she had been there, too — a family picnic among the rock pools west of Porthleven, half a mile from where Flossie had died. She had been twelve at the time.

"That was *you!*" She laughed before she realized she ought to thank him more soberly for his condolences, which she then did.

The scene came back to her with the sharpness of so many childhood memories: a lean, gangling boy with large knees and elbows, being terribly brave about what was, indeed, a nasty gash on his right shin. "I thought ..." she added and then hesitated.

"Thought what?"

She gave an embarrassed laugh. "The same as I thought just now. I took you for a labouring man, dressed like that. And it was the same that day at Porthleven. I thought you were one of the village boys. You were brown as a hazelnut."

Actually he hadn't been brown but bronze — a glorious, golden bronze. She remembered peeping at him slyly when he wasn't looking. Not that he'd taken much notice of her, anyway. She remembered thinking, *Oh, I want skin like that!*

"I *am* a labouring man," he said. "I labour a dashed sight harder than most of that description."

"Even on the Sabbath, I see."

"The armed forces need cloam," he told her, using the Cornish word for crockery. "And poultices. And chocolate that doesn't melt. And art paper for maps ..."

He was explaining why he wasn't in uniform, of course. A lot of people did that, without putting it crudely, in so many words.

She was sorry to have let that happy childhood memory go. "Did it leave a permanent scar?" she asked, interrupting him. "It looked like a very bad gash."

For reply he planted his foot on the granite sill and hoisted his trouser leg to the knee. "See for yourself. Not a mark — a real tribute to your father's skill."

"Did he put in stitches?"

"No. He broke off two stalks of kelp, put one each side of the cut, and bandaged it. They pressed it together. No stitches. No scar."

He still had the most enviable skin — pale bronze now, smooth and hairless. Daringly she touched it, ran her fingertips an inch or so along the bone, where the skin was most gleaming. "Proper job," she said.

He stood erect again and let his trouser leg fall. "Are you going to accept my mother's offer?" he asked.

She looked at him in surprise — and in something of a quandary, for it would seem that his mother had done little more than simply mention her name as someone she had interviewed yesterday. How much should she tell him now? If she did eventually work — on her terms — at Medrose, she'd be seeing quite a lot of this young man. The thought did not displease her but she would not like him to think her deceitful. On the other hand, he might admire her for her discretion in saying little at their first, casual meeting. It was hard to know what to do for the best, but, either way, she realized she wanted his good opinion.

"I rather think it's up to your mother to accept *my* offer," she replied, trying, by her smile, to suggest that he knew very well what she meant.

But he clearly did not. *"Your* offer?" he asked. "She said nothing to me about that."

"Ah, well ..." She returned her gaze to the lake. "As to that, I'm sure she has her reasons."

"Is it something I should know, too?"

"Mister Colston-Smart — how can I possibly answer that? I met your mother for the first time only yesterday. I don't know what she wishes to share with you and what she'd prefer to keep to herself."

"Ah — so there *is* something she's keeping back! Something you know about, too, eh?"

She laughed then, but as a way of fending him off. "You're like a dog with a bone," she said. "Listen! She made me an offer …"

He interrupted. "To become her companion."

But she was not deflected into agreeing — nor into disagreeing, either. "And I made her … not exactly an offer. A modified counter-proposal, shall we say. And I'm now waiting for her to say yes or no to it — that's all I meant. But as to the details, I really think you must seek them from her."

His eyes flickered restlessly over the landscape before them — *his* landscape, as he had made clear at the outset; but whatever he had come out here to investigate seemed now to be forgotten. "She is so headstrong at times," he murmured.

"By nature?" Jennifer asked. "Or is she driven to it?"

She saw no harm in dropping a hint or two that might make the son see life from his mother's point of view.

He looked at her, shaking his head as if to say that the question was much too complex to answer.

"May *I* ask a rather prying question now?" she inquired. "Sort of even things up. You're at liberty not to answer."

He grinned. "Go ahead."

"Why were you leaning against that wall just now? Was that part of your labouring-man's day?"

"Ah — no secrets *there,* Miss Owen. I was engaged on a tour of all our pits, abandoned and working. I want to see how much scrap iron there is. It wasn't worth salvaging before the war. Strictly speaking, it's not worth salvaging now — except that one would hate to think of a British tommy lying dead in France or Turkey or anywhere, all because the metal for the bullet that might have saved him is rusting away here." He pointed at a couple of girders overhead. "Those two lads will come out tomorrow, for a start."

"And how long were you standing there?" she asked.

His brow furrowed and she knew he was trying to decide whether or not to lie to her. To her surprise he reached out and took her by the hand, lightly and tenderly. "Long enough, I'm afraid," he replied. "I am sorry. One wants to help and yet one knows one can't." He stroked her knuckles, almost absent-mindedly. "I had a brother once, you know — a twin. He died of meningitis, not quite two years ago, just before the war."

"I didn't know," she said, barely above a whisper. There was a lump in her throat again and her eyelids prickled.

"So perhaps I can understand a little better than most?" He made a question of it and then answered himself with a shrug.

Hesitantly she raised her other hand, to sandwich his. At the same time she thought how ridiculous they must look — two people who hardly knew each other, standing there like one of those anæmic couples Burne-Jones loved to paint. The humour of the situation rescued her from the bathos of renewed tears.

"They tell you you'll get over it," he went on, "that it'll go away. But it doesn't. Other things overlay it in time — that's true. But it's still there, down in those layers, somewhere." He smiled wanly and removed his hand. The gesture was not brusque; rather it implied that this new, unexpected rapport between them no longer needed such flimsy contact. "Not much comfort, I'm afraid," he concluded. "But it isn't comfort one really wants, is it. One wants to know *why.*"

So he had heard as well as seen her. She found she didn't mind. In fact, she rather welcomed it.

"Well!" He rubbed his hands and became brisk again. "Press on, eh? I do hope you accept my mother's offer — or that she accepts yours. I mean I do hope it's not a case of the immovable object meeting the irresistible force."

She laughed. "Which is which, I wonder?"

"Now you *are* prying." He wagged a finger at her and took a step or two toward the door. Then he paused and half turned back to her. "However, I'll let you into my confidence if you'll let me into yours."

She eyed him shrewdly. "No promises," she warned.

"Just tell me what your counter-proposal was."

"Oh that!" she said off-handedly. "I said I'd accept the position for thirty shillings a week."

Heaven knows what he had expected to hear but he clearly hadn't got within a million miles of anything so outrageous. "A *week?*" he asked incredulously.

"Now you must keep your part of the bargain," she challenged him. "Am I the immovable object or the irresistible force?"

He recovered his poise swiftly. "You don't really need *me* to tell you that, Miss Owen," he said over his shoulder as he walked away.

She turned again to the window to catch him as he passed by outside. "Beast!" she called out as he drew level.

He did not turn and look at her until he was back by the buttress, where she had first noticed him. "I'll say this much, though," he added. "I very much hope we'll meet again — which, I suppose, is the same thing as saying that I hope the immovable object is, for once, capable of yielding with grace."

21 THE SECOND post on the Tuesday morning after that visit to the claypits was late. It did not arrive until nine o'clock. But Jennifer forgave the postman because among the bundle he left them was a brief letter from Millicent Colston-Smart, saying that she would be grateful if Miss Owen would call upon her that afternoon at four. She gave not the slightest hint that she had accepted Jennifer's 'counter-proposal' — but then, as the girl said to her mother, "She wouldn't, would she!"

"I don't see why not," Goronwy replied.

"Pride. Nothing on paper, you see."

"I'd say there's a fair bit of pride on *both* sides, if you ask me, young madam. Now don't you overreach yourself if it turns out you're right."

"I don't know what you mean," Jennifer said testily.

"I think you do, darling. I mean you shouldn't think of her as having caved in. Don't show yourself triumphant. Be matter-of-fact. She *isn't* caving in — she's just accepting a reality, a truth that had not occurred to her before. Namely that you are, indeed, *worth* thirty shillings a week."

Jennifer smiled at that. "So you've also come round to accepting it now, have you?"

"Certainly not! I think it was the daftest thing you ever did. And I don't believe for one moment that she's called you up there to admit she's caved in. All I'm saying is that *if* she has yielded, don't go all triumphalistic, if there is such a word. Behave as if she's just calmly accepting an obvious reality. Be graceful and ladylike. That's all."

"Why do *you* think she's asking to see me, then?" Jennifer said.

Her mother bit her lip and answered hesitantly, "I suspect her son has mentioned your encounter on Sunday, and she's put two and two together and made five in the usual way. She's obviously at daggers-drawn with both the men in her life. People like that — people with more money than they know how to spend — live in a world of secrets and alliances and intrigues. It's second nature to them. She might easily think you went up to Saint Austell on Sunday deliberately to see her son …"

"But that's absurd! Even when I did meet him I had no idea who he was. He looked like an old …"

"*I* know that, dear," Goronwy interrupted, "and you know that. But — it's what I'm telling you — *they* think differently. Mother and son, both. I'll bet that for the first five minutes of your conversation with Douglas he was thinking, 'When is she going to get to the point? She's obviously come all this way and deliberately engineered this meeting, so why is she wasting time in idle chatter like this?' You ask him next time you meet — *if* there is to be a next time."

After this warning it was a wary and not in the least triumphalistic Jennifer who retraced her steps up to Medrose that afternoon. There had been a change in the weather around noon, when the sky clouded over. Rain had started shortly after, quite a heavy downpour at first though it had now died back to a mere spotting. The air was warm and steamy, heavy with those cloying, fungal smells that rise like a miasma after longish dry spells. When she realized she was getting wetter from perspiration inside her raincoat than from rain outside it, she opened all the buttons and flapped her way like a gawky, flightless bird over the last furlong or so.

The odours of rotting woodland floor were almost overpowering in the garden at Medrose. The letter had said to come directly round to the conservatory. As she reached the garden side of the house, Mrs C-S threw up a window and called out a greeting. "Go straight in out of this wet, dear," she said. "I'll be down in half a tick."

It was hard to tell from instructions so brief and loud what sort of mood she was in — but at least she had said 'dear' — not the more coolly formal 'Miss Owen' of the letter she had sent.

The conservatory, which was almost large enough to call a palm house, was pure Victorian in its decoration, all finials and crockets and spiky bits and diamond-shaped panes. It badly needed a coat of paint. Jennifer let herself in by the garden door, only to find, to her dismay, that it was several degrees warmer within and every bit as humid. She hung up her coat and took off her boater to fan her face with.

They could make a jungle film in here, she thought, looking all about her. Would it be too cheeky, she wondered, to ask if George Herbert and she might come up here to make some of their screen tests? Ever since his offer she had kept her eyes open for interesting backgrounds. Locations, they called them.

The maid came in with the tea tray. Mrs C-S was just behind her, speaking before she even set eyes on her guest. "I'm so sorry to have kept you waiting, my dear. I'm all at sixes and sevens today. Move three paces and one drowns in perspiration. You can go, Molly. I'll see to everything."

The girl dropped a perfunctory curtsey and withdrew.

"Now!" Mrs C-S became ominously solemn as she settled herself in a rattan chair and picked up the teapot. "Let's clear the decks, shall we?"

"And batten down all hatches?" Jennifer asked warily.

"I'm sure it won't come to that. Do help yourself to sugar." She smiled sweetly but not broadly. And not for long, either. "You're not surprised that I am a *little* bit cooler toward you this time?" she added, poising her words delicately between a question and a statement.

Jennifer took two teaspoons of caster sugar; they only used granulated at home now, because it was cheaper. "I *would* be surprised," she replied, "if you had not waited to hear what I might have to say."

Suddenly it struck her what she ought to say.

"Well, I am waiting." Mrs C-S took no sugar. "Some madeira cake? Or the battenburg? I suppose we ought to call it 'mountbatten' cake now they've given up their German names!"

Her mother's warnings had misled her: Be humble! Be gentle and ladylike! Her father's advice would have been better: Attack is the best defence! His favourite dictum, or one of them.

Before she could think better of it she opened her mouth and said, "Forgive my asking it, Mrs Colston-Smart, but do you suppose it was a pure coincidence — my meeting with your son near Saint Dennis the day before yesterday?"

The woman almost dropped the cake knife. "Well, my dear!" she exclaimed. "I was rather expecting to ask *you* that question."

Jennifer pressed the point home. "You didn't send him, then — well, I didn't seriously suppose you had. But is it possible you might have said something or other, quite innocently, that made him go there of his own accord and seek me out?"

"I don't think so," she answered reflectively. But her frown said that it was, of course, possible. "Why? Did he say something that made you suspect he had?"

Jennifer shook her head. "That was the puzzling thing. The moment he introduced himself I thought, 'He's been sent here by his mother. This is the second part of my interview!' I didn't mind, of course — it seemed only natural. I mean, it would be awkward to say the least if you took to me and he didn't. But as we continued to talk of quite general matters — the way any two strangers might — I began to wonder when he was going to get to the point. And then, when we'd been chatting away quite amiably for ten minutes or so, he bade me farewell and went his way — leaving me to wonder whether I'd just been subjected to the most subtly gentle interview *ever,* or was the unthinkable true? I mean, had it been a complete coincidence? That's why I asked." She smiled her most disarming smile. "I hope I haven't offended you? That, of course, is the very last thing I'd wish to do."

The woman stared at her a long, uncomfortable while and then said, "I've changed my mind about you, young lady. That really was your first thought, was it — when you realized you were talking to my son — that he was in cahoots with me?"

Jennifer crossed her fingers out of sight in the folds of her dress and said it was. To herself she resolved it would, indeed, be the sort of thing she'd think of in future — that *everyone* was to be suspected of some conspiracy until they proved themselves innocent.

Mrs C-S continued: "I had intended asking you to accept *twenty* shillings a week — which I should still have considered outrageous. I was only prepared to do so because I understand you have some 'celluloid ambitions,' as they call them?" She caught the sudden change of expression in Jennifer's face and said, "Now what is it? Why are you looking at me like that?"

"So you *have* been making inquiries about me! And through them you *could* have learned that I was to accompany the Colletts to the claypits."

The woman relaxed and laughed. "Set your mind at rest on that score at least. I give you my word that I had no part in arranging your meeting. And I speak with *almost* equal assurance for my son — except that he is one of the most devious and secretive young men you could ever hope to meet. Or *not* to meet. Anyway — as I was saying — I've changed my mind about you. If you, at your tender age, already have this gift of suspicion — this nose for conspiracies, even where none exist — then you truly are worth your *thirty pieces of silver.*"

Jennifer let out her breath as if winded. "That was below the belt, Mrs Colston-Smart."

The other was only slightly apologetic. "I've been savouring it ever since it occurred to me in my bath on Saturday evening," she replied. "I had to get it in somehow. I must also tell you what I expect of you in return for such a prince's ransom. You're not eating."

Jennifer took a bite of her cake.

"What do you make of my son, by the way?" Mrs C-S asked abruptly. "I was very pleased to gather that you had said nothing to him of my pet little project."

The girl swallowed quickly and said, "I did tell him how much I'd asked in the way of salary."

"And?"

"He didn't discourage me," she said cautiously.

"You see what I mean — devious! He knew you had less chance of getting thirty shillings than he has of finding gold at Wheal Dream." She sighed. "Actually, I meant what do you think of him as a person? As a man? He has no recreations, you know — only solitary ones like reading and walking — and he spends precious little time on them, even. Work, work, work — it's all he thinks of. He has no friends his own age. Won't join the tennis club. Won't go to dances. I hope you'll be able to introduce him to lots of *your* young friends — especially lady friends. Ones you're not *too* fond of, mind, because he might end up marrying one of them and you wouldn't want to inflict him on a really *good* friend."

Jennifer chuckled. "Will this all be part of my work at Medrose?"

The other did not find it so amusing. "No," she sighed. "It's all a pipe-dream. You won't have any time for fun, either. None of us will, I fear." She raised the cake knife again. "Will you try a slice of the battenburg? It's delicious." As Jennifer held forth her plate the woman went on: "Do you like making lists?"

Jennifer tapped her temple. "In here. My mother's a great one for lists on paper, but what I say is — I say when you write something down it goes out of your head at once. And bits of paper can get lost. And then you're sunk. So I make them here." She tapped her brow again.

"Have you thought at all — here's a real-life test for you now — what changes will have to be made inside this house to turn it into a convalescent home? And if we organized it well enough, could we manage it all between next Monday morning and the following Friday evening? And don't tell me you haven't seen inside the place yet — it's a test of your imagination as well."

Jennifer smiled and leaned back in her chair. By chance she had whiled away the time between waking and sleeping on the past two nights on just such a mental exercise — even while assuring herself she had no intention of taking the position Mrs C-S was offering. "All silver and valuables into the vaults," she began, ticking each item off on her fingers. "Including chandeliers, ancestral portraits, stuffed fish, stags' heads, and anything else that might be used for target practice."

Mrs C-S chuckled. "You *have* been inside my house, I'll swear!"

She held up another finger. "Sheets of plywood to be laid over polished wooden floors. We'll have to consult the head carpenter about the problem of the doors."

"What problem?"

"Well, if you raise the floor level like that, the doors won't open."

The woman shook her head in amazement. "Of course they won't. D'you know, that would never have occurred to me. What's the answer, d'you think?"

"Saw a sliver off the bottom of each door. When the war's over you can replace it with those brass anti-draught strips."

The woman clapped her hands in delight and said, "Marvellous! What an asset you're going to be, Miss Owen. Gobble that cake and come indoors. See the size of the problem for yourself."

"D'you have elegant doors?" Jennifer asked as she followed her inside. "I expect you do. They'll have to be sheeted, too. I think you can get very thin plywood. My father used to make models with it."

The interior of the house held few surprises. Its solid, smug façade had prepared her well for what she found: solid, smug Victorian monstrosities in oak and teak; heavy tapestries like old elephant hide; paintings in ornate frames that must have weighed a ton apiece; wallpapers that aimed at jungle but never rose above the botanic garden; and incongruous things like suits of armour, criss-crossed claymores, pikestaffs, and blunderbusses.

Jennifer's excited monologue trailed away. "I never saw a home equipped with so many implements of sudden death," she said.

"Nor so many reasons for wishing it on someone," her hostess added drily. "Your remarks about target practice are well taken, my dear. I don't think we shall pack *everything* off to the vaults."

And so, for a good hour or so, they wandered from room to room while Jennifer mentally inventoried their contents and tried to anticipate the problems that would arise during the conversion of the house from family mausoleum to convalescent home. Or she tried to. In the end, though, she had to admit it was too much for any one head to hold and that paper lists were, in this case, the only answer.

In that way, though Mrs C-S never quite said, 'The place is yours,' nor Jennifer, 'I'll take it,' she set aside her celluloid ambitions and became bully, bulldog, and secretary to the chatelaine of Medrose.

22 To ALLAY any suspicions in Douglas Colston-Smart's mind — that Jennifer's placing with his mother was now *fait-accompli* and that they were plotting some devilment together — she did not immediately move into the room that was to be hers but stayed on at home and walked up and down the hill each day. She and her new employer passed the Wednesday and part of the Thursday of that week in planning the transformation of the house. Then, when they were quite sure of it in their own minds, they called in George Wallis, master carpenter and prominent local builder of the second generation. His father had, in fact,

carried out the original conversion of Medrose from a modest Regency lodge to its present splendour.

Wallis had a round face and large, sad eyes whose doleful expression was not helped by a drooping walrus moustache. His bowler hat seemed glued to some kind of swivel in his head, for, though he never took it off, he wore it at every possible angle at one time or another as the afternoon progressed. He also wore an apron of white canvas, furnished with long, thin pockets for various tools. The only implement they contained on that day, though, was one of those flat pencils with oblong leads. With it he scribbled almost unreadable notes on scraps of paper torn from old trade calendars. His attitude, which seemed as firmly fixed inside his head as his hat was outside it, was that *anything* was possible but *nothing* was easy.

He began by brushing aside every suggestion they made. "Can't cover up they floors with half-inch ply, missuz," he said. "'Cos the doors won't open, see?"

"Cut a sliver off the bottom," Mrs Colston-Smart said, giving Jennifer a wink when he wasn't looking.

"And when the war's over?" he asked with as much sarcasm as he dared. "And we do take up the ply again ..."

"I've always wanted to fit those brass anti-draught strips," she told him. "The one with the bristles underneath, you know?"

He sniffed heavily and said, yes, it *could* be done.

And so, as the morning wore on, they chipped away at his resistance until, by the end of the day, he was actually asking Jennifer for ideas about tackling this or that problem in the conversion. Indeed, he was so much in the spirit of the thing that, as he left, he told them of a mistake that had been made down at the hospital — which might be to their advantage. The clerk of the works there had ordered sixty-four beds under the impression he had indented for only thirty-two.

"'Tis the way they did list them in the catalogue, see," he explained. They put 'beds, hospital' on one line, then, under it, 'beds, hospital, heads ... beds, hospital, frames ... beds, hospital, springs' ... and so forth — each on one line. And he writ 'thirty-two' anenst the lot — not realizing they was all the spare parts to make a whole bed. That's how they ended up with double, see? I daresay you might get them for a knock-down price if you'm quick."

Jennifer wondered aloud what 'a knock-down price' might be.

He told a passing cloud that he thought five bob a bed might be about the mark.

"I'll see the clerk of the works down there tomorrow," Mrs C-S told Jennifer when Wallis had gone. "His name's Snow, I think."

"Leave it to me, if you like," she replied. "From what I know of that place, I think Matron may have more say in it than Mister Snow."

"Indeed? And you think you have some influence over her?" she asked with kindly sarcasm.

"No, but she knows we're poor now — and I needn't mention your name at all. Think it over, anyway. Meanwhile, there's something more urgent we need to discuss."

"Oh?"

"Your son, Mrs Colston-Smart. If he'll be spending the weekend, or even part of it, here at Medrose, I think we should put up a 'diversion,' as the army calls it."

"To amuse him?"

"To keep him from prying into this and that."

Mrs C-S looked at her askance. "You've been so resourceful this week, my dear, that I dread to think what you might suggest next. Perhaps you know of some overbooked belly-dancers going for a knock-down price?"

Jennifer laughed. "No, but we already have the answer. You remember what you called my 'celluloid ambitions'? Well, Mrs Collett's assistant, George Herbert, who is also something of a dab hand with a motion-picture camera, has managed to lay his hands on such a machine. He's off to serve in France in ten days' time and he's rather keen to take some moving pictures of me pretending to be a cinema actress. 'Screen tests,' they call them."

"And that's not *all* he's rather keen on, so I hear!"

Jennifer shrugged awkwardly. "That's more his business than mine, I'm afraid. I hope I've given him no encouragement. Anyway, he seems to think that if he shows these 'screen tests' to his cronies in the business, I'll be snapped up and carried shoulder high to the nearest cinema stage. Ha ha! But — and this is where I want to ask you a favour — it would keep Mister Herbert happy if we made these tests. And it would also divert Mister Douglas's mind away from the truth if he saw me making them in this house — I mean using the house and gardens as an imposing sort of background." She smiled disarmingly. "But please do say no if you'd rather we went elsewhere?"

23 GEORGE HERBERT stuck both thumbs out at right angles and then placed his hands together so as to make an oblong frame of the same proportions as those of a cinema screen. He closed one eye and peered through this makeshift mask at various randomly chosen portions of the conservatory. Every now and then he made a vague noise, like a half-swallowed *mmm* or a quietly nasal *hnh!* Douglas Colston-Smart watched in fascination; in the same spirit he would observe a car mechanic, a concert pianist, a quick-sketch artist, or any other competent professional. Jennifer was already growing bored, though.

"Does it really *matter,* Mister Herbert?" she asked. "Plants are plants, surely? Especially in black and white."

"Today they're moods as well, Miss Owen," George replied evenly. "Set you against this spiky whatever-it-is and you could be a dangerous vamp. These swirling leaves, like green flames, could help you be a dedicated campaigner — a young Florence Nightingale, perhaps. Put these Gothic windows behind you and you've got to be a saint or a novice nun or something like that. And what I say is, if the background will do half the work for you, why throw it away?"

Then, sensing her impatience, he said, "I'll tell you a story — something the director did on a film we made last year. *The Miracle of Saint Bride's,* it was called. There was this young boy, crippled for the whole first reel. Then comes the miracle and he realizes he can stand up straight and walk. So we had this young boy. Jocelyn Scoley, he was called. About ten. Couldn't act for toffee. But beautiful. Angelic. Couldn't take your eyes off him. The problem was, how to get him to act his delight and surprise immediately after the miracle. So Bud Scoley — he was the director and also Jocelyn's uncle — got this idea. He made the little chap crouch down inside a teachest for a good ten minutes, though it seemed like ten *hours* to the poor lad. Then he started the lights and camera and shouted silence — and, believe me, when Bud Scoley demands silence he gets it! You daren't so much as *whisper* while the camera's rolling, not on one of his movies. Daft, I know — seeing as the film is silent — but that's his rule and God help the one who breaks it! So then Bud beckons the boy out of the teachest and, of course, he stretches like the king of all the world. And while he's doing that Bud says to him, nice and conversational, 'Bet that feels good, eh, Jocelyn?' And of course the poor lad knows the camera's turning, *knows* he daren't say a word, so he just flashes him the sweetest, shyest smile you ever saw. 'Course we all laughed at Bud's cunning. But next morning, I tell you, when we saw the rush print of that scene, there wasn't a dry eye on the set, even though we all knew how it was done. You never saw anything so beautiful, so convincing. Strong men wept." His own voice faltered a little, even at the memory.

Jennifer forgot her boredom, forgot even that she had fallen into that state. She was already regretting her contract with Mrs Colston-Smart. Perhaps what had attracted her most was the element of deception that went with the work — until the convalescent home was up and running, anyway. But the business of making films — or 'movies,' as George Herbert called them — was carried on in a world of *permanent* deception. To her that was like saying 'permanent excitement,' too.

Deception — excitement … excitement — deception. The words themselves melted in her mind, leaving behind them a thrilling aura that now possessed her. Acting, she realized for the very first time — though in some curious way it was as if she had always known it — was the excitement of being other than one was, coupled with the firm knowledge that one remained oneself. It was a perfect deception since it included even the deceiver among its victims.

Seized by this spirit she darted to the Gothic windows and posed before them. "Shall I be a vamp where you would expect to see a nun?" she asked, whipping a bead-fringed cloth off one of the little cane tables and holding it provocatively over her face, like a houri's veil.

"Or a nun where the vamp should hold court, eh?" She dropped the tablecloth and took up a black square of camera cloth, which she quickly arranged as a novice's wimple. Then, with the spiky whatever-they-were as a most incongruous background, she stood, eyes downcast, face composed, the very image of an ardent young woman lost in ecstatic communion with the eternal.

The two onlookers gasped. She wanted to break out of her rôle and say it was all an act, but found she could not. Slowly, as one returning from parley with the infinite, a little bewildered at this world, she raised her eyes and fixed them — now large, cool, and solemn — upon the two men.

"I say!" Douglas murmured, little above a whisper.

George, though he was also stirred by what they had seen, was more professional about it. "Can you do that again, pet?" he asked, picking up the camera and resettling its tripod legs for a 'take' of her as the vamp by the nun's windows.

It was not so startling the second time, of course, yet it fascinated both men to see how she could simply turn it on and off again to order. George would start cranking the camera handle and then, when the rhythm was steady, he'd snap his fingers as a signal for her to begin doing her piece. And it was like turning on an electric switch. Jennifer would slip instantly from her everyday self into a vamp. Or a nun, which was the subject of the next few takes.

She wanted to try her hand at the young Florence Nightingale, too, but George knew how long it would take to move the camera to a darker room and get the lighting just right for the Lady with the Lamp. So she did Florence as an old lady, just before her death (the news of which Jennifer could remember her father bringing to the nursery), receiving the letter from Queen Victoria to say she'd been given the Order of Merit at long last.

'Girl Reading Letter' proved a fertile theme. In swift order she acted: schoolgirl reads letter telling her she has won a place at Oxford; schoolgirl reads letter telling her she has *not* won a place at Oxford; girl reads letter breaking off romance and is heartbroken; girl reads letter breaking off romance and determines on a terrible vengeance; and, finally, orphan reads notice of eviction from humble cottage.

This last, touching scene gave Douglas an idea. "You should also have someone to act *with,*" he said. "Or against, rather. Suppose the landlord turned up in person to evict you from your humble cottage — that is, *his* humble cottage. How would you throw yourself on his mercy?"

"Like this," she said at once, going down on her knees before him. And — greatly to his discomfiture — she threw her arms about his waist and pressed her head to his stomach. She was so lost to the business of acting that he had become just one more prop among so many — the plants, the windows, the furniture.

"I say!" he said, though he actually said no more. He merely laughed with embarrassment.

"Hold it like that!" George exclaimed as he twiddled with various wingnuts on the tripod to retrain his camera on this touching scene.

Jennifer went on pleading to such effect that real tears trembled on her eyelids — and yet none of the usual accompaniments followed it: no lump in the throat, no constriction of the jaw muscles. She was in control throughout. She alternated between showing her tortured face to the camera and gazing up into the prop-landlord's eyes with the most heartrending appeal. And when the prop-landlord resolved back into Douglas Colston-Smart and giggled at the strength of her performance, she punched him quite sharply in the small of the back and said, "Act, damn you!"

And he did.

In fact, he began to see possibilities in her dedication to this business of simulating convincing emotions. And when George at last cried, "Cut!" he turned to him casually and said, "You should throw in a romantic scene or two, don't you think? You know the sort of thing: Vamp kisses man passionately but the moment she rests her head tenderly on his shoulder — when he can no longer see her face — she pulls an expression of loathing and weariness. Something like that, don't you know."

He spoke with studied indifference, suggesting that, if it didn't take too long and if they didn't make too many demands on him, he'd consider lending himself to the charade — all in the cause of art, to be sure.

Jennifer was not deceived, of course; 'flattered' was more the word. Also curious and slightly exhilarated at the prospect. But she didn't wish to say so. Stony-faced she turned to George, leaving the decision to him.

He was not deceived, either. "Here!" he said, taking a step toward Douglas. "You turn the handle — there's nothing to it, really — and I'll show you how."

But Douglas did not budge. "Actually, old boy," he said, "I think I already know how. But you must direct the *finer* points. I mean, should it be like this ... or like this?" And, gripping Jennifer by the shoulders he turned her this way and that, bringing his lips within half an inch of hers in a sort of dummy run-through of two possible embraces.

She turned a smiling face to George and said, "Well? You decide."

He saw he had lost and, with ill-concealed disappointment, mumbled, "The first position, with your nose on the camera side of his." Then, seeking to take all spontaneity out of it, he gave them the most detailed instructions: "His left arm around your shoulder. His right hand touching your left forearm ... slipping away to lightly clasp your waist — go on! Rehearse each movement as I tell you. No, I said *lightly!* Now Miss Owen, your hand steals, also lightly, up his arm ... hesitates ... you want to kiss him and yet you don't want to kiss him ... your emotions are torn in two ... finally you yield. Okay — you don't need to do *that* bit yet. Start again now ..." And so on.

Too late he realized that the film director within him had directed quite a different scene from the one Colston-Smart had suggested. The scene he had created was: Girl wildly in love with boy doesn't wish to reveal her true feelings but is overwhelmed by his advances and impulsively yields to her passion. "But remember," he added belatedly, "you're only pretending. When he can no longer see your face, your expression is full of disgust and boredom."

"No, that's *too* contradictory," she replied. "If I'm *that* sort of coquette, then I'd kiss him like this!" And she flung her arms around Douglas's neck and pressed her lips passionately to his and nuzzled him as if she would devour his entire mouth. Then, just as she was beginning to think how thrilling it was, she forced herself to break their contact and lean her head tenderly on his shoulder while she mimed ennui and distaste.

"So!" she said.

George stopped turning the handle — for he had started the moment their lips had touched (not wishing to run through more takes of these particular scenes than was absolutely necessary). "Perfect," he assured them. "Now let's get the passionate one over and done with. You don't mind, do you — old fellow?" he asked Douglas.

"I think I can just about manage it," he replied jovially.

Jennifer, who had started the day's work at the centre of attention, suddenly felt that *she* had turned into the prop. Besides, she had been stirred by a quite genuine passion at the height of her kiss with Douglas — though whether it had been a passion for him, in particular, or the sort of stirring that might occur if any attractive young man were to kiss her and press their bodies tight together, she could not say. Nor did she wish to find out just yet. "Let's change the young man for this scene," she said, stepping a pace back from Douglas. "You *can* manage to turn the handle, can't you?"

With the same ill-concealed pique that George had shown earlier, Douglas stepped behind the camera lens and yielded up his place upon its other side.

Then, just to pay George back for his earlier fussiness, she made him mime his way through several rehearsals of those same instructions he had insisted upon in such detail — not overlooking his remark that they could dispense with actual contact between their lips during these rehearsals. She held him to that.

Finally, when their kiss came, her earlier question was answered, too. In his own way George Herbert was every bit as attractive as Douglas Colston-Smart; and the press of his eager lips on hers and the firm grasp of his embrace and the exciting pressure of his hard, manly body against hers was every bit as electrifying, too.

So she need not think herself in thrall to either of them — nor to any other young man, either.

24 GEORGE HUNG around long after the last foot of film had been shot − clearly unwilling to leave Jennifer alone with Douglas. She, for her part, wondered that Mrs C-S did not come and claim her back, now that her diversions were over; perhaps she, too, did not want her son to be too long alone with her new 'companion,' as he thought Jennifer to be. Finally, when it was clear even to George that he must go home, he said, in a hopeful, almost begging tone, "It's my day for duty on the beaches tomorrow. Maybe you'd come down for a swim?"

"Are you a lifesaver or something?" Douglas asked, though the question had been directed at Jennifer.

"No. Same-day snaps. We take pictures up to four o'clock, develop them, print them …"

"Oh yes, I know the thing now."

"It's how Collett and Trevarton started out. They nearly went smash the first year and made a small fortune in the second." He smiled at Jennifer and added, "Persistence pays off, eh?"

"If tomorrow's as warm as today, I'll come down for that swim," she promised. "If these Colston-Smarts will let me."

"Should have saved some film for *that,*" Douglas said, holding his hands up to mask the scene as George had done all day − the scene in this case being Jennifer herself. "The cinemas are full of bathing belles."

"No." George sucked a tooth judiciously. "Jenny is high-drama material, not glam."

"Really?" she was stung into saying, and she strutted a small circle, showing off her figure like a mannequin. The wide-eyed response of the two young men was most agreeable.

"I'll, er, take some stills," George promised.

The moment he had gone Mrs C-S appeared and carried Jennifer off to her 'boudoir,' as she called it, leaving Douglas to play croquet solo on the lawn. But after a while, when it became clear that she had no real purpose in taking her away, other than to separate them, Jennifer said, "If you don't give us *any* time together, he'll have every reason to suspect you of plotting something. He'll think you're trying to prevent me from accidentally spilling the beans − which you are, aren't you!"

Reluctantly, then, she let Jennifer go.

As soon as Douglas saw her, he dropped his mallet, saying, "Not tonight, Josephine! You can humiliate me tomorrow if you like. My mother's told me you're like Thor with his hammer. Has she taken you on a full tour of the gardens, I wonder?"

Without waiting for her answer he set off down a path that led along the hillside between banks of rhododendron and azalea and under arches of treelike bromeliads. He paused beneath one of the largest and, as he waited for her to catch up, said, "Did you ever read *The Lost World?* I always pictured it like this."

"Adam and Eve, eh." She had only the vaguest idea of the story.

"Oh no!" He laughed grimly. "Medrose is no Paradise — as I think you're about to learn, Miss Owen. In fact, that's what I wanted to discuss with you."

But she didn't wish to discuss anything of the kind, not even after so blunt a warning as that. She had enjoyed being the focus of attention all day, had enjoyed those kisses, even though they had been in the cause of art, and wouldn't have minded a few more. Not quite so near the house, though. So she accepted his conversational opening for the moment. "I never supposed it would be," she assured him. "Your mother has an amazing amount of energy."

"Quite!" He raised his eyebrows significantly. "That's the problem, of course. It is not always well directed. I trust that whatever I say will go no farther than you, me, and the gatepost?"

You know that already, Mister Colston-Smart."

"Do I?"

"Yes. Have I passed on any of the things she has said about *you?*"

He halted and grinned. "I say — has she? Do tell!"

"If you will release me and let me pass on to her whatever you're about to say?"

He pulled a face at that.

Jennifer went on: "You and she hardly communicate, you know. I could become very useful to you both. You might even end up actually talking directly to each other."

He made talons of his fingers and ran them through his hair. "How frustrating!" he exclaimed. "Can you tell me this much at least — d'you think she's right in whatever she said about me — as far as you can tell?"

"Absolutely not," she said. "Which is why I shall treat anything you say about *her* with a very large pinch of salt, too. How can two people living in the same house suffer from such misjudgment about each other?"

"You don't know what I'm going to say about her."

"I have a jolly good idea, though. Tell me, anyway — I can see you're dying to."

The path opened into a small, bosky grove with two possible exits.

"This was going to be so easy!" he complained, looking first at one path, then at the other, as if they were the source of his doubts.

All Jennifer knew was that the lower path led to a small pond, which supported hordes of biting midges at this time of year. "That one," she said, pointing to the other. "I've never explored along there."

Something about his smile told her she was due for a surprise.

"All right," he said as they set off between clumps of false nutmeg and hydrangea, the latter heavy with pompoms and lacecaps of intensely blue flowers. "Pass on as much of our conversation as you think fit — only tidy it up as tactfully as you can. Now, what did she tell you about me?"

She laughed at his lack of subtlety. "Oh no! You first. Your permission may turn out to be worth very little."

Again he paused and assessed her briefly. "I can see why she took to you so quickly. D'you think absolutely *everybody* has ulterior motives for everything they do or say?"

"Don't you?" she asked in return. "Tell me honestly — what were your first thoughts, out there at Wheal Dream last Sunday, when you realized who I was? Didn't you think it rather too much of a coincidence? Didn't you suspect I'd gone to elaborate lengths to contrive our meeting?"

He hung his head and nodded. "And you thought the same?" he asked. "You gave no sign of it."

"That's because it *didn't* occur to me, not until after. But it *would* occur to me as I am now. I'm no longer the naïve, trusting creature of a week ago. I'm learning."

"Yes." His gaze was solemn now. "And you learn rather fast, I think. I've been observing you all day — flitting between innocent novice and hardened vamp ..."

"But that was acting!"

"Ah," he replied in a tone laden with disbelief. "Good! I hope so, anyway — because I think it would be a shame if you *completely* lost what you call the naïve and trusting sides of your nature."

He resumed their stroll.

She pondered his warning awhile and then said, "D'you mean it would be a shame if *I* lost those qualities or if the people around me behaved so badly I was compelled to lose them?"

He chuckled. "Touché! And here we are at the end of the path." He wafted his hand like a showman unveiling something splendid.

"Oh!" she cried with delight. She had been studying him so intently, keen not to miss his smallest reaction, she had not noticed that the path had opened out into a glade. They were now at the farthest edge of the demesne. And there, right on the boundary fence, was a gazebo — a small, classical temple comprising a circular marble plinth, six pillars, and a dome. Between alternate pillars was a marble balustrade supported by four turned balusters, and at its centre was a circular stone bench, large enough for three at most — and even then they'd have to sit back-to-back, facing three ways outwards.

"It's where the wicked squire used to arrange his assignations with trusting village maidens," he told her. But when she rewarded him with a swift glance of shock, he laughed and added, "See! You haven't entirely lost it yet."

She dug him crossly with her elbow and set out across the glade, saying, "I'll bet the view was too good for such hanky-panky."

Perhaps it had been so at one time, but now, though Penzance itself was still visible, the trees in the neighbouring plantation had since grown to blot out the prospect of St Michael's Mount and most of the bay.

Not too disappointed, she sat on the bench and waited for him to catch up. In fifteen minutes, she realized, the sun would dip below the trees to the west and then the light northerly breeze might have some bite. Nothing too dreadful could happen inside fifteen minutes.

The moment he entered the little temple he fell to his knees and alarmed her into imagining he was about to engage in some absurdly romantic charade. A moment later, however, he had levered up a small stone in the floor and, from the cavity beneath it, he drew forth a bottle and two glasses. "Sherry," he said. "Not a word to mumsie, eh?"

"Is this how the wicked squire began his seductions?" she asked.

"If he had any sense, yes. Say when."

"When."

"I haven't even started pouring yet! You say 'when' when you think I've poured enough. Don't tell me you've never tasted sherry before?"

She shook her head, watching in fascination as the pale, silvery gold liquid swirled into the glass. "I had a glass of hock once. My father always told us that alcohol is a poison."

"When!" He said it for her. "That's quite enough for your first plunge into Demon Drink." He handed it to her and poured himself a slightly more generous measure. "Your health!"

"Toodle-pip!" She clinked glasses with him and took an experimental sip of the alleged demon.

It tasted of … what? Some kind of aromatic vinegar … a touch of honey … and something vaguely spicy. Not unpleasant, but she wasn't sure it would be worth crossing the road for a second helping. Then the afterburn of the alcohol warmed her throat and she began to realize that the beverage had its points, after all. She made an appreciative noise and took a second, larger sip.

"So, what did my mother say about me?" he asked as she savoured it. She just chuckled and shook her head.

"Oh yes!" he said, as if he'd forgotten the bargain. "Well, perhaps you're right to be cautious. I don't have much to say about my mother except to warn you that she is a lady who gets *consumed* by enthusiasms — some of them extremely worthy. The trouble is, they never last very long. She's all passion and no stamina."

"What sort of things?" Jennifer managed to sound surprised — hinting that the woman with whom she had spent the past week had shown no particular passion for anything.

He swallowed the hint and seemed relieved. "Things she can organize, mostly. Last year she tried to organize a gardening society for all those new houses down there ..."

"Where we now live."

"Just so. You've seen the gardens — the size of pocket handkerchiefs, most of them. One packet of mixed seeds and that's the whole summer taken care of! It was absurd. Then there was the Chyandour Art Appreciation Society. And the Nine Maidens Circle — devoted to researching prehistoric life on the Land's End Peninsula. The most successful was her knitting circle for soldiers' comforts last winter — she hasn't even mentioned that to you?"

"No," Jennifer answered truthfully.

"See — she's gone off *that*, already! And that was really quite a success — for a change."

"I see," she said hesitantly. "Or, rather, I don't see — I mean, why are you telling me this? What am I supposed to *do* about it?"

"Be on your guard, that's all. Don't let yourself get caught up in any of her crazes. We've all had our fingers burned — let ourselves be swept along, only to be left high and dry when the wind changes."

Jennifer recalled what the woman had told her of this young man's machiavellian cunning — how he'd never go at a thing straight if there was a roundabout way instead. She realized he must somehow have learned of his mother's convalescent-home project and now he was warning her against getting caught up in the scheme. It was plain to see. But he was managing to do so without letting on that he knew anything about it at all.

She pretended to think it over. Then she said, "Apart from the knitting circle, they were all very *worthy* activities without being terribly *useful*. Perhaps that was the missing element?"

He shrugged, as if to say that it hardly mattered. Then he added, "I think *you* are the missing element, Miss Owen. If she gets the usual bee in her bonnet and launches out on some grand project, she'll rely on you to keep her at it when her natural inclination is to let it go. I just wish there were a hundred *more* worthy activities as yet untried — and that none of them might be called 'useful' at all! Still, I've said my say and that's that. You have been warned."

He cut short her expressions of gratitude: "Now tell me, what did she say about me?"

"That you work too hard and play not at all. You won't join the tennis club nor go to dances nor cultivate young friends ..."

"Oh that!" He waved his hand dismissively. "That's all old hat." Then he remembered what else she had said — earlier, about disagreeing with his mother's opinion. "But you said she's quite wrong. I don't know what you base your opinion upon, considering that you and I only met for ten minutes — if that."

"I think she has no idea what you get up to all week in Saint Austell."

He laughed despairingly. "Oh yes! Saint Austell beats Paris into a cocked hat when it comes to night life and *joie-de-vivre!*" He sang a snatch of *You should see them dance the can-can.*

"At the very least," she pointed out, "your tone shows it's not congenial to you. She thinks it suits you to a tee. So I'm still right. She doesn't understand you at all."

He sidled around the circular bench until they were seated directly back-to-back. Then, leaning against her, he said, *"This* suits me to a tee, Miss Owen."

From where she sat the spiky tip of a conifer was just beginning to stab the flattened orange disc of the evening sun. The touch of him was very pleasant. She set down her glass and writhed gently, moving her spine over his, and leaned her head backward until it came to rest upon his shoulder. "I have no real objection to it, either, Mister Colston-Smart," she murmured and then blew softly in his ear.

He moved it out of her reach as she had hoped he might — not by turning his head away but by leaning toward her. Their eyes met — upside down to each other but that did nothing to hinder the message each held. A moment later their lips were touching, then caressing ... then pressing hard against each other's, urgently, hungrily.

A violent emotion took her unawares. There was a sweet, tingling sensation in her nipples and her innards felt suddenly hollow. She broke free of him and drew a deep breath, but the air was not cool enough to have any effect. He stood up, came round until he was facing her, and pulled her into a standing position, simultaneously turning her like the skilled dancer he was and pressing her back against one of the pillars. Then he crushed his lips to hers once more.

The pressure of his body, hard against her from head to toe, was electrifying. Her limbs trembled and weakened. If he had not been holding her and the pillar had not been there for support, she would have buckled and slipped to the ground. As it was, she abandoned herself to him, hanging around his neck and concentrating every fibre of her being on the magnificent softness of his lips.

"Oh … Douglas!" she murmured when they broke for breath.

"Still here," he replied.

She stiffened. "Is it just a game to you?"

"That's all it had better be for the moment, don't you think?" he asked. She struck him again, this time with her clenched fist.

"Such a she-cat!" he said tolerantly.

She pouted and shrugged herself out of his clasp. The passion died as swiftly as it had kindled. "I suppose I'm just one among dozens," she remarked bitterly.

He pretended to start counting, silently.

She hit him again and then burst into laughter. "You're a beast!"

"I lack my mother's capacity for *sudden* passions," he said, quite seriously now. "But — for that very reason, I suppose — my enthusiasms, though slow to kindle, tend to endure."

The last of the sun's disc vanished below the silhouetted treetops; the warmth it left behind was like the memory of their kiss to her. As they strolled back along the path by which they had come he said, "What's the most interesting thing that ever happened to you, Jenny? May I call you Jenny, or did that 'Douglas' just slip out?"

"I'm always Jennifer at home, but lots of friends call me Jenny. What d'you mean — interesting? In what way?"

"Any way you like."

"I found a baby once."

"Eh?"

"It's true. I often wonder about him. He was about a year old, or not quite. Very healthy. Bonny. Well dressed. And not in any distress. Just lying in a field outside Carleen."

"And no sign of the mother?"

"Not a whisper. I searched ..."

"When was this? How old were you?"

She told him the full story then — how she had searched all around and then taken Moses home ... and how, finally, Martha Walker, their maid at the time, had taken the boy into Helston, to swell the ranks in the union orphanage.

"Did you ever go and see him?" he asked.

She pulled a guilty face. "I've been too ashamed. I've always thought — somehow — that we shirked a responsibility that day. I know all the practical arguments ... and how it would have been socially impossible ... and thank heavens we don't have that extra mouth to feed now — Moses would be only six, poor little mite!"

She halted to fight off an attack of tears, not realizing how emotional she still was. "Poor little mite! Six years old and imprisoned in that gaunt stone building — it's horrible just to think about." Then, with a resigned sort of shrug, she went on, "But I *know* it was impossible, so that's an end to it." Then she managed a chuckle. "D'you know the most extraordinary thing of all, though — his nappy was done up with a brooch — a Victorian bun penny soldered onto a clasp — and d'you know who made that brooch?"

"A jeweller here in Penzance?"

"Jim Collett — the photographer!"

"How d'you know?"

She explained about that, too, and why it provided no clue to the baby's real identity. "Isn't it tantalizing, though!" she said. "Every now and then, just when he begins to slip from my memory, something like that happens and it all comes flooding back. It's hard not to believe that there's *something* out there which doesn't intend to let me forget him. I have this daydream where I become a famous film star with pots of money — and then I make it all up to him."

He remained silent.

"It's a joke," she said.

"I hope so," he replied.

"Why?"

"Because I think you're the sort of person who has to be very careful in her choice of daydreams, Jenny."

She laughed, thinking he was simply being perverse.

"It's true," he assured her. "You could make almost any of them come true. You have the right spirit for it — so you must be *very* careful."

25 IF MRS COLSTON-SMART lacked stamina, she did not once show
it during all that following week. She and Jennifer, who had now
moved into her own room in the house, worked from dawn to dusk each
day and with no sign of flagging on her part. It was an enriching and
fulfilling sort of work, and — thanks to all that careful preparation — it
ran almost too smoothly. They therefore slept soundly enough, untroubled
by thoughts of tasks left undone or milestones yet unreached. 'All in good
time,' they assured each other. Each morning they rose, refreshed, into
the dawn twilight at five, half an hour before the sun itself appeared.
They worked through the daylight hours with only the shortest break for
what Mrs C-S called 'a plebeian luncheon' of hot pasties and heavycake,
all eaten 'fitty-like' in the hand.

Jennifer took some ribbing from George Wallis's workmen at first,
who thought it unnatural for a lady to be wearing dungarees and to be
rolling up carpets and hammering nails into crates and carrying heavy
pictures out to the pantechnicon and other such goings-on. But when she
stopped rising to it, and they saw she did not wilt by early afternoon, they
eased off with the banter; and then they seemed as happy to take their
orders from her as they had taken them naturally from the lady of the
house herself.

George Herbert, who was to leave for London, and ultimately for
Flanders, on the Friday, came up to Medrose each evening after work to
help where he could until knocking-off time at seven. He returned at
eight, properly dressed for dinner — by which time the two ladies were
also bathed and transformed. For the first time in her life Jennifer had
the luxury of a maid to assist her. "We must keep up our standards, even
in wartime," Mrs C-S insisted.

Her invitation to George to join them for dinner, despite the huge
social gulf between them, was soon explained. In fact, she had not one
reason but two. In the first place, a meal without a man to flirt with was,
for her, almost uneatable. She teased him, flattered him, cosseted him,
and cold-shouldered him by turns from first to last. But her second
reason was far less trivial.

"Mister Herbert's a good man," she said apropos nothing on the eve of
his departure. "I know he has no background and his accent leaves a lot
to be desired, but he's bright, ambitious, resourceful — and he absolutely
adores you, my dear."

"Does he?" Jennifer replied casually. "Well, I'm not responsible for that." She didn't believe it, either. George Herbert was undoubtedly interested in her, but the precise nature of his interest was obscure. It was certainly not romantic.

"And what of you — if I may ask," Mrs Colston-Smart went on. "You have no … *inclination* for him at all?"

"I like him well enough as a friend. In fact, I think we could be the best of friends."

"Hmm!" She surveyed Jennifer coolly. "I suppose you know he's going off to the war tomorrow?"

Jennifer's eyes raked the ceiling; George had contrived to work that fact into the conversation several times each day.

"I think it would be a kindness to take him for a little stroll in the moonlight this evening — while there is still a little moon left. I was gazing at it last night. A waning moon in September is always so sad, don't you think? And those young men are so brave. We owe them something, we who stay here all safe and warm at home."

Jennifer decided she had had enough of this persiflage. "Are you trying to put me off Douglas?" she asked.

The woman laughed. "I hope your own good sense will do *that,*" she replied scornfully.

Jennifer wondered if this might be the time to confront her with her son's low opinion of her staying power, but she decided that, on the whole, it wasn't. "I'm not looking for any steady young man," she said. "I mean, any young man to 'go steady' with, as they say."

"Of course not! That's precisely why I suggest a romantic walk in the moonlight with young George Herbert. As he's leaving us tomorrow — possibly for ever — there can be no question of steadiness. Besides, you've enjoyed a similar stroll — though perhaps *enjoyed* is not quite the word to describe it — with my own dear son. And the best vaccination against the sickness of love for *one* man is the pleasurable company of *many*. Only make sure it *is* a vaccination and not an innoculation. You know what I mean?"

For a moment Jennifer was nonplussed. Then, as the penny dropped, Mrs C-S explained anyway: "A light, surface scratch does no harm, but don't let them stick anything into you."

"Mrs Colston-Smart!" she exclaimed, fanning her face as if she were hot with embarrassment.

"It's what your mother would tell you, I'm sure," she responded calmly. "Not so bluntly, perhaps. But, as this house will soon be filled with large numbers of increasingly fit and healthy young men, or so we hope, it's as well to be clear on such matters. May I be frank, my dear?"

"Please do."

"Your blushes become you, but I see they are clearing up quite swiftly. Well ... when I was a gel we were brought up in complete ignorance of ... ah ... a woman's tendency to become incandescent during certain moments of courtship. Nature didn't stop the incandescence but ignorance left one incapable of dealing with it. In theory — and surprisingly often in practice, too — one's gentlemen partner acted as sole guardian of one's honour. He spoke a stern no when we were incapable of saying it ourselves. Mind you, it was in his interests to show such gentlemanly restraint, because if he got the reputation of a cad, all access to the best class of young ladies would immediately be denied him. Where the system worked, it worked well. But where it failed, it exacted a monstrous price of any young girl who fell and 'broke her ankle,' as we used to say. There was a razor's edge between the state of gentility and that of the fallen woman, the one in heaven, the other in hell. I could name you two maiden ladies living not five miles from Penzance who broke their ankles at twenty and who have lived forty years in virtual retirement. In fact, they are only now beginning to be seen at respectable dinner tables. However, it's hard to deny an invitation to someone who's dangling a five-hundred-pound donation to the Red Cross before your eyes! You'll meet her here next week."

Her smile was cynical. "I don't know why," she went on, "but that old system seems to have broken down. Education? The independence you young ladies seem to demand nowadays? Distaste for the harsh old ways? It hardly matters."

She frowned a moment in thought and then changed tack. "Actually, I *do* know why. What happened under the old system was that young girls fell head-over-heels in love with the most unsuitable young men — and for the most trivial of causes. When I was seventeen a young man of no particular merit or charm picked up a glove I'd left in our pew in the cathedral. He came running after us and handed it back to me with such a sweet smile!" She smiled herself at the memory of it. "To him it was nothing more than a friendly smile, of course, but you can have no idea what *I* read into it. 'I've made a *conquest!*' I thought. Our whole existence was devoted to 'making conquests.' For an entire year I pined away for that young man. I wrote myself long, passionate letters in his name and concocted imaginary pages from his diary in which he waxed even more passionate. When he failed to look at me in church I knew just how disordered his heart must be. On those rare occasions when he granted me a faint — and faintly puzzled — smile, I knew how much it cost him. And when he vanished from Truro, never to return, I knew he had emigrated to the colonies in the vain hope of forgetting me and overcoming his ineffable sorrow!"

"And you never saw him again?" Jennifer asked, stirred by the tale even though she knew it was told in mockery. She wondered, too, if the woman had heard of her infatuation for Barry.

"I did, actually. And still do. He broke the ankle of the rural dean's daughter and had to marry her. The bishop got him a place in one of the shipping offices in Falmouth. He's now quite a bigwig in the City — something in insurance. He sails all around this coast in his yacht. Anyway, that proves my point: *All* gentlemen are cads — at least, it's wise nowadays to assume as much. They all want *le beauvoire de Vénus*, if you follow? And girls have to learn by experiment where their own limits lie. In short, a little practice at saying no can't come amiss to any young miss! You'll do young Herbert a kindness and yourself a favour. Let's hope there's a good moon after dinner tonight."

There was.

Mrs Colston-Smart's words had worked a subtle spell on Jennifer throughout that day. She had originally felt disinclined to take a romantic stroll and share a kiss or two with George. She knew he had no genuine interest in her. Or not a loving one, anyway. Not even vaguely romantic. He pretended, but she could feel there was no passion behind it. Now, however, the thought that his real interest might lie in 'the beauty-spot of Venus' intrigued her.

Well, two could play at that game! If he wanted to use her so cynically, it freed her conscience to do the same to him. And wouldn't it be less risky to discover her own limits by experimenting with someone for whom she felt nothing warmer than friendship?

So in that spirit, when dinner was over, the pair of them set out arm in arm across the croquet lawn. As they reached the edge of the bromeliad grove, a vixen yapped somewhere in the woodland below.

"She's at it again," George said. "Same as last night."

"She's looking for a mate," Jennifer said matter-of-factly.

She felt his arm stiffen. "Well!" he exclaimed.

"Well what?"

"You're pretty frank, I must say."

"I hope so," she replied. "Otherwise there's no point. I hope you'll be equally frank with me, George."

"What about?" he asked suspiciously. His arm, which had begun to relax, grew tense again.

"Well, inexperienced as I am, it's quite clear to me that you have no real romantic interest in me ..."

"Jeyses!" he whispered.

"You don't!" she insisted.

"So?"

"So why have you brought me out here?"

He laughed dryly. "I thought you brought me."

"Half-and-half," she conceded.

"So why did you half bring me?"

She chuckled. "I asked first."

He stopped and gave a heavy, theatrical sigh. "D'you think there's somewhere we could sit down?"

"The gazebo," she suggested. "Follow me." She led the way, walking too fast for easy conversation. She had no doubt but that he was doing a great deal of silent rearranging of his thoughts — wondering how much of the truth he dared tell her. Or perhaps *dared* was the wrong word. *Expedient* was more like it. With George, she felt, the expedient thing would always come before the daring one.

"Was it so obvious?" he asked as they crossed the grassy space around the gazebo. His tone was apologetic.

"I don't mind," she assured him. "At least, I don't think I will once you tell me what you're really after." She went up the steps and stood leaning against the balustrade, looking back at him.

He paused, one foot on the bottom step, and gazed up at the stars. "What I'm *really* after ..." he murmured. "If I could tell you that, I wouldn't be the dogsbody who cranks the camera handle. I'd be king of the castle." He stretched a hand toward her, wide open, palm up. "I'd hold you *there!*" he added fiercely.

An involuntary shiver ran up her spine. This was not at all what she had expected. "What d'you mean?" she asked, swallowing audibly.

"You, your leading man, the director, and the poor little devil who cranks the handle — I'd hold all of you *there!*" Again he thrust his open hand toward her.

She took it and pulled him up the steps. "Tell me," she said, her heart going suddenly pittapat. "It sounds exciting."

"It is exciting, Jenny." He came to her and took her face between his hands, turning her into the moonlight. "It's the most exciting thing in the world — power! Power and money."

He was panting with exhilaration now. His spirit fired hers. "Go on," she whispered. "Tell me. Tell me. I want to know it all."

He stared at her in what might so easily have passed for adoration — indeed, it was adoration, though of an entirely impersonal kind. "We're sleepwalkers, most of us," he said. "We're never more than half awake. We eat, sleep, knit, chat, chew, and snore. But when I was working up London, just before the bombs fell, I suddenly came wide awake. I saw how it all worked. You know when you look inside a watch and you think, *Jeyses, how did anyone ever work all that out?* Well, it was like looking at the insides of a watch and understanding, all in a flash, exactly what each little bit of it does. I suddenly got that all-in-a-flash understanding of the film business. I know how it works. I know how it *could* work. I know how I could *make* it work."

"Differently from now?" she asked.

"Yes!" He was ecstatic that she seemed to understand him so swiftly.

She hoped she'd say nothing to destroy that illusion. "With money?" she suggested.

"Not for its own sake. Give me a million and I'd live like a monk — honest. I'd spend it all on *movies* — on making movies my way."

"And how is that different from everyone else's way?" She was amazed at how excited she felt to be so close to the soul of another human being — one so gripped by his ambition that he was willing to bare all in order to convince her, to carry her along, too.

His hands fell from her face and splayed out upon the balustrade. He stared at the woodland and the twinkling lights of Penzance as if they were his audience. "Look at the way it's gone so far," he began, now quite calm again. "Fifteen, twenty years ago all you needed do was put a camera somewhere and crank the handle. People would pay good money to watch 'Passers-by at Hyde Park Corner' or 'A Train Pulls into a Station.' Then they wanted stories, too. So we got all the funny films and tricks and Sherlock Holmes and things like that. And now everyone's waiting for a new Charles Dickens to come along — the storyteller who'll bring the millions in." He laughed derisively. "But it ain't gonna be like that. Charles Dickens hisself could come back and do nothing but write stories for movies — but it wouldn't help. That wouldn't bring in the millions. It's not a new Charles Dickens we need, it's a new Henry Irving … a new Sarah Bernhardt."

He turned to her suddenly and, raising both hands again, sculpted the air around her face, making her blink. "We need what's *here.*" His voice was trembling again. "It's in these magical two inches all around you.

Don't ask me what it *is*, Jenny. All I know is it's *what I want*. You've got something that filters past the camera lens and tells the film you're a thousand times more real than anything else in view ..."

"How d'you know?" she asked scornfully, too embarrassed to let him go on.

"Because I developed the footage we shot — at least, I developed enough of it to know I'm right. And ..."

She interrupted him: "And the rest?"

"Ah! I'm going to leave it with a pal o' mine up Soho — Billy Scott. He's got a decent lab and all that. Also he's pal enough not to go and do the dirty on me."

"For instance?"

"For instance, he'd never show your tests to someone who'd steal you out from under my nose."

Jennifer thought this over and then, taking his arm and giving it a friendly squeeze, said, "Why didn't you just tell me all this, George? Did you think I wouldn't go along with it?"

"Will you? Eh? Will you, gel?" His eyes flooded with hope.

"I'm not saying I will. But if I did decide on it, I'd never go behind your back and ..."

"You'd never regret it."

"Not while this war's on. I must do something more worthwhile."

"Of course. Of course." He spoke soothingly. "It'll only be another year, anyway. And it'll look good in your publicity ..."

Her laughter stung him. He became morose once more. She realized that if Mr Herbert ever became the king of any castle, he could turn very moody and unpredictable. "Why didn't you just tell me?" she repeated.

He sighed. "I'm still not sure I've done the right thing. I'm taking one hell of a gamble — if you'll *pardonner* the French."

"That's not quite an answer."

"What I was going to do was try to make you my girlfriend — or make you think you were."

"Play fast and loose with my feelings!" she said in mock horror — even though she *was* slightly horrified at his frankness.

"Fast, anyway." He laughed pointedly. "I only had tonight to try and pull it off, didn't I!"

She punched him then, rather harder than she had intended. "You're a disgrace," she told him.

"I know." He grinned and winced at the same time, rubbing his arm where her blow had fallen. "At least you know it's the truth. I wanted to keep you thinking you were my girl until this war's over. Then I could come back and ride your coat-tails to the very top of the tree. It's what we're going to do, darlin' — you and me. It's where we're going. D'you think you can manage to get through this next year — till the war's won — without falling in love with anyone? With this Douglas geezer, fr'instance?"

"But suppose I'd really fallen in love with *you*. What about *my* feelings?"

"I think you'd have discovered that being turned into the next Sarah Bernhardt would be more than adequate compensation."

Once more his ruthlessness excited her, almost against her will. To be a kind of partner to someone who was not afraid to reach for the very top of his profession — who was, indeed, all on fire to get there — was a thrill of a kind she had not felt before. "Show me how you'd have gone about it," she said provocatively.

"Eh?"

"Show me how you'd have kissed and cuddled me … what sort of things would you have whispered into my adorable, shell-like ear … et cetera and so on."

He laughed with embarrassment. "I can't — not now."

"You'll just have to grit your teeth and do it, I'm afraid — if you want me to acquiesce in your dreams."

He wiped a stray lock of hair aside on her brow — a gesture so tender that she supposed he was giving in to her request. But he said, "I believe I have, after all, made the biggest mistake of my life in telling you."

"Why?" She was stung into asking it quite sharply.

"Because there's a ruthlessness in you, too, my darling. Billy Scott won't go singing to anyone. But you might. You could go and wheedle those tests out of him and show them to someone who'd see what you've got and pay you a fortune for it. Jeyses, why am I telling you this!"

Yes, she thought. *Why are you?*

"Kiss me, damn you!" she exclaimed.

"Why?" He backed a token inch or two away.

"Because I want you to. I want to know what it feels like."

"Haven't you kissed before?"

"Only boys I thought I loved. I want to see what it's like to kiss a man who's just a friend."

He grinned. "Suppose *I* was to fall in love with *you!* That would be an equal tragedy, you know. It clouds the judgement."

But his earlier reply to the identical question gave her an easy enough answer: "I think you'll find playing Svengali to my Trilby would be more than adequate compensation."

26 THE HUMAN EAR is an exquisitely sensitive organ. Blind people, who rely on it more than others, can often tell if the furniture in a room has been rearranged — just from the change in the acoustics. A ticking clock, for instance, may sound subtly different. All of which must explain how Douglas knew at once that the house had been turned upside down, even though his foot was barely over the threshold; the drastic transformation his mother and Jennifer had wrought had also changed the acoustics beyond recognition. Paradoxically, it had the effect of preparing him for what he was about to see. Even so, though it helped reduce his shock, it did nothing to alleviate his bewilderment. Nor his anger. In mounting fury he strode from room to room, trying to come to terms with what he saw, forcing himself to believe the unbelievable.

All but a handful of pictures had vanished from the walls, as had the halberds, pikes, shields, and blunderbusses. The suits of armour were gone; so was almost all the furniture — certainly all the finer pieces. There were bare light bulbs where electric chandeliers had once gleamed. The beautiful parquet floors and the more accessible wall panels were clad in plywood, and the superb plaster ceiling in the ballroom was now hidden behind a false ceiling of tautly stretched canvas.

Jennifer followed Douglas at a discreet distance as he moved from room to room. He ignored her. When he had seen enough to convince him that the ruination of the house was not confined to a few rooms only, he went to the foot of the main staircase and bawled, "Mother!"

His cry roused alien echoes and lingered in unfamiliar crannies.

"She has a slight headache," Jennifer told him.

Actually, she hadn't. They had simply decided he might be slightly less apoplectic — or control his apoplexy better — if Jennifer alone were to greet him. Now, however, she began to doubt it.

"Is it to be wondered at?" He waved a hand at the spartan desolation all around them.

"It'll look more cheerful when the beds are unpacked and the blankets are on them," she said. "We chose bright red. And the panels on the walls will be …"

"Beds?" He picked the word out of her hasty torrent. "What beds? Are you party to this … this … I suppose you must be." He turned to the stair again and yelled, "Mothaaah!" even louder than before.

"She won't come if you shout like that," Jennifer warned him.

He turned on her then. "How dare you?" he asked, sounding more amazed than affronted. "This must be your doing. She would never have done this off her own ..." His voice trailed off as his eye lit upon a scrap of paper left on a ledge by one of Wallis's men. He picked it up, perused it for a moment, and then gave a triumphant cry. "See — *your* writing, Miss Owen! You *are* behind all this."

"I'm sorry to disappoint you, Douglas ..." she began

He interrupted her. "You are not to call me that!"

"Dougie, then. I'm sorry to disappoint you" — she carried on through his exasperated protests — "but the day I called here for my interview she told me her entire plan to turn Medrose into a convalescent home. I'm just the dogsbody who writes lists for her. All I do is dot the eyes and cross the tees."

"I know whose eye *I'd* like to dot," he said grimly.

"In fact, as from this afternoon, we are now officially the Medrose Home for Semi-Ambulant Surgicals under the overall administration of the Cornwall Red Cross Society. In two weeks' time we shall have ..."

"You knew!" he said, no longer listening to her. "Last week, when we met — you already knew of all this!"

"Actually, Dougie, we met two weeks ago. It is not my habit to kiss young men at the very first ..."

"Stop that," he cried, angry again.

"And yes, I did know it then, too — even before we met."

"And you said nothing."

"I tried to warn you. I told you you hadn't the first idea what your mother's really like. If you credited me with any gumption at all, you'd have realized I wasn't talking idly. The trouble with you is — you think any female my age must be an empty-headed little butterfly."

He strode toward her with such determination that, for a moment, she thought he was going to strike her. But he brushed past and then, grabbing her by one arm, turned her to face the light. "You're right," he said grimly. "I have seriously underestimated you. But no longer, let me tell you. You may swear till you're blue in the face but I shall never believe that *this*" — he waved a hand vaguely about him — "is my mother's idea."

"Ask her."

"Ha! She's probably so much under your spell by now that she fully believes it *is* all her doing."

Jennifer folded her arms and stared at him coldly. She had expected anger, fury, yelling ... all leading up to a slow return of calm and reason.

Perhaps even acceptance. His stubbornness surprised her, as did her own lack of emotion — at least to the degree that she was neither flustered nor provoked. "What are you so afraid of?" she asked.

"You," he replied at once. "Your evil influence over ..."

"Don't be absurd! I meant why are you so worried at the possibility that your mother might have more than a spark of independence and will-power? Why d'you want to see her as a ..."

"Independence and will-power?" He threw up his hands in despair and turned a full circle on one heel.

"Careful with our lovely new floor!" she warned.

He looked down with dismay, thinking she was being serious. When he realized she was just trying to lighten the atmosphere he became angry once more. "Lovely new floor!" he exclaimed, stooping to grab one of its edges. "This'll have to come up again — all of it." He almost overbalanced backward as his fingertips slipped off the edge. "Oh damn!" he added, trying in vain to push a broken fingernail together again. He bit it off and then repeated his curse as a little bit of living flesh came away with it. There was blood on his fingertip.

"Now look what I've gone and done!" she said. "All my fault."

He could see the funny side of it, she could tell by his face, by his unwillingness to meet her eye. But he was a long way from laughter still. It struck her that she was actually beginning to enjoy their squabble; there was in it a kind of intimacy that even their kissing had not achieved. Perhaps he was feeling the same?

He challenged her: "If all this *is* my mother's idea, why isn't *she* down here explaining it to me?"

"Careful now, Dougie!" she scolded. "Are you actually asking for *reasons?* That's dangerous. Once you let reason come in, even by the back door, you open up the possibility of being persuaded by it. Are you quite sure you want that?"

Wrapping a handkerchief round his bleeding finger, he squared his shoulders and replied, "I'll tell you what I want, young madam — I want you packed and gone within the hour. You only live down the road, don't you? So in fact you may go now. This minute. We'll send your things on."

Because he was facing her, he failed to notice that his mother had come down as far as the half-way landing during this last speech. She nodded vigorously at Jennifer, waving her hand to signal that she should pretend to obey Douglas's ridiculous command.

"Very well," she said amiably — and greatly to his surprise. "I'll go out and wait." She blew him an ironic kiss as she strode past him.

"Wait for what?" he called after her.

"For your mother to summon me back — which she will. Aren't you afraid to face her alone?"

"I'd like to see that day!" he replied scornfully.

"I keep forgetting that you haven't the first idea what she's really like." At the door she paused and surveyed him speculatively. "Yes," she decided. "If I were as misguided about her as you are, I think I'd have no fear, either. Toodle-oo!" And she was gone.

She had no intention of going home, of course. But nor did she want to cool her heels, walking in aimless circles on the drive. Instead, she went down across the lawn and through the woods to the little marble gazebo, where she poured herself the second sherry of her life. She sat there, sipping it with slow relish, while she waited for 'Dougie' to appear.

Why she was so certain he *would* appear she could not have said. It was just an intuition that this was where he came when life threatened him with a crisis — not for its picturesque location but for that bottle of 'don't-tell-mumsie' sherry.

She stood where she and George had stood a mere eighteen hours earlier and recalled how she had goaded him into kissing her — which he had done reluctantly at first and then with surprising passion. She was sure it had surprised him, too. Nor had he been entirely pleased at the change. Kings of castles do not welcome chains around their own wrists and ankles.

And, in an odd sort of way, she had also become quite 'incandescent' — to borrow Mrs Colston-Smart's euphemism for it. But it was a sort of second-hand fire, kindled less by George himself than by the strength of his passion. And it was all mixed up with the excitement of being able to stir a man like that. Especially to stir him against his will.

At least, that was how it had seemed here in the dark last night. Now, in the full flood of the afternoon sun, she was less sure of it. George was such a deep and devious man. He might have let the entire thing happen deliberately. He might even have planned it, down to the last sigh and shiver. No, that would lie beyond any human power. And in any case, why bother? All he'd need would be for that little foxy bit of his brain to stay in control — the bit that never slept, never got involved in any of his feelings, and never stopped probing the world for the smallest scraps of advantage. Then he could easily let himself impersonate a man on the edge of losing control.

Wouldn't it be nice, she mused, to live in a world where everyone was open and honest!

But no sooner had the thought struck her than she was moved to say aloud, "It would be the dullest thing ever, you goose!" The fun of life was that nobody ever spoke the whole truth about anything, nor said what was truly on their minds.

Suddenly, the real significance of what had happened last night hit her with such force that she had to lean hard against the balustrade for support. Then, ebullient again, she swung her legs over it and sat on its broad, warm expanse.

All her life — or certainly since she was about twelve — her existence had centred on finding and marrying the right man. It hadn't been drilled into her. No one had made it a daily litany. No one had particularly set out to indoctrinate her with the notion. Instead it had seeped into her soul through a thousand little commonplaces:

"When you grow up and marry someone nice and have a home and children of your own, dear ..."

"These will do for your bottom drawer ..."

"Protect your skin or no man will look at you!"

"A girl with a forward spirit may be popular but it's the modest, quiet ones men marry."

Marry ... men ... home ... children ... modesty ... good looks ... who needed outright indoctrination when life and language bathed a girl in such thoughts from the moment she could speak!

But George Herbert's despair at the thought that she might simply drift down that broad stream — fall in love, marry, have babies, and blah-blah-blah — had changed everything. The alternative he had set before her showed her that there were other ways through life. And even if his particular ambition for her proved nothing but a pipe-dream ... well, it was only one among many.

And *that* was the real significance of what had happened here last night: She could take off those old blinkers that kept her to the path of love, marriage, and domesticity; she could look at *all* the possibilities. The sense of liberation almost overwhelmed her.

"I can do *anything* I want," she said aloud, just as Douglas emerged from the woodland

When he saw her there, sitting on the balustrade, swinging her legs and sipping sherry, he halted. After a moment's indecision he half turned away from her, though he was clearly reluctant to retreat.

"I poured a glass for you, Dougie," she called out.

He strode toward her and again she had the feeling that he'd dearly like to hit her. What a bundle of contradictions he was, too! Perhaps all men were, once you got to know them? Douglas was normally so fastidious, a man turned in upon himself, he did not easily show his emotions. But anger seemed to loosen something within him and turn him into his opposite — a man who'd strike out before he'd say a word.

She found it rather thrilling. Not that she wanted to be hit, but, she realized, she wanted him to get within an ace of it, so that she, by giving the merest tug at the reins of civilization, could bring him back under control. It was the same thrill as that of controlling her own wilder impulses. She remembered a time when her father had shown her pictures of Blondin walking the high wire over Niagara; they had exerted the strangest fascination upon her and filled her thoughts for days. Now she began to understand why.

As Douglas accepted the glass he said, "I shall never, never forgive you for this, Miss Owen. And just you wait till my father hears of it!"

"Oh God!" she sneered.

"What?" he was surprised into asking.

She adopted a childish lilt. "I'll tell my daddy on you — yah-boo! Can't you do better than that?"

"Lord, but you're like a wildcat in a sack!" he exclaimed, still angry but also becoming a little cautious, too.

"Why did you hesitate just now when you saw me sitting here? I'll tell you …"

"You can hardly imagine that I find your company congenial!"

"You wouldn't even have broken stride if I'd been a man — one of your rivals in business, for instance."

"You — a rival!" He laughed. "Don't give yourself airs."

"And don't you delude yourself — you see me as a rival, all right. It's suited you very well to come home to a mother who had nothing better to do with her life than swan around Penzance in her motor and potter along with those pointless little projects you so kindly warned me about. But now she has a *real* purpose before her — in fact, she's *alive* for the first time in years, maybe for the first time *ever!* And you're furious, of course. Ickle Dougie's lost his nice ickle mumsie — and all because of howwid Jenny!"

It was the wrong note. She wanted to see him angry again, to see his fist trembling over her while chevalier and savage fought to control it. Instead, he slumped beside her, facing into the gazebo with his elbows on the balustrade, and said, "You make me feel so old with your enthusiasm. You actually *believe* she's going to persist in this convalescent-home nonsense!" He shook his head as old men do at the follies of youth.

Disgusted, Jennifer said, "I'm surprised you don't insist she should be breast-feeding you still."

That did the trick! His empty sherry glass went spinning out into the sward, and there was his fist, quivering in the air before her. His face was twisted in torment.

Her heartbeat leaped to a sudden sprint. She had never felt so excited in her life. She slipped down and stood before him; what happened to her glass she neither knew nor cared. She was breathing fast, as if she had just been sprinting, and yet she still seemed short of wind. She squared her shoulders and lifted her chin. "Go on!" she dared him. "It's what any other six-foot baby would do!"

His gaze fell briefly to her breasts, which her pugnacious gesture had thrown into prominence. Hastily he raised his eyes once more to her face but now his fury had been replaced by a hunger that was unambiguous — a hunger so naked, so powerful, she could not mistake it. Now he, too, was breathing fast. Then, mirrored in his dark, ravenous eyes, she recognized her own excitement for what it truly was. She knew that the same light shone out of her and that he could see it, too.

Before words could intervene — those weasel usherettes of reason and denial — she put her arms around his neck and kissed him with a passion she would not have believed it possible for her to contain. Until now even her grandest, wildest emotions had always left one small, calm corner where caution might sit; but on that evening every part of her, every fibre of her being, was caught up in one great surge of desire that left no room for caution. She clung to him, ready to yield body and soul.

For what seemed an eternity he resisted that same impulse, though it must have been raging within him just as it raged in her. He stood there, rigid and trembling, with both hands poised — torn between thrusting her from him and gathering her into the sweetest embrace of all.

Indecision forced from him a strangled whimper. She answered it with whimpers of her own, though hardly of indecision. A fire seemed to burn in her breasts and belly and she wriggled her body hard against his, seeking a cure for the exquisite tenderness that suddenly infected every inch of her. She slipped her arms inside his jacket and hugged him till her muscles ached.

He yielded then — the male in him defeating the man. As he folded her in his arms he broke for air, breathing in huge, shivering gulps. But she would give him no respite. She darted her lips over his face, pressing kiss after kiss on his cheeks, his brow, his nose, his chin. And all the while she gasped, "Yes ... yes ... yes ..." in between each loving kiss.

Her hand grasped his and placed it on her breast. She did not do it — not Jennifer. Indeed, there was hardly a Jennifer left to observe such things at all, much less to decide upon them. The female had vanquished the woman, too, so that she was now a blind, sensate bundle of wanting, of provocation, of response ...

His fingers were fiddling with the buttons of her blouse.

It was not fair, the female seethed — men's waistcoats should also unbutton down the back. She fiddled with the lower two and then, overcome by impatience and curiosity, plunged her hand downward, past his waistband, knowing what to expect and yet uncertain of what she might find.

"No!" he cried with a strange urgency, trying to pull away from her.

The thrilling novelty of the situation reawakened her smouldering consciousness, making it possible for her to observe once more, as well as blindly act. She had never felt anything quite like it — such a strange blend of hard and soft — a live bone sheathed in flesh so soft and pliable. And hot! Even as she explored, it began leaping and twitching in her grasp ... and he gave out whimpers as if he had passed beyond torture ... and wet stabs of heat spread over the underside of her forearm ...

In a half-comprehending daze she let him pull away, and draw out his handkerchief, and start wiping and dabbing her arm and hand. "Lord!" he kept mumbling. "I'm sorry ... I'm so desperately sorry!" His face was bright as beetroot.

She raised her other hand to his cheek and touched his lips tenderly. "Don't," she said, just above a whisper.

"Well, it's awful," he said.

"It isn't." She withdrew her moist arm and hugged it to her. She still longed for him but the rawness of her passion had gone, leaving behind something big and warm — and patient.

"Well, I think it is," he said. "Juices and smells and sweat and ... everything out of control."

"We couldn't have lived much longer under the same roof, Douglas."

"All this week I've been making myself promise *never* to ... to inflict *that* upon you."

"There you are, then. We can't go back now."

He closed his eyes as if in pain. "We must never take that risk again."

She ran her fingers back and forth over his lips, light as down. "Do we really need to talk about it?"

He stared at her breasts; she thought, *I don't mind.* Then she threw back her head and laughed.

It shocked him into saying he saw nothing to laugh at.

"Don't you understand?" she asked.

"All I understand is that the world's turning topsy-turvy. I've had enough shocks for one day."

"But it's the *same* shock — that's what I'm laughing at."

He frowned in bewilderment.

"Think about it! The two women in your life — or in your house, anyway — both prove to be as single-minded, as strong of purpose, and quite as ruthless as any man."

It shocked him yet again. "Purpose? D'you mean you *intended* ... that ... what we just did?"

She repeated herself: "Do we have to talk about it?"

He walked a few paces from her and retrieved his glass. "Where's yours?" he asked.

She hunted for it and found that — incredibly — it had fallen on its foot and still held most of its contents. She raised it and toasted him, tossing it back in one fiery gulp.

"How many was that?" he asked. At last he dared to reach out and button up her blouse.

She laughed again. "I'm not giving you *that* excuse, my lad! It was my first. First glass of sherry, I mean." She took his arm and turned him toward the house. "And the other thing, too, actually — just in case you were wondering."

"It was for me, too," he replied. "Just in case *you* were wondering." He halted in indecision. "I say — what about these sherry glasses?"

"What about them? Time your mother knew of your secret vice — that one, anyway. Are you *really* so angry at what we've done to Medrose this past week, Douglas?"

"I'll forgive you anything if you never call me Dougie again. I suppose I'm most angry at the fact that I wasn't consulted."

"And if you had been?"

He nodded, conceding the point without another word. "Funny," he said as they reached the croquet lawn. "I had prepared such a different homecoming this weekend. A little surprise for you, in fact."

"For me? How exciting!"

"I hope you'll still think so. D'you know what I discovered on Thursday?"

Discovered? Thursday? George's last night. Her heart skipped a beat.

"I was in Helston on business," he went on. "So I dropped in at the workhouse and looked through the orphanage records. My father was an inspector for the Board of Guardians before the war so I have a certain 'in' there. I wanted to bring you news of your foundling, Moses. And you'll never guess what *I* found."

"What?" She took a new grip on his arm, surprised at how badly she wanted to hear his reply.

"You say it happened about five years ago?" he asked. "You're quite sure of that?"

"The fifteenth of June, nineteen-ten," she told him. "A Wednesday, it was. Why?"

"That's what I thought — mid-nineteen-ten, anyway. But just to be sure we went through the records of foundlings for nineteen-oh-nine *and* nineteen-eleven as well. Three whole years. It made no difference. As far as they're concerned, your infant Moses simply doesn't exist."

She stopped and stared at him, quite sure he was pulling her leg.

"True," he assured her. "The entries are pretty detailed, you know. Where found, by whom, dates, times, circumstances, distinguishing features of the child, clothing ... and so on. Not a single foundling from Godolphin or Carleen during those three years. And did you say it was a maid called Walker who carried him in there?"

"Yes — Martha Walker — *and* she came back and told us it had all gone smoothly. The records *must* be wrong."

"Well, I can assure you that no one by the name of Walker has *ever* handed in a child to the Helston Union. Nor was the name Owen there, either. So she didn't hand it in under your name instead. Isn't it intriguing! Where is this Martha Walker now?"

"She got married. In fact, she left us that same week, I think. She married a Billy Tre ... Tregorran? Tre-something. Over to Falmouth." Understanding dawned on her. "I'll bet she took the baby as an excuse to pop over to Falmouth and see her beau. She could have handed the baby in at Falmouth workhouse instead."

He shook his head. "Wrong union. They'd never accept the charge."

"Well, I don't know, then. Perhaps she lied. She could say he was found in Penryn or somewhere inside their union."

He conceded the possibility. "I'll be over that way on Tuesday," he said. "I'll look into it — see if any male baby was handed in on ... the fifteenth of June?"

"Sometime that week, anyway. She could have left him with her mother. But I'll bet that's what happened."

She wished she felt as confident as she made herself sound. She also wondered why it mattered so much to her after all these years.

But it did.

27 AT DINNER that night Douglas repeated his tale of the Moses mystery for his mother's benefit. Jennifer saw how it intrigued the woman and she had the first glimpse of that mercurial nature of which he had warned.

"How exciting, Jennifer!" she kept saying. "What can it all mean?"

The more bubbly she became, the more dismissive Jennifer found it necessary to be. "It means the maid used the child as an excuse to go over to Falmouth and visit her mother," she said. "And she spun the local union some tale and they took it in there. That's all."

"It doesn't sound like any union *I* know," Mrs C-S replied. "For foundlings they want chapter and verse on anything and everything."

"I'm surprised that no one checked back with your father," Douglas added. "Especially as he was the local doctor. He'd be expected to know a thing or two — which females in the district were in an interesting condition and so on."

Jennifer shrugged. "Perhaps they did." She suspected that Douglas, having originally prepared this news as a surprise for her, was now using it to distract his mother from the convalescent-home project.

"But they couldn't have," he pointed out. "As far as the Helston Union was concerned, no such child existed."

"I mean the Falmouth Union. They might have inquired of Daddy but *I* wouldn't have been told. They kept everything from me. I was so miserable at losing him, anyway. He was *my* find."

"And you're still miserable, aren't you, dear," Mrs C-S stated firmly.

"No!" Jennifer laughed to cajole her out of this absurd notion. Once she got an idea fixed in her mind …

"You are. I can tell. Never mind — we shall do something about it to set your mind at rest."

"My mind *is* at rest — at least on that particular matter. If it's disturbed at anything it's at the knowledge that our first casualties will be arriving in ten days' time. But if I never hear the name of Moses again, I shan't lose a wink of sleep."

"You're only saying that to be brave," the woman insisted. "But Douglas will make inquiries in Falmouth next week, won't you, dear? You'd do that for Miss Owen's sake?"

He smiled knowingly at Jennifer. "For Miss Owen's sake? Of course I will, Mother dear."

Later that night, when all the house was quiet with that creaky silence which goes with emptiness, she put on her dressing gown and tiptoed along the carpetless corridor to his room. But when she tapped on his door she heard him spring out of bed and race across the floor. A moment later she heard the key turn in the lock. She smiled, thinking he was *un*locking it to let her in. In fact, she was wondering what sort of man locked his own bedroom door in his own house, when the question was answered for her: a man who did not wish to be visited by an inquisitively ardent young lady at dead of night.

Angrily she returned to her own room, where she considered making her way along a broad granite ledge, aided by large stems of well-rooted creeper, all the way to his window. But the picture it conjured in her mind made her laugh at last. "It's not the world my grandmother knew," she said as she climbed back into bed.

But, as she lay there, alone and waiting for sleep, she began to wonder about that. Her grandmother may have known just such a world, too — but simply never have talked about it.

The frustration of that locked door left her filled with a desire whose nature and object she could not doubt. She only had to think of slipping into bed and cuddling herself up against Douglas to know what this was all about. She shivered just to think of it, and her breathing was flustered, and strange ripples of warm and cold ran all through her. But why? She had never slipped into any man's bed in her life; she had only the vaguest notion of what they might do together; and yet every particle of her was filled with longing for it.

What unknown force inside her could be driving her like that? A kind of madness? Or something that everyone felt — or everyone except Douglas, damn him!

She recalled jokes that girls had sniggered about in school — about the mad women in the asylum who'd tear the clothes off any man rash enough to go among them. Was this the first step into that dread state? Was that why Douglas was so terrified? Did he know all about it? Perhaps the Colston-Smarts had one such unfortunate kinswoman already tucked away in an institution.

She didn't *feel* any degree of insanity within her, incipient or otherwise — but then, mad people never did. They always knew they were the only perfectly sane person in the world. To prove she still had all her brain cogs working, she began reciting the seven-times table, which she had always found the most difficult one. When she couldn't remember what seven nines make, she gave up. It didn't prove anything, anyway.

Finally her thoughts turned to the conundrum Douglas had presented her with earlier that day — the disappearance of little Moses, from the official record if not from the world. She had made light of it then, for reasons of her own — because she resented the way he had delved into her life like that ... because too many new, exciting things were happening and she didn't want stuff out of the past getting in the way ... but mainly because she knew jolly well that he was using the mystery to distract his mother and take her mind off the convalescent home. Now, however, alone in the dark with nothing but her thoughts for company, she began to worry that something dreadful might have happened to the little boy.

If, as seemed likely, Martha Walker — or Martha Tregear as she became only weeks after the finding of Moses — hadn't taken him to the Helston Union, then there were only two possibilities: Either she and her husband adopted him themselves or she had, indeed, handed him in at some other orphanage, not necessarily Falmouth.

A moment later a third, chilling possibility occurred to her: Martha might simply have abandoned Moses once again, just as his real mother had done.

She tried telling herself it hardly mattered, anyway. There was nothing she could do about it now. The child was either alive or dead. If alive, he might not be living in the lap of luxury but at least he'd be under a good roof and clothed, shod, and fed after a fashion. He'd survive to make whatever he could of his life. If he were dead ... well, he'd be dead and that was that.

Again she tried to put the whole business from her mind, but it would not give her peace. The uncertainty plagued her. If only she knew for certain what had happened ...

But, of course, that was the very notion Douglas had implanted in his mother's mind. It was what he wanted them both to start thinking about, worrying about, become obsessed about — to the detriment of the convalescent home.

Her gloom deepened when she realized that, even if she managed to steer Mrs C-S's mind away from the Moses mystery, Douglas would only find something else to divert her. He wasn't the sort to give up at the first fence — nor at the hundred-and-first fence, either.

Her concern at this possibility surprised her. Why should she care whether the convalescent home thrived or failed? She was Mrs Colston-Smart's companion — and on a jolly good wage, at that. If the woman waxed hot and cold on a *hundred* projects, it was no business of a mere companion to bother her head about it, one way or another. She should just get on and … be companionable. The convalescent home wasn't *her* idea. Two weeks ago she hadn't even heard of it. And yet the mere thought that Mrs C-S might now get cold feet and start chasing some other chimæra filled her with anxiety.

Perhaps the thing to do would be to *encourage* her employer to take an interest in the Moses story, but on the sidelines, as it were — as a sort of diversion when the business of the convalescent home allowed. Saying no and mind your own business, however tactfully one might dress it up, would only encourage a woman like that to interfere more and more.

And so, at breakfast the following morning, when Mrs C-S returned from Communion, Jennifer said that yesterday's mention of Truro Cathedral had reminded her how long it was since she last saw the place, and so, with Mrs Colston-Smart's leave, she would worship there today.

She was barely out of the room when she heard Douglas say to his mother: "She's going to try to discover what really happened to the baby she calls Moses." And Mrs C-S laughed and said, "Dear boy! D'you think I didn't realize that the moment she spoke!"

28 As IT happened, Jennifer did attend morning worship in the cathedral, partly because her conscience said that the fewer lies she told the better, but mainly because it suited her with the train times. She saw Hector among the dragooned squads of boys from his school. She even managed to catch his eye once but he seemed more embarrassed than pleased to see her, so she left it at that. When she hastened back up the hill to the station, who should she see waiting on the branch line platform for Falmouth but Mrs Collett.

"Hello, dear," she said brightly. "Heard the news?"

Jennifer stared at her blankly. "What news?" The woman was so pleased that, for an absurd moment, she thought an armistice might have been declared while she was in the cathedral.

"Why, a whole shipload of our boys is coming into Falmouth sometime this afternoon or evening. No one will tell you a thing, of course."

"Not … wounded?" Jennifer asked — though Mrs Collett would hardly be so delighted if that were the case. Except that the slaughter was so great, you heard women praying for their men to come back armless, legless, blind … anything but dead.

"No! On leave. They're shipping all the Cornish boys from Cherbourg to Falmouth." Her face became solemn for a moment as she added, "I rather think the straits of Dover are busy with hospital ships at the moment. They try not to bring the wounded back through the same ports and stations as the fresh lads going out — at least not at the same times. I think Mrs Colston-Smart is starting her convalescent home just in time." She gave a little smile of friendly provocation. "But isn't that what brings *you* here?"

"What?"

"Well, *who* d'you think I've come all this way to meet?"

Jennifer blushed, though thoughts of Barry Moore were the last thing on her mind that day.

"There!" Mrs Collett patted her arm. "I'm only teasing. I know that never amounted to anything more than a schoolgirl infatuation. I wonder if you'll even like him, in fact. Still …" She waved all such thoughts and words away. "Here's our train. I adore this little branch line to Falmouth. It was the first I ever rode on — when I was seventeen, can you imagine! An engineer told me the wooden bridges were due to collapse at any moment, but they're still there a quarter of a century later!"

They climbed aboard the Ladies Only and, while they waited for the engine to shunt out onto the main line, pass them, and shunt back onto the branch line to be coupled at the other end, Jennifer explained why she was going to Falmouth that afternoon.

Mrs Collett was suddenly interested. "If this Martha Tregear can shed any light as to how *my* bun-penny brooch came to be pinning that baby's nappy …" she began.

"But only the true mother would know that," Jennifer pointed out. "Martha's even farther down in the chain than me."

"Of course! Stupid of me. Still, you never know. She might have discovered something meanwhile. Someone may have seen it and told her something about it — you know what Cornwall's like. We all live in each other's pockets."

The train pulled out on its half-hour journey to Falmouth; no one else had joined their compartment.

Mrs Collett eyed Jennifer speculatively. "What are you hoping to learn in Falmouth today, if I may ask?"

"Oh, that Moses is alive and well and we can all forget about him!"

"We?"

So then Jennifer had to explain how the story of Moses had become entangled in the domestic power games at Meldrum. "I shouldn't be saying all this," she concluded guiltily. "Mrs Colston-Smart is my employer, after all, and I hate servants who tittle-tattle."

"Don't we all — unless they tittle-tattle to *us,* of course! Actually, you've told me nothing I hadn't already heard from young Mister Herbert. How we miss him!" She stared quizzically at Jennifer. "Or don't we?"

The girl sighed. "Can I talk to you about him, Mrs Collett?"

"By all means, my dear — and d'you think you could find it in you to call me Crissy?"

"Aunty Crissy?" Jennifer offered.

The other shook her head. "Anything but that!"

"Very well — if you insist. It'll feel very strange, though."

"That's the way with anything new, Jenny — or d'you prefer Jennifer?"

"Jennifer usually, but Jenny with you. Jenny and Crissy — they go pretty well together."

"I hope so. What perplexes you about George Herbert, then?"

Jennifer screwed up her features in frustration. "Nothing — in one way. I mean, he has this one absolutely over-riding ambition — which, at the moment, he has fixed on me, though I have no illusions about it. I know he'd drop me the moment it looked like not working or if he found someone better ..."

"He's not going to do that in a hurry — find someone better, I mean."

"Really?" Jennifer looked at her hopefully. "You're not just saying it?"

"No, dear. I've seen your tests — or the footage he developed in our lab before he sent the rest to ... well, to London."

"To Billy Scott, I know."

"Oh! He told you that? I am surprised."

"He told me. But he said it was a mistake because I could wheedle the film out of Billy Scott and go on to fame and fortune without him."

"And wouldn't you?"

Jennifer shook her head. "I don't have his burning ambition, you see. He really is consumed by it."

"I know. Don't you find it exciting? Especially as it's all to do with you."

"But it isn't to do with me! If he was a different kind of enthusiast — suppose he'd invented ... I don't know — a new kind of aeroplane or something — he'd be just as enthusiastic about that machine as he is about me. D'you see what I mean? I'm just the *thing* that will help him achieve his ambition."

Crissy stared out of the window awhile. "Of course," she mused aloud, "if you *know* that's the case ..." She left the rest of her thoughts hanging.

"I can plan around it — is that what you mean? If he treats me as a *thing,* no matter how precious a thing, I'm free of any moral obligation to him, eh?"

"I can see the thought has already crossed your mind, dear. Did you reject it out of hand?"

Jennifer shook her head.

"Good," Crissy went on. "I think you'd be quite right to give as good as you get — no better and no worse. As long as you don't start using *everybody* for your own purposes, which is what George will do, of course. He can't help it."

Jennifer gave a brief, embarrassed laugh. "His plan was to make me fall in love with him — can you believe it?"

"Very easily. 'Monomaniacs' they call them — men like that. Obsessed by a single ambition. I've met a few down the years — in fact, I married one once, though he's mellowed down a bit since. Once he achieved his ambitions. No, actually, it's not fair to compare my Jim with a towering monomaniac like George Herbert. No achievement is *ever* going to satisfy that young man. He may think so now. 'All I want is my own film company, Mrs Collett,' he told me. But the moment he gets it he'll want to double its size. Then he'll want to buy up other companies and swallow them up ... and on and on until he *is* the British film industry."

"And after that, the world!" Jennifer concluded.

"Just so. You agree? Well, the thing I was going to say — about all such monomaniacs — is that they don't regard themselves in the way *you* regard *your* self or I, me. We've got little critics who sit up here" — she tapped her brow — "hauling on the reins most of the time, telling us we're going too far, making us blush. Young Herbert cannot blush."

Jennifer chuckled. Crissy Collett had put her finger on almost everything that had puzzled her about George. "I think *his* critic sits up there, doing the opposite — pushing him over the edge all the time, telling him to risk more. So when he says something ridiculous, like 'I'm going to be Mister British-Film-Industry before I'm through,' we laugh, but at the back of our minds we can't help thinking there may be some truth in it after all. He *could* be."

"Indeed he could."

"What's to stop him — if he goes at it hard enough? And you can't deny he's pushing for all he's worth."

Crissy eyed her companion speculatively for a moment. "I'd love to know what he did — or said — to put such thoughts into your mind, dear." She smiled her most disarming smile. "Of course, that doesn't mean you're obliged to tell me!"

"Oh, I don't mind — in fact, I'd love to hear your opinion, too. I think the moment when it all fell into place was when he said it would do my career as a film star — ha ha! — no harm to spend the next year or so nursing wounded soldiers."

"Did you laugh?"

"No, that's my point. I was completely swept up in his ideas by then. I thought, *Yes, he's right, and how lucky I am to have someone as far-sighted as him to ... you know — guide me!* Later, of course, I came back to earth. To me, it's still castles in Spain. To him, it's the place he's already living in, here and now."

Crissy stared out of the window while she absorbed these thoughts. The broad mudflats of the Devoran valley, wrecked by centuries of tin vanning, trundled by. Downstream a low-flying swan played pattacake-pattacake with its own reflection on the shimmering tidal mud.

"It doesn't always work for him, though," she said at last. "He'll tell the world he's going to rise to the top — and we laugh and say he probably will. He'll tell you he's going to make your name, or whatever stage name he chooses for you, a household word — and you laugh though you know he very well might. But when he tells *himself* he's going to make you love him — so that you don't do anything foolish until the war's over and he can get on with his ambitions — it doesn't work at all. *You* see through it at once. Was he really so bad an actor?"

Jennifer made a hopeless gesture. "No! Once I'd challenged him with it ..."

"You *challenged* him?"

"Of course."

Crissy looked at her with new admiration. "Good for you! Sorry, I didn't mean to interrupt."

"Once he'd agreed it was a stupid idea from the start, I ... well, I behaved a little childishly, I'm afraid." She smiled self-accusingly. "I thought to myself, 'Why is it such a stupid idea? Why couldn't he genuinely fall in love with me? Have I got two heads or something?' So I challenged him to actually show me how he'd have gone about 'winning my heart'! It was all rather childish."

Crissy let out a peal of laughter and clapped her hands in delight. "Poor fellow! He has no idea what deep waters he's trying to paddle in, has he — trying to take over your life while you're still living it! What did he do?"

"Wriggled and squirmed and tried to get out of it, of course."

"But you persisted?"

Jennifer nodded. "And then he said, 'Oh, very well ... since you force me to it ...' and so on. A big show of reluctance. And then he started to kiss me et cetera — very badly. All very wooden. But then" — a faraway look stole into her eyes — "something happened."

"To you or to him?"

"To him. It was as if ... well, as if it suddenly became the real thing."

"Passionate!" Crissy's eyes gleamed as she leaned forward eagerly to hear more.

"No. Shocked! He pulled away. And he could hardly breathe. And he wiped his lips like this, as if I'd poisoned him with something. And he looked at me — it was bright moonlight, so I could see his expression quite well — he looked at me as if I had suddenly turned into some old witch or wild animal or something."

"Oh, Jenny! How did *you* feel?"

"Suspicious."

No word could have surprised Crissy more.

Jennifer went on: "I just looked up into his eyes, thinking, You're still doing it, Mister Herbert! You've planned even this bit. You knew you couldn't carry off the pretence, so you're doing it this way, instead — pretending to be all shocked and horrified to discover you really are falling in love with me! But then, the very next moment, I was thinking, No, no man could be *that* devious. So then I didn't know what to think." She laughed. "So I stopped thinking altogether!"

"And?" Crissy insisted. "Or would that be too indiscreet?"

"We ... couranted awhile, as the saying is."

"But there was no corresponding passion on your part?"

Jennifer held her gaze steady and said, "No *romantic* passion, anyway. I'm sure of that."

"Ah!" The smile was all-understanding, all-condoning. It said, *Welcome, Jenny dear — we have all been there.*

Jennifer plunged in at the deep end. "Is it so wrong?" she asked. "I mean, a conventional bit of me says it is, but as for the rest ..."

"Yes? As for the rest ...?"

"Well, it's just sort of neutral. You remember on our way back from the claypits, when we were talking about the difference between painting and photography? About how a painter can say a tree is 'wrong,' and a photographer can say it's 'wrong,' and a forester can say it's 'wrong' — but they'll all mean different things by *wrong?*"

"Yes?"

"Well, none of us asked what nature herself would say, did we! I don't think nature would say a tree could be either right or wrong. She'd just say it's a tree, take it or leave it."

"And what about *human* nature?" Crissy asked. "Don't you think human nature would say *think* about it first? Then you'll understand *why* you should take it. Or, of course, leave it!"

After a short silence, Jennifer said — somewhat tactlessly, "Things seem to be so different these days."

It stung Crissy into saying, "Oh yes! I'm *really* on the scrap heap!"

"Oh, but I didn't mean to imply …" a horrified Jennifer stammered.

But the other went on: "You really think it is different nowadays, don't you." She raised her eyes to heaven and gave a single, ironic laugh. "Where boy and girl are concerned, it's been no different since Adam and Eve ate of the Forbidden Fruit in Eden. Now *there* was a tree on which nature must surely have had an opinion!"

"Did you …" Jennifer began hesitantly. "I mean did girls in your day … you know?"

"Some, yes."

"Many?"

Crissy sighed. "Most, I suppose."

"Mrs Colston-Smart says they were so closely guarded that they'd think the faintest smile from a stranger was a sign of undying love. So they'd fall for all the wrong people."

The hint of a comparison — the suggestion that Mrs C-S might have imparted more wisdom on this topic than herself — caused Crissy to shed the last of her reticence. "In *her* class, perhaps," she replied, trying not to sound contemptuous. "I'm talking about us, the great majority. My mother took in washing and I had to go into service. No one chaperoned us. We had to do our own fending-off."

"Or not — as the case may be."

Crissy laughed. "You *are* a terrier! I fear George Herbert may have met his match in you — the only difference being that he's driven from up here." Again she tapped her brow. "But your drive lies much deeper — too deep for even you to see. I wonder which is the stronger?"

The tension inside Jennifer was now so great that she had to fight an impulse to stand up and pace about the pocket-handkerchief gangway between their seats.

"I can only tell you my own experience," Crissy went on. "And that of people who confided in me. Like you, I wondered about these things until what had started as mild curiosity turned almost into an obsession. Fortunately, by that time I was within a few weeks of marrying, anyway, so … we 'jumped the starter's gun,' as they say."

"And?" Jennifer was on the edge of her seat.

"Well, it was wonderful, of course. I quite understood why the grown-up world had conspired to keep the secret from me. But it wasn't so utterly out of this world as to make me forget everything else ... I mean, it cured the obsession. It took its place among other pleasures like swimming, reading, music, and so on — which is where it belongs, of course, just one of life's many pleasures."

"Ah," Jennifer said flatly.

"Oh dear! Is that not quite the answer you were hoping for?"

The girl shrugged. "I don't know that I was hoping for any *particular* answer, actually. But what does one do if one *isn't* within a few weeks of tying the knot?"

"Well, you don't have to go all the way, you know. You can discover a great deal about yourself, your feelings, your ... how shall I put it? Your *needs* — you can discover a lot without taking that final plunge. It's something every woman has to decide for herself. When I was about your age I became great friends with a lady of impeccable respectability. She took me to London once — the first time I ever went there. We stayed with her widowed aunt — at whose dinner table one evening a young barrister attempted to seduce me. I was so innocent, I had no idea. I mean, I truly thought he wanted to show me his etchings! But this lady I'm talking about — this lady of impeccable respectability — intercepted his note to me and forbade my going. She explained why, of course, and I was jolly grateful. And I thought that was the end of it — until, on the train back here to Cornwall, she confessed she had kept the appointment in my place and had spent a very enjoyable afternoon in the bed he had prepared for *my* reception!" She laughed at Jennifer's expression and said, "Are you hoping to catch a fly?"

Jennifer remembered to close her mouth then — at least until she exclaimed, "And weren't you furious?"

"No." It was Crissy's turn for surprise. Then she said, "Actually, you're making the same point as I was: horses for courses. Each woman has to decide for herself. Dip a toe in the water, then a foot, an ankle, a calf, a knee ... then you decide where to draw the line."

"Why were you surprised just now, though? Look at it another way — your respectable friend deprived you of the chance to learn all about it from someone who was obviously very experienced. He wouldn't fumble and fume and stammer and get it all wrong and then try to hide from you in self-disgust ..." She paused, realizing she was giving away rather too many of her own secrets. "I mean, I suppose something like that *could* happen," she added hastily.

"I wouldn't know, dear." Crissy was not deceived for a moment. "Both Jim and I were absolute beginners, but tolerance and a sense of humour pulled us through — plus the fact that we adored each other. I can't imagine going to bed with someone like that young barrister, no matter how experienced and suave he might be. But I don't for one moment criticize my friend for doing so. She had her career before her — which would have come to an abrupt halt if she'd married. So she had to take those pleasures where and when she safely could. And, as she said at the time, I think, there was absolutely no danger of falling in love with a cad like that! So there you are, you see. *She* couldn't possibly go to bed with a man she might grow to love, but for *me,* love is the very first condition. But I don't rank myself as more noble or virtuous than her because of it. The question for you is, are you like me? Or like her? Or are you somewhere in between?"

29 THE LIBRARY was shut, of course, but the police station, a hundred yards farther up the Moor, was open and the sergeant on the desk let Jennifer browse through his copy of *Kelly's*. To her dismay it listed five Tregears, all in widely separated parts of the town. None had the initial B or W. However, by showing the right degree of distress and fluttering her eyelashes the requisite number of times, she wrung from the sergeant the news that a young Willy Tregear had 'come to his attention' many years ago over a small matter of some apples missing off their boughs and that he had dragged the boy's ear home — the rest of the boy following pretty smartly behind — to a courtyard off Market Street. He warned her that it was pretty rough and advised her not to linger there.

She didn't truly believe him. Market Street was at the beginning of Falmouth's main shopping thoroughfare, full of shops that Crissy Collett would call 'eminently respectable.' A courtyard so close by could hardly be a sink of iniquity.

But as she went under the archway and up the narrow, cobbled passage, she began to see he had spoken the truth. Coming as she did from a village, and knowing only the most salubrious end of Penzance, she had little idea of the poverty that can exist literally side-by-side with wealth in any town in the kingdom.

The buildings in the little yard were from Shakespeare's time and had probably been unfit for human habitation for the past century or more.

Even the sunlight that filtered down between their overhanging upper floors and the back walls of the shops had a different quality — thin and hazy, though it was rich and autumnal in the street she had just left behind. She almost tripped over a broken hobbyhorse, so grimy she would not have touched it with tongs.

In the back of one of the buildings a man was shouting abuse at a woman — at least, Jennifer assumed it was a woman because, although she never replied, the list of things she was useless at suggested as much. Some of them were embarrassingly personal.

A mangy cat rose to its feet on a nearby windowsill, arched its back, and moved from shade into sunlight before settling again. A bow-legged mongrel dog eyed it speculatively but lacked the energy to test his hopes. But for those two animals she thought she was alone in the courtyard — until a bundle of rags and straw at the farther end stirred, broke wind, and fell still again. The straw turned into matted blonde hair and the rags resolved into a skirt of kinds. A claw of a hand reached out, scratched where no female should scratch in public, and left her right limb in what would have been indecent exposure if it had not also been so repellent. A bottle glinted in the shadow at her side. Jennifer gave up any thought of asking her for directions.

At that moment a voice behind her said, "Oh, good!"

She turned to find a young man coming up behind her, a sailor by the cut of him, for though he wore no uniform, he had the roll of a seaman and was shod in the rope-soled sandals they favour, even ashore.

She could not imagine that he lived here but a moment later the mystery was explained. "The sarge sent me after you, miss," he said. "I'm PC Dempsey, by the way. I'm off duty — as you might guess!" He spread his hands apart as if they had been concealing his civilian dress until now. "But he said as I was passing, I could just keep an eye on things. The Mrs Tregear you're looking for lives in that one."

He pointed to the house beside the one from which the shouting was coming. Then he went up to it and knocked hard at the door.

The brawling stopped. Then came the sound of breaking glass. PC Dempsey hammered even louder on that door and shouted, "Stop that, you two — unless you want your wrists measured."

The silence was unnerving.

There was a shuffling in the passage of the Tregear household, then, after two or three bolts were withdrawn, the door opened outward, forcing them back a pace or two.

"Yes?"

A squat, square old woman raised a brawny arm across her forehead to shield her eyes from the glare of the enfeebled sun. "Stand back where I can see 'ee," she snapped.

"You know me well enough, ma," Dempsey said. "There's a young lady here inquiring after your son Billy." He checked with Jennifer to see if the sergeant had given him the right details.

"'Aven't got no son Billy," she told him. "Nor never did 'ave, neither."

The drunken woman at the end of the yard stirred again. Mrs Tregear saw it and, paying no heed to her visitors, picked up a pail of water — apparently kept immediately inside her hallway for just such a purpose — marched across the intervening dozen or so paces and flung it over the sleeping creature. "Piss off, you!" she shouted. "This is a respectable courtyard, this is."

"Now then, ma ..." Dempsey began.

The wet, bedraggled creature — sleeping no more — rose to her feet, screaming abuse, and hurled herself at her attacker, nails out for blood.

Jennifer looked at the constable in amazement. Surely the fact that he was off duty didn't prevent him from intervening? "Aren't you going to do something?" she asked when it became clear he was not.

He confirmed it with a shake of his head. "Domestic brawl," he said evenly. "We get no thanks for interfering in family fights."

"Family?" Jennifer stared at the two combatants, who were actually more bark than bite at that moment.

"She's the old one's daughter — or daughter-in-law."

"Fucking useless bag o' bones!" The old woman spat at her assailant.

Dempsey stepped smartly between them and grabbed the mother-in-law by her jaw. "Just you mind your tongue, ma," he said sharply. "There's a lady present."

The daughter-in-law noticed Jennifer for the first time. And Jennifer, stricken with horror, stared back, searching those filthy features for something she might recognize. This ... this *thing* from the lower depths could not possibly be the Martha Walker who had once worked for them in Carleen — not sensible, jolly Martha, who couldn't stop talking about the wonderful young man she was about to marry. And yet, in some grotesque way, it *could* be the same. Something about the eyes ...

"Miss Owen?" the creature whispered, mortified. "Miss Jennifer?"

"Martha?" Forgetting everything — even the errand that had brought her there that day — Jennifer went to her and threw her arms about the stinking bundle. "What's happened? Oh, dear Martha — what's become of you!"

The woman burst into tears — huge drunken sobs that racked her body. The stench off her was appalling.

"What's happened?" Jennifer repeated.

The sobbing continued and she had to wait for it to subside before she repeated the question for the third time.

"What hasn't!" Martha said glumly.

Jennifer became aware that they were alone. She let go of the woman and looked around. Dempsey was standing at Ma Tregear's door, giving her some kind of mild lecture. Jennifer made a hasty gesture at Martha, indicating that she was coming back, and went to talk with the constable.

"I'm sorry about all this," she said. "Look, I know you're off duty, so I won't trouble you further, but if you could just tell me where the Salvation Army is — or some charity where I could take her and get her generally cleaned up?"

The man bit his lip, running down a mental list of charities, most of which would not have given a cup of water, let alone a bath.

"She used to work for my family," Jennifer added. "Before the war."

Dempsey glanced at the old woman, who immediately snapped, "Oh no — not in 'ere!"

He sucked at a tooth. "It could get her off your hands for good, ma."

The point struck home. The woman hesitated.

He pressed home: "You got any old clothes of hers in there? You've surely got a bath fast the wall out the back?"

The woman licked her lips.

Now he was relentless. "There's water in the pump and a shaving or two of soap in the scullery, I shouldn't wonder?"

She was no match for him. At last she stood aside, snapping balefully at Jennifer, "Come-us on, then. Sooner started, sooner ended, I s'pose."

He, too, looked at Jennifer — who, after a puzzled moment or two, realized what he was waiting for. "Oh please!" she said. "Do go on. You were going sailing, I imagine? I can manage now."

"Which I certainly can't!" He gave an embarrassed laugh.

"You've been so helpful."

"What'll you do?" he asked.

She shrugged. "What I can. Clean her up. Sober her up. She was one of the best maids we ever had. She can't have forgotten everything. We need more staff where I'm working at the moment."

He turned and looked at the scarecrow that was — or once had been — Martha Walker.

Her eyes followed his. "I know," she said morosely.

30 GORONWY STARED at Jennifer with a mixture of baffled pride and consternation — a combination of emotions familiar to any mother with a strong-minded daughter. She looked from her to the bedraggled Martha Walker and then back again. Martha, despite a heroic cleaning-up and a suit of clothes that would have been passably respectable on any other scarecrow, still did not look like the sort of person anyone would invite indoors. Goronwy had not recognized her at first, and when she did, the contrast with the fine, healthy maid she remembered did nothing to recommend her now.

"You can't just *do* this, darling," she said.

"What?" Jennifer asked. "What's so unreasonable?"

"You don't come near us for a couple of weeks ..."

"Eight days," Jennifer insisted. "And I called in last Wednesday, only you were out."

"And rifled through all your clothes — no, no! Don't let's start all that. The point is — the first time I see you since you started up at Medrose — and you must *know* how I'm longing to hear all about it — I mean, I'd have expected to see you at least for a few minutes each day just to hear how you're getting on — but, no ..."

"I'm sorry." Jennifer was angry at being wrong-footed. "You're right. I should have."

"What's half a mile, after all?"

"Yes. I know. I've said I'm sorry. We've been busy. I've been exhausted. But even so I should have ..."

"Not *too* busy to ..." Goronwy gestured toward Martha and let the rest of the sentence hang.

"If you'll only let me *explain!*"

Goronwy folded her arms. "I'm waiting."

"Must we stand out here — talking over the garden gate like a pair of ... I don't know?" She was aware, as her mother was not, that Flora, Colin, and June were watching in wide-eyed amazement from their bedroom window upstairs.

Goronwy glanced dubiously at Martha.

"Oh, very well!" Jennifer turned on her heel and, taking Martha by the arm, set off up the hill toward Medrose. "We'll go where we're wanted," she called over her shoulder — sounding a great deal more confident than she felt.

"Leave I," Martha said miserably. "I aren't worth no dam' hurry between 'ee."

"I'll be the judge of that," the girl snapped back.

"Jennifer," her mother said quietly, so that the word barely carried the half-dozen paces that now separated them.

Her daughter paused but did not look round.

"Come back, darling. We have to talk about this. Walker can sit in the scullery for the moment."

Jennifer returned then and, putting her arms about her mother, gave her a powerful hug. "I'm sorry," she murmured. "Perhaps you'll understand when I've explained."

"I hope so." She slipped from her daughter's embrace and opened the garden gate.

Jennifer stepped back and ushered Martha in ahead of her. "I'll cut her a slice of heavycake," she said.

"Remember there's a war on, dear."

"Two wars," Jennifer replied grimly. "I don't mean us, I mean ..." She pointed at Martha's back.

Goronwy's spirits fell yet further when she heard her daughter saying, "Now if you feel you're going to be sick again, Martha, go out in the back garden. Right? On the grass for preference."

When Jennifer appeared in the parlour, Goronwy said, "It really is a bit much, darling. What's this about vomiting?"

"Well, you saw the condition she's in. She's only just sobered up in the last half hour."

"She can't sleep here. Her hair is *alive.*"

Jennifer nodded morosely. "We'll probably have to cut it right back. I did my best. You should have seen her when I found her. At least her clothes are clean and I did bath her all over."

"You *what?*"

Jennifer waved away all questions. "I don't want to be reminded."

"I should hope not! What is Mrs Colston-Smart thinking of — requiring you to ..."

"It's nothing to do with her. Well, it is in a way. But she hasn't *required* me to do any of this."

She sat in the only armchair; Goronwy spread herself on the sofa.

"You remember when Martha took baby Moses in to the Helston Union?" she began.

"Yes?"

"Well, she didn't."

Her mother frowned. "I'm sure she did. Did she tell you she didn't?"

"I haven't been able to get a word out of her. In fact, I haven't even tried. She's like a wild animal. She's lost all trust in … well, in anyone. Especially herself."

"So how do you know she didn't take Moses to …"

"Because Douglas Colston-Smart made some very thorough inquiries."

Goronwy sat bolt upright. "What on earth has it to do with him?" She frowned. "Are you doing all sorts of machiavellian things up there?"

Jennifer sighed. "Only in self-defence, I assure you. The thing is, Douglas is absolutely furious …"

"It's 'Douglas,' is it!"

Jennifer closed her eyes, miming superhuman patience. "Yes, it's 'Douglas,' and yes, he *has* kissed me." She wondered what her mother would say if she knew what else had happened between them! Just for a moment she saw herself from outside — as if she had left her own body and was watching the scene from some vague hovering point above them. What did it matter what she said? What did *anything* matter?

She realized then how exhausted she was — and steeled herself to be extra vigilant against letting anything slip out.

Her mother was staring at her, anxiously biting her lip. "I hope you know what you're doing, darling."

Of course, Jennifer realized, she was thinking that a marriage into the Colston-Smart family would be a feather in her cap — and a considerable boost to the Owen family fortunes, too. So maybe a *little* risk was well worth taking.

"Don't worry, Mummy," Jennifer said. "It's as Zack Hosking says — the boatbuilder down Newlyn, you know? 'You do do your best by 'er,' he says. 'You do build 'er so sound as what you can and you do give 'er good balance for all weathers. But once she'm laanched on the morrow tide, she'm on 'er own.' Or words to that effect."

Goronwy was not reassured. "When did Zack Hosking ever say such a thing to you?"

"Not me. He said it to Mister Collett. Anyway, to get back to Douglas — he's absolutely livid at what his mother has done to Medrose …"

"Which I've heard all about — though no thanks to you!"

"I'm sorry! I can't keep saying it. I'll write it out a hundred times, if you'd prefer that."

"This kiss — was it serious?"

"Yes!" Jennifer answered in a weary monotone. "Your wedding invitation is in the post!"

"Don't be flippant!" Goronwy responded angrily. "Courtship ... marriage ... these are serious subjects. I'm surprised you need reminding."

"Courtship, marriage, babies, housekeeping, blah-blah-blah! These are not the *only* serious subjects."

"Not to the president of the Royal College of Physicians, perhaps — but they are to *you.*"

Jennifer closed her eyes and silently counted 10, 9, 8 ... "Anyway," she went on when she felt calm again. "Douglas loathes what his mother has done up there — his mother *and* me. He thinks I'm the driving force behind it. He has no idea what his mother's really like. He thinks she's a spoiled, empty-headed woman who flits about the world like a butterfly, never sticking at anything for more than two minutes ..."

"Well, she does rather have that reputation, dear. I've been hearing things since you started up there. People are so *generous* with bad news! All the little projects she's started and then abandoned."

"I know. I've heard all about them, too — and from guess-who. But this time it's different. Believe me — it really is different. You should *see* the transformation — not just in the house but in her, too. And poor ickle Dougie is fwitened."

"Dougie?"

"I call him that when I want to annoy him — which is most of the time. He is insufferable! Never mind all those convalescent soldiers who *need* a place like Medrose ... never mind the fact that his mother was going out of her mind with the triviality of her life — with her husband away all the time and her son away all week and all her friends doing *something* toward the war effort — none of that matters a scrap to him. He just wants the place to be like it always was for those few hours when he deigns to drop by. If it could all be packed away in mothballs meanwhile — including his mother — he'd be just as content."

"Does this have anything to do with Martha Walker? I thought that was what you were going to explain?"

"I did — remember? Douglas making all those inquiries about whether or not Moses was placed in the Helston Union?"

"Oh yes — it's so confusing. Why should he do such a thing?"

"Well, of course, he hasn't the slightest interest in Moses. Nor in Martha Walker, come to that. But he knows how his mother can't resist a bit of real-life mystery. So he's dangling it in front of her — to distract her from the convalescent-home project. He'd love her to start on a wild-goose chase for Moses. He said he'd continue his inquiries in Falmouth this coming week. That's why I went over there today — to forestall him."

Goronwy smiled knowingly. "I believe you, dear — even though thousands wouldn't."

It was Jennifer's turn to frown in bewilderment.

"I met Mister Collett on the way back from church," her mother explained. "He told me about the troopship coming in ... and his wife going to meet it ... and *who* might be aboard!"

Jennifer stifled a pretend-yawn. "I knew nothing of that until I met Crissy Collett on the train."

"Good heavens! *Crissy* Collett — we are getting free with people's Christian names!"

"And, from the moment I clapped eyes on poor Martha until this minute, I'd completely forgotten about the troopship — *and* 'who might be on it.'" She eyed her mother as if she saw a stranger sitting there. "Aren't you even slightly curious about Moses?"

"Not really." Goronwy sighed. "But I suppose Walker told you all about it on the way here."

"Nothing. I told you — she's only *just* sobered up. I'm not even sure she'll remember the incident when I do put it to her."

"You're not really interested, either. Or are you?"

"I am, as it happens. He was such a bonny little baby."

"Well, if it's bonny little babies you want, dear, you'll have to work at getting a husband to make them with — not go off on wild-goose chases all over Cornwall."

Jennifer ignored the barb. "Besides, I've *got* to be interested. I've got to find out what happened. Otherwise, like I said, it'll be Mrs Colston-Smart who'll be whisking me off on wild-goose chases."

"But why should that worry you? You're paid to be her companion in *whatever* she may do — and you're paid jolly well, too. You mustn't try to run her life, you know. Will you get time to see Barry Moore if he *is* home on leave?"

A profound depression settled on Jennifer. "This is like every drive home from every dance you ever took me to," she said. "Why should I 'get time' to see Barry Moore?"

"Well, it does seem extraordinary that you'd spend every waking hour last winter knitting garments for the man — and now you ask why should you even see him!"

"No, I mean why *should* I see him? You made it sound like a smart thing to do."

"Well, it would do no harm, darling."

"Harm?"

"I mean, if you just met for tea on the promenade or something ... and if Douglas Colston-Smart should get to hear of it ...? A little rivalry, no?"

Jennifer sank her head between her hands. "I think," she said, "when I get Martha's hair cut off tomorrow, I'll have my own removed, too."

"Why?" Her mother laughed anxiously.

"So that I shan't be tempted to tear it out by the roots!"

31 JENNIFER'S VAGUE design for the rescue and rehabilitation of Martha Walker involved finding her a place, however menial, in the Medrose establishment. That being her long-term aim, she did not wish to wreck it by accepting the obvious short-term solution to her problem — where to place the wretched woman for the night. The obvious location was in the stables at Medrose, but the rest of the staff would never forget it and would probably never work happily with her if that were how she first came to join them.

Even Goronwy saw the point in the end and so, with great reluctance, agreed she might sleep in the garden shed and use the outside bucket lavatory. And she'd give her breakfast, too. *And* — after a little arm-twisting — she said she'd call at the nit-nurse's house and arrange for her to come and fumigate Martha and do something about her hair. Fortunately she knew Nurse Musgrave quite well since she'd recently done the girls' heads at Heamoor.

Jennifer hugged her and told her she was an angel and promised to be a more dutiful and loving daughter ... and left for Medrose in much better spirits than she had been all day — certainly since finding Martha like that.

It did not last, however, for now, with her immediate problems behind her, she faced the two big ones: how to get Martha placed respectably and how to prevent Douglas from distracting his mother over the fate of baby Moses.

She found Mrs C-S standing on the terrace, holding a nail-bar, and staring uncertainly at a large packing case someone had left there. It dwarfed her.

"Fancy making deliveries on a Sunday!" she exclaimed. "They use this war as an excuse for everything. I'm sure they were being paid double-time." She kicked the crate lightly. "And I'm sure it's double what we ordered, too."

"What is it?" Jennifer joined her.

"Blankets. We must get them indoors immediately, in case it comes on to rain. The whole place is going to stink of moth balls. I hate it. I can hardly breathe already."

"Where's Mister Colston-Smart?"

"He's on some blackout committee. They think zeppelins may be able to get as far as Falmouth docks, so it's not only seaward-facing windows now. Where d'you think this crate comes apart?"

Jennifer took the nail-bar and inserted its flat tongue between the lid and the body. It creaked and yielded a half inch or so. With the curved bit she hammered it back, leaving one nailhead proud. She stuck the forked tongue under it and pulled it out.

"Aren't you clever!" Her admiration was genuine.

"That's how they undid the crates for the beds," Jennifer explained.

She pulled a few more and then, like an impatient child, Mrs C-S said, "My turn! My turn!"

She pulled the last three to her own ecstatic accompaniment. Then, with dusk falling fast around them, they carried armfuls of bright red blankets into the drawing-room, spreading them over sofas, chairs, and whatnots and pulling faces at the powerful reek of camphor. When they had finished, Mrs C-S said, "Well now! Let's sneak down to the kitchen and make a nice cup of tea and you can tell me all about your discoveries this afternoon."

"I can tell you that now," Jennifer said as she followed the woman down the passage. "Nothing."

"Nothing at all?"

"Nothing of any consequence. I found Martha Walker but she's been very ill lately and I didn't feel I could press her ..."

"Very ill? You didn't leave her there, I hope?"

"No, no. I brought her back with me. My mother's caring for her now. Martha left our employment five years ago, it's true, but one still feels a sort of responsibility — especially as she was one of the *best* maids we ever had."

Mrs C-S digested this while Jennifer filled a kettle at the tap.

"Very ill, I think you said?" she wondered aloud. "But nothing contagious, I hope?"

Jennifer realized it would count against her if she were later shown to have withheld the truth. "A self-inflicted illness, I'm afraid," she said, and she mimed the act of swigging at a bottle.

"Oh!" The tone went from sympathetic to coldly censorious in under one second.

"That's why I had to bring her back to my mother's. She was such a *good* servant, you see. The *best* and *most abstemious* we ever had — as I said. So, in its way, her fall from sobriety is an even greater mystery than the whereabouts of little Moses."

"As long as that's the *only* fall from which she has suffered," the other said primly.

The kettle began to sing on its bright-blue corona of gas flames.

"Also," Jennifer continued in a more down-to-earth manner, "I thought that if she wishes to rehabilitate herself, she might prefer to do it in a sympathetic household like my mother's, where she's well known — and was once greatly esteemed. In other words, she can have her old job back — but at a lower wage, of course."

"Ah!" The tone went from censorious to interested in under half a second and Jennifer knew she had found the right cord to pull.

Mrs C-S left the matter there for the moment and returned to the earlier point of interest. "She didn't say a word about Moses?" she asked. "Not the smallest hint?"

"To be quite honest, Mrs Colston-Smart, I can't be sure she'd even remember the incident if I were to mention it. But I didn't want to press her too soon. She'd probably invent some tale and then she'd feel obliged to stick to it for ever. Whereas if I can win her confidence ..." She left the rest unsaid.

"Yes, yes!" Mrs C-S was unhappy at having to agree.

Jennifer realized how very eager she was to unravel the mystery of baby Moses — and how close Douglas had come to achieving his purpose. Indeed, he might still pull it off if she did nothing to frustrate him.

The kettle came to the boil. As she made the pot of tea she laughed. "I wonder what your son would have done if he'd gone to all the trouble of tracking down poor Martha, only to find her lying drunk in the gutter!"

"Oh, I'm glad he didn't!" Mrs C-S responded. "He'd have given up on the spot."

Jennifer smiled a knowing smile — and made sure the other noticed it.

"He would have," she insisted.

Jennifer passed her her tea with a shrug that implied, 'I disagree but I have no wish to argue about it.'

Mrs C-S eyed her suspiciously. "You seem to know something I don't," she said coldly.

"Well ..." Jennifer's tone was mollifying. "Let's just say I have my own opinion as to why your son is showing such an unlikely interest in the fate of a foundling baby he never even saw."

The woman's expression on hearing this was a curious blend of suspicion and curiosity.

"Well!" Jennifer sighed as if forced to speak against her better judgement. "It does strike me as strange that he should make such a *thing* about it — immediately after all that sound and fury to do with the conversion of this house!"

"I don't see the connection."

"No. And I'm sure he's hoping you never see it. But wouldn't it just suit him down to the ground if you gave up your plans for Medrose, even at this late stage, and set off looking for this mare's nest instead?" She shrugged again. "That's my opinion, anyway."

Some moments of deep thought ensued. Then Mrs C-S laughed. "He never could play bridge properly, either! By heavens, we could string him along, though, couldn't we? Now we've tumbled to his game."

"I think our best answer — or riposte, is that the word? — would be to play the card he fears the most."

"Oh yes — let's!" she replied enthusiastically. Then, after a short silence, "Which one is that?"

"Go full steam ahead with the convalescent home — and continue showing a keen interest in *his* inquiries into the fate of baby Moses."

32 THERE WAS A flurry of telephoning in the small hours of that Sunday night. The troopship that arrived in Falmouth that day had been expected to contain a number of wounded men in need of minor surgery. Several hospitals had been prepared to receive them — and, indeed, had received them, only to discover that they were *ex*-minor-surgery cases sent home to convalesce. Lady Cleer, president of the local Red Cross, was 'terribly, terribly sorry,' but if Mrs Colston-Smart could possibly see her way to accepting them ...? Now? Yes, within the next few hours ...?

Poor Millicent Colston-Smart could hardly explain that she had wished for her son to be out of the way when the first convalescents arrived — enabling her to pile one fait-accompli upon another. She said, yes, of course, put the telephone earpiece back in its cradle, and almost suffered a collapse. In the stress of the moment she forgot to ring off so the next call to the Penzance exchange came directly to her. A voice, speaking in conspiratorial haste, said, "The brandy's in the usual place."

Then there was a click ... and silence.

Only then did she realize she had forgotten to ring off. Jennifer appeared, yawning and heavy with sleep, while she was cranking the handle. "Who was it?" she asked.

Millicent, laughing feebly, said, "The brandy's in the usual place!"

Realizing that the situation must be serious, Jennifer went at once to fetch the reviving spirit. A few moments later she returned with the decanter and three glasses.

"No!" Millicent said. Then, "Oh, why not! We shall certainly need it before this night is out."

By the time Douglas came down for breakfast, Medrose was a mighty ant heap of activity. Servants he had never seen were pulling beds from their crates, which the gardener and two boys were assembling on modern factory principles. Other servants, also unfamiliar to him, were carrying them off to the drawing room — or what had until last week been the drawing room — and furnishing them with uniform mattresses and bedclothes.

And yet they were not entirely unfamiliar, these new maids. Indeed, it was the familiarity of one that gave the clue as to the rest. "Hallo, Doug," she said brightly. "I say, isn't it absolutely spiffing — something for us girls to do at last!"

"Sibyl?" he asked incredulously.

"Who else?" She laughed. "D'you want introductions all round? Clarrie, Faye, Deidre, Ruth ... Don't tell me these uniforms make us *so* unrecognizable!"

Jennifer was in her auxiliaries uniform, too, so he almost passed her by with the same vague nod he had given the others — who, in another life and another world, were all the daughters of family friends, girls with whom he had swum, ridden to hounds, and played tennis for as long as he could recall.

Jennifer took him by the arm and led him to the butler's pantry, where his breakfast had been laid. "This is the family dining room from now on," she explained, and went on to tell him of all that had happened since four o'clock last night.

While she heaped his plate with his favourite breakfast dish — kedgeree of halibut — he stood in the doorway, staring morosely out at the bustling scene around him. What struck him now was not so much the transformation of the house as of these, his childhood friends. Ruth Skewes had always been such a languid girl; she would give up the hunt for a lost tennis ball after less than a minute. And Clarrie Barnes would never stick at anything for more than ten minutes without saying, "I'm *bored!*" And

Sibyl McLaren couldn't lift a finger for herself if there was a servant within earshot to do it for her. And yet here they were, bustling around like little songbirds at nesting time. "What is happening to everyone?" he wondered aloud.

Jennifer held the plate beneath his nose and said, "Almost everyone. Now sit down and eat your food like a good fellow while I tell you what I discovered yesterday in Falmouth."

He listened with half an ear — which she took to show he had given up any serious hope of distracting his mother with the Moses mystery. The other ear-and-a-half was cocked for all the activity in the dining room and drawing room beyond. It was as if he needed to be reassured, every couple of minutes, that none of it was a dream, that the house, his friends — the whole of his world — really was being stood on its head.

"When are they coming?" he asked at length. "These so-called ambulant surgical convalescents?"

Even as he spoke there was the unfamiliar sound of a motor bike drawing up outside.

Jennifer raced to the front door, where she found a dispatch rider waving an envelope at Michael Ivey, a boy-simpleton from one of the nearby cottages. The man had two white discs around his eyes, where the goggles had kept back the dust. The sight of a uniform reassured him and he handed her the envelope at once.

Jennifer passed it on, unopened, to Millicent, who joined them at that moment. The man summarized the situation anyway. "There's twelve of them in two ambulances, ma'am," he said. "I left them going down Marazion and came on ahead. They'll be here in ten, fifteen minutes, I shouldn't wonder."

Millicent plied him with questions — how badly wounded were they? Could they all walk or did some need chairs? And so on. Douglas, who had wolfed his breakfast, stood behind her and watched in renewed amazement. The dispatch rider replied that they all could walk, some on crutches. All the details were in the envelopes. He licked his lips and added, "Thirsty weather, missiz."

Jennifer took him round to the kitchen for a cup of tea. Michael Ivey tried to join them but she told him he had to pick two buckets of stones before he'd get his reward. While the man enjoyed his tea and fuggan cake, she scribbled a note for him to take to her mother on his way back; she explained the situation at Medrose but promised to come down as soon as she could, to tell her all the news and to do something about Martha Walker.

The two ambulances were coming slowly down the drive as she returned to the front door. The auxiliaries were all assembled there, together with some of the maids, making almost one for each patient. They watched in horror, which they struggled to conceal, as the doors opened and the nurses helped the men disgorge. Some had ears and other bits of their faces blown away. Some were missing an arm or a leg, or at least a hand or a foot. One or two had shrapnel inside them still, too difficult or hazardous to remove.

But if the watchers had expected a subdued motley, haggard with pain and unmanned by the horrors of the trenches, they could hardly have been more wrong. A man with an eyepatch and two crutches balanced himself precariously on one of them while he jabbed a comrade in the back with the other, saying, "Har, Jim, me hearty! Now us'll find Flint's treasure, eh!" And he ran his one good eye over the waiting girls.

His comrade spun round and, with every appearance of ferocity, waggled the stump of his arm in his face and snarled. "Just 'ee wait till I gets me 'ook, Silver. See 'ow free thee art wi' thy crutches then!"

And they all burst out laughing, until one of the ambulance nurses reminded them they hadn't got all day.

When they were all on the ground, Millicent gave a brief speech that began, "Welcome to what was my home and is now yours ..." It went down very well.

As they were led indoors for the customary tea-and-a-wad, during which their individual needs and other particulars could be assessed, Douglas took his mother aside and said, "You really are serious about it, aren't you."

"Never more so," she replied. "But the east wing remains the family wing. You can shut yourself away there, if you wish ..."

"No, that wasn't ..."

"Most of the girls can cycle home when they're off duty. Faye Carminowe will ride, of course. And ..."

"No, I meant ..."

"Deirdre Stratton will sleep in the old housekeeper's parlour because poor Lilly Stratton has had to go back into hospital."

"No, listen — I want to say that if you *are* serious, then I'd like to help."

His mother just laughed. "You mean you want to take the whole show over — as usual!"

"Of course I don't. But ..."

"Your father would be the same."

"He's going to be furious when he hears of this."

"And no doubt some good-natured son or other will make sure he does — and soon!"

"I write to him twice every week — about the business — as you very well know. I can hardly *not* mention it!"

"That's what I said."

"I give up!" he shouted angrily as he walked away.

"Was that just a teeny bit harsh, Mrs Colston-Smart?" Jennifer asked while they followed the hobbling group into the mess hall, as the dining room was now to be called.

"You don't know his ability to ... there should be a special word for it: 'To appropriate something by excessive help.' When he was fourteen he begged to be allowed to weed my flower border — the one beside the conservatory that no one else is allowed to touch. Foolishly I yielded because to get a fourteen-year-old boy to take the slightest interest in a garden is a minor miracle in itself. And then later that same afternoon, when friends called to take tea with us, I heard him say, 'Come and look at my border.' He's doing the same to you over your search for baby Moses." Millicent smiled at her to show she was really joking when she added: "Actually, dear, you have something of that same quality, yourself, so perhaps you understand him better than I do."

But a steely glint in her eye showed she was only half joking. Jennifer regarded herself as having been warned — in the nicest possible way.

The new arrivals were soon settled in and, fortunately, a warm though thin September sun made it possible for them to walk in the garden, lie in the grass, or sit on the terrace, and generally bask in the kind of peace they had not known for twelve gruelling months.

The auxiliaries settled to their work with a will, writing letters, reading yarns by H.G. Wells, Conan Doyle, and John Buchan, darning socks, or carrying water and towels for the barber, who had come up from the town to shave the men. Jennifer was just thinking that this might be an appropriate time to ask for leave to go home, to deal with Martha, when Mrs Colston-Smart came looking for her.

"Tell me if I'm going mad, dear," she said, "but we seem to have lost one of our convalescents."

From among the papers the dispatch rider had brought she handed over a summary list of the men who were, or ought to have been, in the two ambulances that morning.

Jennifer scanned no more than four names and then froze. "Barry Moore," she whispered. But hadn't Crissy told her he was just on ordinary leave?

"Yes — so I'm not going mad. Goodness, how quick you are! I suppose you know all their names already. Well, he's not here, is he!" After a pause, in which Jennifer said nothing, she added, "My dear! You've gone quite pale. Do you know this Lieutenant Moore?"

She nodded. "I did ... a long time ago. When I was a child. He's Mrs Collett's nephew, you know."

"Ah! So it's possible he's been dropped off to stay with them. What a muddle! I wish they'd tell us such things."

"Shall I go down and see? They only live ten minutes away."

"I'll telephone them now." Millicent walked a few paces away and then turned. "On the other hand — we could kill two birds with one stone — since you're going that way, you could also call in on your mother and see if this ... whatzername?"

"Martha."

"See if she's fit for work. If she could just wash the dishes without smashing too many? She would come cheap, you said?"

Five minutes later, still in uniform, Jennifer was on her way down to ... well, to the Colletts? Or to her own home? It was, she realized, some kind of test of her true feelings.

No it wasn't! That was absurd. Martha Walker wasn't going anywhere; Barry Moore, on the other hand, might simply have called by at his aunt's. He might even now be setting off for his parents' home at Ludgvan. The most sensible thing to do, regardless of all other considerations, was to make sure of that errand first.

She saw him when she was still several houses away. He was going nowhere. In fact, he was sitting on the front steps, staring out over the bay. His right leg was in plaster and he was poking delicately down inside it with a stem of dry grass. She told herself not to be so ridiculous but her heart began to race all the same. He was just a ... just a *person*. Nobody special. A silly little schoolkid who happened also to have been called Jennifer Owen had once nurtured a silly pash for him, even though he'd given her not the slightest grounds for it. Now if she, the new Jennifer Owen who had grown up in place of that little idiot, were to make a fool of herself all over again, she'd embarrass him dreadfully. She took half a dozen of the deepest, quickest breaths she could manage and tried to frame herself to behave sensibly.

"Good afternoon, Mister Collett," she called out in tones of ringing confidence the moment she arrived at the garden gate.

The moment the words were out, of course, she realized her error and lost her tongue.

"Mister Collett is down at the shop."

"Mister Moore, I meant to say."

"Ah!" He peered at her. "Miss Owen, if I'm not mistaken?" He threw away the grass and rose to his feet. Ignoring her protests that he was not to stir himself, he came hobbling down the steps to greet her. "At last I can thank you in person for some comforts that were the envy of the entire regiment."

"Oh, please! It was nothing, honestly. I feel guilty at not sending you any more. I will try."

The moment their eyes met, she knew.

She knew it had been something more than a girlish 'pash.'

She knew that same *something* would bind her to this man for ever. Even if she were never to reveal her feelings and he were to remain no more than a casual friend of hers, it would make no difference. She was trapped already.

She knew it was madness to let such wild, unreasonable feelings rule her, but that simply made madness attractive.

She knew that somehow, some day, they would belong together. The time would come when he'd say, 'If only you had told me how you felt that afternoon — think of all the suspense and uncertainty we'd both have been spared!'

She knew she'd do no such thing.

She knew that no matter what other experiences she might have, what other conflicting intimations of love the future might bring, this moment would be the one against which she would weigh them all.

She knew she loved Barry Moore, had always loved him, and always would. He was so handsome it almost hurt her to look at him.

"I can guess why you're here," he said. "I'm sorry. It was thoughtless of me." Seeing her puzzled frown he added, "My aunt told me you work up at Medrose now. Besides ... the uniform gives you away."

So he and Crissy had been talking about her! Oh, what had they said? What had *he* said? She'd have given anything to eavesdrop on their conversation. "The ambulance nurse should have told us you stopped off here first," she replied.

"And I should have made sure she did. That's what pips on the shoulder are for — for thinking ahead. Anyway, now you're here, what are you like at scratching? D'you think you could cure an itch down here on my ankle? It's driving me mad not to be able to get at it."

He pulled another straw of grass and returned to the front steps. She followed him, thinking, *It's as if we've known each other all our lives.*

She sat on the same step as him and patted her lap. "Turn round sideways and put your foot here," she said.

The moment he did so she began unlacing his shoe.

"Eh?" he said.

"Don't fidget! I'm only going to try to get at it from below," she explained. "Nearer the ankle."

"Well, thank heavens they put us in clean things this morning. Most of us arrived from France quite disgustingly verminous."

His stockinged feet smelled of carbolic soap and shoe leather.

"What happened?" she asked, stroking the hard plaster. "Were you shot at by a sniper?"

"No." His laugh was embarrassed. "A horse knocked me down and trod on my leg — smashed the bone. And me a farm boy! I have to get back soon — if only to prove I didn't do it deliberately. Ooh, that's good! You've got it — just there."

"One hears whispers about that sort of thing, people who wound themselves deliberately, to get sent home."

"We shot a man last week for that very thing — gashed his hand badly on a tin of plum and apple. Personally, I don't think it *was* deliberate but the colonel said we've got to nip that sort of thing in the bud — make an example of the fellow. So he died for the good of his country one way or the other."

Something told her he was testing her. He might even have made up the entire story, which did not sound like British justice to her — nor like the way the finest army in the world would behave, either. If she were squeamish, he would think less of her. She didn't work it out in so many words but the idea was strong enough to make her swallow her indignation. "It must be pretty awful over there," was all she said.

"It's no picnic," he agreed. "Could you be an absolute angel and take off the sock as well — and scratch just below the ankle?"

She complied, thinking how odd it was that if it were his hand and a glove, rather than his foot and a sock, she would never let it rest where it was now.

Nor would he — or would he?

When she resumed her scratching with the stem of grass, he flexed his foot this way and that, moaning, "Oh! O-o-h! That is *so* pleasant ... you have no idea, Miss Owen!"

The incidental (or was it accidental?) caressing of her thighs and ... well, nearby regions, was *so* pleasant, too. "I'm glad," was all she could trust herself to say.

"Enough!" he exclaimed when he could not decently prolong it further. "Or I'll lose all desire to go back to Flanders."

He moved his foot toward her knees and handed her his sock, saying, "D'you mind?"

"Whereabouts in Flanders are you, exactly?" she asked a little huskily as she pulled his sock on again.

"Not allowed to say," he replied. Then he added, with a laugh, "Just to the south of Ypres — Wipers, as we call it. The battles there have certainly wiped out ..." He hesitated. "Well, it must end soon. It cannot possibly go on like this for more than a few more months. You've seen the casualty lists?"

"Daily."

"Enough said, then. Have you got ... someone over there?"

"No, why?"

"That's usually why people look at them daily."

She decided that the best way to cope with these new, raw feelings was to dress them up as a joke. "I look for *your* name, as a matter of fact, Mister Moore. I think, shall I go and buy some wool? Is it worth my while? And then I think, let's see first if you still want *anything* in the way of knitted comforts."

"Ho ho ho!" he laughed, not in the least deceived. Then he pinched the material of her sleeve between thumb and forefinger, murmuring, "It's true though — put a uniform on a person and he grows callous at once. Or she."

She wasn't going to be lured into more aplogies. "It's a way of coping," she told him coolly. Then, after a pause, "You pass from humour to seriousness very swiftly."

"I'm sorry."

"No, it's good. It's a good trait. People think humour is frivolous, but it isn't. It's the greatest defender of ..."

"I remember you now!" he exclaimed, lively once more. "Leedstown, was it? Or Carleen? Carleen, yes — practising for the Leedstown match. You were there with ..."

A troubled look came into his eye.

"Flossie Penhaligon," she said quietly.

"Yes." His eyes sought the distant horizon. "Awful!" His expression was inscrutable. Then he looked at her again, smiled, and said, "But I remember *you.*"

"And I, you." She hoped her ears weren't as pink as they felt.

"What were you — fifteen? Sixteen?"

She did not disabuse him.

"Lots of girls that age have the angelic sort of beauty I saw in you that day but few of them keep it until … well, your present advanced years, for instance. I'm glad you've managed it."

"Really!" she said.

"Am I embarrassing you?"

"Dreadfully." She laughed. "But don't let that stop you."

"My aunt told me about the tests and George Herbert and all that. Apparently, they were …"

"Goodness gracious! My ears should have been burning all morning long, it seems."

"Oh no! I distinctly recall two or three occasions when we spoke of other matters."

"Enough!" she said firmly as she knotted his shoelace and set his foot gently down.

He gripped her wrist and forced her to look into his eyes. "Don't take it too seriously, eh?"

"What?" she asked.

"Anything. Life. People. Hope. Anything."

There was an immense sadness in his eyes. She did not want explanations — only for him to go on holding her wrist like that. "I know," she said. "It can all vanish in less than a second — and without anybody intending it. I'm sure that zeppelin pilot didn't *intend* my father's death."

"You understand." He nodded and let go her arm.

Without thought she turned her hand upward and gripped his as he withdrew. "What is it *really* like?" she asked. "Over there?"

After a moment's thought he said, "Only a poet could do it justice. Dante? Milton? Someone of that stature. Blake, perhaps — who else could cope with so many thousand deaths each day? The rest of us wallow in triviality — pull it over our eyes, stuff it in our ears. Anything to …" He closed his eyes and raised his arms to push away imaginary walls closing in all round him.

She took his hand again as soon as he returned it to his lap. "Don't *you* go mad," she said. "Just think of … this — all this — waiting here for you." She gestured at the bay, the houses all around, the bright afternoon sky … stopping just short of including herself.

He raised the hand she held and with it touched her cheek. "I will," he promised quietly.

33 Mrs Sturgess, the nit-nurse, had pretensions to be a hairdresser, too. So when Goronwy Owen said of Martha's hair, "Of course, it'll *all* have to come off," the would-be coiffeuse contended with the nurse, and won. "Oh, I think we can save most of it," she said, more confidently than the nurse would have allowed. "You'd like to save as much of it as possible, wouldn't you, Walker?"

Martha shrugged listlessly. "Can't say as I'd really mind one way nor yet t'other, missiz."

"Well, I do. I won't have people thinking I'm a butcher." With sinking heart she patted the lank, lifeless mat of tangled hair. Almost every strand was studded with the empty cases from which nits had hatched, some of them months ago. "However, it's going to hurt a bit," she added. "So just make your mind up to it, eh?"

Martha appealed to Goronwy. "Would there be such a thing as a drop of gin in the house, ma'am — just to dull the pain?"

Goronwy shook her head firmly. "Fight pain with pain, my girl. Gin won't help you out of this mess."

Half an hour later, her whole body shivering from the torment she had endured, a past-caring Martha stared at herself in the looking glass — and burst into what would have been tears if she had had any left to cry. The image that confronted her was of a forgotten woman, dead these many years and buried in a past beyond recall — until just such a ghost as this arose to remind her. And, of course, accuse her.

Mrs Sturgess was insulted but Goronwy, who remembered that same Martha Walker, understood at once and, suppressing her distaste, put an arm around the woman, saying, "Perhaps one *small* glass of gin, eh? You've been so brave."

It did nothing to ease her craving, of course, but its illusory promise helped dull the agony from her scalp, turning it into nothing more than a sort of stinging ache.

At mid-morning a cup of tea and some dry toast was all Martha felt she could keep down. Then Goronwy took her to the parish relieving officer to find a more suitable dress than the dirty, rather funereal outfit in which she had arrived, which must have been worn by a grand lady in mourning back in the 1870s.

This time, when Martha saw herself in the mirror, she did not burst into tears; she just stared in disbelief. New clothes and a revived head of hair

— and, to be sure, a little milk of human kindness — did more for her spirit than would a whole vat of that other spirit she still thirsted after.

"Well, Walker," Goronwy said, "d'you think you stand a chance of beating the old demon now?"

The woman's only response to this was a hint of a nod and the shyest of little smiles.

Goronwy took her hand and rubbed it between her own. "Long way to go, though."

Another nod but this time no smile. "I shouldn't never ought to have left 'ee," she said.

"We can never know such things in advance. Don't talk about it if you'd rather not. Though nowadays they say that getting things off your chest is the best way of putting them behind you. Are you Miss Walker, by the way, or Mrs Tregear."

"Tregear!" she sneered. "That's a name I never wish to hear no more."

"Yes, but legally? Oh well, Walker it is — if you say so. Is *he* still alive?"
Martha just shrugged.

Goronwy explained that she had classes at Heamoor after lunch, then two private pupils after tea. If Martha felt up to a little light work, there were all the children's stockings to darn and cauliflower to pick and prepare for their dinner.

And that is what Jennifer found her doing when she called after leaving the Colletts' that afternoon — and a more reluctant parting she had never endured. For a moment she could only stand and stare, wondering if Time were not playing some trick on her. The transformation that had come over Martha during the past twenty-four hours was so vast that a supernatural explanation seemed as likely as the more obvious one.

"Martha?" she asked, for the second time in as many days — but this time as a joke. "What a change, eh!"

The maid bit her lip and smiled guiltily, as if she had been collared in some masquerade.

Then Jennifer caught sight of the gin bottle on the table and said, "Oh? What's this?"

"I put 'n there," Martha said swiftly. "Your mother hid 'n away but you can't hide the likes o' that from the likes o' we. So I put 'n there where I can fight 'n."

"You know best, I suppose," Jennifer said with resignation. "The main thing is to *want* to fight it."

Like wanting to fight love! she thought, knowing what a one-sided contest that would be.

"Well, there's work for you up at Medrose House, the new convalescent home just on top of the hill from here — if you feel up to it? Maybe not today. Start on Thursday for a short week, eh?"

Martha smiled to herself.

Jennifer asked why.

"You'm thinking like a working maid, miss — start Thursday for a short week!"

"Ah, well, we're all working maids now. You'll be surprised who you'll meet up there, mending clothes, making beds, slopping out. Such are the times we live in now."

Her voice, mouthing these platitudes, seemed hardly to belong to her. Another Jennifer lived a secret life inside her now, exulting in the discovery of love — knowing at last what love truly was — wanting both to share that knowledge with all the world and yet to keep it the deepest, darkest secret ever.

"How are 'ee doing all this for I, miss?" Martha asked.

"Well ... I mean to say ... you once worked for us ... I mean, more than that, you were part of our household — almost part of the family ..." The explanations trailed off and she said, more quietly, "I also want to know what happened to that baby I found — remember?" She could tell by the woman's face that she did, indeed, remember; but she continued talking to give her time to compose herself — and to cut ahead of any convenient lie she might attempt. "We nicknamed him Moses and you carried him into the Helston Union — or said you did. But our inquiries there show no such entry in their records. No foundling from Carleen or Godolphin for the whole of that year, in fact."

Martha listened in mounting dismay as her avenues of escape were closed down one by one.

"So what *did* become of him, Martha?" Jennifer concluded.

With careful deliberation the woman set down the stocking she was darning. "Your little brothers and sisters'll be home wanting their tea soon, I daresay," she mumbled.

"Martha?"

"I don't *know!*" was the anguished reply.

"What d'you mean, you don't know? You left here with Moses and you came back without him. You must know what you did with him, surely?"

"I took 'n to Falmouth!" she shouted. "So 'elp me God, that's what I done. Nor I don't care what *she* may tell 'ee. I took 'n to Falmouth and she ... I don't rightly know *what* she done wi' 'n, poor li'l cooze! She sold 'n, I 'ope! Else ..."

"Or else what?"

"It don't bear thinking 'bout, miss."

"*She* is Mrs Tregear, I take it — that awful old woman I met yesterday? Your mother-in-law."

Martha nodded glumly. "I thought Billy and me could rear 'n for ourselves, see. 'Cos the doctor — your father, miss — 'e 'zamined I once and 'e warned I not to 'speck no babbies. So I thought Moses was, like in the Bible, you know, sent down from heaven, special-like, what with me getting married so soon and not 'aving told Billy what the doctor said." She rested her arms upon the table and sank her head into the space between them. "A barren cow," she added.

A sense of foreboding came over Jennifer. Even from this jumbled beginning of an explanation the outlines of what had happened were distressingly clear. "Listen, Martha," she said gently, "I wouldn't have asked if I'd known it was such a painful tale. Not so soon as this, anyway. And my main question is answered, after all. To go any further than this would just be prying."

But Martha now had the confessional bit between her teeth. "First she said 'e was put to Billy's sister, over to Mylor, till after we was wed. But I found that was a lie. Then when I tried to explain to Billy 'bout what the doctor said, well, 'e 'alf killed I. He thought he *'ad.* Done I in, I mean. That's how 'e skipped the country. Joined the merchant navy."

"And does he still believe he killed you?"

"No, 'e come back — just after the war broke out. How many years ago was that?"

"Last year."

Martha stared at her in disbelief.

"Honestly. Look!" Jennifer pointed at the calendar on the wall. "Nineteen-fifteen, see — Monday the sixth of September. A day none of us is ever likely to forget, I think!"

"Last year?" She was still unable to believe it. "Was it only last year?"

"And when he came back and found you still alive? How had you been living — if that's not too ..."

"I were back in service. 'Twas all I could do — or so I believed. But 'e 'ad other fancies," she added grimly.

"Well! Look, it's really none of my business, Martha. It seems that the person to ask about baby Moses is ..."

" 'E said if I couldn't make babbies for 'n, I could make money instead. 'E put I up one o' they 'ouses in Vernon Place. You know — one o' *they* 'ouses. Where the sailors do ..."

"Martha — it's all over now. It's behind you, honestly. There's no point in distressing yourself …"

"And when I ran away, they copped I half way to Helston and brung I back and did chain I to the bed."

Jennifer closed her eyes but swirls of light pursued her into the dark. She wondered if she were about to faint.

"I'm no good, miss," Martha went on. Her tone was quite flat and unfeeling now that she had emptied her conscience. "You shouldn't ought to be a-helping of I, the way you are. I aren't worth it. I aren't worth the spit, as the Chinaman said."

"What Chinaman?"

"The one who do own that 'ouse. Mister Lee." She shuddered even at the mention of the name.

"Well, you should be proud to be worth nothing to a man like that. You're worth something to *us,* I can tell you. Threepence an hour, to be exact — plus board, lodging, and ale."

Mrs C-S would kill her! Those were the terms under which she could engage *any* scullery maid. A girl like Martha, down on her luck and with no other prospect of respectable and regular work, should be glad to do it for twopence, or even less.

"You shouldn't ought to be a-helping of I," Martha repeated.

But Jennifer could see how pleased she was beneath her gruffness.

Martha continued: "But 'twon't do 'ee no good to go asking 'bout Moses of *she,* miss. When I found out Billy's sister never clapped eyes on the babby, I asked 'er what she'd done wi' it. And 'er said, 'What babby? You never 'ad no babby, you barren old cow.' And no matter what I said — and Billy, 'e backed 'er up of course — no matter what I swore, she did say there never was no babby. So if you'm minded to go ask she, 'er'll tell 'ee 'tis all a pack o' lies. But 'tin't. I *did* bring babby Moses there and she *did* get rid of 'n somehow."

The younger children came bursting into the house at that moment. Flora, now eleven, flung her arms around her elder sister and hugged her almost in two.

"Steady the Buffs!" Jennifer laughed and gasped all in one. "You only saw me last night, you know."

"Not to hug," Flora said. "You smell of soap."

June, now eight, came close, sniffed, and walked away, ostentatiously holding her nose.

Colin, six, said, "Is it true one of the wounded soldiers only's got half a face? How could you not have the other half? What's there instead?"

"Come up and see," Jennifer said on the spur of the moment.

Martha shot her a baleful glance and she realized the poor creature assumed she was just trying to get her younger brother and sisters away from the Fallen Woman.

"They'll just let us stand and look at them?" Colin asked incredulously.

"What d'you think it is?" Jennifer asked him crossly. "A zoo? Even there you'd have to pay. No — you silly sausage! But they'll let you play cards and they'll tell you stories and one of them might mend that old kite of yours if you asked him very politely."

"You mean we can go up and play with them?" Flora asked. She was thinking how envious all the other girls in her class would be when they heard she'd been playing with the wounded heroes of Flanders.

"Not like you'd play with dolls, no. But you can help them convalesce."

"What's that?" Colin asked. "Is it like converse?"

"That's part of it. Now come on — if you're coming at all. I don't mind one way or the other."

They dropped their satchels and lunch boxes here, there, and everywhere and went racing to the door. When Jennifer joined them she looked back over her shoulder and said, "Thursday, then?"

"Thursday." Martha smiled at last. "Start on Thursday for a short week, eh?"

34 MILLICENT TOOK the news — or utter lack of news — about Moses far harder than Jennifer had done. Indeed, Jennifer had been more relieved than anything to realize that no further search was possible. She had done her best and now she could close the book on the whole affair. But Millicent seemed to take it as a personal affront that 'we' — as she now put it — had done so much and got so far, only to end at a blank wall.

"I know!" she said brightly, a week or so later, "what if I were to go and see this Mrs Tregear? You can't, of course. She's seen you and wouldn't believe a word. But if I went and told her some story about the gypsies stealing a child from our family ..."

"But gypsies don't steal children — only in penny dreadfuls."

"But that's all they read, people of her class. She'll believe it. And I'll tell her there's a substantial inheritance awaiting the little boy — if only he can be found. What about that? Threats will get nothing out of her but if we can play upon her greed ...?"

"She'd find a suitable six-year-old boy and produce him like a shot — that's what greed would make her do."

"She'd have to produce the brooch as well."

"And how difficult would that be? There must be tens of millions of bun pennies still in circulation. Any handyman could solder one to a brooch-pin."

Millicent wrung her hands, paced the room, breathed heavily, and said, "Well, you're a great help, Jennifer!"

"I hope I am, Mrs Colston-Smart. I hope I'm helping you not to waste time and money, not to mention nervous energy, on what is clearly a pointless quest."

"I shall put a private detective onto it," she said firmly.

"And it won't take *him* more than an hour to realize he, too, can produce some likely six-year-old street urchin who's been in and out of orphanages and foster homes and has no memory of anything else. He'll string you along until he sees you're growing tired of it — sting you for all he thinks he can get out of you — and then produce the child. It'd be the easiest thing in the world."

There was another spate of heavy breathing while Mrs C-S stared at her balefully. "For a well-brought-up girl of tender years, you are amazingly cynical, Jennifer. That's all I can say."

Jennifer smiled as if she took it as a great compliment. "And we'll hear no more about 'my' baby Moses?"

Trapped, resigned, she said, "Where's the point?"

Jennifer added bolts to bars. "That question could be asked even if your private detective produced the real Moses together with incontrovertible proof of his authenticity. *Where's the point?* What would you do then? Adopt him? Sponsor his education? Or just take him off the hook and throw him back in the lake? I wish I'd never mentioned him to anyone. I wish I'd never found him at all."

"Well, at last we find *some* point on which we can agree!" She spoke in the tone of one who produces a final, crushing argument, but neither woman was deceived by it.

"Good." Jennifer gave a little sigh of relief — which annoyed Mrs C-S all over again.

"I remarked the other day on your tendency to take over other people's endeavours and projects. I do hope you will try to curb it."

"If you feel that *I* have acted in that way over any of *your* endeavours and projects, Mrs Colston-Smart," she said pointedly, "then please allow me to ..."

"Bringing the Walker woman to work up here, for instance. What d'you call that?"

"I call that 'responding to your suggestion.' I distinctly remember your asking me ..."

"Not at threepence an hour!"

Jennifer fought an impulse to say, 'Take the difference out of *my* wages if it's so important to you!' but instinct warned her never to give an inch with someone like Mrs C-S. Instead she weighed in with, "She's worth two of any other scullery maid. You said so yourself. You said we could hardly keep her at such menial ..."

"Never mind what I said. Anyway, I'm not really talking about trivial little things like that."

"Why bring it up at all, then?"

The woman stared at her in amazement. "My goodness, child — you're like a terrier."

Jennifer attempted a placatory smile. "I'm sorry. But if I don't fight my corner, who will?"

"You mean I'd walk all over you."

"And you would, too — wouldn't you!"

"All I can say is that you're a very different young woman from the one I interviewed out there on the terrace ... was it only three weeks ago?"

"And it's a very different post from the one I thought I was being interviewed *for*. Look, if you want some meek little scribe who'll trot along at your heels, making lists and never taking any of the work off your hands, then just say so. I don't want to fall out with you. I admire you more than anyone I know. I think you're doing wonderful work here — and you've certainly biffed your prig of a son right in the eye! But, admiration or no admiration, I can never be that meek little scribe you seem to want — that's all."

Millicent turned away to dab a small tear from her eye — not even a tear, really, just a slight excess of water. She had always considered herself to be a mistress of emotional manipulation but how could she compete with *this?* Jennifer was such an adept in the art, such a *natural* practitioner, that she probably wasn't even aware she was doing it. "I don't want a meek little scribe, dear," she said when she felt she had regained control of her voice. "I want someone just like you — except ... just a little more consultation, perhaps?"

Jennifer, glad she had stood up to the woman, now saw she could yield a little without giving an inch. "I'm sorry." She hung her head. "I shall try to use a little better judgement in future."

"Come! Give me a kiss and we'll forget all about this."

They kissed, cheek-to-cheek, and Millicent added, "Perhaps you'd look upon me as a courtesy aunt, Jennifer? Aunt Millicent, eh?"

Jennifer, genuinely delighted, mumbled that she didn't know what she'd done to deserve the honour. Millicent smiled and said nothing as to that; for all her natural aptitude, the girl did not seem to realize that she was now a sort of honorary member of the family — and that *family* rows are always fought without gloves. She, herself, had often wished for a daughter in place of Douglas; now she wasn't so sure.

They went on to discuss important but emotionally neutral matters and decided to tell Lady Cleer that they were now ready to take in up to twenty-six further ambulant convalescents — ten officers in one dormitory and sixteen other ranks in another. They would have to eat in the same mess hall, though it could be divided by a curtain.

As Jennifer went to the telephone to place the call she saw a young officer sitting at the window, tilting back in his chair, with his feet on the sill. She was about to tell him off when the plaster cast around his right leg gave him away.

"Lieutenant Moore?" she called out, her mission temporarily forgotten.

He gave a start, sat up straight, and took his feet down off the sill. "Sorry," he said. "Drifted miles away."

"No one told me you'd arrived." She sat on the arm of the chair nearest him. "How's the leg?"

"I'm afraid I just walked in by way of the terrace. Itching again. Actually, I was wondering if I might go on your ration strength here? I just moon about at home, arguing over old matches with my father. And if I stay with the Colletts, I do nothing but think about how close Medrose is, and … my comrades. And you, of course."

His laconic delivery and devastating smile almost felled her. There were about a dozen things to say and she couldn't articulate one of them.

"And I couldn't help overhearing that you now have room for officers."

"Golly, yes!" Stung by the reminder she sprang to her feet and made once more for the telephone in the brigadier's study. "Of course you can have a bed here. I'll be back in half a jiff."

Lady Cleer was delighted with the news and warned them to expect the extra beds to fill within the next ten days.

When Jennifer returned to the dining room, Barry was standing at the french window, looking out over the terrace. "It's starting to drizzle," he said. "A real Cornish day."

"D'you want to see your room? Have you brought your kit?"

He smiled at her. "Are you sure this isn't one of those decisions you ought to consult with the memsahib about?"

"You heard that, too? I wondered about that while I was on the phone. We can walk in the conservatory if you want the exercise."

"I wouldn't be keeping you from your duties?"

"Walking and talking with convalescents *is* one of my duties." She grinned and stuck out her tongue at him.

"My crest was never so fallen," he responded with equally mocking humility. But as they entered the conservatory — which she was pleased to see they had to themselves, for the moment, anyway — he became serious again, saying, "You certainly gave as good as you got."

"You have to with her. I've seen her trample all over some of the other girls because they're too well-mannered to speak out for themselves."

"You're absolutely right. My company sergeant-major is just like her — he'll bully anyone who lets him. But there's one private in my platoon who stood up to him from the beginning. The CSM tried everything in his power to break the man — and a CSM is a bad enemy to make in the trenches because when we go over the top and advance across no-man's-land, he's the chap who brings up the rear, with a drawn revolver, and shoots any coward who turns and runs. Anyway, he tried to break Private Cudden's spirit every way he knew. But nothing worked. I tried to tick him off about it — told him to ease off. But he said, 'I'll be the making of that man, sir. There's greatness in him — you'll see.'"

"And was he right?"

"Judge for yourself. When the CSM fell during an advance last spring, who was it went out through a hail of enemy sniper and machine-gun fire and brought him safely back? Private Cudden — our first VC in this war!"

"And now he calls the CSM 'Uncle John' — or whatever his name is?"

Barry laughed. "Not him! Cudden swears he only did it because he thought the fellow had the platoon's daily rum ration in his hip pocket! But that's the British tommy for you." He looked shrewdly at Jennifer and added, "Is it possible Mrs Colston-Smart is doing the same for you — in a more feminine way, of course?"

In her embarrassment Jennifer did not quite know how to reply.

He persisted. "When you came up here for that interview she mentioned, d'you suppose ..."

"Heavens, you *were* eavesdropping!"

"Unashamedly. When you came up here first — at the very beginning — d'you think you could possibly have stood up to her like that — the way you did just now?"

"If I'd known as much about her as I do now — yes. Why are you so interested, anyway? Just because you happened to overhear one ..."

"No, no — I assure you. I've been interested in the subject since ... well, certainly since this war gave me time to think. To take stock of life."

"What subject? I don't know what you're talking about any more."

"I'm talking about our attempts to take over each other's *lives*. Not just 'endeavours and projects,' as the memsahib put it ..."

"You mustn't call her that."

"They already do call her that — you see, you don't know everything that goes on here. Anyway, I'm interested in people's desire for power over others, which is what's at the bottom of it all. In fact, I can prove it." He fished in his breast pocket but then thought better of it and did the button up again."

"What?" she asked, intrigued.

"Nothing — just a poem I wrote when I was orderly officer one evening. One of our quieter evenings."

"Oh, *do* let me see. I absolutely adore poetry — at least, I would if I had more time."

He was not truly reluctant, only shy. Thus encouraged he fished in his pocket again and this time produced a small notebook bound in green calf, with a silver propelling pencil down its spine. "I'd been reading the Bible," he explained. "You get pretty superstitious out there and one of the tricks is to open the Bible at random and read the first verse that catches your eye. The word 'battle' occurs in various combinations eighty-nine times in the Bible, so there's a fair chance of finding an omen. Anyway, I opened it this particular night and, instead of finding omens of war, I found this."

He kept his hand over the lower half of the page while she read the rubric at the top:

Ruth to Naomi: Whither thou goest, I will go; and where thou lodgest, I will lodge: thy people shall be my people and thy God my God.
Ruth 1, 16

"Yes?" She was puzzled. "And?"

"It set me thinking. Is *anybody* quite that humble? Remember how ''umble' Uriah Heep took over his employer's business? I thought, what if Ruth did that to Naomi? And then I wrote this poem about it. Actually, the title came to me first — *Ruthless!* After that I just had to write it. D'you see?"

He uncovered the rest of the page and she read:

Ruthless
I will take my place humbly
in your house.
Lovingly I will take your children
to me.
I will so faithfully obey you
your people will say,
"She is most becoming."
I shall become your house,
... your ways,
... you.

I shall take your place humbly
in your house.
Lovingly I shall take your children
in your house.
And then my ways shall be your ways,
my word, your command.

The hair prickled on the back of her neck as she read the last two lines. "See what I mean?" he asked.

35 THE LETTER was from *Captain* George Herbert; Jennifer could hardly believe it — a captain with a cockney accent! That would flutter the dovecotes in any officers' mess he visited. No, surely he was just joking? But she remembered the George Herbert who had revealed himself that night, before he left to join up; then anything seemed possible. He anticipated her reaction, anyway.

Don't faint, petal [he began]. All war artists are captains or higher. Mine is temporary, acting, unpaid. That is, I'm paid as the newest subaltern on the scale, which is still the best spondulicks I ever had, mind. Royal academicians are made up to majors at once, but I think that's only because the sight of someone with silver hairs but still with only three pips on the shoulder is too pathetic. Anyway, that's not what I'm writing about — which is urgent.

The thing is, darling love of mine, I was wrong about how being a nurse and looking after convalescents and that would help your career in films after the war. There'll be thousands of heroines like you and it won't mean much. This is what people told me passing through London.

Also, Billy Scott says your footage is sensational. Let me put it another way. SENSATIONAL! D'you know what I mean? Funny, no one can say what IT is, not in so many words, but when we see it on the screen, we can all agree THAT'S IT! And you've definitely got IT. Billy also says the war has pushed the demand for films with beautiful English roses up through the clouds and you should waste no time. Beautiful English Rose is you by another name, and smelling as sweet, if I may make so bold.

No prizes for guessing what this news has done to me! I'm stuck here now and I can't get out of it. I thought if I could get just <u>slightly</u> gassed ... but then I met two blokes who had been and it stopped being funny. So I'm stuck here, like I say, for however long it takes.

I could make a song-and-patter about all what you owe me and don't you never forget it. But I won't. You're too fly for that, anyway. The thing is I can't stand in your way no longer. You deserve your place at the top, pet. You're a good kid and it's all yours for the taking. So take it. The film is yours — all the stuff with Billy and, I think, about ten foot I left with Mrs Collett. Free, gratis, and for nothing. And if, when you're up there and I come back from the wars and I'm still down here — and you reckon you can put a thing or two my way — well, I shan't think none the worse of you for returning the favour. D'you follow me?

Bless you, my child, as the bishop said — and who should know better?

See you when this lot's over.

George.

Excuse the writing. It's not mine. (Joke)

It put Jennifer in a quandary. She read and reread the letter a score of times over the following days, always hoping that some little word or phrase would finally tip the balance and make her mind up for her. But nothing of the sort happened.

In the end, and with some reluctance, she showed it to Barry.

He was now one of eight officers convalescing at Medrose, which also had its full complement of sixteen ORs. All of them knew there was something special between 'the *young* memsahib,' as she was inevitably called, and Mr Moore — who simply had the good fortune to arrive first. So none thought it especially strange when she took him aside in the billiards room one day and fell into earnest consultation over what looked like a military letter from France.

It had been raining at dawn but a drying wind had sprung up so that by now, mid-morning, the grass had dried underfoot. At first they wandered this way and that around the lawn, keeping within its confines.

"We have a phrase in the army," Barry said. " 'Coming the old soldier' — meaning putting on the swagger because of your length of service. D'you think Captain Herbert could be, one might say, 'coming the old Cockney,' just a little?"

"Why?" Jennifer asked impatiently. She was far more eager to discuss the letter than to analyse its author.

"This bit about a rose, 'smelling as sweet.' From *Romeo and Juliet.* I'll bet he knows that, too. I never met the man, of course. I only know what my aunt and uncle have told me — and what I can glean from this letter."

"What did they tell you?"

"That he'll go far. You know Aunty Crissy's family was split up when her parents died? She was younger than you are now but she fought tooth and nail to get them all back together again — and she won. It's hard to believe now but Uncle Jim told me she just *burned* with that one ambition. It consumed all her time and energy. And he told me George Herbert had that same quality — except that it's more on the inside with him. On the surface it's all camouflage. He wants people to take him for any old Tom, Dick, or Harry — so that he can outflank them before they tumble to the truth about him. That's what I mean by saying he's 'coming the old Cockney'."

After a longish silence on her part he said, "Well? Penny for 'em."

So then she told him what had happened — and not happened — between George and herself on that final night, back in the summer — how he'd tried to entrap her by pretending to be in love. "The thing is," she added, "he did it so badly, I think it was deliberate. I mean he deliberately bungled it so that I'd see through him. And *then,* of course, in an absolute *flood* of honesty, he cast the real net over me, which is this promise of stardom."

Barry gave the letter another cursory glance. "This seems to rule that out," he said. Then, watching her closely, he added, "There is another possibility ..."

"What?"

"He might genuinely be in love with you — and not know how to cope with it."

She shook her head. "I'm sorry to say it but I don't think he's capable of love for anybody."

"That's my point, really. He probably thought the same — until you came along. Falling in love isn't always the wonderful, welcome event the poets say it is. So he tried to ... what's the word? Not 'besmirch' — *belittle!* He tried to belittle it."

His comment that love was not always welcome worried her. Was he talking obliquely of his own feelings? Also, it had to be admitted, she herself did not exactly *want* to be in love with him. Her life, just at that moment, held too many other exciting prospects — the most exciting one of all being set forth in the letter from George. And then again there was his reputation ... and what had happened to Flo Penhaligon ...

Again her silence forced him to speak. "When you say he's not capable of love for anybody — not even himself?"

She chuckled. "Even that would get in his way."

"Does that make you sad?"

"For him, yes. But not for me. The last thing I want in all the world is for ..." She hesitated.

"For *anyone* to be in love with you!"

"For *him* to be in love with me. I don't understand him more than *that* much." She stretched out her little finger. "But even that little bit doesn't inspire me to want to know more. It'd be like trying to hold a conversation with someone who only speaks Chinese or something — a person like that. Yet I am fond of him, you know."

"What sort of person *would* you like to be in love with you?"

Seeking escape from this inquisition — even though she did not wish it to end! — she turned from him and took a few steps down the path to the bromeliad grove, out of sight of the house. When he caught up with her he touched her arm.

She shivered at the contact and turned to face him. "Not any *sort* of person, Barry. How can you ask such a thing?"

It was the first time she had called him by his Christian name to his face. He stared at her and swallowed audibly. She realized he was in something of a state, too.

"Because I dare not anticipate the answer," he said. "I know what I found sewn into one of the bobbles on the scarf you knitted me, but I also realized how ..."

"When?" she asked, thinking, *Of all the stupid questions ...!*

"Yesterday. But I realized how long ago it was sewn in there — and how much has happened in the meantime — so, as I say, I dare not anticipate ... anything."

Further words were pointless. She turned to face him fully, sank her head to his chest, put her arms around him, and hugged him in something akin to desperation.

He took her head between gentle hands and turned her face to his — and suddenly the sky was God. Their lips touched and melted into one another. She would never have imagined that the touch of another human being could feel so sweet. The essence of him poured through that exquisite contact and filled every part of her with a wild, unfocused kind of longing. She moaned and moved her head this way and that, seeking an even more ecstatic fusion between them there.

"I've never forgotten you," he murmured as soon as they broke to draw breath. "Not for one minute."

"What d'you mean?" She rested her head hard against him, not much caring what he meant.

"I forgot your name — everything else — but the image of that beautiful young girl on the Flow at Carleen that afternoon has haunted me ever since. I can't believe ... *this* — that I'm actually holding you in my arms at last. I was sure you'd quite forgotten me ..."

"Never!"

"Well, I didn't dare believe that — until I found that ... that dear little bit of embroidery yesterday. I've been in a torment ever since. I resolved to say nothing unless you spoke first — and then a hundred times, last night, this morning, I've had to force myself to keep that resolve."

"Silly," she murmured, hugging him even tighter.

"Did you still have those feelings when we met again last month — out on the steps at my aunt's and uncle's?"

"Of course."

"Why didn't you say something? Think of all the agony and suspense we'd have been spared!"

He did not really understand why she laughed at that but he joined in, all the same.

However, the laughter died just as swiftly when she said, "I have to know about Flossie Penhaligon, Barry."

He stiffened at once. "She was with you that day."

"You know what I mean. You don't want to make me say it, do you?"

He slumped against her with a sigh and then pulled away from her. "It's true," he said.

When his eyes held her like that she lost all judgement. "Well then ..." was all she could say.

"Have you never done anything so stupid you'd give the rest of your life to *un*-do it?"

"All the time!" She tried to lighten the mood but its solemnity was too powerful. "No, not really," she said, chastened.

"She wanted so much — and so did I, of course. One doesn't know the power of these emotions until ..."

Now his silence prompted her. "Until?"

He laughed with little humour and quoted her back at herself: "You know what I mean. You don't want to make me say it, do you?"

"In this case, yes."

"Why? What point would it serve?"

"Because you've changed. You *have* changed. And it's thanks to what happened between you and Flossie. You were in love with her, too? That surely goes without saying?"

He closed his eyes and nodded. "Is there somewhere we could sit down? This plaster cast ..."

She thought of the gazebo and opted instead for a fallen log just beyond the grove. It held no past associations to disturb her. She took off her apron and spread it for them both. "It needs a wash, anyway," she said. When he was seated she went on, "You're going to treat me differently, because of ..."

"You bet!" he exclaimed.

"Because of what happened with Flossie. But if all we ever do is mutter and hint darkly about these things, we could be piling up endless misunderstandings for the future."

He stared at her awhile and then said, "In some ways you're very like her and in other ways you're quite the opposite."

She shrugged. "Go on."

"Comparisons won't annoy you?"

"That's stupid! Comparisons are part of life. We all compare everything and everyone all the time. I'll help you. Flossie was eager not to stick in the same rut all her life. She wanted *something* out there." Her hand swept the horizon. "More! She wanted more than life would ever let her have — probably. So you don't need to tell me how I'm like her! But how am I quite the opposite?"

"You're only partly right, Jenny. May I call you Jenny?"

Impulsively she kissed his cheek. It seemed to unlock some of his reserve at last. "She wanted *more,* as you say, but she had no idea *what* more. She just took anything that came along. She'd seize on it and try it to death ... worry it to bits. 'Is this it? Is this what I'm looking for?' That seemed to be her way. But it's not yours. You want *more,* too, but you have a pretty good idea about where to get it."

"But even then, I'll still be asking, 'Is this truly what I'm looking for?' It's not so very different."

"It is, believe me. I've seen it. A burning desire to *go* somewhere is utterly different from the same burning desire to *leave* something behind. George Herbert has a burning desire to *go* somewhere, and so ..."

"Forget George Herbert!" she said crossly.

"... and so have you. But Flo tried everything — short cuts, mostly."

"I don't follow."

"You know she was addicted to laudanum at one time?"

Jennifer shook her head.

"And that she later drank herself into a coma? Your father attended her that time. And then her next addiction was ..."

"You?"

He closed his eyes and nodded. "As mine was her." He gave a brief, dry laugh. "I keep thinking I've managed to put it all behind me — and then I find I haven't. And, of course, I never will."

"I understand." She took his hand and squeezed it.

"I hope you don't, Jenny. I hope you never do — except in a general sort of way — the way you understand things in books. But I hope you never understand it *here.*" He rammed his fist into his stomach.

She thought of those feelings that had almost overwhelmed her with Douglas in the gazebo that time. *Shall I tell him?* she wondered.

While she hunted for words he went on: "The thing is — the thing no one tells you — is that there comes a moment when everything inside you is shouting no, no, no — telling you it's madness — and the rest of you knows it's true but there's absolutely nothing you can do about it. Were you ever at a shipwreck? You see people standing on the clifftop shouting no into the teeth of the gale. It's as useful as that. The storm sweeps you on, however you struggle to resist."

She thought it over a while and then said, "So — do you decide you'll never go within five miles of the sea again — or do you build a proper lighthouse ... lifeboat station ... all that sort of thing?"

She did not dare look at him directly while asking this but he put a finger beneath her chin and turned her face to his. "I have never met anyone like you," he murmured. "It's frightening."

"Frightening?" The word surprised, and did not entirely please, her.

He nodded. "Because you look so demure and ... English rose, yes! I won't say his name for fear of another explosion, but he hit it exactly. You look as if the brush of a butterfly's wing would bruise you. But underneath it all you're adamantine. Or Cornish granite."

"Stop this!" She gave his hand a playful slap.

"You and G.H. have a lot in common, you know. He comes the old Cockney, you come the young English rose, but inside you're both granite. Neither of you will yield an inch if there's something you really want out there."

She drew forth George's letter and waved it under his nose. "This isn't yielding?"

"Not a bit. He's just taking two paces back to jump a little higher. If you do act on his suggestion, don't for one moment think he's let you go."

There was another little pause and then she said, "Actually, you know, 'Rose English' would make a good stage name."

36 NOVEMBER brought a series of violent storms to the western approaches. Most of them had moderated to a mere gale by the time they reached the mainland but even that was formidable. Several houses in the town lost every slate they had, and the harbour was closed for most of one week. It was said that the men on the Wolf Rock Light were down to starvation rations. But the really spectacular sights followed after each storm had blown itself out. For when the winds were westerly they had a fetch of a thousand miles or more — long enough to let them pile up mountainous bluffs of grey-green water and hurl them at everything that stood in their path.

If all the world's navies had assembled in the bay and fired every shell and torpedo and depth charge in their armouries at the feet of the cliffs, they would still not have produced a sight as awe-inspiring as dying wind and immortal ocean achieved between them in those hours when the gales passed on and the waters came rushing up behind.

The best views of all were to be had from the gazebo. Even the Mount and the bay were visible from there now, after the storm had played havoc with the neighbouring plantation. The patients crowded there and quarrelled with each other for a turn with the one pair of binoculars that Medrose possessed (four other pairs having been handed over to the War Office in a patriotic flush at the outbreak of war). Jennifer and Millicent saw how this awesome display of nature's power held them in thrall and so, when the next storm blew itself out, they were ready with a treat — a charabanc outing to the north coast. There the cliffs were at least twice as high, and ten times as desolate, as those around Mount's Bay. And there, too, the swell would be greatest, since the storm had blown from the northwest.

More than half the patients signed up to go along. And so, after a good breakfast and medical inspection, eight officers and ten ORs, each clutching a democratically identical packed lunch, piled into one of 'Churley's Charas' — as it proudly advertised itself in two-foot letters down its side — and, accompanied by Clarrie Barnes, Faye Carminowe, and, of course, Jennifer herself, set off for Gurnard's Head for luncheon and then on to Cape Cornwall for tea.

As the conveyance chugged through Penzance and meandered up onto the wide, wild moors of the Land's End peninsula, they sang 'Hush, here comes a whizzbang!' and 'They were only playing leapfrog' and 'When this lousy war is over.' And they laughed a lot, and tried not to think too deeply about the meaning behind the meaning. But when they reached the summit of their brief journey, where, apart from the thin ribbon of road, the hand of iron-age man is everywhere more apparent than any contribution from a later age, an odd sort of hush fell upon them. They were passing the circle known as the Nine Maidens — said to be petrified village girls who had violated the Sabbath by sneaking away to the moors for a ring dance; a passing saint had punished them by turning them to stone.

From the silence in the bus as they passed this macabre site you'd have thought something of that ancient magic still persisted there. In reality, it was the magic of the entire landscape that stilled their tongues and drew their eyes to a silent feast of colour: Flaming heather, deep-green furze that was dotted here and there with sulphur-yellow blossom, and patches of golden, sun-bleached grass tumbled and rioted down the long, sloping flanks of the hill, a mile or more to the sea. Here and there small ramparts of grey and ochre rock reared in futile opposition to the dithering tide of vegetation. Perhaps, as some said, they were relics of bronze-age mines for tin and copper. By now, though, they were as primeval to the eye as the rolling downs themselves.

Jennifer watched Barry, drinking it all in as the charabanc rolled the last few bumpy furlongs down to the coastal road. "What are you thinking?" she asked.

He was slightly embarrassed to confess it. "It struck me that if we could only kidnap all the generals and politicians and bring them here — show them this — and then say, 'Now tell us what it's all about!' ... then there might not be a war to go back to."

"Oh, I say!" a brother officer cried out — a Mr Cardew Silk of the 10th Royal Hussars. "What talk is that? No war to go back to? Not afraid are we?" He laughed and looked about for support, though he found little.

"Were you there at Second Wipers, Silk?" another officer put in.

"Just missed it. Damn shame. Can't wait to get back for a good biff at the Boche." This time the lack of support amazed him. "Don't you chaps agree? Surely?"

"What did you do before you joined?" yet another officer asked.

"You're missing the view," Jennifer told them. She wished she hadn't opened her mouth now.

"I was still at school," Silk replied a little defensively, adding, "Not that I'm much of a scholar, mind. But I gave up a chance of stroking the college eight at Henley in order to enlist, you know."

"Coxing, more likely," someone suggested, to general laughter.

"I heard that!" He looked around belligerently but no one owned up to it. "What's wrong with you chaps? Would you actually *like* the war to be over before we can get another crack at it?"

"Yes," Barry said at once. "And only someone who's never been in an actual battle could sneer at being afraid like that."

"Who says?"

"I do. Nobody told me but I'll do you a favour, young 'un, and tell you — and I've been over the top a dozen times this year already — fear is part of every soldier's survival kit."

"I say, steady on, old chap," one of the others put in. "Others are listening in, you know. What?" He nodded his head significantly toward the ORs in the seats behind.

Barry turned to him. "You think they don't already know it?" Without looking back he called over his shoulder, "Corporal Walters!"

"Sah!"

"How many battles have you fought in?"

"Too many, sir."

Barry faced him then. "Good man! So tell me — what happens to the soldier who feels no fear?"

The corporal was an old enough soldier not to wish to be drawn into an argument among officers. He simply drew a finger across his throat and nodded heavenward.

"I don't think this conversation is at all what the doctor ordered," Jennifer said.

"Quite so!" Silk clutched at any straw now. "We really ought not to subject Miss Owen and the other young ladies to these masculine revelations." He beamed at the nurses in turn, as if expecting their gratitude for such protection.

Fortunately the vehicle came to a halt at that moment and the driver slid back his little communicating window and said, "You want for me to drive on down, Miss Owen, or do 'ee want to walk? I reckon 'er'd carry five but not more on that rough road."

She thanked him and said they could all walk. She made sure she alighted immediately before Silk so that she could fall in easily at his side, without its seeming deliberate. He was at first surprised, but not for long; he soon began to smirk as if to say he understood perfectly well why, having heard how brave he was — or intended to be when given half a chance — she would naturally seek his company in preference to the others'. It annoyed her but she did not want him to feel isolated and resentful — and that was not just for the sake of *his* feelings, either, but for the effect on the general *ésprit de corps*.

"It must have been a terrible wrench, Mister Silk," she began. "Having to give up Henley in order to volunteer. Are you keen on rowing?"

"The only thing I stayed on at school for," he told her. "*Two* extra years. Got elected to Pop, too."

She recalled something another officer had told her: 'An Old Etonian will never tell you he went to Eton, of course. Yet I never met one who doesn't manage to find *some* way of letting the fact slip out sideways within the first minute of one's acquaintance.'

"*Ginger* pop gets *my* vote every time," she said. "Listen — you mustn't take all this badinage too seriously. We do our best to keep you all occupied ..."

"Where are we going?" He looked about him suspiciously, surprised to see how far she'd led him away from the group.

"Just down this track to Gurnard's Head. All roads lead to Gurnard's Head, don't worry."

"What's so special about Gurnard's Head?"

"You'll see when we get there. As I was saying, it's hard to keep you all occupied. Lots of football and cold showers would delay your convalescence but anything less gives you time and energy for all this cavilling. So I give this smug little lecture on sweetness and tolerance to everybody. Don't take it too personally."

"It's that Moore fellow you ought to talk to," he grumbled.

"I have. And I shall again."

"Putting subversive ideas into the OR's heads like that. The man's a thundering disgrace."

Jennifer didn't know why she said it, but she did: "He may be the man I marry one day."

If she expected his embarrassment, she was spared it. He looked at her speculatively. "Only *may* be, eh? D'you mean to say there's room for a little doubt there, what? What?"

Amazed at this turn in the conversation, she could only stare at him and murmur, "Why?"

"Well ..." He actually twirled one of his little waxed moustaches. "You could do worse than yours truly, you know. I think I could help you — and you could certainly help me."

"How?" She laughed, but not unkindly. "Or dare I ask?"

"Depends," he drawled. "A lot of marriages head straight for the rocks because there's too much *feeling* around. Too many hot emotions, if you follow. Now I'm a pretty unfeeling sort of chap, myself — except when it comes to patriotism and honour and things in that department. But in the personal-feelings department, I'm pretty cooled off. So, whether you marry Mister Moore or not, I'm perfectly sure you'll marry *someone*. A lot of girls won't be able to because the chaps just won't be there — unless the survivors turn Muhammedan or something. But you will, I'm sure of it."

"Thank you," she felt she had to say. By now she was wishing she *hadn't* led him so far from the others, even though their paths were now converging once more.

"Don't thank me yet. You haven't heard the offer. But if you'd like to learn all that matrimonial doodah — how to dance the matrimonial polka, as they say — without embarrassment and all that hot, emotional stuff getting in the way — Cardew's your tutor!"

She stopped and stared at him a long while. He just smiled, preened the other little wax prong, and stared back.

"Did you really just say that?" she asked.

"You wouldn't be the first. I wish I'd taken testimonials."

"How old are you?"

"Twenty-two. I began when I was sixteen. Helped my housemaster's daughter ..."

"And you go through life making this offer — this *brazen* offer — to all and sundry?"

"Not quite. I know how to be a gentleman, you know."

"Whatever *that* may mean!"

"It means I don't leave any embarrassments behind. As I was saying, I helped my housemaster's daughter cross the Rubicon in the month before *her* marriage. Several times, in fact. She was like a shrieking little filly to start with, scared out of her wits. But you should have seen her on the great day itself! Sailed into marriage. Sent a card from Florence. Utter bliss. All thanks to me."

"Well! I don't know what to say. I've never ..."

"Don't need to say anything. Just think about it. Shan't force myself upon you."

"Oh, well, I'm grateful for that!"

He laughed pleasantly. "Funny old world, isn't it — once you get out of the nursery and take the plunge."

"As, indeed, I'm discovering."

"Haven't offended, I hope?"

"Not in the least, strange as that may sound."

"And you don't actually *dislike* me?"

"No. That's the strangest thing of all — I don't." She was glad, nonetheless that he didn't ask what her feelings might be.

Just before they rejoined the others he said, "Listen. I can't bear all these packed lunches and army rations. I've had a hamper sent down from Fortnum's. Got a taxi bringing it out here from Penzance at one. Pheasant, game pie, *pâté de foie gras,* stuff like that. Would you and the other ladies care to join me?"

A thought struck her. "Have you made this same offer to any of them?"

He winked. "I told you. I know how to behave like a gentleman."

"And — just as a matter of interest — how many ladies accept your generous offer?"

After a moment's thought he replied, "One in five?"

There were by then nine auxiliaries at the convalescent home — ten, counting herself. "Busy little bee!" she said.

He laughed. "Passing from flower to flower!"

When they reached Gurnard's Head he, and everyone else, saw why she had brought them there. The narrow headland, which projected almost half a mile into the Atlantic, had a sheer fall of two hundred feet on its western flank. Those with a head for heights took turns to crawl on their bellies to the very edge of the rock and stare directly down at the wild, angry sea as it hurled vast walls of blue-green water at the foot of the rampart. Each impact was so violent that they could feel its thunder through the soles of their feet, and suddenly the mighty rock did not feel quite so mighty any more. With each assault the water broke into a mass of seething white foam that reached long, clawing fingers up the face of the cliff and charged the air with a fine, salty drizzle, refreshing to the taste but clammy on the skin. The dying wind still roared about them, making sustained conversation impossible — which was just as well, Jennifer thought, because she could see Barry was eager to discover what she and the egregious Silk had been discussing so earnestly.

From there, too, a six-mile stretch of the north-coast cliffs was visible, from Zennor Head in the east to Pendeen Watch to the west. And the same majestic waves were battering away at every yard of it, rearing in vast plumes that seemed as airy as steam until they fell back upon the seething white waters below.

"Amazing!" Barry pointed out the gulls to her. "How they ride the swell so calmly, just beyond where the trouble starts."

"They're generals and brigadiers to the last little feather," another officer said.

"To the last *white* feather," put in a third.

"Is there *no* escaping this war?" Jennifer shouted.

They looked at each other, then sadly at her, and she realized that, indeed, there was none.

And still they lingered there, enthralled by a display of power so unimaginably superior to anything that humankind could deploy. But at last the chill, and the prospect of a packed lunch in the lee of some sheltering cove, brought them straggling back to the mainland, where Clarrie Barnes and a corporal from a cooks' platoon had stayed behind to brew a canteen of tea.

As they sauntered up the narrow cwm of rock that linked the headland to the rest of Cornwall, a car came lurching and bouncing slowly down the track toward the parked charabanc; groaning gears and squeaky brakes were all that held it back from a headlong rush toward the sea.

"*My* lunch, I believe," crowed Silk, clapping his gloved hands as he strode out to take possession — a laird of the manor striding over his own ancestral turf.

Brother officers and other ranks watched in amazement, not to say envy, as he paid off the taxi driver and took out the hamper, which was vast. It needed the pair of them to lift it out and set it down. He opened the lid like a stage magician and drew off a sparkling white cloth to reveal a feast of golden-brown piecrust, pâté jars, fruits, jelly, salt beef, and half a dozen bottles of châteauneuf du pape, mouthwateringly purple and wicked. "Come on, chaps," he said, enjoying himself hugely. "Give your packed lunches to the boys. They won't say no, eh, fellows?"

A mighty cheer went up from the men.

Men! Jennifer watched the little tableau in astonishment as they lined up in parody of a rugby-football lineout and waited for the throw-in, which followed at once. As each man caught a paper bag he gave a whoop of triumph and ran off up the field, warding off mere token tackles from his comrades. *A gang of men will make a game of just about anything,* she thought. She could imagine them bayoneting the enemy in the same devil-may-care spirit.

And what when the war was over, when such fellows came home from the trenches — back to the ledgers, the workbenches, the shop counters of civilian life? Suddenly the prospect of post-war England was not quite as inviting as heretofore.

Cardew Silk was now a splendid chap, of course, a good egg, a spiffer. "Won't you join us?" he asked Jennifer while the others, including Clarrie and Faye, spread the cloth upon the sward and set forth the contents of the hamper.

"No, thank you," she replied, clutching her packed lunch a little more tightly to her. She glanced toward the men.

"Be sensible! They won't respect you for it," he told her in his by now infuriating drawl.

"How *can* you tuck into such a feast while they have to eat a dull old bag of sandwiches?"

"Because they expect it. Darwin was wrong. Officers and ORs are descended from entirely different missing links or whatever his theory was. They don't respect an officer who tries to be one of them. That's why we wear our hair down to the shoulder while they're shaven to the bone. They drill like machines while we slouch around. That's the way it is. Sorry." He held a bottle approvingly up to the light. "Never throws a deposit. Favourite of the French railways, you know. You'll be missing a dashed fine wine."

He spoke this last as Jennifer went over to join the other ranks, who were delighted to make room for her among them.

"No taste for the high life, miss?" Corporal Walters joked.

"How does a scene like that make you feel?" she asked as she took her first bite of ham sandwich. And a jolly good ham sandwich it was, too, she was pleased to discover.

"That's officers for you, miss," a sergeant by the name of Ward said. "By rights we sergeants shouldn't be hobnobbing with *this* scum, either." He gave a private a playful kick.

The private reminded him that scum rises to the top.

"Dregs, then," the sergeant replied at once.

They all laughed.

"The war has rubbed a few edges off of everyone, anyway," the corporal put in.

"Not quite everyone. Not the Old Etonians among us." Jennifer let her eyes rest rather obviously on Silk and the carousing officers. In turning back to see how they responded she noticed that Corporal Walters was on the point of adding something.

Whatever it was, though, he thought better of it and the conversation turned instead to the possibility of getting up a scratch game of football on one of the more level fields beside the road — officers *vs* the rest.

Jennifer said she could only allow that if there were no tackling; a player would have to pass the ball as soon as an opponent touched him.

"Might as well play with women!" a private grumbled.

"All right," she said. "Jolly good idea. The three of us will play on the officers' side, to make their numbers up a bit."

The notion was intriguing enough to everyone for even the most reluctant to give it a try. Jennifer persuaded the doubters among the officers by saying it was the only way to make sure the ORs played a gentle enough game. Her head would be on the block if anyone came back from this jaunt with fresh injuries.

The farmer was squared with a tot of medicinal brandy. Empty wine bottles and officers' hats served for goalposts. The football, which Jennifer had not seen smuggled aboard the coach, was the genuine article, as was the whistle with which Sergeant Ward refereed the game. The three women scored the first four goals in quick order, by which time the ORs realized that they were not the shrinking violets that well-brought-up ladies are supposed to be and that chivalry has its limits. After that they were treated as roughly as any of the others. Jennifer was glad to retire, at her own suggestion, to the goal, where she could spread her feet wide and, thanks to her long skirts, save the goals in a way no man could — or would dare.

Half an hour later the game ended with honours more or less even, at 20 − 18 to the ORs, and everyone in a state of happy exhaustion. The low cloud, which had been scudding across the sky all day, began to break up and let the sun shine through. They took a vote as to whether or not to go on to Cape Cornwall and decided they were happy enough where they were. Some went off on walks; some returned to the cliffs, to marvel at the sea again; most just lay down in the lee of a ridge or rocky outcrop and, pulling their caps over their eyes, fell asleep. Cardew Silk, Jennifer noticed, took Faye Carminowe aside and engaged her in a lengthy and earnest conversation.

"Come on," Barry said at her elbow.

"What?"

"We could walk to Zennor along the cliffs and return by the road. It'll only take an hour."

"I can't leave them so long. You're all in my care, officially, anyway."

"Where then?" he asked.

"Why should we go off anywhere?"

It was a cruel question. She saw the hurt in his eyes. "Because time is short," he said.

She turned and gazed at Faye and Silk, heads earnestly together, and realized that her reluctance had nothing to do with a change in her feelings for Barry — nor, really, with her sense of responsibility. It was that she did not wish to let those two out of her sight.

But was that because she felt it her duty to protect Faye from the seductive offer he was doubtless making?

Or that she did not wish the girl to steal a march on her?

37 A WALK TO Zennor would have been too ambitious a project even if Jennifer had not been responsible for the whole party. She and Barry went back to the headland — not to the precipitous cliff edge where they had all stood and marvelled that morning but to the northeastern corner, where several 'giant's armchairs' had been carved into the rock by frost and smoothed by rain.

"When we were children," she said as she clambered into one, "we used to call this 'King Arthur's seat'."

"Well, if you're King Arthur, who am I?"

"I'm Guinevere," she told him, patting the rock beside her. "There's room for an Arthur here still."

"Wasn't she the ..." He paused and then said, "Oh, no, that was Tristan and Isolde."

She guessed he had been going to ask, 'Wasn't she the unfaithful one?'

After a pause he said, "Everything's war, war, war. I can't even look at these waves without thinking of wave after wave of men going over the top. The war mucks up everything. How can we plan?"

"Barry." She took his hand and folded it between hers in her lap. "If you're wondering how you can ask me to wait for you, then ..."

"How can I possibly do that?" he interrupted. "Honourably, I mean."

"I was about to tell you — there is no need. No power on earth can stop me. Of all the things you might think of to worry you in the trenches you can cross that one off the list."

He sank his head on her shoulder, which was uncomfortable for them both, since he was a lot taller. She pushed it away and leaned hers on his shoulder, which felt much more natural. "How can I *ask* such a thing?" he persisted.

"I know," she sighed, pretending to misunderstand him. "How can one *ask* water to be wet or grass to be green?"

"What was Silk on about?" he went on casually.

"Nothing. He was mostly listening to me giving my standard lecture on the need to get along with everyone. He said I should tell it to you, too, and I said I would. He probably thinks that's what I'm doing now. Did you know he went to Eton?"

"Did he tell you so?"

"They never do, do they — OES — but they manage to let something slip so as to leave you in no doubt."

He chuckled. "What — in his case?"

"He told me he got elected to Pop. I told him I like pop — expecially ginger pop." She laughed. "He thinks I'm beyond the pale now. Even so, he'll be annoyed I didn't catch his meaning. He'll be desperate for some other way to let me know."

"He's telling Faye Carminowe and she'll tell you — that's why he took her aside."

"Of course! That explains it. I couldn't think what *else* he might want with her. She's much too horsey for him." A new thought struck her. "Actually, I think Corporal Walters knows something about our Mister Silk of the Prince of Wales's Own. He was about to blurt it out and then thought better of it. But I saw it in his face."

"How would Walters know anything about him? He's in the Green Howards. Different part of the line."

"But Walters's parents — I've just remembered — live in Windsor, which is right next door to Eton. That's where they could have met."

"Hah! There you have it, then. *Do* pass on whatever he knows — unless it's greatly to his credit, of course. He gained quite enough points with this lunch-hamper extravaganza."

"But he has style, you must admit. He told me he was wondering if Fortnums would send hampers up the line once he gets over there."

Barry did not react to that. After a while she said, "Penny for 'em?"

"I was just thinking what an ugly thing jealousy is," he replied. "And yet unavoidable, too. When I saw you walking with Silk, after we got off the charry, I could have killed him. I might have guessed you were reading him the riot act but even so ... I mean, it's quite unreasonable, I know."

"I'm glad you realize that."

"It's going to be the same when I'm back at the front — I'll think of you here with other officers and other men ..."

"Is that a promise?" She squeezed his hand gleefully. "If so, *I* promise I'll worry about Mademoiselle from Armentières."

"*And* Mister Douglas Colston-Smart," he added.

"No, I shan't worry about him," she said confidently.

"You know jolly well what I mean."

"I don't," she replied. "I jolly well don't. Of all the people who might induce me break my vows to you, *he* is the least ..."

"Ah! So you do admit there are *some* people who might induce you 'break your vows'!"

She pulled away from him and stared out at the northern horizon, where dark clouds were gathering.

"Eh?" he persisted.

"It must be something Celtic in the air, or in the rock — this obsession with fidelity and honour. I never thought you'd be like this."

"Nor did I — but then, I've never been in love like this before."

She reached up, pulled his head down to hers, and smothered his words with kisses. Then words were superfluous anyway. After a while, still locked in a kiss, she took up his hand and carried it to her breast.

He snatched it back as if she had scalded him but she caught it again and carried it back, giving out a little moan whose meaning he could not possibly mistake.

Reluctant at first, then with increasing ardour, he caressed her there. It was not as exciting as she had expected. Forbidden things ought to be very exciting, she felt.

He loosened one of her buttons and slipped his fingers inside. When he touched her nipple the most delicious sensations radiated through and through her. His breathing was growing disordered, too.

He undid more buttons, changed positions slightly, and slipped both hands inside her blouse, where, by crossing them, he managed to caress both her nipples at once. The feeling was unbearably sweet. She had to break off their kiss, but not their embrace, in order to fill her lungs. She breathed rapidly, deeply, panting like a dog, but still she could not get enough air. She put her lips to his again and tried to devour him there.

Finally, when she was ready to tear off all her clothes and surrender herself to him completely, he began caressing higher up her chest, up to her shoulders and the base of her neck. The wildness of her impulse was tamed but its intensity remained as a memory she knew she would never forget. When she had gathered the shreds of her feelings about her once more, he took his hands out of her blouse and started caressing her behind her ears and up into her hair.

"That was close," he murmured.

"Listen," she said. "When you go to take leave of your parents ..."

"Yes?"

"I could take some time off — I'm overdue a half day, anyway — and come with you."

"Why?" he asked, thinking she meant to see his parents, too.

She dug him hard with her elbow. "Why d'you think?"

38 THE CONVALESCENTS made their own beds each day. In fact, they were required to do as much of their own housekeeping as they could manage — and then to push themselves a little beyond that limit. The weekly change of sheets, however, was a task for the auxiliaries, who inspected them for wear and tear, and for the housemaids, who bundled them for the Penzance Steam Laundry every Friday.

On the Friday after the charabanc outing Faye Carminowe and Jennifer were engaged in that particular task. They enjoyed it because it required almost no mental effort, which left them free to talk without interruption.

"We're pretty lucky, don't you think?" Jennifer said. "Being able to live cheek by jowl with so many men ... and talk with them and all that."

Faye raised an amused eyebrow. "And all *what*, pray?" she asked.

"Well, before the war what chance had we to mingle with them? The odd picnic or ball ..."

"Hunting ..."

"Yes. Just a few hours at a time. Snatched conversations. A lot of ribbing and teasing. No *real* conversation. I used to be afraid of them."

"Jenny!" Faye laughed. "I can't believe you were ever afraid of anything — least of all *men.*"

Her friend's flattering perception of her came as a surprise. She accepted the compliment, though, and went on: "I felt nervous, then. You know — as if they were ... foreign or something. Of course, they still *are* foreign but not unfamiliar-foreign, if you know what I mean."

"Some of them are very *familiar*-foreign — if *you* know what *I* mean."

"Yes, well, even that's part of it. I mean, if any man had presumed like that before the war, I'd just have died of embarrassment or frozen with shock or something. But now ..." She dug her elbow hard into an imaginary man at her side and stuck her chin out pugnaciously. "All in a day's work."

"Or play. I know what you mean. Of course, I have two older brothers but it's still not the same, is it. The difference is that here it's our *job* to be with them, to help them start walking again, to write letters for those who can't, et cetera. It's not a few hours of leisure taken out of a day devoted to other things — the way a picnic is. Or a hunt. This sheet's past it, don't you think?"

The centre portion passed much more light than the edges.

"Sides to middle?" Jennifer suggested.

They threw it on a separate pile.

"And all the different *sorts* of men, too," Jennifer went on. "We'd never have had the chance to make such comparisons before. There's Trooper Davy, who's obviously never going to fight again, desperately trying to conceal his disability and pretend everything's going well. And there's Private Mears, malingering for all he's worth. He could have gone back last week if Doctor Fothergill wasn't so blind and gullible. You only discover things like that by living cheek-by-jowl with them."

The stable clock struck eleven.

"Come on!" Jennifer added. "We should be in the officers' dorm by now. Where does the time go!"

Faye was staring out of the window. "Also," she said, as if she had not heard Jennifer, " one begins to see how the differences between them and us aren't quite so clear cut as you'd think. I knew it from my brothers, I suppose — except that one never thinks one's brothers are typical of all men. At least, one *hopes* they aren't!"

"In what way?" Jennifer shook a sheet at her. "Wake up!"

"Think of the rug RSM Laws is making — I mean, a *regimental sergeant-major* making a rug! And so beautifully, too. Of course, he'd say you shouldn't do anything unless you do it well. But Corporal Walters told me that man could boil a kettle just by shouting at it. He said when he reads about cannon balls bouncing across the plain at Waterloo, he thinks of the RSM's voice booming across Ramillies parade ground at Aldershot. And yet there he is making that beautiful rug and waiting for his ankle to mend. *And* — this is the point — look what he's started! Edwards and his poker work ... Floyd and his sampler ... Mister Moore and his poetry ..."

She gave the latter example in the same offhand tone as the rest but the glint in her eye challenged Jennifer to rise to it — which she did: "Oh, but he was writing poetry ..."

"Joking!" Faye interrupted the moment she had achieved her purpose. "What I'm saying is that once an undoubtedly *manly* man like the RSM is seen doing something as apparently effeminate as making a rug, it's like prison doors opening and they're all at it. But why not before? What is it about men in gangs that they have to become ... well, you know, like a pack of dogs?"

They went up the corridor to the officers' dormitory, leaving two piles of sheets behind for the maids to deal with. Jennifer peeped into the room first, to make sure it was unoccupied. "Speaking of manly NCOs," she said, closing the door and lowering her voice, "I think Corporal Walters knows something about Mister Silk. D'you remember our outing to Gurnard's Head — when I went and ate sandwiches with the men?"

"You missed a jolly good spread, you giddy ass!"

"Never mind that. The conversation naturally turned to Silk and his grand gesture and ... I can't remember the exact words, but someone spoke about his being a proper toff and so on. And I'm as sure as can be that Walters was about to disagree but then he saw me looking at him and, for some reason, changed his mind. I'd *love* to know what he might have said."

"But how could Walters ... I mean, they're even in different regiments, foot and horse."

"But Walters's parents live in Windsor. I looked up his next-of-kin in his papers. And Windsor is next door to Eton, where Silk went."

Faye grinned as all sorts of possibilities opened up. "Perhaps he thought you'd take it amiss."

"But why, for heaven's sake?"

"Perhaps he thought you and Silk were beginning to spark — after your long *tête-à-tête* with him."

"*Long tête-à-tête!*" Jennifer echoed scornfully. "Five minutes at the outside. These sheets are black! Whose bed is this?"

Faye looked at the ticket over the bedhead. "Lord Hall's. We might have guessed. An aristocrat who won't wash! I'm surprised the others don't take him out for a regimental scrubbing. They jolly well would do if he was an OR."

"Anyway," Jennifer went on, "Silk spent a jolly sight longer than five minutes with you. After the picnic. Don't think I didn't notice! What were you talking about?"

Faye hesitated, which told Jennifer all she wanted to know. Then the girl drew a deep breath and said, "Probably the same as he was talking about to you."

They stood upright, frozen in their action, eyes locked, each daring the other to say it first.

It was Jennifer who broke the silence. "Did he say something about being pretty cooled-off in the romance department?"

Faye broke into a broad smile and let out her pent-up breath. "Yes. And all about the headmaster's daughter — how grateful she was?"

Jennifer laughed. "That was rapid promotion! She was only his housemaster's daughter when he spoke to me. Perhaps he thought I wasn't sufficiently impressed."

"And were you — impressed?"

"By the sheer nerve of the man. I told him that Mister Moore and I were, you know, *possibly* going to marry one day — thinking Silk would turn tail and run for cover, especially since he'd just lost one scrap with Barry. But not a bit of it!"

Faye collapsed in a chair and shrieked with laughter, making Jennifer waddle on her knees across the bed to clap a hand over her mouth. "Mrs C-S will hear us!" she warned. Then, when the young woman made an effort and curbed her merriment, she asked point blank, "So did he offer you a sort of tutorial in conjugal relations, too?"

Faye, blinking tears from her eyes, nodded. "The thing is, he was so matter-of-fact — almost blasé — about it … I mean, he made it sound such a trifling choice between yes and no that I almost caught myself saying yes."

She watched her friend closely to see whether this rather ticklish confession raised an echo. Jennifer, who had not been aware of the slightest impulse to respond positively, realized she could not leave poor Faye dangling alone on the limb. "Part of me, yes," she said carefully. "Not that it would ever come to an actual acceptance, of course."

"No, of course not."

"And yet one is bound to be curious."

"And the fact that one couldn't *possibly* feel anything of a tender nature for the man," Faye added. "That's also in his favour. But d'you know what I found most tempting of all?"

"What?"

"He may not have said anything to you about it, but I asked him if he made this generous offer to all and sundry and he said only to pretty girls or something gallànt like that. And then I asked how many said yes."

"And he said one in five!"

Faye looked at her in surprise. "No. One in four! His lies are obviously getting more desperate by the day. It'll be a royal princess and one-in-two by now! He was talking rather earnestly to Ruthie Skewes yesterday. I'll bet he told her one in two!"

Jennifer clapped her hands and laughed with delight at the thought. Then, remembering their duties, she said, "Come on — we're *way* behind with this."

It was the purest sop to conscience, however, for, once these particular floodgates were opened, the reservoir simply had to empty itself.

"It's funny isn't it," Jennifer said as they tackled the next bed with renewed vigour, "but the thought that one wouldn't be the only wicked girl to say yes ... I mean, the thought that you'd be one of many *does* somehow make a difference. All we like sheep!"

"We ought to call his bluff," Faye said, taking up a new tack. "If he really was trying to seduce Ruthie yesterday ... and we don't know who else he's tried — maybe all of us. We ought to ask around."

"And then?"

Faye rolled her eyes while she thought. "Yes!" she shrieked — bringing another warning from Jennifer to keep her voice down. "Next time he takes a bath we could open the vacant-engaged door bolt with a screwdriver, the way Wallis's carpenter showed us to do in an emergency, and all troop in — all of those he's made this offer to — and just line up round the bath and say we're ready!"

Jennifer thought this such a splendid wheeze that she jumped up and down on the spot in her excitement — which gave Faye the chance to pass the warning back where it came from.

After that they raced through the rest of the sheets with the speed they ought to have shown from the outset.

Barry Moore's was the last bed. Naturally, Jennifer folded it more lovingly than the others, which was how she came to notice the discoloration. "Pus?" she asked in horror. "He hasn't complained of an infected wound." She showed the mark to Faye — who blushed and looked away and said, "Jenny! Really!"

Jennifer looked at the stain again and then threw the sheet hastily on the pile. "Golly!" she said.

"That," Faye said slightly pompously, "is what makes any sensible girl think twice about Cardew Silk's oh-so-generous offer. And twice and twice and twice again!"

39 THE SEVEN auxiliaries looked at each other in amazement now that each knew her own scurrilous secret was fully shared by all the others. "Every single one of us?" Sibyl asked. She was especially annoyed because Cardew Silk had told her she was the only one at Medrose whom he'd even consider helping in that way — on consideration of which, after long and careful thought, she had, within the past hour, decided to accept his generous offer. And now Jenny Owen had spoiled it. She had sacrificed her reputation in her own sight, and all for nothing!

It had been a delicate weekend for the two originators of the plot to unmask the Silkworm, as they now called him. Clarrie Barnes and Deirdre Stratton had at first denied the accusation — as they saw it — quite vehemently. But when Marilyn le Grice, the most recent recruit to their company, admitted very loudly that the Silkworm had, indeed, approached her, they belatedly owned up to it, too. It was the manner of Marilyn's confession that changed their minds.

"The effrontery of the man!" she sneered. "As if one needed *tuition* in that particular area of life!"

The others all gaped at her.

"You mean," Faye said hesitantly, "you've actually ... you know ... *done* it?"

"Of course not!" She was not outraged, just dismissive.

"What's it like?" Ruth asked.

Marilyn stared around at six pairs of eagerly focused eyes. "I haven't!" she insisted.

"Well, then," Jennifer spoke for them all. "What d'you mean one doesn't need tuition? How d'you know?"

"Who taught you to breathe? Who teaches cows or bitches or hens ... or female bluebottles, for that matter, to do it? Yet we've all seen them *at* it, haven't we? The gall of that man — I tell you, I very nearly hit him. I'd like to teach *him* a lesson. And not in his favourite subject, either, but a lesson in humility."

"Ah!" Faye's eyes lit up and she went on to explain the scheme she and Jennifer had hatched the previous Friday, with just that aim in view.

Marilyn caught the drift of it before Faye was half way there but, rather than interrupt, she went over to the notice board, where a copy of the week's bath rota was pinned. "It's tonight!" she called out as soon as Faye had finished explaining her idea to the others. They were all a little nervous, of course, but if everyone took a part, it would be different. "He's down for nine o'clock," Marilyn added.

"Half-past-eight now," Jennifer said, tucking her watch away again.

The header tank above the hot-water cylinders began to chirp and burble. They were in a cupboard in the ironing room next door, separating the auxiliaries' dormitory from that of the maidservants. But since the walls in the attic were only plaster on a common stud, the tank and cylinders might as well have been in the room.

"That could be him now," Ruth said. "Starting early."

"Or one of the scullery maids drawing a sink of washing-up water," Sibyl pointed out.

"But the officers' bathroom has a geyser," Jennifer reminded them.

"Ha!" Marilyn clapped her hands. "And its chimney goes up through our bathroom. We can feel when it gets warm. Bags I!"

She skipped down the passage to their bathroom, which was right at the end.

"I'm supposed to be helping Mrs C-S prepare for the brigadier's homecoming." Jane looked at her watch again. "But I wouldn't miss this for worlds."

"Her husband?" Clarrie asked.

"Who else?" Ruth sneered.

"Well, there are lots of other brigadiers — at least half a dozen at Western Command alone."

"When is he due?" Ruth asked Jennifer.

"The end of this week — so far as anything is certain in this war. It could be next month, for all we know. 'Expect me when you see me,' his telegram said."

"Anyway," Deirdre sought to pour on a little oil, "whenever he may be coming, it's not an official inspection or anything like that — thank heavens!"

"Well — yes and no," Jennifer said carefully. "It's not an official war office inspection, true, but in a way it's even worse."

And she went on to explain what a struggle Millicent had had to turn Medrose into a convalescent home. "You've no idea how petty those two men were — her husband and her son. Just because they were putting their all into the war, they expected her to sit like Penelope and ..."

"Douglas Colston-Smart?" Deirdre asked scornfully. "What's *he* doing towards winning the war?"

"A lot," Jennifer responded. "China clay goes into lots of things apart from porcelain, you know — poultices for wounds, cocoa drinks, bread, ammunition. And many a railway is laid on chips of Cornish granite."

"China clay in cocoa?" Sibyl asked, holding her stomach as if about to be sick.

"Gives it that creamy thickness. You ask Mister Colston-Smart. He'll amaze you with all the things that use china clay."

"I think he's ever so good-looking," Faye confessed shyly.

"So does he!" Sibyl told her. "When I was fourteen I had the most idiotic pash on him and he was so beastly to me. I'll never forgive him."

"He didn't know what to do — at that age," Jennifer said. "You mustn't be so ..."

Faye giggled. "That's because he wasn't a dog or a tom-cat — or a male bluebottle ... all those things Marilyn said!"

They all laughed rather nervously at this reminder of what excitements lay in store that evening.

"If he doesn't start to bath soon," Jennifer said, "I'll have to miss it."

"You're just trying to get out of it," Sibyl accused her.

"All right!" Jennifer's tone was challenging. "I'll stay. I'll go with you. And then see what Mrs C-S says when she finds out why I was so late! It'd be much better for you if I were keeping her occupied."

"That's true," Ruth admitted grudgingly. "Still — the more the merrier, you know."

However, Marilyn came dancing back at that moment, crying, "He's there! He's there! I heard him light the geyser and then I went down to the half-landing and peeped and I saw him go in — bare legs under his dressing gown — so he's already ..."

"You're sure it was him? They do swop bath rotas among themselves."

"No one else has a red and black silk dressing gown like that!" Marilyn said confidently.

"They borrow each other's dressing gowns, too."

"Ah, but *I* manicured his feet today. I'd know those pale, spindly shanks anywhere!"

"It's *pedicure* if it's feet," Sibyl pointed out.

"Look!" Marilyn was exasperated. "He's down there. Take my word for it. All pink and ready in his birthday suit. So are *we* ready?" She held up a screwdriver and repeated, with a different emphasis: "I mean, are we *ready!*"

There was a nervous licking of lips and canvassing of each other's eyes.

"I need to plant a sweet pea," Deirdre said.

"No time for that," Marilyn snapped. "Put a cork in it."

"You are awful," Sibyl told her, but even she laughed.

"What could men put in it?" Ruth whispered to Jennifer as they followed Marilyn, their undoubted leader in this escapade, down the stairs on tiptoe.

"Propelling-pencil lead?" she suggested.

"A birthday-cake candle," Faye added to an explosion of giggles — swamped by a chorus of shushes, mostly from the gigglers.

"I shall never look at either propelling pencils or birthday cakes in the same light again," Ruth complained as they reached the foot of the stairs. They gazed about them uncertainly.

"Ask a stupid question ..." Sibyl sneered.

Everybody said shush again.

And in a fair imitation of silence they glided along the corridor to the bathroom, where their quarry lay all relaxed and unsuspecting in a tubful of sudsy lather.

It all happened rather quickly.

Marilyn used the screwdriver to open the indicator bolt and pushed the door open just as Jennifer glanced behind them — and saw to her horror that a fully dressed Cardew Silk was standing watching them — and with a matching expression of horror on *his* face.

Without even pausing to think she turned again and thrust her way past a bewildered Marilyn. Accosting the stranger in the bath, she cried, "And what is the meaning of *this?*"

The others fled, leaving her and Marilyn alone with ... well, Jennifer had seen enough photographs of the brigadier to know him at once. But still she pretended not to.

"I ... I ..." he spluttered, sitting up to force his nether half beneath the foam. "I could ask the same of you!"

"You're new," she said, slightly mollified. "But that's no excuse. The others should have told you. There is to be *no* swapping of bath times without letting one of us know. How can we keep good order and military discipline here otherwise?"

"But I ..." he tried again and then gave up. "Millicent!" he bawled at the top of his voice.

"You've got no discipline at all," Jennifer scolded. "What are you? Cavalry, I shouldn't wonder. You're the worst."

"Millicent!"

"Still, I suppose we'd better scrub you now we're here. Come on le Grice. Give a hand here."

The brigadier looked at her in amazement. "Le Grice?" he asked. "Little Marilyn? Oh, my God!"

And he buried his head between his knees and submitted to having his back scrubbed rather vigorously by the two harpies who had so importunately invaded his privacy.

"Brigadier?" A scandalized-sounding Marilyn pretended to recognize him at last.

But it was too late. For the second time in as many minutes a voice boomed from the door: "And what, pray, is the meaning of *this?*"

"It's none of my doing, dear, I do assure you," her husband boomed from between his knees. "Could you call your two wardresses off ...?"

She strode across the bathroom and snatched the brushes from them. "I'll speak to you later," she said.

The voice was cool enough but the glance that went with it would have silenced enemy guns.

40 EACH GIRL swore on her honour — the very commodity Cardew Silk had sought to compromise — it was not she who let the cat out of the bag. Nonetheless, it was inevitable that the word should get abroad somehow, and, by the following afternoon, the Silkworm had been posted on to another, unspecified, convalescent home. He was accompanied, no doubt, by suitable cautions to its matron. Jennifer had to apologize to the brigadier, not for invading his privacy but for giving him the impression that the auxiliaries at Medrose were in the habit of scrubbing the backs of officers in the bath. He managed to keep a straight face while she did so.

"He's much nicer than his son," she told Faye afterward.

Faye was still miffed at the way Marilyn had taken over the bathroom escapade, even though Jennifer explained it was a jolly good thing the brigadier had recognized her, otherwise he might have gone into a rage and anything could have happened.

"It was your quick thinking saved the day," Faye said, unwilling to give Marilyn credit for any part of it.

"My dear, I didn't think at all! That was pure instinct. If I'd thought about it for one second, I'd simply have turned tail and run — honestly. But you really shouldn't be peeved at Marilyn, you know. She didn't *mean* to shoulder us aside."

Faye looked all about her and, lowering her voice, said, "I'll tell you who *is* peeved at what's happened — Sibyl McLaren. I think she'd already decided to ... how to put it? Climb into the Silkworm's cocoon."

"No!" Jennifer grinned and stared, wide eyes to wide eyes. "How d'you know? Has she said anything?"

"Not to me. It's just her general surliness. Also, she asked Mrs C-S if the Silkworm had been sent far away."

"Oh, I know the answer to that," Jennifer said carelessly.

"You? How?"

"Ah, that'd be telling."

"Oh, go on — please!"

"Why do *you* want to know?" Jennifer asked archly. "Still thinking over his offer, are we?"

"No!"

"Then why the sudden blush on the tips of your ears?"

"I don't know. The cold. It's just nice to know things that other people don't — especially when Mrs C-S has taken such pains to stop us finding out. Anyway, why did *you* want to know, eh? You must have done or you wouldn't have bothered finding out."

"It's very simple. I keep the records of all the ambulance trips. The driver left out the destination on his worksheet — on instructions — but he did put in the mileage. Thirty miles there and back. Now you tell me where the Silkworm's gone. Isn't it funny — I haven't the slightest interest in knowing the answer ... I mean, not *personal* interest, you understand — not while Barry's here. But the minute *they* try to prevent us from finding out, I can't rest until I've discovered the secret. Rather symbolic, what!"

"You mean ... the other thing — the Big Secret."

"Yes. Anyway, now you know where he's gone."

"Camborne-Redruth? You're sure it couldn't be Helston?"

"That'd be only twenty-six miles, even if he drove the long way round through Carleen. But you know the biggest joke of all?"

"What?"

"You know where the convalescent home in Redruth is?"

"No."

"At Little Sinns! It's the one that's run by the Quakers."

Faye stared at her in amazement. "Not the home for wayward girls?"

"Yes!" She laughed delightedly. "Of course, they moved the girls to Truro in 1912, but that's the building. *Also* rather symbolic, what! Think of the Silkworm lying there in a dormitory that once slept two dozen wayward girls! He'll go out of his mind."

The following day she and Faye had split duty, with the afternoon off. It was Jennifer's habit on such days to go home and help her mother with the housework. They had a daily who came in to do the cleaning and the laundry but that still left the ironing and mending, to say nothing of cooking and general repairs. That particular Tuesday being cold and fine, she decided to screw steel angles across the corners of the downstairs sash windows, which were getting a bit wobbly. Faye asked if she might come along.

The Carminowes had a small country estate over to Perranarworthal, on the western side of the Devoran river valley. Her father, Colonel Carminowe, was — or in peace time had been — master of the local hunt. Faye had only ever visited houses like the Owens' in the way of charity, when one of the deserving poor fell ill or on hard times. She was not so tactless as to say so but her eager curiosity almost said it for her. She stood on the threshold and peeped gingerly within, rather as a child might explore a new play house.

"No goblins," Jennifer assured her with some amusement. "D'you think you'd be any good with a putty knife."

Faye watched in surprise as her friend opened her late father's toolbox and laid out a gimlet, a screwdriver, a dozen brass screws, four steel corner braces, some putty wrapped in oilcloth, and the aforementioned putty knife. "Don't you think you should get in a little man to do that?" she asked.

"That's what I meant by 'no goblins,' really," Jennifer replied. "What you call a *little* man would charge very *little* under tenpence an hour. Besides, there's no art to it."

Watched by an admiring Faye she set about the first window. She pinned the brace with her thumb, marked the four screw holes with the point of the gimlet, routed the holes with vigorous twists, and almost fell backwards when she jerked the last one out.

"You do it like a real workman!" Faye said.

Jennifer basked in what she took for praise until her friend added, "You even make the same sort of mess on the carpet!"

"Oh ... yes. Well, I'll clear up after me." She put the brace against the frame and slipped the first screw into its prepared hole.

"They all say that! Who taught you to do this?"

"No one. I just watched one of Wallis's men patching up the conservatory lights with some of these things. It's hardly one of your mystery crafts!"

When she'd finished the first brace Faye asked, "What was that you said about putty?"

Jennifer took her outside, leaned a step ladder against the window sill, and showed her how to rake out the decayed bits between the glass and the frame — also how to prime the exposed gaps with thinned-out red-lead paint and spread the fresh putty with the knife. "If it was our own house, we'd do it properly. We'd rake it all out, but since the landlord's too mean to pay for anything, we'll just do the minimum that will get us through the winter."

"It's jolly spiffing fun, isn't it," Faye said after a while, speaking through the partly opened window. "My mother would have a fit if she could see me now."

"D'you really think so?" Jennifer responded. "I suppose I could say the same about mine, except I don't think she would. Our parents' generation has changed more than we have, because of the war. Even to each other. Molly Pengilly was telling me this morning that the brigadier would never have taken the changes at Medrose so calmly back in the old days — and she's been with them since she was twelve."

"That's because he can see how it's changed her, Mrs C-S. Before the war she was either rushing madly about with some fatuous bee in her bonnet, poking her nose into everything, or she was languishing at death's door with an illness that kept the entire household in thrall. The only reason my mother let me take up this work was — apart from the fact that Lady Cleer as good as blackmailed her into saying yes — was to let me see such appalling behaviour at first hand. Talking of hands, does this stuff wash off one's fingers?"

"Turps gets it off. We've got some rubber gloves somewhere."

"No, I like the smell. You'd almost think you could eat it."

Jennifer finished the other lower corner and said that Faye was going to have to excuse the view of her boots for about ten minutes because she was going to do the top corners next. But Faye told her two could play at that game and, climbing up the ladder, said, "Boo!" through the gap at the top.

They worked away as before, chatting all the while. When they moved on to the next window Faye said, "You know what you told me this morning, about not being interested in the Silkworm's kind offer — not while Barry Moore is around …?"

"Yes …" Jennifer responded cautiously.

"Did you mean … well, what *did* you mean?"

"What did you think I meant?"

Faye gulped audibly and said, "Golly!"

"D'you think that's dreadful?"

"I think it's dangerous. You know the reputation he has — and his father before him."

"The Ludgvan Bull, yes. But Barry has changed. Anyway, I'm tired of talking about it and wondering about it and giggling about it and ... not *knowing*. Besides, he's being posted back to France next week."

"To the front?"

"No, his brigade is in training. He'll be on rear-echelon duties until the spring at least — thank heavens. He'll be quite near his cousin Rosalind as a matter of fact."

Faye caught the slight edge in her voice and said, "Oh? Was there ever anything there?"

"Nothing serious, I think, not on his side, anyway."

"And hers?"

Jennifer shrugged.

"Still — even something frivolous can turn into something serious in the stress of war."

"Oh — for this relief much thanks!"

"Sorry." Faye smiled penitently. "Only pointing out the obvious. And d'you think one way to hold him might be ... you know? I don't think that ever works, actually."

"I was thinking of completing my training at the hospital and then applying to go over and join her."

Faye gazed at her in a disbelief that was more jovial than surprised. "Really!" she said.

"It was just an idea," Jennifer admitted. "And then as soon as I think I've made up my mind I have a complete reaction against it. I think, why *should* I reorder my entire life for his sake, and why ..."

"For *his* sake?" Faye echoed in amazement.

"All right — for the sake of being near him."

"And her — Rosalind. Is that Rosalind Collett?"

"Yes, the photographer's daughter."

"Oh, I've met her — blonde girl ... strikingly handsome. I didn't know her socially, though."

Jennifer laid down her screwdriver and gazed at her in a show of despair. "If you've any more comfort to offer, dear, just pour it all over me here where I stand!"

Faye laughed and blew her a kiss. "Sorry again. Just ..."

"I know — just stating the obvious. Anyway, I think why should I upset the course of my life just to be near him? And her."

After a moment's thought Faye said, "The real question is, '*What* course would it be upsetting?' Does your life have a course at all?"

Jennifer nodded, closed her eyes, and hung her head.

"Don't take it to heart so," Faye went on. "I only ask because it's very much on *my* mind too these days. What course does *my* life have?"

Now it was Jennifer's turn to look amazed. "But you're an heiress in your own right, aren't you?"

"Just so — but that's not exactly a *course* in life, is it! I'll inherit my grandmother's fortune when I'm twenty-five — or earlier if I get married."

"May one ask ...?" Jennifer said delicately.

"The will was probated so it's no secret. Fifty thou' in the funds plus a house in Westmoreland and another in Eaton Square."

Jennifer whistled between her teeth.

"You are funny," Faye said.

"In what way?"

"When the rest of us were paralyzed with fright to see the Silkworm standing there — and us wondering who on earth we'd just burst in upon — you go charging in without a qualm. No panic, no hesitation. One would think you're the most determined and self-reliant person *ever*. But when it's something really big and important — like what to do about the rest of your life ... Nothing! Just dither."

Having no real answer to this, Jennifer stared at her in dismay. "Thank heavens you're my *friend*, Faye," she said at length. "God knows what you'd say about me if you weren't. And don't tell me you're just stating the obvious."

"Even though I am doing precisely that!"

"So what d'you think I should do? Volunteer for France?"

"Heavens, no! Volunteer to be a film star!"

Jennifer was both disappointed and impatient. "They'd never take me. That's just a silly pipe-dream."

"Oh, sorry, I didn't know you'd already tried. What did they say when they turned you down?"

Jennifer just looked at her wearily and said, "Ha ha!"

"If you don't at least try, you'll never know."

"And what do I live on while I'm trying?"

"Your wits. Of which you have plenty. You could do evening waitressing, couldn't you? Washing up? Make sandwiches in those all-night canteens? There'd be dozens of things if you only looked. If it's *really* a question of money, I'll lend you fifty quid — which is little enough to me. And you can repay me if you succeed."

"Oh ... Faye ... look — I didn't mean to ..." Jennifer stammered.

"Yes, yes — okay — take all that as read. My point is it's not the lack of oof that's holding you back, is it!"

Jennifer felt trapped. "If I were less happy in what I'm doing ... if it weren't for Barry ... you know — I don't want to upset the applecart." After a pause she added, "What if I fail?"

"You won't. And *that's* pointing out the obvious, too!"

"But *if* I do? I could never repay fifty quid."

"Oh yes, you could. Keep a diary of everything that happens — all the people you see — what they're like — what they try to tell you — all the false starts — the charlatans — everything. Let me read it when you come back. It'd be worth fifty to me. God, you've no idea how lucky you are *not* being an heiress!"

For reply Jennifer kissed a fingertip, reached the hand out through the slit of a window opening, and planted it on her friend's brow.

"So!" Faye went on. "When's the big day? When are you going to let Barry Moore have his wicked way with you?"

"Aargh!" Jennifer pretended to scream. "I thought you meant the really big day — you know, going to London."

"Well, we both know you're never going to do that! I meant the *other* big day. When will it be?"

Jennifer shook her head in amused exasperation. "I don't know. Before he goes back to France, obviously. And then again it may never happen." When she saw that Faye was about to press her again she added, "I'll keep a diary on *that,* if you like. How much would it be worth to you?"

Faye never replied because at that moment a voice from the street said, "'Allo, 'allo, 'allo — what have we here, ladies?"

Faye spun round, Jennifer craned to look past her — and there at the gate stood Corporal Walters.

"Come in and have a cup of tea," Jennifer called out. "Give us the benefit of your experience." To Faye she added, "He was a carpenter and joiner before the war."

Walters needed no second invitation. "Did the length of the prom in eight minutes today," he announced as he entered. "I'll win the war single-handed if I don't watch myself. Ah!" His eyes fell on Jennifer's handiwork. "I thought that's what you were doing. Did you cramp those sashes before you put on the braces?"

"Cramp?" Jennifer asked uncertainly.

"It's all right. You don't *need* a cramp, not if you offset the screw holes an eighth of an inch. That'll pull the cheeks in, as the dentist said to the dowager." He laughed. "You didn't do that, either, did you."

Jennifer shook her head. "Does it do any harm?"

"Not exactly harm. It just makes the sashes difficult to move." He tugged at one, which moved with jerky reluctance. "Like that."

"Oh!" Jennifer slumped in a chair. "And my mother was going to be so proud of me!"

"It's all right," Walters replied confidently. "There's probably enough paint on these to sink a dreadnought. Lend us that driver."

He took the screwdriver and prised out the sash divider, which, in turn, enabled him to pull the sash clear of its frame. He wedged a couple of screws between the sash cord and its housing, trapping the weights at the top. Then, rummaging through the toolbox, he produced a coarse rasp, with which he began filing away at the edges of the sash.

A shower of paint flakes and sawdust fell to the carpet. Jennifer and Faye exchanged glances, which he caught in the corner of his eye. "Lucky someone else made such a mess here before me," he remarked. "Is there any danger of being handed a cup of tea, as the Irishman said?"

The kettle was already mewing at the back of the stove. It needed only a minute on the gas to bring it to the boil. By the time the two women returned with the pot and some jam sandwiches, he had the sashes back in place and moving freely again. Then he showed them what he meant by offsetting the gimlet holes so that the screws would draw the sides of the frames inward — so that they'd get it right next time.

"Well!" Jennifer said as she passed him his cup. "I suppose the lower decks are full of the Mister Silk affair?"

"Well, miss ..." He scratched his neck diffidently.

Faye guessed correctly at the cause of his discomfort. "It's true," she said. "To spare your blushes — it's true — about the offer he made to all the auxiliaries."

To their surprise, Walters shook his head and laughed. "Wouldn't you know it!" he murmured.

Jennifer decided to grasp the bull by the horns. "Come on, Walters," she said, "you know something about that man. You almost blurted it out that day at Gurnard's Head. You might as well tell us now. He's gone and it can't do him any more harm than he's already done himself."

The man looked at her shrewdly. "I knew you seen it, miss. I knew you was going to ask it sooner or later."

"Well, I've asked it later rather than sooner. Why — would sooner have been better?"

He shrugged. "I suppose the result would have been the same. The thing is — you know how he claimed he went to Eton?"

"You mean he didn't? I *knew* it!" Faye began.

But he cut her short. "In a way he did, miss — the same Eton as what I went to, which was the board school — the elementary, that is. Not the board*ing* school, or the college, as we call it. We was in the same class, him and me. He never recognized me but I'd have knowed him anywhere."

"But where did he acquire that accent?" Jennifer asked. "It was *so* upper class — didn't you think so?" She turned to Faye, who nodded reluctant agreement.

Walters chuckled. "That's old Charlie for you — that's his proper name, by the way — Charlie Shortis. Gawd knows where he got 'Cardew Silk' from!"

"Same initials," Faye pointed out. "C and S — criminals often do that, I've read."

"Is he a criminal?" Jennifer asked excitedly.

"Next best thing," Walters told her. "He's an actor. That's how he does all them accents. He can do any accent you want — always could do. I saw him once fool a bunch of Scotch lads that he was Scotch, too. Never been near the place but he just listened to them a few minutes and then he could come right out with it. Amazing."

"But the money," Faye objected. "The hamper from Fortnum and Mason ... the taxi ... none of it was cheap."

"Ah ... well ..." Walters was uncomfortable again. "There was a number of rich old ladies up Lunnon town who was, shall we say, very appreciative of his attentions. Say no more. Also, he's acted in a couple of films — *Nights in Araby* was one. And *The Man in the Moon.* I never saw them myself but they say he was good. Anyway, I don't believe Charlie Shortis lacks for the readies. But you can see why I didn't want to queer his pitch, I hope, miss?" he asked Jennifer. "Him and me coming from the same school and all — and him doing such a good job of fooling all those other officers."

"Not to mention the army itself," Faye put in. "But surely the Tenth Hussars look very carefully into people's backgrounds, even in wartime. Or perhaps it's different when there's an emergency on?"

"He's got a very persuasive tongue," he said. Then, seeing the glance the two women exchanged, he added tactfully, "Well, I mean, in some directions, anyway."

The conversation turned to more mundane matters and then Walters left them. They stayed on to wait for Goronwy and the younger Owens to come home for their tea.

"What a saga!" Faye commented when they were alone again.

"It makes me wish I'd got to know him better," Jennifer replied.

41 IN CORNWALL every day is a lottery with the weather. You can get snowfalls in June, whereas in winter, in the middle of a week of hard frosts, there may be an odd day when you can go about in short sleeves. The end of the third week in that November brought just such a day; following a frost on Thursday and a Friday of blustery drizzle, Saturday dawned calm and clear. The sky was as crowded and restless as the Cornish landscape itself, with bright, pastel-coloured clouds hanging like tattered drapes in disorderly ranks, the most distant of which seemed to lie far above and beyond the sea horizon.

Jennifer stood at the hillcrest, a couple of hundred yards beyond the Medrose gates, waiting anxiously for the first sight of Barry in his parents' gig. She did not want anybody — especially Faye — to see her going off with him and then go and snigger her secrets to the others. She had been on night duty since Thursday and ought to be asleep in bed by now, but that was, of course, impossible. Today was, after all, their last day together before he returned to France ... their last chance ...

No! It was fatal to start thinking like that. She set her mind resolutely against such thoughts. The war had given the word 'last' a double finality, adding dread to mere nostalgia.

First, then?

But she did not want to think of firsts, either. Both words — last and first — pulled events out of their proper context. They interrupted the smooth flow of life. They distorted experience. *I might as well marvel that this is the first time I ever stood at this corner on a November Saturday!* she told herself. It was absolutely true but what of it? If you lived life properly, *every* event — no matter how new, unique, unprecedented, et cetera — should be like that. Nothing should be plucked out of it and made special.

Certainly, things that hadn't even happened yet — and might never happen, either — should not be made special.

Though the air was balmy, the ground still held the proper cold of winter and she had to march on the spot to revive the circulation to her toes. Why was he so late? She looked at her watch again. He wasn't late. Her watch had stopped. She held it to her ear. It hadn't stopped, either.

And there he was! Coming from Gulval whereas she had expected him to come up the hill from Chyandour. They'd *see* him from Medrose! She tried to signal to him to duck low as he passed but he thought she was simply waving a greeting. Then she remembered the thick belt of cypresses beside the road and relaxed again. For all of five seconds.

"Don't get down," she called out as he drew near. "I'm quite capable."

In fact, she trotted toward the gig and, with a skip and a jump, flung herself in the seat beside him, putting her arms about him and hugging him as if life depended on it.

Laughing, he started to turn the gig around on the proverbial sixpence.

"No!" she cried, sitting up again and tugging the reins in the contrary direction. "Let's go down to Chyandour. Don't go past Medrose again."

"Why not?"

"Because. To humour me."

"Yes, O my mistress." His voice was laden with martyrdom but he did as she bade.

"Someone will see us if we go that way," she explained.

"They've seen us together before." He turned the horse down the hill toward the seafront.

Contented at last, she took his arm and hugged herself against it, wondering if the soft pressure of her breast upon the back of his arm stirred him.

"The weather's going to be kind to us," he said.

"Are your parents expecting us for lunch?" she asked.

He grinned and nodded his head backward. There, nestling in the body of the gig, she saw a battered old picnic hamper. "D'you know what Time is?" he asked.

"About ten past ten."

"No. Time with a capital T. Time is the only thing that stops you bumping into yourself along roads like this — roads you travel frequently."

She considered his words and then laughed. "You're right. I never thought of it like that. Suppose you *could* bump into yourself, though. Think of all the pitfalls that lie ahead — that you could warn yourself about. 'Don't take that place at Medrose!' Or, 'Do take that place at Medrose!' Or, 'Don't muddle the medicines next Friday, you idiot!'"

"Did you?"

"I gave Private West cascara instead of cough mixture, poor man!"

Barry laughed. "Still, it would work. I'll bet he *daren't* cough today!"

She dug him in the ribs and told him he was awful.

"It wouldn't just be our own selves we'd meet," he pointed out. "We'd meet each other, too, if Time didn't keep us apart. Jennifer of 1917 might meet Barry of 1914, who remembers her only as a beautiful half-child-half-woman. What does she tell him?"

"Especially if Barry of 1919 is standing nearby to contradict her! And all the other Barrys and Jennifers, past, present, and future. It'd be worse than the Tower of Babel. Besides ..."

"Hang on," he interrupted. "Would a future self be wise to offer any sort of counsel at all? They wouldn't be all-seeing gods. They might know that this or that choice was a mistake but the alternative might have been even worse and they wouldn't know that. A future Jennifer might bump into you now and say, 'You were a fool not to try that career in films.' But all she'd really be saying is that your choice of staying here at Medrose didn't work out too well. She couldn't possibly know what a career in films might have done to you. It might have done things that would make life at Medrose seem a very heaven. See what I mean?"

She hugged his arm tighter and leaned her head against his shoulder, not caring who saw her now, as long as it wasn't Faye or one of the other girls. "What put such thoughts into your mind?" she asked.

He took a deep breath and exhaled until he slumped. "The uncertainty hanging over us all, of course," he replied. "The way a whizzbang can fall out of the blue with one's name on it. I was thinking what wouldn't I give for a crystal ball to see my own future in? Then I realized the grim truth. I could step out of the path of that whizzbang — and walk smack into a sniper's bullet."

"But the crystal ball could show you that, too — if it was a good, British-made one, of course."

"So I avoid the bullet only to take a piece of shrapnel. I escape that, only to put my foot on a mine ... It's like chess. One can only see three or four moves ahead."

"I think it's best not to look ahead at all," she said firmly. "Just give the future the best guess you can and meanwhile live each moment to the full. That's my philosophy."

"Hedonism," he said. "Eat, drink, and be merry for tomorrow we die."

"Good thing you brought the hamper!" Her gaze flitted hither and thither over the bay, for they were now at the foot of the hill and turning left toward the edge of town. "And I'm glad there isn't another Jennifer in sight to wag a finger at me and utter warnings like the Three Witches."

Now that they were on level ground he urged the horse to a trot. They bowled along, talking happily of this and that, until she suddenly noticed they had taken the St Ives road, which was not the direct road to his part of Ludgvan.

He saw the fact register with her and said, "Have you ever been to Chysauster? I thought we might go there."

The name rang the faintest of bells. She shook her head.

"It's an almost intact village from the Iron Age." He pointed northward, into the hills. "They lived in stone huts shaped like giant beehives but now it's just the foundations — low stone walls in little circles and grassy humps. Your Mrs C-S and her band of nuts did some digging there before the war — looking for Celtic gold." He laughed. "They soon discovered what any farm hand could tell them about digging — it makes you aware of muscles you didn't even know you had."

"Is that where we're heading?"

"No one goes there in November," he said. "And the remains of the walls are just about high enough to screen one perfectly." He leaned his head down to touch hers and nuzzle her scalp gently. "From any stray breeze, I mean," he added.

They left the horse with Eric Polglaze, who farmed the land at the foot of Chysauster hill and who knew the Moores well — well enough to give Barry a solemn wink as he led the horse away.

The path to the ancient settlement led steeply up around the headlands of two fields, which meant that there were three hedges to clamber over as well. There were no drains, so a long, linear pond of rainwater had collected on the uphill side of the middle hedge; but Barry set down the hamper, straddled it, and lifted her over as if she were thistledown. She relished his strength, the firmness of his grip, the limber ease of his action.

The village had been built on the southwest-facing flank of the valley, not quite at the hillcrest but high enough to offer a splendid view over Penzance and the coastline from Newlyn down to Mousehole — far more spectacular than the one from the gazebo at Medrose, whose domed roof could just be seen, nestling among patchwork fields and woods below.

Barry went directly to the largest of the dwellings, where he laid the hamper down with a sigh of relief. Jennifer turned round to see him in silhouette against the sky, stretching his aching arms toward the watery sun. "Primitive man!" she called out. "Do you live here, pray?"

He beat his chest like an ape. "I live here *and* prey," he responded with a voice full of menace.

"Don't you pray on your knees like a good Christian?"

"No! I prey on all primitive maidens who pass this way — and there's nothing Christian about it!"

"Eek! Help, somebody!" She crammed her fingers in her mouth and stared at him in terror.

He laughed. "Come and look at this."

She abandoned the game and went to join him. As she drew near he went down on one knee. She assumed it was for another game, one more chivalrous this time, but he said, "See this stone?"

It was a large, flat boulder, level with the grass at what must have been the front door — indeed, the only door — to the house. It was flanked by low walls that would have formed a lobby or passage into the circular living space beyond.

"The threshold?" she guessed.

"More than that. They used to keep a little fire burning here — kept alive by embers from the main fire in there. It purified all who entered and it stopped evil spirits from sneaking in on their coat tails — or whatever clothing they wore."

"How d'you know?" she asked warily.

"They still do it in some parts of the world. Shall we make a fire?"

"Oh? D'you think we need purifying?"

"Well, I could do with a purifying draught of tea."

During the previous summer there had been a heath fire on the moorland above the village. The furze and ling were beginning to regrow but there was still plenty of half-burned wood, sun-bleached and dry, ready for kindling. Within ten minutes they had a merry blaze going, not on the threshold stone but in what would have been the main hearth of the dwelling. Shortly after that the water in the billy-can began to sing and give out muffled little explosions.

"Doesn't it make your hair stand on end?" he asked, reaching his hands toward the blaze. "Fifteen centuries ago there were people sitting here, exactly where we're sitting now, and there was a fire burning here" — he leaned forward and touched the hearth with a reverence that was almost religious — "on this actual bit of stone. I mean this ... this ..." He touched the stone again and then words failed him. He shivered. "Don't you think it's ... awesome?"

She shivered, too, borrowing something of his sense of wonder.

"And it's not just *any* ancient people. They were our ancestors, the original Cornish, who built this deserted village. Some small drop of their blood is surely running around inside you and me even now! We have an ancient claim to these stones, this hearth, this sky." He grinned at her. "Blood and territory, eh — how they *grip!*"

"We're home," she said.

"Home," he echoed, reaching out both hands toward her.

She moved the billy-can to the side of the fire and went to him. "Yes," she said. "Now!"

42 HE ATE as he had made love — eagerly and yet savouring each morsel or moment. She watched him eating as part of her, shocked by the novelty of it all, had watched him making love to her. No, that wasn't quite right, she realized. Part of her had watched the pair of them making love. It was weird. It was like nothing she had ever imagined and yet it had felt like something she had always known.

Perhaps it was that drop of ancient Cornish blood in her veins, which must have known dozens, if not hundreds, of such couplings to have survived down the centuries like that.

Also the way the pleasure had possessed her, from her scalp to her toenails ... that was something she had not expected. And the way it lingered on in her shoulders and hips, where the bones of her limbs joined to her body; it was the sort of delicious relaxing pleasure you get when you wake up after a sound night's sleep and stretch as hard as you can, only it went on and on. It was like a solo hymn to youth and vigour.

"Are my legs bandy now?" she asked, pressing her skirt down hard between them.

"Why?" He gave a baffled laugh. "Honestly, I never know what you'll come out with next."

"Sally Pask once told me you could always tell a woman who'd done it because her knees wouldn't touch together afterwards." She moved her legs together. "Mine still touch. Are you sure you did it properly?"

"Really!" He laughed with embarrassment this time and stared up at the sky.

"Why are you blushing? Are you now ashamed of having done it?"

"Of course not! But ..."

"Well, stop blushing then. Maybe we should do it again, just to make sure there's no shame."

He kissed a fingertip and reached out to touch it to her lips. But she seized it, snarling like an animal, and gnawed at it as if it were a bone.

He let her bite harder and harder until it truly hurt. Then he pulled away and said, "We can't, anyway. Too risky. I only had one of those rubber johnnies."

"You shouldn't have thrown it on the fire then."

"One can't use them twice. That's the most dangerous thing of all."

"I wish you had let me see it. Why didn't you?"

"Yuk!"

She lay back in the dry, yellow grass of winter and closed her eyes.

He ate the core of his apple and dropped the stalk among the embers before he stretched himself out, leaning on his elbows to bring his head just above hers. "Jenny," he murmured.

"Mmm?"

"I love you."

Keeping her eyes closed, she felt for his lips with hers.

He kissed her briefly and went on, "I love you so much I don't know how I'm going to survive even the first hours of our parting, never mind the weeks and months that follow on."

"Shall I help?" she asked.

"How?"

She opened her eyes then and stared deep into his. "There will never, never, *never* be any other man but you. It's going to be hard for me, too, but I'm not even thinking about it yet. We've decided we're living for the moment today, remember?"

"It goes without saying ..." he began.

"No it doesn't," she interrupted him. "You have my absolute permission to say it."

"Well, there will never be anyone for me but you, too. In a way there never has been. I mean, I've always carried that memory of you — hopelessly, as I imagined. But it was always there."

"And what about all those other girls?"

"There weren't all *that* many."

"You've been most careful not to number them while I've known you."

He shrugged, trying to suggest it had all been terribly casual. "Three or four dozen ..."

She sat up, bumping her nose against his in her shock. "But that's ... that's about one a month!"

"One a week sometimes, actually. But look at it like this — it only proves how casual they were, doesn't it!" He brightened as a new line occurred to him. "In a way, I was just keeping in practice, ready for you." He smiled and watched her hopefully.

"For me, eh?" she echoed dubiously. "You mean for what we did just now? You kept in practice for that?"

"Certainly not!"

"Oh! You mean you've *never* done it before? Ha ha!"

"Well ... obviously ..." He looked away uncomfortably.

"With how many of them?"

"Too many," he answered with a sigh.

"Oh! So where does that place me! I'm *one* too many, I suppose?"

"God!" He groaned and rolled away from her. "I'm never going to win, am I — no matter what I say. Suppose I'd said I didn't do it with enough of them? I wish I'd done it with them *all!*"

"And so you do, don't you!"

"Of course — whatever you say. Actually, the reason I wish I'd done it with them all is because, from now on, there's only one love for me and no other woman in all the world is going to get *near* her, in my eyes. So I've missed my chance."

Smiling through a sudden wateriness in her eyes she threw her arms about him and, pulling his face back to hers, said, "You haven't. You can have all the chances you want — as long as you take them with me."

Part Three

New Life after Little Sinns

43 WHEN WAR broke out they said the boys would all be home by Christmas. It had been repeated as a grim joke toward the end of 1914 — 'They meant *next* Christmas, of course.' But when that next Christmas approached it was no longer a joke of any kind. As if to rub it in, on the Sunday before Christmas Day the Germans launched an attack on the Wipers salient with phosgene, a gas far more lethal than chlorine, which both sides had been using up until then. Fortunately Tommy was well equipped with gas masks and well drilled in their use; also the wind was strong that day and the gas soon dissipated. Even so, more than a hundred died and ten times that number were taken ill. And Medrose began to receive a new kind of convalescent — one sound in limb but not in wind, who fought for every breath and needed frequent back-rubs and help through fits of coughing.

There was, too, a more subtle difference between the new breed of wounded Tommies and the earlier crop: They would not talk of the war. Friends, the food, lice, letters from home, the sarn't major ... the perennial topics of soldiers everywhere — yes; but of the war itself, the daily Armageddon of the front line, they said nothing, not even to each other when they might have supposed themselves to be alone.

Jennifer and her fellow auxiliaries understood then that what had been a topic of horror in July — the ultimate horror for most of those men — had now passed beyond the power of words to evoke it, handle it, contain it. The slightly frenetic gaiety of earlier months was replaced by a mood of taciturn grimness, in which Christmas itself made only a temporary, though welcome, dent.

Millicent and Jennifer were still only half way to understanding this change when they planned the seasonal festivities. They reasoned that, since the men could neither go home nor be joined by their families, it was for them, the staff at Medrose, to provide as homelike an atmosphere as possible. Jennifer's younger brothers and sisters were well used to coming up to play among the heroes of Medrose by then, so she got them to select a group of their schoolfriends, all of whom were to be invited to a party on the day after Boxing Day. It was an extra Christmas for them, in effect.

Outwardly it all went down well. The terrace became a pirate ship, manned by half the convalescents, who wore eye patches, spotted bandanas, and brass curtain rings tied to dangle from their ears, and who flourished wicked-looking cutlasses whose plywood blades were hidden beneath silver lacquer. 'Cap'n Flint,' their leader, othertimes known as Gunner Ashley, had his right hand stuck into a bully-beef tin on which he had soldered a porter's hook; with several of his teeth blacked out he struck terror into the heart of every child there, even the blasé fifteen year olds who came with Hector. And Trooper Mitchell, who lost a leg at Loos, was, of course, a natural for Long John Silver. They couldn't find a parrot for his shoulder but everyone agreed that a stuffed pheasant looked much more dignified.

The remaining convalescents were jolly Jack Tars of Nelson's navy. Their task was to board the ship, kill its pirate crew, and take their treasure as a prize. Their first attempt was — naturally — a failure. And so was the second. It was only when 'Admiral Nelson' (who looked suspiciously like Captain Rafferty, RFC) turned in desperation to the children and asked for their help that the pirates were routed at last. They were made to walk the plank, of course, pushed along it by gleeful six-year-old savages of both sexes wielding yard brooms. At the end of the plank, with many a piteous scream and groan, they fell into an ocean of grass and drowned for a brief while.

Then came the hunt for the pirates' treasure, which had been cunningly hidden in two dozen places around the garden, each with its own cryptic clue — and, by the most extraordinary coincidence, there were two dozen children to locate it, each with the help of one convalescent.

Then came tea and cake and jam and jelly, and party hats made by the men, and lucky-dipping into a bran-tub, and shying at an aunt sally, and — for some — the time-honoured ritual of being sick in inconvenient places to cries of, 'Never mind, darling. Dry your eyes. I'll clear it up.'

"Just like home, really," as one of the men said afterwards.

But later still, when Jennifer stumbled upon a solitary Trooper Mitchell, crying his eyes out in the bromeliad grove — from which she retreated hastily before he saw her — she realized that the very meaning of the word 'home' had, for many, changed beyond recognition. For *too* many. The men with the darkness had arrived that year, and it would take more than a jolly children's party to drive them away.

And yet, as people endlessly told one another from the depths of grief, life goes on. The saddest must eventually eat, and must then answer the most trivial questions, like, 'Scrambled or fried?' Farce and tragedy were never more than a whisker apart. Sometimes, indeed, they were hard to *tell* apart. Jennifer did not know whether to laugh or scream in frustration when Douglas buttonholed her early in the new year to say he had more news of baby Moses. They still called him that, though by now he would be six or possibly seven.

"Persistence pays off," he said nervously. There was an unaccustomed hesitancy about him.

"Obviously," she replied. "In some directions, anyway." When he made no reply, she said, "Well?"

"D'you think we might be friends again?" he asked, not looking her in the eye. In fact, the moment the words were out, he turned aside and stared out of the window. It was five o'clock — late in the twilight. "Blackout soon," he murmured to himself.

"I thought we were friends already," she replied.

"Only in the sense that we haven't actually quarrelled. No screaming fits. But you've been pretty distant with me, don't you think?"

"Is that to be wondered at — after what happened in the ..."

"I know, I know!" He held up both hands as if to ward off her speech — and almost as if the word 'gazebo' had scarlet lights all around it. "I was a fool. You cannot know how much I've ..."

"My dear!" She touched his arm so gently he had to look to confirm it. "I was talking about *me*," she added. *"I'm* the fool. I'm the one to be ashamed ..."

"No!" He turned to face her, eyes now alight, and gripped her arms below her shoulders. "That's what I mean. I've been thinking about it ever since — about the appalling way *I* behaved. Like a silly little boy. I was just wondering ..." Uncertainty returned to claim him and he let his arms fall. "D'you think we could possibly begin again where we ... I mean ..." He stumbled to a halt as he saw her shaking her head. "No?"

"Life has moved on since then, Douglas."

"I'll let you call me Dougie!" He laughed to cover his seriousness. "Call me anything you like."

She smiled, grateful for that small relief. "We can still be the most tremendous friends."

"Oh, yes!" he said bitterly.

"I mean really close. I do *like* you. Very much. We can go to dances together, you as my partner. And cycling and stuff like that. I'd really adore it."

"But ... only platonic," he said glumly.

"Why not? I'd love to have a man-*friend* — you know? Someone I could open my heart to and be at ease with because I know there's no ... you know — nothing behind it. Wouldn't you like to have a girl-*friend* like that, too? Someone you could talk with, easily and openly."

He drew a deep breath and said, resignedly, "If it's all I can hope for ... so be it. There's a dance at the Queen's tomorrow?" His raised eyebrows and hopeful tone made it a question.

"I'm on duty till eight. Then a meal and a quick bath. Nine, shall we say? From nine onwards I'm all yours."

He jibbed at her choice of words but said nothing. Instead he forced a smile, rubbed his hands, and answered, "Well, that's capital! Actually, we could dine at the Queen's. May I invite you? Then we could go earlier — at half-past eight."

"Thank you, kind sir." She bobbed a curtsey. "Now what's all this about Moses?"

"Oh," he said airily. " 'Twill keep, 'twill keep. I thought you weren't too interested anyway."

She took a paper knife from the desk and advanced on him menacingly.

"Kamerat!" He held up both hands. "I've been working on that Mrs Tregear. Not directly. I mean, I haven't approached her in person but through a fellow I know who works in Falmouth docks — a chap called Phil Diver, who is, funnily enough, a marine diver by trade. We've used him to fish stuff out of flooded claypits. He was quite close to Billy Tregear before he vamoosed. It's taken him some time to get anything out of the old woman because, of course, he couldn't show too keen an interest. Anyway, the long and short of it is that she sold him to ..."

"Sold him?"

"Yes. Not into slavery or anything dramatic like that. He was a very bonny baby, I'm sure."

"And beautiful! Almost too beautiful to be quite real."

"Just so. Well, there was this couple who'd recently lost a baby of their own and they ..."

"When? What were their names? Actually, Martha Walker should hear this. D'you mind if I call her?"

He barred her path when she was halfway to the door. "I'd rather she didn't know I had anything to do with this," he said. "Tell her by all means but make it seem you, or Mrs Collett, or someone else did all the digging. All right?"

"Fair enough." She went and knelt in one of the window seats to draw the blackout.

"The couple was called Hosking and ..."

"Oh well — *that* should make them easy enough to track down!" she said sarcastically, for Hosking is to Cornwall what Jones is to Wales and Smith to England. "What were they baptized?"

"She *thinks* he was Edward. She doesn't know the wife's name at all — just Mrs Edward Hosking. It could also be Hoskin, of course, or Hoskins. The woman's illiterate so a g or an s more or less is neither here nor there to her."

"And why not Hodgkins? Or Hopkins. Or Hastings!" Jennifer asked, still in sarcastic vein. "I don't mean to grumble, my dear, but we're no forrarder at all. You didn't say when all this happened."

"Almost immediately after Walker took the baby over to Falmouth, it seems. Within weeks, anyway. Billy Tregear did most of the negotiating — and took the lion's share of the fee, the old lady says bitterly."

"How much was it?" Jennifer asked.

"Fifty guineas!"

She sat down with a bump. *"Fifty!"*

"Guineas." He nodded. "So they were people of some affluence — which should narrow down the number of Edward Hoskinses to look for. The needle in a haystack turns out to be a knitting needle at least. Let's hope it's not lacquered the colour of straw."

"Oh — and one other thing," he added as she went to the door to break this news to Martha. "She says she's pretty certain they came from around Saint Ives."

"Oh, Douglas!" She ran to him. "I could kiss you!"

He grinned. "No objection here."

"If only we hadn't agreed to keep it utterly platonic!"

44 PEOPLE WHO CAN afford to buy a baby for fifty guineas are likely to have their names in *Kelly's Street Directory* and similar publications. Jennifer checked. There were plenty of Hoskins, and Hoskinses and Hoskings, living in St Ives, which, for directory purposes, included the posh suburb of Carbis Bay. But there was not an Edward among them, even though some properties as far out as Lelant and St Erth were listed. There was one Edwin Hoskin, which looked hopeful — and he was connected to the telephone. But what could Jennifer do? She could hardly ring him up and ask if he and his wife had illegally purchased a foundling boy about six years ago!

She considered going in person to St Ives on her next afternoon off and making some discreet inquiries. But afternoons off were increasingly rare and precious. She knew what a hard time her mother had in trying to run the household and look after four fairly demanding children, *and* earn a living, so she took every opportunity to go down there and help where she could.

Faye, who had enjoyed that afternoon she and Jennifer had spent repairing the windows, came with her if she could arrange the same hours off. The little family living on little money in its little play-home fascinated her. It was 'real life,' she said. To live in a house without servants represented some kind of unattainable ideal for her; of course, she meant no living-in servants, for not even the poor-as-churchmice Owens would consider managing without their daily to do the really tedious work, like cleaning the grates and setting the fires, scouring the pans, and sweeping and dusting. Also they sent their big wash — the sheets and pillowcases and Hector's shirts — down to the steam laundry, which seemed an extravagance until you reckoned *all* the costs of employing a visiting wash-lady: the coals and soap, the lamp oil and wicks for the light, the wear on the mangle and washboard, the tea and the heavycake. Also, since the woman left as soon as it was all hung out on the line, there would be no one there to rescue it if it came on to rain or if a neighbour lit a bonfire. But there were still all the smalls to wash and mend. And that was a chore Jennifer liked to take off her mother's shoulders. Sometimes Faye helped, too.

They arranged matters so that, on the night before Jenny's afternoon off, she would send word to her mother, who would fill the copper and light the fire just before she left for school the following morning. She soon had it down to a fine art. By the time the girls arrived the water would be more than half way to the boil and the fire had burned down to a respectable glow, needing only a bit more kindling and some small coals to complete the work. Meanwhile they did the more delicate fabrics in the cooler water.

Faye would flake the soap with a potato peeler while Jennifer dissolved the starch and prepared the rose-water rinses for the blouses and handkerchiefs. Then they could set about the actual laundering, with sleeves rolled up, hair tucked away in mob caps, and dresses protected by oilcloth aprons — and lots of laughter at the transformation. They looked like a pair of reformatory girls.

"If George were still here," Jennifer said, "we could get him to take a photo of you and send it to your mother."

"She'd have a fit!" Faye answered delightedly. "Talking of George …"

"No, don't." Jennifer took a few gallons of hot water from the copper and poured them into the washer. This grand machine, which had followed them from Godolphin, had a hinged lid with a paddle beneath it. When turned back and forth, back and forth, by a cranked handle on the upper side of the lid, it swirled the laundry this way and that, doing the work of the traditional wooden dolly. Half a dozen pebbles in the water, each about the size of a hen's egg, helped pound the clothes and halved the quantity of soap each wash required. You could also slot a mangle in along one side of the machine; this let you lift the clothes straight out of the water and into its rollers. There was a tray beneath it that could be tilted to spill either way — back into the wash tub if the water was still fairly clean, or forward into a slop pail if it was too dirty to re-use for the next, cooler, wash.

Faye scattered a handful of her snowflakes and said, "Bags I first swish of the paddle."

She started turning the handle vigorously, to work up a good lather, while Jennifer looked for buttons dangling on worn thread, which might come off and get lost in the spirited paddling and pounding Faye was about to give them.

"If not George Herbert, what shall we talk about, then?" Faye asked.

So Jennifer told her what Douglas had discovered of baby Moses's further history; the bare facts of her chance discovery of the little boy were by now common knowledge at Medrose.

"And are you going to follow it up?" Faye asked excitedly.

Jennifer sighed. "I don't know. I don't see much point in it."

Faye opened the lid and they put in the blouses and lace handkerchiefs.

"We forgot the blue bag!" Faye held it up guiltily.

Jennifer took it from her and dropped it in an enamel bowl filled with tepid rose water. "It goes in the rinse," she said pityingly. "You'll never make a washerwoman, Faye Carminowe!"

Faye laughed and repeated her question as she resumed her paddling: "One, two, three ..." She counted as far as twenty, changed arms, and then lost interest in counting altogether. Again she repeated the question, insistently this time.

And Jennifer repeated her original reply: "I don't see a point in it."

"Well, you're the one who started it. Wasn't it you who sought out this Mrs Tregear in the first place?"

"Yes, but that was only to stop Mrs C-S from going off on a wild-goose chase — which was why Master Douglas pushed *his* nose in, to distract his mother from setting up the convalescent home."

"Oh really? I didn't know that. But why?"

"Because he's such a stick-in-the-mud. The war brought excitement and responsibility to *him* — with the brigadier going off to France and so forth — but he wanted Medrose to be frozen in time, preserved in nineteen-fourteen aspic. As far as he was concerned, his mother was part of the Medrose furniture. He's come round to accepting the changes now, but the ball he started rolling in the beginning — the quest for baby Moses — has since come to develop a momentum of its own. Unfortunately, everyone else involved seems ten times more interested in solving the mystery than I am."

"But don't you think it's exciting? A real-life mystery right on your doorstep? Hoo — my arms!"

"Not really. Shall I spell you a while?" She took over the handle and cranked the paddle more slowly and steadily than Faye had done. "I mean, even supposing I did find him — what then? Suppose he *was* adopted by this Edwin Hoskin of Carbis Bay, and I go over there to see the man ... explain my supposed interest, blah-blah ... and he invites me in to meet the boy. What then? It could be dreadful. They could have turned him into a sickening Little Lord Fauntleroy, or he could be a fat, pampered young toad. Even a perfectly ordinary boy of six is hardly the most inspiring thing in the universe. We all know what they're going to turn into." She reached her free arm behind her and, by way of proof, held up Hector's football shorts between a fastidious thumb and forefinger. "Yuk!" She threw it back on the heap.

She opened the lid while Faye, ready with the wooden tongs, lifted out a blouse. As the steam cleared they tweaked open the collar of it, dipping their hands in cold water between each scalding tweak.

"It's done," Jennifer said after inspecting the collar for stains. "So will the rest be, then."

She screwed the wingnuts on the mangle, tightening it only to its gentlest setting, and set the tray to spill back into the machine. "Now watch out for the buttons," she warned. "That mother-of-pearl cracks so easily."

She wound the handle slowly so that Faye could flatten each button before it passed between the rollers.

"You know why Master Douglas doesn't object so much these days?" Faye said.

"Because, like all stick-in-the-muds, he's got used to a new bit of mud to get stuck in."

"No! I don't think he'd have objected from the outset if he'd realized it would mean filling the house with half a dozen nubile young spinsters of our class. It must be every eligible bachelor's dream — the way we all fight for his attention. All except you and me, of course."

Jennifer laughed at this fantasy.

"It's true," Faye insisted. "Lady Cleer told my mother, who was one of the last she approached. She had it down to a fine art by then — how to persuade a mother to let a marriageable daughter go to work in intimate contact with a transient population of young men. She said, 'Before you say no, dear — and I can see it in your eye already — I should tell you that Sibyl McLaren, Constance Skewes, and Maude Stratton all said no at first but they all changed their minds when they heard that the convalescent home is to be at Medrose.' And, naturally, my dear mama got this picture of Dorothy, Ruth, and Deirdre, too, all setting their caps at one of Cornwall's most eligible young bachelors while I languished at home, quite out of the race. She wasn't going to let pre-war notions of propriety stand in the way of *that* chance!"

"And you?"

"Well, I'm certainly not setting my cap at *him!*"

"Actually ..." Jennifer said thoughtfully.

"What?"

"No — it's a bit grisly."

"Go on. I don't mind."

"Well ..." She sighed. "The way things are going — the way they're being slaughtered over there in France — rather a lot of us are going to be left on the shelf when it's over. And I think a lot of pre-war notions of propriety will go out of the window before we're done."

Faye sniggered. "Well, that's what they were for, all those prohibitions — to stop us being *done!*"

Jennifer dug her with her elbow and tried not to smile.

"Talking of which ..." Flora went on.

"Don't."

"You already said don't once. You can't have another. One don't per day — that's the rule.

"Who says? There should be one more lace hanky in there."

"*I* says. Oh yes, here it is. Are you going to add more hot?"

"No." She tested the water. "We could do the woollens in this. It's cool enough. If the copper's boiling, you could chuck in the whites and the rest of the soap flakes."

"And the blue bag?"

Jennifer realized she was teasing just in time to stop herself screaming. "Go ahead — see if I care. Throw the whole block in," she said airily. She laughed. "Actually, *blue* sheets would look rather swell, don't you think? Decidedly risqué, what?"

"No — pink!" Faye stretched luxuriously, reaching up to touch the rafters of the little outhouse. "Or scarlet — yes, scarlet! Perhaps we'll all have to have scarlet sheets in the man-hungry years ahead. I say — wouldn't it be a wheeze to write a book of etiquette for such times, when two women are chasing every man! I mean, it's bound to affect morality, isn't it. Girls can afford to be very high-minded when it's ... what were the figures before the war? A hundred and four men to every hundred women? Something like that. Our haloes would blind the saints in those days. But let the numbers fall to *fifty* men for every hundred women and you'd soon know us by our cloven feet and forked tails!" After a pause she added, "I think I've been very good — not pestering you to talk about it for the past ... month?"

"Two months. Two months and one day."

"Don't you think I've been good?"

"No, I think you've been shy." She saw the chagrin in Faye's eyes and relented. "No, perhaps that's too unkind. You've been *very* good — so why spoil it now?"

"Because I want to know."

Jennifer busied herself with sorting the woollens.

Faye persisted. "You can't stay silent, Jenny. You've already used up today's Don't card."

"All right, then," Jennifer said easily. "Let's talk about it."

Another silence ensued.

"When?" Faye asked impatiently.

"Tomorrow," Jennifer replied.

"But that's not fair! You'll be able to play another Don't card then."

"Precisely."

"You beast! You ought to be a lawyer. Women can be lawyers now, you know." After a moment's thought she went on, "Actually, you know, when they try to talk you into signing a film-acting contract, they'll be in for rather a shock!"

"Look, there's nothing to talk about," Jennifer said at last. "It's exactly like you always thought it would be — only even better. And you already know it's got to be fun or they wouldn't make such efforts to prevent it, would they!"

"And it really, honestly *is* fun?"

"With someone you love, yes. With someone like Cardew Silk I imagine it'd be pretty ..." She lolled out her tongue and pulled a face.

Faye stared at the steamed-up window as if she could see the horizon. "I wonder how one gets to *be* in love?" she mused.

45 IF JENNIFER thought she had laid the matter of baby Moses to rest, at least until such time as she had the leisure to pursue it further, she reckoned without Millicent's kaleidoscopic mentality, her insatiable curiosity — and her rich network of friends and acquaintances. For her it was a matter of three telephone calls and a few simple requests couched in such terms as, 'not a word to the parties themselves ...' and, 'be as discreet as only you know how, my dear ...' and, within the week, she was able to announce to Jennifer that the Edwin Hoskinses had a boy of fourteen and girls of seven and five.

"You're absolutely sure it *was* a boy you found, dear?" she asked, clutching at a straw.

Jennifer suppressed several even more ribald answers and assured her he had, indeed, been 'every inch a boy.'

Millicent smiled at that but saw no way to overcome its finality. However, she found one last straw to clutch at. "Mind you," she said, "the illegal transaction took place in nineteen-ten, at which time an Edward Hoskin or Hoskins might well have been living at Saint Ives. We should go to the library and get out the old directories for nineteen-ten. They could have moved away since."

"Yes, indeed," Jennifer said wearily. "They might have moved to the moon. They could very well be staring down at us this very moment, smiling at our folly."

"I'm sure there's no call for you to be pert with me, my dear," the other replied sharply.

"I'm sorry if I appeared pert. That was not my intention. But you know how it is. If a woman is absolutely positively certain-sure she left her earrings in a particular place on her dressing table and she finds they aren't there ... well then, they could be anywhere. She's at a loss where to start. Her utter certainty has closed off all other possibilities, even though, as she's just proved, that certainty was unfounded. It's just like that with Moses. For five years I was certain he languished in Helston. Then we were certain we'd run him down to Falmouth. Then we had absolutely positively certain spoor leading to Saint Ives. And look what a dance that has led us! We have to draw a line somewhere. The way I see it — the baby was cherished enough for someone to pay an outrageous sum for him. His adoptive parents are clearly people of means. He's vastly better off than he would have been in the Helston orphanage ..."

"Yes, yes!" Millicent cut short this recitation for she saw its conscience-saving conclusion well enough. "Have you told any of this to Walker?"

Jennifer sighed. "Not yet."

"Don't you think you should?"

"I don't know. Do *you* think I should? Her drinking was mainly to drown her guilt over what happened to the baby — that's one thing I really *am* sure of. I wanted to be able to say, 'See! It's all turned out for the best.' I wanted to be able to take her to Saint Ives and *show* her the boy — from a discreet distance, of course. She's been heroically abstemious since she came here ..."

"Ha! She knows it's her last chance — that's why."

"Whatever the reason, it can't have been easy ..."

"And if she feels any guilt, it's about the scarlet life she led."

"I doubt it, you know. They drift in and out of it. What we think of as the scarlet life is just pale pink to them. No — it was what she did, and didn't do, to the baby."

"But why should a coarse creature like that entertain such fine feelings about the fate of a baby? They're easily got among women of that class."

"Not by her."

Millicent pressed her lips tight together, as if to hint that she could say much more but wouldn't.

"If you'd rather she left ...?" Jennifer said, though she had no idea how she might finish the sentence.

"No, no," Millicent replied hastily. "She's cheap and she works well. Let her stay."

"Cheap?" Jennifer was amazed. "That's not what you said when I ..."

"I know." She waved the words away. "But you don't know what this war has done to female wages. The world's gone mad. Our maids and cooks leave the town by every train, to go and work in factories up in England. And the ones who stay can demand more and more, of course. So Walker can stay, by all means."

"I was wondering if she couldn't move up from the scullery to the kitchen at least? She was quite a good cook for us in the old days — on cook's day off, you know."

Millicent put an arm round her shoulders and led her to the door, a friendly way of saying that their interview was closed. "Let me pass on an invaluable piece of advice my mother gave me," she said. "Never darn a stocking until it has developed a hole! In short, leave well alone."

But Jennifer felt an almost proprietary interest in Martha's reform and so could not leave well alone. So, on the pretext of telling the maid about

Moses's good fortune, she visited her in her room over the stables. It had been a dormitory for stable boys in the days when up to a dozen horses had been kept at Medrose.

"It's only me, Martha," she called out as she went up the rickety old stairs. She was prepared to make complimentary and encouraging remarks, no matter what she found beyond the door, but the scene that met her eyes robbed her of words for a moment.

She would not have believed so much could have been made of so little. The carpet was a bright red horse blanket; the table was a tea chest papered with wrappings from Christmas presents and covered by a square of chintz — a sample from a draper's catalogue; three other samples were tacked in overlapping diamonds on the wall; close by was the lid of a biscuit tin with a coloured view of the Leaning Tower of Pisa; the bedspread was a patchwork that must have cost hundreds of hours in needlework alone; but the most astonishing thing of all was also the cheapest and simplest — a second tea chest that stood just inside the door. Martha had painted it black and on it had arranged a piece of tortured driftwood, scoured smooth by the sand and bleached silver by salt and sun. Nestling in its curves were three granite stones of a kind common on Cornish beaches. They were either large pebbles or small boulders, about the size of an ostrich egg and every bit as smooth. One was a light, sandy grey; the other two were darker. All three had fine white lines of quartz running around them, like randomly drawn great circles, intersecting at equally random angles.

Lost for words, Jennifer could only stand there and run her hands over them, marvelling at the precision of those lines. It was hard to believe that any blind process of nature had produced them. Of course, she had experienced something of those sentiments before, on finding such stones strewn about the beach or shimmering at the bottom of some rocky pool; but she would never have believed that the mere act of carrying them home and giving them the sort of setting normally reserved for glass paperweights, toby jugs, and other bricabrac could transform them in such a fascinating way. "They're beautiful, Martha," she murmured at last. "This whole room ... I can't believe it!" She smiled at the woman. "Can you?"

Martha's head wobbled all over the place in a fit of embarrassment. "'Ardly, sometimes. I can't afford no better, see."

"Oh, Martha — if you could!" She surveyed the room again and let out her breath sharply. "Still, that's not what I came to say. I came to tell you the good news about baby Moses."

"Oh, 'im." Her face fell at once.

"It's good news, honestly."

"Oh, ah?" she responded dubiously.

"Yes. Listen! Shortly after you left Moses with Mrs Tregear she received a visit from a couple called Hoskin or Hosking. Does that name ring a bell with you? Did you ever meet them?"

Martha shook her head, not very emphatically but it was an undoubted no, all the same.

"They were obviously quite well off because they made her an offer for the baby."

The woman's head jerked up at that.

"It's true. Heaven alone knows how they got to hear of it. I suppose if you're childless and rather desperate, there'd be ways. Anyway, they got to hear of Moses and came to see your mother-in-law ..."

"'Ow come you do know all this?"

Jennifer wondered how much she could honourably divulge. In the end she decided that accurate details were the only things that could allay Martha's understandable suspicions. "There's a man who works in the docks there — who has also done work for the Colston-Smarts — in their china claypits — who was also a friend of your husband's ..."

"Phil Diver," Martha said.

"Very well," Jennifer conceded. "He got the story out of Mrs Tregear. Apparently the Hoskinses, or whatever their exact name was, paid her fifty pounds for Moses and ..."

"Ha!" Martha exclaimed scornfully.

"They did," Jennifer insisted.

"That what she told 'ee, is it?"

"More than that. She gave his exact name — Edward Hoskin — and she said he was from Saint Ives."

"Ah?" She showed the first crack in her disbelief. "You've been there, 'ave 'ee? Seen the boy?"

"No. Because they don't live in Saint Ives any longer and we don't know where they've moved to. But" — she took a chance on a lie — *"Kelly's Directory* for that year does show them as living in Carbis Bay, in Boskerris Road."

It impressed Martha not at all. "And you think that ole cow and Phil Diver can't go up the library and look in the d'rect'ry for that year, and this one, and find someone with a name like Hosking who was there in nineteen-ten and is now gone? 'Twouldn't take they five minutes to work that out! If she swallowed nails, she'd ... well, they'd come out corkscrews.

Edward Hoskin! 'Ow d'you think she picked that name, then? And 'ow are 'ee ever going to find 'n now 'e in't there no more!"

Jennifer was shattered. It had all seemed so certain and so hopeful. "What d'you think happened to Moses, then?"

"Think! I'm as certain as what you're sitting there that she smothered the poor little cooze — which is mebbe the best thing could've 'appened to 'n. Fifty pound! Where did that go to, I wonder?"

"Well," Jennifer said bleakly, "we'll just have to find this Edward Hoskin who used to live in Carbis Bay, won't we."

The really depressing thing was that it was quite true. Now that Martha had put such doubts in her mind, she'd have to follow the trail, true or false, if only to set her own conscience at rest. Worse, she'd have to pretend to believe the story, if only not to hurt Douglas's feelings, for he had been so proud of his detective work and what it had unearthed.

"And good luck to 'ee!" Martha said.

"Well!" Jennifer forced herself to be brisk and businesslike again. "That was only one of the things I wanted to talk to you about. I also wanted to ask you if you're happy here?"

The moment the words were out she realized it was the wrong question to ask — or, at least, the wrong way to phrase it. Panic filled Martha's eyes as she looked about the room she had done so much to make a home. "Why, miss" — she gulped heavily — "I 'ope as I do give satisfaction?"

"You do, Martha, of course. Mrs Colston-Smart is very pleased with your work — and if she saw what a transformation you've made here, I'm sure it would only double her satisfaction. Nobody thinks you've had an easy ride here. But that's the point. You know, and I know, that you're cut out for something much better than scullery maid. Look at your hands! They're ten years older than you, despite all the goose grease."

"I don't want to cause no trouble, miss," Martha put in. "By rights I shouldn't even be scullery maid, not after what I done."

"By rights you should be in the kitchen — at the very least. In time you should have a kitchen of your own. I don't think you should let a few mistakes in your past blight your life for ever and ever."

"A *few* mistakes!" Martha laughed scornfully. "'Tis more'n a few. You got no idea what I done."

"Why don't you tell me, then?" Jennifer suggested.

"Ha!" was all she said to that.

"It often helps to share one's guilt, you know. Sometimes, when you let other people look at it, they can show you it wasn't anything to be guilty about at all."

"Hmm!" It was still contemptuous but less vehement.

"Unless, of course, you actually *want* to go on feeling guilty. We had a woman in the hospital when I was down there who actually enjoyed cutting herself."

"I never cut myself," Martha said — and that was all she would say on the subject.

Jennifer reverted to her original topic. "It's not that anyone here disapproves of your work — much less do they disapprove of you. It's just that you could do so much better, Martha. Wouldn't you like a little more money to spend? Get some more pictures to hang up? Buy yourself some pretty clothes?"

She couldn't say no, of course. "How?" She licked her lips nervously and hung on Jennifer's reply.

"Well, even as a scullery maid you could get five bob a week more at an hôtel like the Queen's."

"With a character, yes."

"My mother would give you one."

"For nineteen ten!"

"And so would Mrs Colston-Smart. In fact, just asking for one would set her thinking. She might offer you more money straight away and you wouldn't even have to move."

"I like it here, Miss Jennifer."

"That's obvious." She waved a hand around her. "But you'd like it even more with another five bob a week, eh? Think it over, anyway." She prepared to go.

"That other thing you said ..." Martha added as she opened the door to go.

"Yes? What in particular?" She'd said so many things, she couldn't be sure which the woman might mean. No doubt her next words would make it clear.

"'Bout being fond o' misery and that ..."

"Well, that wasn't quite what I said — or what I meant. I meant to say that if we've done wrong, it's right for us to punish ourselves, but it mustn't turn into a habit. Every punishment, no matter how severe, must come to an end, sooner or later. Whatever wrong you think you did, you've surely punished yourself enough." When Martha just sat there woodenly she prompted her: "Eh?"

She sniffed. "Even half-a-crown a week'd be something, now."

46 IT IS CURIOUS how certain decisions in life — often the most important ones — depend on a precise sequence of quite random events, which, if they had happened in a different order, might have led to quite different decisions. So it was in Jennifer's life on Leap Year's Day, 1916. In Cornwall, the end of February marks the beginning of spring, and a bright, blustery spring day it was when the first of those random events took place.

She was down at the railway station seeing off a batch of convalescents on the up train. It was really Marilyn le Grice's turn but she was in bed that day with a nasty chill. After waving the men goodbye she was to wait twenty minutes for the next down train, which would bring two new convalescents for Medrose. However, these timings were very approximate; military and other priority traffic on the rails had played havoc with the timetable.

For instance, the up train should have been standing at the platform, getting nice and warm, for twenty minutes before she and her little party arrived; but the platform was empty. In fact, they stood there a full five minutes before the down train even pulled in sight. At a snail's pace it crawled into the terminus, where it disgorged several dozen passengers. They straggled wearily down the platform, glad to have put the train and what had clearly been an uncomfortable journey behind them. The guard strode among them, officiously telling intending passengers not to board until the cleaners had had a chance to sweep the aisles and corridors. No cleaners were visible, however.

When Jennifer complained that it was hardly wise to keep newly restored convalescents waiting out in the raw air, the man grudgingly allowed them aboard. This parting at Penzance station was always a sombre time. It was the moment when the men realized that their recuperation was finally at an end and that they were headed, most of them, straight back to those earthly infernos whose names already struck a chill into the whole nation's heart: the Somme, Wipers, Menin, Bapaume, Messines …

Jennifer tried to fill those parting moments with activity — checking their travel warrants, their packed lunches, and all the other things they should have around them. Since everything had already been checked up at the house there was never any hold-the-train sort of panic, but it helped to fill the time and to postpone any maudlin brooding until she, at least, could no longer witness it. On that particular day nobody came to clean the train. The guard blew his whistle, and Jennifer only just managed to get off before it had gathered a dangerous amount of speed.

In landing on the platform she stumbled and was caught by a prosperous-looking gentleman wearing the type of coat called a British warm, embellished, in his case, with an astrakhan collar. "Oy-oop!" he exclaimed as he set her back on her feet. "Can't have this — the star of my next picture breaking her ankle on the very first day!"

"I beg your pardon?" she asked as she put her bonnet straight.

He was about sixty, with an interesting, battered sort of face — battered by life, not by pugilism. He tipped his hat, a dark, velvety homburg, and said, "Miss Jennifer Owen, I presume?"

"Yes?" She eyed him warily.

Now he swept off his hat and kissed her gloved hand. "Cass Potter," he said and waited for her reaction — as if he had said, 'Harry Houdini' or 'Sir Henry Irving' or someone equally famous. "What?" he said when it became clear his name meant nothing to her. "Never heard of the Global Imperial Film Company?"

She shook her head. He was as cockney as George Herbert — unless, like George at times, he was 'coming it' a bit.

"Strewth!" he said. "Where to start? *Nights in Araby?* See that, did you? *Sinbad the Sailor? The Man in the Moon? Bride in the Bridewell?*"

Some of the titles rang a vague bell but she shook her head to each and said apologetically, "I haven't really seen many motion pictures since the war started, Mister Potter."

"What have you seen then, gel? You got to stand out here, have you? Can we go somewhere for a cup of tea?"

"Only the station buffet," she told him. "I'm supposed to wait on to collect some new convalescents. I'll show you where the buffet is."

He chuckled. "I was drinking pints in that buffet before you were born, young lady — except, come to think of it, it wasn't there then." He took her arm gently and steered her down the platform. "You know Collett and Trevarton, of course. You know how they started — with the Shilling Picture Company? D'you know who gave them that idea, and who was the salesman who turned disaster into triumph for them?" He dug a finger into his breastbone as he spoke. "Yours truly — Cass Potter. They hadn't the first idea, poor lambs. I pulled their irons out of the fire for them. I made them what they are today — but it's nothing to what I'm going to make out of you. Billy Scott was right about you, love. The camera don't lie. You haven't signed up with anyone else yet, have you?"

Jennifer thought, *He talks too much. He gives me time to think.* "You're the first who's come here in person," she replied.

He let out an explosive sigh of relief.

She added, "I should warn you, though, I think the work I'm doing with convalescent soldiers is far more important than ... well, anything I might do in motion pictures."

"Movies, love. We call them movies, because they move the soul."

"Don't you have any luggage?" she asked suddenly.

"All sent on in advance," he replied grandly, adding, "Or someone will swing for it."

"D'you know George Herbert?" she asked next.

"Been like a father to that boy," he replied at once. "Next question?"

They arrived at the buffet door, where she asked an inspector when the next down train would arrive. He peered up the line and said, "Twenty minutes." They peered up the line, too, but saw nothing to warrant his words. Perhaps he and the signalman had a private semaphore code.

"Nice and warm," Potter said as he ushered her inside the buffet. "Hallo, Maureen!" he called out to the stout lady behind the tea urn. "You still watering the beer, then?"

The stout lady peered at him suspiciously and then let out a squeal of joy. "Cass!" she exclaimed. "Is that really you? After all this time!"

So he wasn't lying about past connections with Penzance.

Unless he'd slipped down here and bribed the barmaid as soon as he got off the train. Funny, she'd never have thought such scurrilous things about anyone else, but there was something about Cass Potter that invited the most vigilant suspicion.

The two of them — barmaid and movie mogul — hugged awkwardly over the counter. He told her she was still a good handful; she told him he was awful. Then, honours even, she turned to Jennifer and said, "Watch out for this one, Miss Owen. He's got more twists than Harry Lauder's walking stick."

"Now there's a man we can all admire!" Potter said at once. "Look at the work he's doing entertaining our boys. He never stops. I'll have a pint of Rosewarne's best to drink his health by, Maureen, my love. Miss Owen will have a cup of tea the way only you can make it." He smiled at her and winked at Jennifer. "Yes — Harry Lauder," he went on while the barmaid busied herself with the order. "What a man, eh! He could be doing something really useful like ... well, hospital porter, say, cheering up the one or two lads who come his way. But does he? Not him! He cheers them up by their thousands, instead. Did I say thousands? *Tens* of thousands. I shouldn't be surprised when this lot's over if he didn't end up with a kay tee for all the good work he's done."

"Katie?" Jennifer asked.

"No. Kay tee — a knighthood. *Sir* Harry Lauder, he'll be. Sounds funny now but there's not a serving soldier would grudge it him." He sniffed and stared Jennifer in the eye. "Makes you think, eh?"

She laughed. "It certainly does, Mister Potter. It makes me think of the vast, unbridgeable gulf there is between Harry Lauder — never mind any knighthood — and little Rose English, whom nobody's ever heard of."

"Including me," he said, baffled. "Who's she when she's at home?"

"You see! Makes *you* think, eh?"

He frowned. "You?"

She nodded. "My stage name."

He took her head between his hands. She found she didn't mind. George Herbert had once done the same; it was the impersonal gesture of a sculptor, quite lacking in intimacy. He turned her this way and that, observing how the light fell across her features. "Yes!" he said ecstatically when his eyes had drunk their fill. "Rose English — that's you to a tee."

"But not to a *kay* tee?" she quipped.

He chuckled. "You'll do, darling," he said. " 'Cos you're quick, see. You're the kind what lasts. You've got the stamina where it counts." He tapped his forehead. "There's lots of pretty gels in the movies but most of them are pure cotton wool from 'ere to 'ere." Or he might have said, 'ear to ear,' for those were the parts of her he touched.

Maureen set down her tea and his ale. He pulled out a fiver, then some loose change. "You're doing all right these days," she said. He told her he couldn't grumble.

"Well, now!" He turned to Jennifer when the barmaid had gone. "To be serious ..."

"You mean you haven't been serious until now?"

"Just listen. The time for small talk is over. I *was* going to dazzle you with promises ... tell you the world's your oyster ... all that malarkey. Get you signed up and then gradually break the awful truth to you. But I could see inside two seconds that wasn't going to work. You're too smart, for one thing, and for another, you're not hungry enough."

"Hungry?"

"For fame. For money. Don't pull a face. That's not an insult. It's good. It means you won't throw away your life like what some girls I've seen do. They listen to some sweet-tongued geezer who promises them they'll be up there with Lilian Gish and the Barrymores only first they've got to do, you know … this and that — mostly *that!* — and they end up doing *only* that. You know what I'm talking about?"

Jennifer nodded.

"Good gel. You're gonna meet lots of sweet-tongues like that before you rise above their level. Just a word of warning in your pink little shell-like." He winked. "So I'll level with you, as we say. The Global International Film Company …"

"Global Imperial, surely?"

"Yeah — whatever I said." He grinned disarmingly. "It's an office measuring six by four at the wrong end of Wardour Street. Third floor up. It's got one telephone but …"

"Those films you mentioned …" Jennifer interrupted.

"Movies."

"Those movies you mentioned …"

"They're real enough. It doesn't cost much to *make* a movie, you know. Hundreds are at it every weekend — amateurs. Thousands, for all I know. But that's how cheap it is. The big costs come later — distribution — getting it into the big movie houses where it can start earning big money. That's where I've failed so far — I admit it. I know just about everything there is to know about *making* movies." He laughed sarcastically. "I blinking well ought to — the numbers I've made. And I've had one or two small successes — mustn't be *too* humble. *Nights in Araby*. That one did quite well. So did *Bride in the Bridewell.* Small successes but they kept the wolf from the door. The real problem is — I've got no star. Everyone in the business is saying we need writers. *Stories* — that's what brings the people in. Rubbish, I say. They go to see stars. They've got stars in their eyes, see? Why does Griffith keep using Lilian Gish? Because she's a good actress? Nah! She *is* a good actress but that's just a bonus. He uses her because she's got this very special face. You look at her up there on the silver screen and her face is twenty foot high — but that's not what people see. You walk into a movie theatre half way through a movie and you get a shock. 'Blimey!' you say. 'There's a woman with a face twenty foot high and flickering enough to give you a headache.' But if that woman is Lilian Gish, you've forgotten all that inside ten seconds. By then she's a pal. She's as real as the girl next door only a thousand times more glamorous. I've been making movies ten years now and all that time I've been looking for an English Lilian Gish — a face that makes you forget she's just a dim, flickering image up on the screen. And when George Herbert told me to go and see what Billy Scott was holding for him — I mean, the minute I saw your face there on the screen

— only *this* small, of course, but it's the same difference — the minute I saw you, I knew my search had ended."

"Very flattering," Jennifer said awkwardly. "The train'll be in soon, if the inspector was right. I ought to go out and wait on the platform."

"I'll come with you." He gulped down the rest of his pint. "Waste not, want not."

Outside, the inspector came up to her. "Miss Owen — they've just rung down from Medrose to say that the two men you were to meet on this next train are coming tomorrow, instead."

She thanked him and turned to Potter. "I'm sorry. Now I have to go back to the convalescent home at once."

"Walking? I'll go with you as far as the Colletts' — they still live up Chyandour, do they?"

Outside the station he pulled his scarf up higher round the back of his neck and fell in at her side. She made her pace slower than usual but he was lithe for his age and she soon had to step out to keep up with him.

"Where was I?" he said. "Oh yes. Billy Scott. He's showing your tests all over London, you know."

"Goodness!" she exclaimed. "Shall I soon have to meet every train?"

"No, they're too high and mighty for that, most of them. You might get the odd one. But most of them will just write, promising the sun and moon and stars as long as you don't mind them being made of cardboard to start with. I just thought I'd steal a march on them and come in person." He guffawed. "I can show you what *real* cardboard looks like!" Then, serious again, he went on, "I've never been as convinced of anything in all my life as I am of this. My only difficulty is — I can't promise you anything except that if you throw in your lot with me and we make this movie together and it does as well as what I know it will — well then, you'll have me strapped over a barrel, as the archbishop of Canterbury might put it."

"And if it doesn't do quite as well as you say?"

"Well then, you won't have lost nothing — 'cos I haven't promised you nothing, have I!" Without prompting from her he turned into Lanoweth Road — which showed he did, indeed, know where the Colletts lived. "So is it yes or no?" he asked.

"I'll have to think about it," she replied.

"'Course you will, pet. At least it's not no. Take all the time you want."

Time alone may not be enough, she thought.

She did not know it then but several more of those life-shaping random events were going to play their part as well.

47 JENNIFER'S MIND was in a whirl all that day. She caught herself on the point of making so many mistakes she was astonished she didn't do herself, or one of the men, a serious injury. At nine o'clock that evening, however, she had the rest of the day, such as it was, to herself at last. Without pausing to eat — taking only a bully-beef sandwich left over from the officers' tea — she raced down the hill to the Colletts' to learn what more they could tell her of Mr Cass Potter.

It was amazing, she thought, how quickly one got used to the blackout; and yet it was, after all, the natural state of the world at night. The streets were going to seem like theatrical sets when the war was over.

Her knock was answered by Rosalind, who stamped her foot and said, "Hell! *I* was going to surprise *you*. Now you've been and gone and spoiled it!" But she flung her arms around her friend and hugged her hard. "I've got two weeks, pet," she murmured. "Isn't it wonderful!"

'Let's have a look at you." Jennifer held her at arm's length and turned her into the light from the hall, dim as it was.

"Lights!" came an officious cry from the stygian dark outside.

Jennifer took a couple of paces into the hall and pushed the door shut with her foot. "No discernible change," she said. She looked at Rosalind's ring finger and found it empty. "No change at all."

Rosalind laughed. "And you?"

Jennifer took off her glove and showed a naked finger, too. "Mind you, I could have had *two* rings there if I'd said yes."

"Oh, I've said yes since last we met!" Rosalind laughed again but looked slightly apprehensively over her shoulder. "Not exactly to the wearing of a ring, though."

Jennifer bit her lip, naughty-girl fashion. "Do tell!" Then, serious again, she went on. "Actually, don't be miffed, but I'm even more desperate to hear whatever you or your mother can tell me about a man called Cass Potter, who ..."

"What did I say!" Crissy called out from the upstairs landing. She poked her head over the banister rail. "Welcome, stranger! I knew you'd come tonight."

"I'm sorry, honestly," Jennifer replied. "It gets more hectic every day that passes."

"D'you think she heard?" Rosalind whispered as her mother came down to the half-landing.

"D'you think she *doesn't* know?" Jennifer asked in response. "You should talk to her sometime." She went to the foot of the stair and kissed Crissy on each cheek.

Crissy eyed the pair of them critically. "I wonder if you're both old enough yet for a glass of port? A small one, perhaps. Have you eaten, by the way?" she asked Jennifer.

"Just a sandwich. I'm *dying* to hear about Cass Potter."

"All in good time. We're about to have some Irish stew — just a meal in the kitchen. You're welcome to join us. We'll have the port after. Jim's out somewhere being a blackout warden. He won't be back till gone eleven, but there's nothing you need to know about Cass that I can't just as easily tell you. Also," she added with a backward glance at Rosalind, "I baked some saffron cake today in honour of our prodigal daughter."

There was a twinkle in her eye as she spoke the word 'prodigal.'

"Killing the fatted saffron cake?" Jennifer said. "It doesn't have quite the authentic ring."

"Barry sends his love," Rosalind said.

Jennifer spun round and halted so swiftly that her friend almost bumped into her. "You've seen him?" she asked excitedly — then, in quite the opposite tone, "He's not wounded?"

"No, he's still in rear-echelon. Billetted quite close by. Not all that *rear*, actually. Poperinghe. We can hear the gunfire, though we're out of range of most of it."

"Yes, yes!" Jennifer said impatiently.

Rosalind burst out laughing. "It's not fair! I was going to spin this out and tease you to death and I find I can't do it. Let me tell you — Barry's really met his match in you!"

"What d'you mean?" Jennifer protested. "I haven't even *looked* at another man."

Daughter and mother exchanged surprised glances. "That's not at all what I meant," Rosalind said.

"But how interesting that you should think it was!" Crissy put in.

Jennifer was covered in confusion. "Well — everyone knows his reputation," she muttered.

"For breaking hearts," Rosalind replied. "That's what I meant. *You* have broken *his* heart for a change."

Jennifer, too happy to continue the skirmish, did a little dance on the spot. "I shan't apologize for it," she said truculently. "He broke mine long ago, so we're quits. Tell me about Cass Potter."

"First tell us what he's offered you," Crissy countered.

While they supped on the stew Jennifer told them, word for word as near as she could remember, everything that had passed between her and Potter that morning. "The thing is," she concluded, "I shouldn't even have been there. It was Marilyn le Grice's turn only she went down with a chill. D'you think that's Fate's fickle finger at work?"

"The thing you should know about Cass Potter," Crissy said, "is that he's as straight as a die and just about the best friend anyone could ever hope to have. He'd hate to hear me saying it. There's nothing he'd love better than to be called the most notorious scallywag in London — or crook, not to mince words. But his honesty always gets the better of him, so he keeps up this verbal pretence all the time. That's the best I can tell you. The worst is that he really is being honest with you. He'll manage to scrape together enough to make this movie, but he won't be able to pay you much for your part — if anything. He'll be gambling on you and you'll be gambling on him."

"Is it true he rescued your business — Collett and Trevarton, I mean — when you first started?" Jennifer asked.

Crissy smiled. "Is that what he told you? He did in a way. But the *idea* was Jim's, which was pure genius. Nobody had ever just gone out and taken people's snapshots, up and down the promenade — and had them developed and printed and ready to buy at the station on the same day. Jim thought of that." She turned to her daughter. "You can be truly proud of your father for that."

"I am, I am," Rosalind protested.

"Good." She turned back to Jennifer. "But, fair dues to Cass Potter, we set about it completely the wrong way and it was he who put us straight. We would have got by without him but he it was who helped us lay the foundations of the vast fortune you see around you here today." She waved a hand about their modest kitchen and laughed. "No, but he was a tower of strength," she added seriously.

"He mentioned something about other movie companies writing to me," Jennifer said.

"Yes, it might be a good idea to see if they make such an outstanding offer that you'd be an idiot to refuse. You needn't feel guilty. Cass is quite versatile. He'd spin round on a sixpence and be your agent instead, I'm sure. Also — I don't know if he told you this — but he's having trouble finding his leading man."

"No, he didn't say a word about that. In what way — *finding?*"

"I mean finding out where he is. He just seems to have vanished off the face of the earth."

"Perhaps he enlisted?"

"No, the army's turned him down — and the navy — more than once, apparently. He was desperate to join up, poor man. Oh, his name's on the tip of my tongue. A very strange, unstable sort of fellow altogether, but on the screen he has this burning conviction." She hit her forehead with her fist, as if to dislodge the syllables. "You saw the film, too, Rosalind — *Nights in Araby* — he played the sheikh. And he also played that officer in *Bride in the* …"

"Charlie Shortis," Rosalind replied. Then, catching Jennifer's expression, she added, "What did I say?"

"You said Charlie Shortis," Jennifer said in amazement. "Also known as Cardew Silk."

"That was in *Bride in the Bridewell!*" Crissy said. "What a memory you have! But why did you pretend you hadn't seen any of Cass's movies?"

"I haven't."

"Then how did you know Charlie Shortis played Lieutenant Cardew Silk in *Bride in the Bridewell?*"

"Of the Tenth Royal Hussars?"

"I think so. *You're* the one with the memory around here."

"So that's where he got the uniform," she murmured. "A theatrical costume, eh?" And she went on to tell them what *she* knew of Cardew Silk, alias Charlie Shortis — including the embarrassing scene with the brigadier that had led to Charlie's banishment to the former girls' reformatory at Little Sinns.

For some reason Crissy thought that especially funny; she laughed until the tears ran. "Cass must hear this at once," she said as she wiped her eyes. "Come to the phone with me."

When she got through to Cass at his hôtel she handed the set to Jennifer, who simply said, "If you're still looking for Charlie Shortis, Mister Potter, he's probably still swinging the lead and masquerading as Lieutenant Cardew Silk of the Tenth Royal Hussars at a former girls' reformatory — now a convalescent home — near Redruth. Have you got pencil and paper? I'll spell it out for you."

There was a chuckle at the other end. "Little Sinns," he said. "It's all right, darling. I could walk there in the dark."

"You do know Cornwall well!"

"You ask Crissy Collett how I come to know that particular place — she'll tell you. But now you tell me — how come *you* know all this?"

Jennifer explained, much more briefly than she had for the Colletts. "You don't seem too surprised to hear it," she concluded.

"Nothing about that man would surprise me," Cass said. "By the way — I suppose they explained — he'd be your leading man. Unless you was to object. But he's good. More than just good. You should ought to try and see some of his movies before you decide." He cleared his throat cautiously. "Or have you already decided?"

"Mmm — three quarters."

"What's holding you back?"

"Well — if these tests I made with the Colletts and George Herbert really are as sensational as you make out, and if someone with a lot of money thinks the same as you, and if they ..."

"That's a lot of ifs, darling."

"I know, but just supposing. If they offered me a lot of money ... I don't know — a hundred pounds or something, well, wouldn't you rather be my agent in that case?"

He laughed richly. "Listen, love — another word in your rose-pink shell-like: Nobody ain't gonna offer you a hundred. Lilian Gish herself don't get that much."

Jennifer put the phone down and rang off. What did he take her for? She might not be very interested in the world of movies but *everyone* knew that Miss Gish got *thousands* of dollars per movie, never mind a paltry hundred.

The phone rang again. She picked it up.

"Five," Cass said desperately. "That's the highest I dare go."

"Five!" Jennifer repeated flatly. "Pounds or dollars."

"Pounds of course."

"Five pounds!" She put the phone down on him again.

This time it stayed silent.

"Did he make any comment about Little Sinns?" Crissy asked when she returned to the kitchen.

"He said you'd explain how he came to know the address so well."

The phone rang. Rosalind went to answer it.

Crissy started to explain. "When my parents died and our family got split up, my elder sister, Marian, made some injudicious remarks which were interpreted as showing she was in danger of moral turpitude. Actually a more delightfully innocent young lady ... who was it, dear?" she said when Rosalind returned. "You forgot to ring off."

"He's hanging on. It's Cass again. He says six pounds, but that's really as high as he can possibly go."

Jennifer pulled a disgusted face. "Really! He must think I came down in the last shower! Just six pounds for making a movie? I'm getting a steady thirty shillings a week at Medrose. Why should I jeopardize that for a measly six quid!"

"It's six quid a *day,* dear. Didn't you know that? All movie payments are *per diem.*"

Jennifer's jaw dropped. "A *day?* My God — and I talked of a hundred! No wonder he said ..." She closed her eyes and shook her head, still barely able to believe it. "I said no to five pounds a day — *twenty times* what I'm earning now!"

"So I'll say yes?" Rosalind asked.

"Yes." But as her friend turned to go she said, "No!" Then, lowering her voice in case it carried as far as the telephone, she murmured. "Let's just see if he'll go to seven."

Rosalind looked at her in admiration. Crissy laughed and said, "You'll do, maid!"

"You were saying," Jennifer reminded her, "about your sister Marian? She's Barry's aunt, too, of course."

"Yes. Actually, I want Roz to hear this."

Her daughter returned shortly, wearing an amused expression. "He says you must think you're a star already."

"But he didn't say seven?"

"Give him time and he might."

Jennifer turned to Crissy again. "Yes? You were saying that Marian said something ambiguous — what?"

"Oh, I can't possibly remember. But they took it to show she was in danger of moral turpitude. I was about to say a more innocent young lady never breathed, but actually, innocence of that kind does leave a girl open to all sorts of threats of moral turpitude — which is why I'm against it. I'm all for a little judicious experience." She directed these remarks at her daughter, who squirmed with embarrassment. "Anyway," she returned to Jennifer, "they sent her off to Little Sinns — which was actually the best thing that could have happened to her, because the lady warden there — your Aunt Harriet," she explained to Rosalind, "only a courtesy aunt," she added to Jennifer, "she got Marian a very good place in a fine house in Hampstead."

"Ah!" Jennifer grinned. "Did she also meet a young barrister there who wanted to show her his etchings?"

Crissy looked daggers at her. "I told you that story in the strictest confidence, young lady."

Rosalind caught the whiff of embarrassment at once and said, "What's all this?"

Crissy, still vexed, said, "If I don't tell you, *she* will. It's not funny, Jennifer. There's nothing to smile at."

Jennifer, however, was quite unabashed. "One tale like that will do more than all your vague, liberal talk about being in favour of 'a little judicious experience,' et cetera. Honestly."

Crissy stared at her but could not stare her out. "Perhaps so," she said at last, and quite mildly. Then she told her daughter the story more or less as she had told it to Jennifer on the train to Falmouth.

"Golly!" Rosalind was both delighted and impressed. "It happened even in those days, then!" she said.

"Even in *those* days!" her mother echoed ironically. "I suppose each generation thinks it alone has discovered the secret. Still" — she became brisk and businesslike again — "enough of this. Did Cass tell you anything of his plans?"

Jennifer shook her head. "It would mean going to London, I suppose?"

"Not a bit. He was very taken with the *location* — as they call it — of your tests."

"Medrose."

"Yes. He was even more impressed when I told him so — because the story he has in mind involves a young auxiliary who falls head over heels in love with a young convalescent officer ..."

"In the Tenth Royal Hussars?"

Crissy laughed. "Why not? He already has the uniform."

48 JENNIFER WENT out early next morning — for a walk, she said. In fact, it was to have a very early breakfast with Cass Potter at the Queen's Hotel. She had barely taken her seat when he informed her that six *guineas* was his absolutely last and definitely final offer, take it or leave it, she was bleeding him dry. Jennifer tried not to show how eager she was to take it.

"Now for the old bat," he said. "What's her killer's heel?"

"Killer's heel?"

"Soft spot, weakness ..."

"*Achilles* heel!" She laughed. "You know — after Achilles, son of ... I don't know. Some Ancient Greek or other. A god dipped him in a river, which made him immortal — except for his heel, which was where the god held him. Shoddy upper-class workmanship, see — any humble *potter* could have told them how to dip him all over."

Cass was listening too intently to laugh. "There's a lot of good stories from Ancient Greece," he mused "But back to Mrs Colston-Smart ... where's the A-chill-es heel there?"

Jennifer thought quickly. "Novelty," she said. "That'll win her over. Tell her it's something new. *Is* it new, by the way — making an indoor movie in a private house?"

"Most amateur movies are done that way — and don't they just look it! The trick here will be to make Medrose look like any respectable studio."

"How will you do that?"

"Lighting, mainly. Fifty kilowatts of carbon arc — and that's just for the highlights on your face!" He laughed, so that she didn't know whether or not he meant it.

"It sounds a lot," she said. "We've only got ordinary lighting at Medrose, plus an electric hot cupboard in the butler's pantry. Very swell!"

He explained that they'd have their own generator.

She said that would mean noise and smell. "Best not say anything about it," she decided. "Just keep harping on about her being the first. Tell her she's doing today what other grand ladies will be doing tomorrow."

Cass smiled at her. "You really want to do this movie, don't you!"

"Now I've agreed — just try and stop me! The other big problem, of course, will be to get Charlie Shortis — actually we'd better call him Cardew Silk from now on. We don't want to add impersonation to his list of crimes. The problem will be to get him back here. The girls were all highly amused at his antics, but that's in private. You know what hypocrites we are. In public they might feel they have to appear outraged rather than amused."

"Could we say he knew he was going to take part in this movie and only came here in disguise — harmless disguise — to, you know, soak up the atmosphere ... get into the part?"

"That depends. Does the part call for the seduction of six auxiliary nurses, one by one?"

She meant the question sarcastically but he tugged at his lip and said, "Dunno. What d'you think? Six might be a bit much? One or two, maybe? One?"

She was astonished. "You mean you don't *know?* Don't you have a script or something?"

"I've got a story," he replied defensively.

"Well?"

"Well, you know the first thing you do with a *story.* You change it."

"Why?"

"I dunno. There could be a million and one reasons. The cameraman says it won't work. The distributor got out of bed the wrong side that day. Could be anything."

"I give up!" Jennifer waved him away. "Call on her anytime today. Pretend we've never met and you've just seen these pictures of a fabulously beautiful home and some voice inside you said the whole world's got to know about this place and its gracious owner and the wonderful work she's doing — such a shame to hide her light under a bushel — blah-blah. Let her think it's more fact than fiction and that Medrose and the convalescent home is the real centre of the story."

He pulled a dubious face. "She's bound to mention you — I mean you're in every frame of those tests practically."

"You can say, off-handed, that you spotted quite a passable nurse or housemaid or something in some of the scenes. If she were still around, she'd make a decorative addition to the movie — you know. Play it down." She looked at her watch. "I must go. Give me twenty minutes start on you. Actually, the best time for you would be eleven this morning."

"The best of times and the worst of times!" Cass said. "There's another one we could do — *Oliver Twist* — out of copyright, isn't it?"

She corrected him: *"A Tale of Two Cities."*

"That, too! It's a golden future, darling! Who needs writers?"

But his quip about the best of times and the worst was nearer the mark. Jennifer ought to have realized that a man like Cass Potter and a grand lady — Jennifer's own words — like Mrs C-S would never hit it off. She could be utterly charming to the lower orders as long as they were at the receiving end of her boundless charity. She could sit by their beds or their wheelchairs for hours and become completely absorbed in their quaint preoccupations and domestic worries. If some jumped-up nobody in the town council had demeaned one of 'her' brave lads in some way, she'd take up the cudgels on his behalf and she'd usually carry all before her with no mightier weapon than her pen — backed, to be sure, by an intimate knowledge of how power was brokered in most English institutions. But when a member of those same lower orders — a man who was clearly no stranger to criminal thoughts and ways — came with an offer to put *her* on the social-historical map ... well! Sparks flew, and fur, and a choice epithet or two.

Jennifer, who used her precious lunch hour to meet Cass in the Railway Bar, found him sunk deep in gloom. "I think we'll have to call the whole thing off, darling," he said. "What with paying you a small fortune, I can't afford a studio. I needed that free location." He smiled at her.

"Don't *you* worry, though. The vultures will be after you soon enough. Nothing in the post this morning? I'm surprised."

Jennifer was on the point of telling him to forget her wages when she realized that would suit him very well. She'd been talking with one of the officers that morning and he'd said the British would never yield the Messines ridge to the Hun. "We've invested too much blood in that precious earth," he said. It made her think of Cass Potter, investing so much money in her — 'bleeding himself dry,' as he said. At least it would make sure he wouldn't simply drop her at the first mishap; he'd push all the harder to get his investment back. So instead she said, "Let me have another go at her — see if I can talk her round. I'll meet you back here at seven. I'm off early this evening."

"I'll take you to the pictures," he said. "They're showing *Nights in Araby* at the fleapit."

If only she had said she'd meet him when she had good news to report. She might then have taken a day or two at it and she just might have wheedled and flattered Mrs C-S into reversing her decision. But that quite unnecessary deadline of seven o'clock that same evening made her rush her fences and try to win by mere logic alone.

"Just think," she said enthusiastically, "future generations are going to have tons and tons of film showing the horrors and heroism of the front line — and generals looking important, and battleships ploughing through the waves, et cetera, et cetera — all stuff like that. Also soldiers being treated in big general hospitals. Queen Mary going round the wards, and so on. But what about little convalescent homes like this? The country is full of generous, patriotic owners — the *real* aristocracy of England — who have thrown open their doors to convalescents. But who's taking films of them? Amateurs — that's all. And their stuff is terrible. People aren't going to want to look at lots of wobbly pictures with all the heads and feet cut off. They'll choose the film made by a pro, with proper lighting and good, steady camera work. The name of Medrose will ..."

"People!" Mrs C-S interrupted scornfully. "Who *are* these people? How are they going to *choose* this film or that film — as if they were library books!"

"Museums, for one," Jennifer told her. "Films are historical documents now. In the future, museums will have specially darkened rooms where they can show films of historical importance. And then there are books. You talk of libraries. Well, there'll be hundreds of picture books about this war. There already are, I'm sure. And they can take still photographs out of a film, you know. The name of Medrose will become ..."

"What is *your* interest in this, Jennifer? Why so keen all of a sudden?"

"Well ..." She waved a vaguely dismissive hand in the air. "I just happened to meet Mister Potter at the Colletts' last night. Apparently he was their partner years ago, when they first came to Penzance. He's come down here now because of Medrose — because he saw the tests that George Herbert ..."

"Yes, so he told me. He also said there'd be a part for *you* in it. That's your real interest, isn't it!"

"A tiny part, perhaps. The same as the other girls, you know." She smiled disarmingly. "He promised me the earth, of course, but he was just being gallànt."

"Hmm! Well, dear, I'll think about it. You're as persuasive as you always are when you want to get your own way."

Jennifer began to protest at that but Mrs C-S waved her to silence. "I'll write and ask the brigadier his opinion. It may take a month or so. I hope Mister Potter can wait."

And that was the best Jennifer could get out of the woman. She suspected that even if Mrs C-S finally said yes, it wouldn't advance them much. She'd never agree to Jennifer's taking a starring rôle; and as for allowing Cardew Silk to return to Medrose ... it would be absolutely out of the question.

On her way to break this depressing news to Cass, down at the Railway Bar, she half formed an alternative plan — remembering the old saying about the mountain and Mahomet. She gave him no details when they met; she simply broke him the bad tidings and asked him if he could wait just one more day. "I have the germ of an idea and I need to develop it a bit more — and ask one or two people one or two things."

"Like what?"

"Like favours."

"Schtumm, schtumm, eh?" He laid a finger to his nose and winked. Obviously he thought it more of a joke than a practical possibility.

She drank a half of Rosewarne's Export to each of his two pints, and even that made her a little light headed. He told several stories of filming mishaps and curiosities, which left her feeling she was already part of that exciting and exclusive world. In short, the Jennifer who left the bar that evening was not the usual cautious, level-headed girl of that name — otherwise what followed would never have happened. Perhaps the unaccustomed drinking on an empty stomach, together with the gossip from a world she was soon to embrace, was the second of those random events that were to shape her life from that month on.

There could be no doubting the next of them though — which happened when she ran into Martha Walker, standing there in a provocative stance outside the taproom door.

"Why, Martha!" she exclaimed. "What on earth are you doing here?"

She wasn't aware of it but Martha had been talking to a sailor, who, ignoring Jennifer, said, "Come on then, lass. Make up thy mind or I'll go to yon one over there."

'Yon one over there' was a woman of an unmistakable type, common around railway stations and dock gates — the sort that Jennifer, like all respectable ladies, chose never to notice at all.

Martha took the sailor's arm and walked off with him. Over her shoulder she called back, "I'm doing the only thing as is left me, Miss Owen." And she waggled her backside in a most provocative manner.

"No!" Without even thinking, Jennifer rushed forward and struck the sailor a sharp blow with her rolled-up umbrella. "Be off, you scoundrel!"

"'Ere!" He turned round belligerently but, after one look at her expression, he took to his heels and ran to 'that one over there.'

"Now look what you've gone and done," Martha exclaimed and burst into tears.

"Come on, dear." Jennifer took her arm gently and turned her toward home. "We'll say nothing about this little lapse. It'll be our secret, just you and me."

"Oh, ah?" The woman stood her ground. "And 'ow am I to live, I'd like to know — with no work and no character?"

"But you have your work at Medrose." Jennifer wondered whether her previous drinking mania had destroyed part of her brain, leading to moments of amnesia like this.

"I 'ad," she said with emphasis. "Till 'er turned I off."

"Who turned you off?"

"'Er, Mrs Colston-Smart." She sniffed. "Mrs Coldstone-Heart, I do call she."

"Very good!" Jennifer laughed briefly. "What d'you mean by 'turned you off'? Did she dismiss you?"

Martha nodded. "For disloyalty, 'er said."

"In what way?"

"'Er said I'd applied for a place at the Queen's and I never did. I only asked if they had a place open and 'ow much it'd pay, like."

Anger at this high-handed action by Mrs C-S deflected Jennifer from asking why, even so, Martha, with all her skills and her newly won sobriety, had chosen to go back to making her living on the streets. "We'll just see about that!" she said grimly as she grasped the maid by the arm and propelled her toward Chyandour and the long climb up to Medrose.

Time and again on that breath-punishing hill, Martha said she 'didn't want to make no trouble.' In the beginning Jennifer told her there wasn't going to *be* any trouble; but by the end, after she had extracted more of her story out of the maid, she changed her tune. "Believe me, Martha," she said grimly, "you haven't seen *anything* you could properly call trouble, yet."

It was not the best mood in which to approach Mrs C-S for the second time that day. Nor was, "What is the meaning of dismissing Martha Walker without a word to me?" the best opening line. From there it could only get worse.

"Hoity-toity! I shall employ whom I like and dismiss whom I like, miss — a fact that should urge a certain degree of caution upon *you*, if I may say so."

By now Jennifer was shivering with rage. But she took the firmest grip she could manage and, outwardly calm at least, said, "I don't consider it at all helpful to utter threats of that nature. Do let us try to conduct this interview in as civil a manner as possible."

Mrs C-S was speechless for a moment. "Do you *dare* to lecture me, you ... you ..."

"I simply ask for information. Why was Walker dismissed so hurriedly — and in such a furtive manner, too? Why did you not do me the least courtesy in saying something before I finished my duty? I gather it happened at four this afternoon."

Tight-lipped but slightly more in control of herself, her employer answered: "I had already endured quite enough of *you* for one day. And I do *not* have to supply you with reasons as to why I employ or dismiss ..."

"Ha!" Jennifer interrupted. "That's at the heart of it, isn't it — me! You're getting at *me* by dismissing Walker. And you haven't even the courage to ..."

"You? My dear little thing — you really are getting above yourself these days. You're behaving like a film star already."

"That's it! That's it!" Jennifer smiled with sarcastic sweetness. "Now it's out in the open. You can't bear that thought, can you!"

"I do not intend to bear this ... this stream of unbridled contumely for another moment."

"You had no intention of letting Cass Potter make our film here. You were just going to string him and me along for a month or two and then say no."

"Oh, so it's 'him and me,' is it! And *our* film'! I thought as much! You ran into him casually at the Colletts'! Ha! He only offered you a tiny part! Ha, again! You were both lying in your teeth. You want to sweep me into the corner and take over Medrose for some fiction in which *you* are the heroine of the hour! Ha, once more! Well, Miss Owen, I shall refuse to play your little game — so you can just stew in your own juice. You and he deserve each other, I'm thinking."

Jennifer took a deep breath and said, "I shall save you the trouble of dismissing me. I shall go and pack now and I'll send for my box tomorrow — mine and Walker's."

She saw the older woman hesitate for a fleeting moment, but then she swept from the room, saying, "Nobody is indispensable."

"And *I* am nobody!" Jennifer called after her.

She had almost finished her packing when there was a knock at the door. She drew breath to call out 'Come in!' but Mrs C-S was already in. "Jennifer, dear," she simpered, "this is absurd. You and I shouldn't fall out over a little nobody like Martha Walker. So I'll tell you what I'll do: I'll pay her a month's wages *and* give her an excellent character. There! And I'm sure your mother will do the same — which will gloss quite happily over the years in between. But your work here is too important to be broken off over a little tiff like this — so what d'you say?"

Jennifer sat down on her bed, closed her eyes, and slumped. "It wasn't a little tiff," she said.

"No." Mrs C-S paced the room. "It wasn't. You're right. It was a big one. But it has cleared the air. We both said things we regret, I'm sure. I know I did. We'll know we have to be more careful in future — that's all. Do say you'll stay? You're the backbone of this place, you know. I've been meaning to say this for some time — I think your wage should go up to two pounds a week."

Jennifer clenched her fists tight. Was ever anybody faced with a harder decision than this?

"And that's what I propose," the woman concluded.

"I really do want to make this movie," Jennifer said quietly. "Not just for vainglory, though that's part of it and I'd be silly to deny it. But I really do think it could help our lads and encourage other girls to volunteer as auxiliaries — or even go into full-time nursing."

"Well, I shan't back down on *that!*" Mrs C-S said sharply. "I've eaten quite enough humble pie for one day — and I have yet to see you taste a single spoonful."

Jennifer shrugged hopelessly. "That's all there is to be said, then."

"You won't find anywhere else to make this film, you know. I'll make sure every convalescent home in the West Country is closed against you."

It was on the tip of Jennifer's tongue to point out that one or two of them were beyond the reach even of Lady Cleer and her charmed circle. But prudence ruled her and she said nothing — except, "I'll send up for those two boxes tomorrow. I haven't taken any of the silver but you're free to inspect them for yourself."

Mrs C-S swept from the room without a further word.

Jennifer went over to Martha's room and saw, to her satisfaction, that the maid had packed everything, even the view of Pisa's Leaning Tower and the stones she had picked up on the beach.

"What now, Miss Owen?" she asked.

"Now you're going up in the world, Martha," Jennifer said with far more cheer than she felt. "You're going to be a film star's dresser!"

49 JENNIFER SAID, "If the mountain won't come to Mahomet, you know ... I mean, why don't we go to where Cardew Silk is? Make the film at Little Sinns."

This suggestion was greeted by a silence, which Crissy was first to break. "Well now ..." she said encouragingly.

"But it's an old *reformatory,*" Cass interrupted before the idea could gain ground. "I know that place. It can't hold a candle to Medrose, with all them gardens, that glasshouse — and the ferny trees, whaddyacallem — bromides!"

"Cass!" Crissy objected. "You haven't *seen* Little Sinns for a quarter of a century. It has beautiful gardens — which are Harriet Martin's legacy. True, it has no views of the sea ..."

"Oh, we can fake *that,*" he said contemptuously. "But all that red brick! You know how black it'll photograph." He sniffed. "We could limewash one bit, I suppose, and shoot against that."

"Also," Crissy added artfully, "think of the *dramatic* possibilities. You could make a positive virtue of the fact that the place had once been a reformatory for wayward girls. The auxiliaries could all be wayward girls who were reformed *in that very institution!* You could have little scenes where each girl remembers her wicked past and contrasts it with her angelic present. It would make an uplifting tale of virtue rewarded — all those pretty young girls repaying their debt to society — a tale of how war can purify and uplift as well as blight and destroy ..."

" 'Ere!" Cass laughed. "Are you writing this thing?"

"Who else? Someone's got to. That hotchpotch you showed me last night wasn't exactly inspiring."

"It was only the *story*," he said defensively. "Anyway, I like this new idea much better. Reformed naughty girls'd work a bit cheaper, too, maybe. I like it! Is Harriet Martin still there or did she move when the reform school moved?"

"She moved with the school — *but*, funnily enough, she has gone back there recently. She retired from the school before the war — when her aunt died and she inherited quite a bit. Then, when war broke out, she joined forces with the Quakers and suggested they should reopen the old building as a convalescent home with herself as its administrator — honorary, of course."

"Which means," Jennifer said, "that it's outside the control of the Cornwall Red Cross. Mrs C-S will make quite sure that no convalescent home connected with them will open its doors to us."

Cass chuckled as he turned to her. "What about you, darling? Fancy playing a fallen woman, do you?"

"An *ex*-fallen woman," she replied, thinking, *I know where to get a tip or two if necessary!*

"Okay — supposing we do leave them walls alone — no whitewash. The dark blue dresses will just vanish. They'll have to wear white."

"But that's so impractical," Rosalind objected, a second ahead of Jennifer and her mother.

"Not for a movie, darling. You're thinking of real life. Also, you know, white's the colour of purity. All them penitent girls — pure at last. It's what we call 'symbolic' in the business. But it'll mean making all them dresses in white — or bleaching them. Will they bleach? And who's going to make them?" He looked hopefully around at the three women.

"Martha can," Jennifer said. "It'll keep her out of mischief and let her feel useful. At least it's better than scouring pots and pans."

"She can use my sewing machine," Crissy said.

"And who's going to ask Harriet Martin?" Cass went on. This time he looked hopefully at Crissy, who said, "I think you should leave the overtures to Jennifer. Harriet Martin has a soft spot for ambitious young girls with get-up-and-go. And you, Rosalind, can accompany her and do the introductions."

"Can we go in Daddy's new car?" Rosalind asked eagerly. "I can drive now, you know. I've been driving all over France — well, all over Flanders, anyway."

Crissy ducked the answer. "You'll have to ask him about that. Also there's the little matter of petrol. You'd have to persuade someone to let you have two or three gallons."

"Let's go by train this time," Jennifer said — having no wish to see her career as a film star end before it had begun, and herself with a broken leg, or worse, in a ditch. "We can go for a spin to Land's End or somewhere at the weekend."

And so they took the first local train after lunch to Redruth, some twenty-five minutes up the line.

"When I'm a big star," Jennifer said as they settled in the compartment, "I shall have three cars — a nippy little Renault for getting about town, a Vauxhall Prince Henry for speed on the open road, and a modest little Rolls-Royce Silver Ghost for all other occasions."

"How d'you know so much about cars, pet?" Rosalind asked. "I've never even heard of a Prince Henry."

"Just keep your eyes and ears open, that's all."

Rosalind stared out of the window as the marshalling yards passed by. "You will be a star, too," she said. "You want it so much. People always get what they …"

"I do not," Jennifer protested. "You've no idea how close I came to saying no to Cass Potter."

"But only because you doubted he'd be able to carry out his promises."

"What I want more than anything — really-really-*really* want — is for Barry to come back, safe and sound, when the war's over. Actually, I wouldn't mind if another horse trampled him a bit — as long as the injury wasn't permanent, of course. Except that he'd be so ashamed, he'd be impossible to live with. Isn't it awful when you go down and look at the casualty lists and he *isn't* there, and you say, 'Thank you, God!' And there's a woman standing beside you, crying her eyes out — what do we say to God about her?"

Rosalind sighed and stared out over the bay. "I suppose he writes to you every day?" she said.

"A little bit. He only posts it once a week, though." She hesitated and then added, "His latest came this morning, in fact."

"Ooh!" It was on the tip of Rosalind's tongue to ask what was in it but courage failed her. Instead she asked, "What sort of thing does he write about? I mean … I don't want to *see* it, but …"

"Not 'arf! — as Cass says."

"I just can't imagine what sort of letter he'd write. Does he write anything like he speaks?"

"You don't know how he speaks," Jennifer pointed out. "Not to a girl he loves."

"We tried to kiss once. It was so funny. We just had fits of giggling. I don't think boys and girls who grow up together can ever be in love."

"How long ago was that?"

"A couple of years. Why?"

Jennifer relaxed. "I could show you a bit — but promise not to laugh."

"Of course I shan't laugh. You mean you've got it on you?"

"I always carry his latest." She drew it from her handbag and hunted for a suitable portion.

"You're blushing!" Rosalind said.

"I couldn't possibly show you that bit." She turned to the next page. "Ah yes — this will do." She folded the top and bottom back to reveal but a single paragraph. She went and sat beside her friend, holding the sheaf firmly pinched between finger and thumb for her to read.

Rosalind promised not to try to read the rest but Jennifer would not let go. She read:

The importance of love's little gestures! Because you have kissed me, my whole life is redeemed. Because you have kissed me, I am renewed. Life literally began again for me in that magical moment when our lips first met. If I seemed to hesitate it was because, in a curious way, I did not want it to happen. Instead, I wanted it to be <u>about to happen</u> for ever. Because once a thing has started — since all earthly things are finite — its end is already implied. But the about-to-happen has a wonderful kind of immortality. There can be no end in sight for what has not yet begun. And this is the pain of love — that it must someday end. We know, you and I, that of all the countless millions of lovers who have sighed their hearts toward each other down the millennia, not one of them has loved with such intensity as I love you and you love me. And yet ...

"And yet what?" Rosalind asked.

Jennifer looked and saw she had folded it a little too high on the page. "Well, you just wanted to see the *sort* of thing he writes. So now you have." She started to tuck it away again.

"Is it all so ... well, high flown?" Rosalind asked, disappointed.

"Oh, read the whole bloody thing, then!" Jennifer thrust it into her hands before she could have second thoughts. "But don't you ever dare tell him."

She read avidly, eyes wide, mouth open. Several times she caught her breath and half turned to Jennifer before the attraction of the words drew her eyes back again. When she had finished she fanned her face with the sheets and said, "Golly!"

"It all depends on his mood, you see, from one day to the next," Jennifer said.

"Yes! He's certainly very ... ah ... I mean, talk about sacred love and profane love!"

"The only profanity is to do it without love."

"Where does he say that?" She looked at the letter again.

"No, *I* say it. Love sanctifies all. Love justifies all."

"Obviously!" She stared out of the window again. "So you and Barry really did ... you know ..."

"Yes. Are you surprised?"

Rosalind laughed awkwardly. "Not at him, of course. But I am at you — a little bit. The risk, et cetera."

"He used a rubber the first time. After that he said there wasn't enough to ... anyway, what about you?"

"I've never been in that situation. Or not yet. I mean, I've never been in love like that."

"So what was all that about the other night, when you said you've often said yes but not to an engagement ring, or something like that?"

"Well ... you know ..." She glanced at the letter as if it somehow gave her leave to be unusually frank. "Fingers and things." She closed her eyes and flushed bright pink. "I lost my maidenhead at least."

Jennifer was about to make some jokingly superior remark when she realized that, give or take a few months, her own response would have been identical to Rosalind's.

That, more than anything else, made her realize how much love had changed her. They said it laughed at locksmiths. Well, it certainly opened doors, some of which had not even been apparent until she passed through them and stood on the far side. Like now.

But how could she say anything along those lines without sounding intolerably patronizing? Instead, she said, "What you said just now — about always getting something if you want it enough. That's what true love is. It makes you want it enough. Everything else seems shallow and trivial beside it."

"Well." Rosalind sighed contentedly. "That certainly hasn't happened to me, yet. I always feel it's about to happen — and, as Barry proves, that's quite a happy state."

"I feel as if Barry and I are already man and wife, you see. That's why I feel absolutely no guilt about our going all the way."

"And when you write back ... do you write every day, by the way?"

"No. Once a week, after getting his letter — so I'll write tonight. I write more than he does, though."

"And are your letters as ... you know ... equally frank?"

Jennifer shook her head. "It's not necessary for me. I mostly tell him news and stuff about people. Referring to *that*, I just say things like I miss his *touch*, or the *dear weight* of him." She chuckled. "It's what we lovers call *symbolic*, you know!"

Rosalind laughed too. "Dear Cass!" she exclaimed. "Isn't he an absolute hoot sometimes!"

"He's never going to make any money, you know."

"What?" Rosalind was too astonished by this calm assertion to ask anything more specific.

"That's where your theory breaks down. Or perhaps not. Perhaps there's something in him that wants to destroy what it builds — the way little boys will build elaborate sandcastles just for the pleasure of jumping on them and smashing them to bits."

"But all his movies make money," Rosalind objected.

"Oh yes. He'll never starve, either. But I'll bet you that if George Herbert were to make this movie and if it earned him *exactly* the same amount of money it's going to make for Cass Potter, he'd use it to build up a thriving film company. *And* he wouldn't forget its name from one day to the next! Now *that's* symbolic, if you like!"

Rosalind stared at her with a sort of despairing amazement. "You're amazing! You say things like that with such conviction — even if you're wrong, one can't disagree."

"But I'm right."

"In that case, why aren't you making movies with George Herbert instead? Why do anything with Cass?"

Jennifer shrugged. "Let's see if this one's a success, first. And if George still wants me when the war's over, then I will."

"Assuming Barry lets you."

Jennifer seemed bewildered for a moment, as if she had forgotten who Barry was; then all she said was, "Ah."

Rosalind laughed. "That never struck you, did it!"

"Well ..." She moved her head about vaguely and shrugged again. "Cross that bridge when we come to it."

"If there's still a bridge to cross by then."

50 THEY DECIDED to walk from the station to Little Sinns, which lay just over a mile from the centre of Redruth. The road led down into a valley beside a poisoned, lifeless brook whose banks were crowded with one-man tin workings, most of them derelict. At one time, it was said, twenty venturers prospected this stream for waste tin along its four-mile run to the sea; and, such was the inefficiency of the mines' extraction processes, the last man in the line made as good a living as the first — and there was 'plenty left for the pilchards,' as the saying went. Now, however, most of the mines themselves stood silent and ruined, killed off by cheaper tin from the empire. The war was bringing about a small revival but it was slow and uneven.

When they arrived at a bend in the road Rosalind said, "There it is!"

The grim building, almost half a mile away, near the top of the hill to their right provided a bleak and forbidding prospect; but not the one that Cass's words had prepared her to see. "It's not built of brick at all!" Jennifer cried. "It's granite."

"So it is! Anyway, brick or granite, it's pretty cheerless, what? I always imagine the opening scenes of *Oliver Twist* happening there — except that's all in Yorkshire, of course."

Jennifer, staring up at the building, was lost for words. Perhaps the most important few weeks of her life were going to take place in that gaunt institution, which was a cross between a prison and something vaguely ecclesiastical. Surely some mystical aura ought already to surround it — something caged within it should speak directly to her at this most significant moment? She strained to feel it but caught nothing.

"Cat got your tongue?" Rosalind asked.

"Just trying to catch the atmosphere of the place."

In another ten minutes or so they were approaching the front entrance to Little Sinns. Their laughter announced their arrival, at least to the porter, who came out of his lodge and waited until they were within speaking distance. "Miss English?" he said then.

Jennifer and Rosalind looked quizzically at each other.

"Miss Rose English?"

The penny dropped and Jennifer stepped a little forward of her friend. "How did you know?" she asked.

He chuckled. "The telephone's a wonderful invention, so they do say. Miss Martin, she's expecting of 'ee." He nodded toward the front door.

"It *is* red brick at the entrance," Rosalind said.

" 'Es," the porter chimed in. "The board o' guardians got th'offer of a load going cheap, half way through the building, so they axed the architect to change the plans a bit."

"You were here then?" Rosalind asked in surprise.

"My dear soul, I was here when this was all just fields, maid. I was borned in a room as stood just *there.*" He pointed to a spot in the immaculately raked gravel, half way to the front door.

"And were you porter here when it was a home for wayward girls?"

He nodded. "See that chimbley?" He pointed to a tall smokestack on the western skyline, probably at Chacewater. "And that 'ill?" Carn Brea, of course. "And that tall tree on the harizen." That was on Trewithian Downs, three or four miles away. "And the sea." He jerked a thumb over his shoulder, toward the only remaining point of the compass. "I never went farther than they four points in all my life," he said proudly.

"Never went to Truro — or Penzance?" the girls asked.

He shook his head. "Nor never yet wished to, neither."

They stared at him as at some Rip van Winkle while he beamed back, delighted at their amazed silence.

Then Rosalind said, "I don't suppose you remember my mother — Crissy Moore as she then was — who used to ..."

" ' Course I do, maid," he replied scornfully. "And 'er sister Marian. She come 'ere scores and scores o' times, your old woman."

"D'you recall the first time she came?"

He drew his breath in sharply, a gesture that means yes in that part of the world. "A Sunday, it was," he said. "When the girls weren't left to 'ave no visitors, see? And she stood at that very window and cried 'er eyes out, poor li'l giglet ..."

"Jenny, petal ..." Rosalind broke into his flow. "Would you mind going on alone, since you are already expected? I'll catch up in a mo."

Jennifer walked across the immaculate stretch of gravel and rang the bell, trying to imagine how Crissy must have felt, standing on that very spot, ringing that very bell, a quarter of a century ago. It gave her gooseflesh all over again, just to contemplate it. She remembered Barry having a similar reaction to lighting a fire on a fifteen-hundred-year-old hearthstone. She thought her own response more meaningful, though, because more personal.

But when the door was opened she could only stand there and wonder if she'd come to the right house after all, for who should be on the other side of the threshold, grinning like a little devil, but Faye Carminowe!

"Thank heavens I caught you," she said, pushing Jennifer back off the step. "Listen — I want you to support me in a little white lie. Will you?"

"But ... I mean, what are you doing here? You haven't come to take the Silkworm back to Medrose, I hope? That'd be ..."

"No — listen. I work here now. And it's ..."

"Since when? I mean, it's only two days since ..."

"Just *listen!*" Her own loudness startled her and she looked guiltily over her shoulder. "There isn't much time." She drew a deep breath and tried again. "I'm working here now. I couldn't stand Medrose a single day without *you,* see! No, seriously, the atmosphere there is awful. Mrs Colston-Smart's in a foul mood all the time. And Douglas came back the night you left and he really went off the deep end with his mother — which didn't help matters. So I just said napoo, toodle-oo, good-byee! But the thing is, I had to tell a little white lie to get the place here. I said I did all the ration indenting and petrol-and-mileage reconciliations at Medrose — you know — all the things you did."

Jennifer goggled at her.

"Well, I *could* have done them," Faye said defensively. "I saw you do it often enough. I know *how* to do them. Anyway, Miss Martin just fell on my neck with gratitude. She says her own girls have hearts of gold and are willing to slave their fingers to the bone but they're a bit simply furnished, most of them." She tapped her brow and winked.

"What does your mother say to this, Faye? You won't be able to ensnare Douglas from here."

"Ha ha! She doesn't know yet. Anyway, I'm over twenty-one. Are you going to work here?"

"Not as an auxiliary."

"I know that. I mean are you going to make your film here? Is that why you've come? Don't look so surprised. I mean, you obviously can't make it at Medrose now ... and since the Silkworm is here ..."

"He *is* here! Thank heavens!"

"... it didn't take much for a genius like me to work it out. One day I'll find your baby Moses for you, too. By the way, I told Miss Martin your name was to be Miss English Rose from now on."

Jennifer threw back her head and laughed. "Did I tell you that, too?"

"Yes. Have you forgotten?"

"I don't know — so much has happened." She flung her arms around Faye and hugged her. "But I am glad to see you here."

"Come on." Faye took her wrist and dragged her back to the front door. "She probably knows you're here. That porter tells her everything."

"Just one thing more — how *is* the Silkworm? Does he know *we* know all about him?"

"I'm sure he doesn't. I certainly haven't said anything. He hasn't said much, either, but I've noticed him watching me. Trying to size me up." Her eyes danced merrily.

"Size you up?"

"Yes, he's wondering if I've come here to take up his kind offer. Poor Sibyl! She'll be sure that's why I'm here — and she'll be so *green!*"

With echoing footsteps they crossed the large entrance hall, which, despite the potted plants all around, was still as bleak as its original architect had intended.

Just before they came to the door of Miss Martin's study Jennifer reacted to something Faye had said earlier. "Little white lie?" she echoed in a fierce whisper. *"Little* white lie? It's a whopper! You know what you are, Faye? You're *a wayward girl!* You're right where you belong at last — in here!"

Faye stuck out her tongue, knocked at Miss Martin's door, pushed it open, and said, "Miss Rose English."

51 MISS MARTIN still looked every inch the reformatory superintendent, with her silver-gray hair gathered tightly into a bun — so tightly, in fact, that you felt sure it must be stretching her skin all the way down to the soles of her feet — and her piercing eyes, which stared at you through steel-rimmed glasses. Those glasses seemed to confer upon her the power to peer into your very thoughts.

And yet, somehow, Jennifer knew the woman was going to say yes from the moment they met. She was beginning to realize that humanity was divided into yea-sayers and nay-sayers. Of the two, the nay-sayers were the trickiest for they divided yet again into the honest and the devious. Honest nay-sayers frowned and ground their teeth and tugged at any beard or whisker they happened to have about them and generally looked sour from the beginning; but the devious kind smiled encouragingly and accepted all your reasons for saying yes before, with many a sigh and many a sorrowful shake of the head, they overtopped you with ten times as many reasons for saying no.

But some instinct told Jennifer that, despite her outward severity, Miss Martin was a yea-sayer to life and its many adventures. She was, after all, that same woman who had once said a joyful yea to a gentleman who wished to 'show her his etchings' — Jennifer was almost certain of it. And yea-sayers don't come more yea-sayery than that.

Even so, the woman made her spell out Cass's plans to the smallest detail. Jennifer imagined she would be mainly interested in the way the physical business of making a movie would disrupt the regularity of life at Little Sinns — the crew, the paraphernalia, the noise of the generators, and so forth — but she seemed to take all that for granted. She actually thought it would do her convalescents and auxiliaries more good than harm to appear as what Cass called 'extras' in the drama; after all, as she pointed out, amateur dramatics were already part of their recovery programme there. She was much more interested in the moral aspects of the movie.

Jennifer hastened to assure her it would be of the highest tone and that not even the archbishop of Truro himself would cavil at it.

But Miss Martin interrupted her. "You misunderstand me, Miss Owen. You see, I *know* Cass Potter of old. He likes to think himself the world's cynic but in fact he's a soft, sentimental old dear. I don't want my girls being turned into pure sugar — indeed, not even sugar, but saccharine copies ... Talking of which, may I offer you some tea?" She pressed a button on her desk without waiting for an answer, saying, "And it will only be saccharin, I'm afraid."

"Everywhere, these days," Jennifer said vaguely. "But I'd love a cup of tea — just milk, no sweetener."

"Sweet enough already, eh!"

An auxiliary came to the door and Miss Martin ordered tea for three.

"You know Rosalind came with me, I suppose?" Jennifer said.

"Yes, she'll join us soon. At the moment she's trying to dig up something scurrilous about her mother and aunt from Davies, out there in his lodge. She'll soon give up, though."

Jennifer thought, *Yes, if this were still a reformatory and I were a new arrival, I'd start to believe you had mystical ways of finding things out!* She said, "I know what you mean about Cass Potter, though. He has this idea, you see, that, since Little Sinns was once a home for wayward girls, it would be dramatic to make it part of the story that the auxiliaries are all ex-... what d'you call them? Inmates? Pupils?"

"Girls," Miss Martin said. "Ex-girls, just as one would with old girls from any other good school. In fact, there's no need to pretend. All of them *are* ex-girls — except for your friend Miss Carminowe, of course. Is she to have a part in your play?"

"That would be for Cass Potter to say."

"Ah, yes — Cass Potter. Let me guess what he has in mind. He wants to show my ex-girls as Florence Nightingales reincarnate ... angels with lanterns, going round the wards in the small hours, mopping fevered brows ..."

"... and repaying their debt to England," Jennifer put in.

"And in between, no doubt, recalling some of the more titillating moments of their wicked, wanton past! Yes — you see, I do know Cass Potter quite well."

"Actually, it was Mrs Collett who suggested it. Cass wanted to make the film at Medrose with all the aristocratic girls there. Noblesse oblige, et cetera."

"Yes, I know Mrs Collett, too, dear good soul that she is. Now there's a woman who really *is* as tough as a box of rivets. She resorts to sentimentality to cover it up. The end result is the same, of course. However, you may tell both of them that I'm afraid I cannot permit a play with such a trite and untrue theme to be made under this roof."

Jennifer's heart sank. "I think Mrs Collett only wanted to show that war could purify and uplift as well as hurt and destroy."

"And d'you think it can?" the other asked sharply. "Have you been purified and uplifted by your father's quite senseless death in London last year?"

The question rocked Jennifer. It must have been quite a telephone conversation between Miss Martin and Crissy Collett, she realized.

"No." Miss Martin softened again. "There is nothing to be said in favour of war — though you may be sure our screens will be flooded for the next few years with cinematic plays that glorify its encouragement of patriotism, heroism — the ultimate test of manhood, and so forth. I won't have it. You tell Cass Potter this: He has a chance — here at Little Sinns — to tell a story, a true story, of war's horrors, of the depravities that follow in its wake, of the monstrous atrocities it ..." Her voice broke and words failed her. She swallowed, drew a deep breath, and went on: "He can tell a story here to relight the beacon of civilization in this sea of new barbarism. He can snatch a brand from this monstrous fire now raging across Europe and with it light the conscience of the world. Whew!" She fanned her face and smiled apologetically. "Sorry, but we've had some particularly gruesome cripples sent to us lately — armless, legless, blind ... one only wonders that they aren't insane, too."

Jennifer closed her eyes to evade that pitiless stare. The idea stirred her; the challenge of it was exciting; but ...

"Well?" Miss Martin said.

"I agree. It's a powerful idea ..."

"Because it's true."

"An exciting challenge, too."

Miss Martin smiled. "I hear a big *but* coming."

Jennifer sighed. "Well, I can see a *story* in Cass's idea. It almost writes itself ..."

"That's because it's a cliché. The clown who cannot laugh ... the whore with a heart of gold ... the wickedness of stepmothers ... all such stories write themselves. We must persuade Cass Potter he's bigger than that."

Jennifer remained silent. It wasn't that she disagreed with a word the woman had said — she just didn't think it would make a movie. But how could she say as much without throwing away any chance of filming at Little Sinns?

"You're still not happy?" Miss Martin prompted her.

"I think it's deeper than that. I mean, it's not as simple as cliché versus truth. The movie Cass wants to make is about *real* people. But a movie about the horrors of war would be a movie about a message — a *manifesto,* as the politicians say. Any real people would be all cut down to suit the message. And Cass's plot *needn't* be about clichés, either. Especially as *you* are here, Miss Martin. *You* could see to it that your ex-girls aren't romanticized. You could insist that the awfulness of some of the things they have to do here is not glossed over. And you could ensure that their reminiscences about their wicked past are true to the life — who better! And, actually — come to think of it — our message about the horrors of war can be carried as well. Only it will come out unobtrusively, between the lines — or between the scenes — as it were. People will pick it up unconsciously, you see — which is much better than grabbing them by the buttonhole and bawling it in their ears. Also, don't forget ..."

"Yes, Portia!" Miss Martin interrupted with a light laugh. "You're very convincing. I don't mean you've convinced me — except to the extent that I'm willing to give it a try. You tell Cass Potter that you've broken the ice pretty well and that I'd like to see him too for a good, hearty chinwag about this cinema play of his. Now" — she sat well back in her chair and folded her hands in her lap — "tell me something about yourself before Rosalind comes."

Jennifer felt she had been turned inside-out by the time she and Rosalind set out on the short walk back to the station. "But I don't really mind," she added. "It's all in a good cause."

"The cause of Jennifer Owen," Rosalind said, not unkindly.

"Whose mother started it all in the first place?" Jennifer countered.

52 WHEN MISS MARTIN finally said yes it was like slipping the drive belt onto some mighty machine, full of complex parts that moved in bewildering but perfectly meshed interactions. Telegrams sped between Penzance and London; bankers' drafts, letters of credit, contracts, and heads of understanding were delivered with every post; packing cases began to arrive at Redruth station, filled with arc lamps, cameras, dollies, reflectors, tripods, and other trappings of the movie-making business. Cass no longer looked like a genial if slightly shady banker for he had put off his British warm with the astrakhan collar; in its place he wore a sort of colonial hunting outfit — jodhpurs, a slightly-too-large khaki jacket with big appliqué pockets, and, where a colonial might wear a pith helmet, a tweed cap with the peak turned to the back, covering his neck.

In this outlandish get-up he certainly stood out from the rest of the crowd — which, he maintained, was the first duty of a movie director. His second rule, though he never enunciated it, seemed to be to keep one and all in a high old state of creative confusion. All this activity seemed to give him a new lease of energy, at which Jennifer could only marvel. In a single five-minute period she saw him suggest a way of relocating the generator so that it had better access to cooling water, decree three minor but important changes to the sample uniform that Martha was running up on Crissy's sewing machine, and rewrite the captions to one scene that Miss Martin had rejected as 'pure saccharin.'

Jennifer realized that Cass's earlier appearance as a slightly down-at-heels impresario struggling to *seem* rich had been a sham; money was certainly flowing freely now that the film had actually started. Whatever qualms she might have had about her 'outrageous' demand for high wages were now stilled.

But when one worry goes another takes its place. The moment she relished least was having to meet Cardew Silk again — more than meet him, in fact, for he was, of course, to play the lead opposite her. That, in turn, meant they were to fall in love, that he was to kiss her passionately in several scenes, and that he was at last to die with his head cradled on her bosom — a conjunction of which he would, no doubt, take every advantage. She wondered how she was going to be able to engage in so many intimate acts with him, and both of them knowing what even greater intimacy he had once proposed to her. She did not doubt that she *would* play her part; she merely wondered how.

He was not, in fact, a patient at Little Sinns. Miss Martin's experienced eye had sniffed out the malingerer within half a day and had extracted his full story from him by sundown. Her first thought had been to hand him over to the military police but when she learned that he could be shot for impersonating an officer in wartime, she cured his wounds overnight and employed him as a medical orderly, instead — in which position she promised to maintain him until the moment had passed when a hue and cry might hound him down.

"He isn't entirely sane, you know," she told Jennifer. "One must be a little tolerant. Not that he's certifiable, mind, but he inhabits that awkward no-man's-land between eccentricity and outright lunacy. He's certainly *very* eccentric."

Hesitantly Jennifer asked if she knew precisely why the man had been expelled so peremptorily from Medrose.

The slight but knowing smile that twitched at the corners of her lips was answer enough.

Emboldened, Jennifer went on, "And weren't you afraid he might ... you know, with so many of your ex-girls here?"

"Firstly, my dear, they are *ex*-girls, you know. Secondly, they're all grown-ups now, fully capable of taking such decisions for themselves — as were you girls at Medrose, I must say. Ganging up on him like that was very schoolgirlish, in my opinion."

Jennifer swallowed hard and stared at her. "You mean ..."

"You know very well what I mean, my dear," Miss Martin said. "There's no need to say it in so many words. Actually, I confess I'm looking forward to seeing him in uniform again — especially that short-jacketed one they call, rather inelegantly, a 'bum-freezer.' His face is handsome enough in a vacuous, upper-class sort of way but from behind, in those narrow-waisted, tight little trousers, he's absolutely the berries — or hadn't you noticed?"

"Upper-class?" Jennifer asked, to avoid the embarrassment of a direct answer — which, of course, led to her sharing all that Corporal Walters had revealed of the Silkworm's past.

Miss Martin listened with undisguised glee. "Oh, Jennifer," she said when the tale was told, "isn't life just so *interesting* once you get beyond those clichés we were talking about the other day! Cardew Silk of Eton College is really just Charlie Shortis of ... well, of Eton! Who would have thought it?"

"He's a good actor then."

"Yes, that too!"

Jennifer met him for the first time since what he called his 'expulsion from Eden' that same afternoon. "Hallo, you old scoundrel," she said, hoping to set a new seal on a new relationship.

It took two or three seconds from the moment he recognized her to the moment when he had composed his face into a suitable expression of melancholy. She witnessed the transformation with amazement. It was like watching a lightning sketch artist turn a general-purpose eggshell of a head into one with a precise character and expression, all within seconds. "I've been desolated, princess ..." he began.

"Enough of that!" She cut him short. "There are one or two things I'd like to have clear from the very beginning, if you and I are to play opposite each other."

"That was the only thing which prevented me from putting an end to my miserable existence, princess. When I heard that you and I ..."

"Cardew!" she said peremptorily. "If you don't stop this persiflage at once, I ... I'll ..." She floundered for a moment until inspiration struck her. "I shall start calling you Charlie Shortis!"

That worked; he came to heel in an instant.

"Walters told you," he said gloomily, still in his upper-class voice. "Bloody traitor — pardon the French."

"Bloody good friend, I'd say," she countered. "He told me nothing until after you'd gone. He could have had you shot at any moment. Don't you realize you could be shot for what you've done?"

"I'd play the scene well," he said coolly as he straightened up before an imaginary firing squad. "No blindfold, thank you, General." He pushed away the imagined offer. "I want to see the whites of their eyes." He dropped the besom with which he had been sweeping the back courtyard, stood up even straighter, arms behind him, and jutted his jaw pugnaciously.

"And I want to talk to you seriously," she said.

"Oh *what?*" he asked in a surly tone.

"Just this — and let's get it quite clear before we even begin: If you take advantage of our intimate scenes — by which I mean that if you attempt anything beyond what is strictly required by our profession — I shall advertise your origins to everyone at Little Sinns."

He turned pale. "You wouldn't dare!"

"You dare, I dare," she replied. "But play your part professionally and I'll go to my grave rather than reveal it. Though" — she spoke now in a kindlier tone, taking his arm and leading him an aimless little stroll — "if I may say so, I cannot see why you should feel the way you do."

"What d'you mean?" He was sulky still, but also intrigued.

"I mean that if I were you, I'd be far prouder of having come from your origins and arriving at where you are today than I would be at having come from Eton College and *descending* to where you are today!" She took up the besom and thrust it into his grasp. *"If* you see what I mean?"

He stared at the thing as if his hands had never held it before and said, "Mmm."

"Pax?" she suggested. "Professional pax?"

"Okay," he replied.

At last the day dawned on which they were to start filming in earnest; appropriately enough it was All Fools Day, too. Until then they had merely carried out little technical tests — for make-up, dress, lighting, and so on — which had occupied most of that March at Little Sinns. Since Martha was now wardrobe mistress to the 'unit,' Rosalind had appointed herself as Jennifer's chaperon and dresser — an office that came to an end in the middle of the month, when it was time for her to return to France. Crissy had then volunteered to take over all her daughter's services, except, of course, for makeup, which was nothing like what anyone outside the movie business would call by that name. Movie makeup involved painting the face a rather ghastly white and almost blackening the lips and parts of the eyes; it was therefore done by a professional from London, a woman who had worked on many of Cass's previous films and could 'tell them a thing or two' — or so she kept darkly promising.

Crissy turned up on that first morning of proper filming with a little packet in her hand. "Just a talisman," she said while Jennifer unwrapped the paper around it. "We hope it'll bring you better luck than the last wearer ..." Her voice trailed off as she saw Jennifer gape in surprise.

It was a brightly polished Victorian bun penny soldered to a brooch pin. "How?" was all she could say as she continued to stare at it — almost as if she feared it would vanish if she looked away. "Does this mean you've also found ..."

She could not say it in so many words but Crissy understood what she meant, anyway. "Oh no, dear, it isn't *that* one," she said quickly. "I'm sorry if I gave that impression."

"When you said 'the last wearer' ..."

"I was going to say 'the last wearer of such an ornament.' My husband made it last night. It's very easy if you have a clean penny, some solder, and a brooch pin. I hope you like it? I was a bit doubtful, myself — for obvious reasons — but he seemed to think it a good idea." Jennifer's continuing amazement disconcerted her slightly.

"It's lovely. Tell him I'm so grateful." She laughed. "I'm another babe launched on an unknown sea, so it's very befitting."

Cass spotted it at once. "What's that?" he asked as she walked onto the set. "That's not in the props list." He started riffling through his own personal chaos of papers.

"It's just a talisman," she explained. "Mister Collett made it for me last night. There's no reason I can't wear it, is there?"

He came closer and peered at the brooch. "I like it," he said. "We can use it. We'll change the story. Give it to Silk so's he can give it to you in his dying moments."

She stared at him in perplexity. "But why? It doesn't play any part in the story. Anyway, he doesn't die until the final scene."

"That's right. That's what we're shooting today — the final scene."

"Oh." She was nonplussed. "I assumed we'd start with scene one."

General laughter greeted this remark.

Cass waved them to silence. "We always shoot the last scene first, darling. It locks us in, if you follow — so's we all know where we're going. Otherwise, you know, we could stray ... anywhere."

Having seen something of his improvised methods so far, she could understand the logic of that. Also she was relieved to be getting the head-cradled-in-bosom bit over and done with while her warning was still sharp in the Silkworm's mind. "But why does he give it to me?" she asked. "Are we going to change the earlier story to give it some significance?"

He thought about that and then said, "No. It'll be what we call a teaser — something you don't explain. People will go out the cinema saying, 'What was that brooch he give her? I didn't understand that.' And it'll nag with them and stick in the mind. And then, if *Little Sinns* is a success, we can ..."

"Is that its name now?"

"For the moment. Don't keep asking questions or we'll never get going. That brooch will be like a peg on which we can hang the further adventures of Nurse ... what's your name now?"

Jennifer sighed. "Last time I was told anything about it I was Rose English playing Nurse English — the idea was that I'm playing my real-life self. Remember? Of course, that was three hours ago, so God knows what I'm called by now."

There was more general laughter, this time directed toward — but not against — Cass himself.

"The brooch is our hook into the further adventures of Nurse English," he said firmly. "Give it to Silk and let's get on with this scene, okay? I want one strong light across him, Bill, and a dim light with a naked filament to reflect off his eyeballs in the dark. Can we see that effect?"

Since they'd spent an hour the previous day testing it, Bill already had the lighting set up. Cardew Silk took the brooch from Jennifer, lay back in his bed, and cradled his head in her arms as chastely as anyone could wish. Bill killed the general lighting and switched on the specials. Jennifer gave a little gasp for the effect was quite extraordinary. The hair prickled on the nape of her neck as it seemed to her that she really was holding a dying man in her arms. She did not notice that the cameraman was already cranking his handle; she thought this was just a rehearsal.

The rule was that nobody spoke on the set except Cass, who kept up a constant stream of directions and encouragement: "Watch Silk, darling, take your cue from him as his life ebbs away ... good ... Lower your eyelids, Silk ... not so fast ... that's it ... and Rose, now you *see* he's dying. Look up at the light — straight into it — like you're saying to God, 'Why? Why?' That's it — oh, yes! Ma-a-arvellous! Now Silk, you stir a little. And Rose, darling, you ... good gel! Don't need to tell you much! Breathe in deep, Silk — this is your last gasp ... that's it!"

Bill whispered urgently, "The talisman!"

"Oh yeah!" Cass punched himself on the brow.

But Cardew Silk was already struggling to get one feeble hand into his pyjama pocket. Jennifer was still all a-tingle with excitement at the conviction behind his performance; it required very little acting on her part to brush a stray lock from his brow and let her knuckles stray tenderly down his cheek. She knew it was going well because Cass stopped directing so minutely from then on, simply letting their own momentum carry them forward.

There was a moment of panic for her when at last his trembling fingers drew the brooch from his pocket. Was she supposed to recognize it? If so, did it recall happy memories, or sad ones? And if not, was she merely curious ... or something stronger — puzzled? Alarmed, even? Damn Cass and his brilliant improvisations! But Cardew, bless the man, must have sensed her dilemma and at once gave her the lead she lacked. His shy smile as he held it up into the light told her this was an act of tenderness, evoking some powerful emotion they had once shared. She accepted it from him as if he were giving her the most precious jewel in the universe, pressed it to her lips, and closed her eyes.

To her surprise (and, judging by the gasp that went up all about her, to the surprise of most others, too) she felt a tear roll down her cheek. A real, wet tear!

Then, for the first time, she heard the camera being cranked and, realizing who and where she really was, she froze.

Later Cass said that final stiffening of her whole body, as the life passed out of Lieutenant Silk of the 10th Royal Hussars, was one of the finest pieces of acting he'd ever seen.

When she thought how much the scene had owed to Bill's expertise with the lighting, and how much her 'finest piece of acting' owed to sheer panic, she realized how little praise she was actually due; but she held her peace and accepted it all, nonetheless.

The death scene was, indeed, the last of the dramatic scenes. But Cass had another brilliant idea at that moment. If 'Rose English' was going to play her 'real life' self in *Little Sinns,* it would be more effective to run the cast list at the end of the movie — more of a surprise. He could, of course, run it over a 'frozen frame,' as they called it, of that moving final scene — especially with the glistening tear on Rose's cheek. He probably would do that, but, just in case it didn't work, he decided to shoot what he called a 'winding-down scene' showing the ordinary life of the convalescent home resuming once again.

"We'll cross-fade the special lights to a general all-over effect, Bill," he said. "And you, darling, you're kneeling beside the bed, see — praying. And then one of the other auxiliaries comes in ... who's free? Any auxiliary there?"

In fact, they were all busy with real inmates but a carpenter, who was standing near the door, called out to one who was passing, "Oy, ducks — wannabe a star before all your mates get the chance?"

"Let me see now, it's Ann Hotchkiss, isn't it?" Cass asked as the girl came shyly among them.

She blossomed at being recognized.

He explained what he wanted of her — how she was to come into the room, hesitate a moment, then realize that the officer had died, go slowly to the bed and pull the sheet up over his face, then touch Nurse English gently on the shoulder. He told her they'd just run through it once or twice as a rehearsal — till she felt comfortable with it — but, as with Jennifer's scene, he tipped the wink to the cameraman, who filmed the whole scene.

And Ann Hotchkiss was good, Jennifer realized — too damn good. She was going to steal the final scene of the movie if it were ever used. *What can I do to get it back?* she wondered furiously.

She thought of dabbing a handkerchief ostentatiously at her eyes but somehow that didn't seem dramatic enough. Also too crude.

The solution came to her at the moment the girl took hold of the sheet and began to draw it up over Cardew's face: She let the brooch slip from her nerveless fingers.

Ann Hotchkiss saw it, of course, and hesitated a moment, wondering if Jennifer had made a mistake. Then, as if the brooch meant something to her, too, she raised a hand to her mouth and recoiled in something close to terror.

"Marvellous!" Cass called out encouragingly. "Now go forward again. Keep looking at that brooch. Reach out for it like you're afraid it could be boiling hot. Yes — that's good. Now touch it ..." And so on.

Only Jennifer, watching her through the slits of her praying fingers and seeing her response from no more than three feet away, realized that her initial terror at the sight of the brooch had owed nothing to whatever native acting ability the girl might possess. She had quite genuinely *recognized* it — or thought she did, just as Jennifer herself had thought she recognized it half an hour earlier. And the terror that followed had been quite genuine, too.

For the second time in five minutes Jennifer froze and the nape of her neck tingled.

53 AFTER THAT auspicious beginning the pace of filming never slackened. Cass slowly — and deliberately — abandoned his technique of secretly filming what he called mere rehearsals. Collett & Trevarton developed each day's footage overnight so that he could show unedited prints of the previous day's work to the actors first thing the following morning. When the largely amateur cast saw that the 'rehearsals' weren't half as bad as they had feared, they gained sufficiently in confidence for Cass to start saying things like, 'That was good, darling, but the bit where you turn and recognize him — remember? — I want you to take that at about half the speed what you took it at. Okay?' And, in time, he progressed to saying, 'You can do a lot better than that, pet. Tone it down. You're not acting on stage — trying to reach people up in the gods, half a mile away. You're twenty foot high and sitting right in their laps. Underplay! Underplay! Underplay! What did I say?"

And the embarrassed actor or actress would have to say, "Underplay."

"Right! Underplay — the very word! I wish I'd thought of it myself."

And so, by mixing jokes, criticism, cajolery, and encouragement, he coaxed from each the best that he or she could give.

For Jennifer, who was the chief recipient of this treatment, it was the customary baptism by fire. Indeed, at times she felt she was entirely surrounded by flames, for not only did she have to face whatever Cass was dishing out that day, but always at her back she felt the blaze of curiosity at Ann Hotchkiss's strange behaviour when she clapped eyes on the bun-penny brooch. She longed to ask the woman, straight out, what it had meant to her and why she had reacted so strongly, but she knew that would be the worst possible approach she could make. Nothing would be more likely to make the woman close up like a clam.

Her behaviour could mean so many things, from the utterly innocent to the deeply implicated. Crissy Collett had said the original brooch had been stolen from them — most likely by a respectable female friend with a touch of kleptomania. If so, she had probably returned it to them — or half returned it — by leaving it lying conspicuously where they might find it. Or where someone else might find it, too. That someone else could so easily have been Ann Hotchkiss. And that might be the beginning and the end of her involvement in the affair.

Would that give her a guilty conscience large enough to prompt such a response more than half a decade later?

Probably not, in normal circumstances. But under the emotionally charged conditions of acting in her first-ever scene in her first-ever movie — when her nerves would already be stretched to screaming point ...? It was possible.

At the other extreme it was also possible that she, once a wayward girl, had herself borne and then later abandoned the baby Moses — along with the brooch she had stolen or somehow acquired. Her extreme response on seeing what she thought was the selfsame ornament would then need no special pleading to fit the facts.

And in between these extremes there were, no doubt, half a dozen equally plausible or implausible explanations. The trouble was that the plausible ones might be lies from start to finish; the implausible ones could be the pure, unvarnished truth! Unfortunately, those that involved either the abandonment or the later abduction — or both — of Moses were the very ones that any sensible woman would deny and do all in her power to conceal.

She simply had to find out more about Miss Ann Hotchkiss — and without arousing the woman's slightest suspicions.

On the pretext that her long sessions of make-up were boring and she wanted to be able to chat with the others, she moved from her 'star' dressing room to a more democratic seat among the rest of the girls.

Once there, she took the seat next to Ann Hotchkiss and made sure to leave the brooch lying carelessly but conspicuously on her dressing table, where even the most casual observer could not fail to see it.

The trouble was, everything could be read in two ways. The woman picked it up, quite casually, and said, "That did give I a turn when I seed 'n that time!"

Jennifer's heart skipped a beat at the thought that her bait had been so quickly snapped up. "Oh?" she responded, equally casually, as she offered a cheek to Gerty McGuire, the make-up lady. "Why so?"

"I 'ad one just like it once. My ol' man made it for I years ago."

"Mrs Collett's husband made this one for me — for good luck, you know — the night before filming started."

"Oh, I do know this ain't mine." She laid it back among Jennifer's things. "Mine 'ad a nick on the Queen's cheek. Yur, see?" And she drew her fingernail diagonally across Victoria's face.

And that was where Jennifer decided to let this first conversation lapse — slowly, slowly; softly, softly.

Was the woman lying — trying to put some distance between herself and the only brooch in which Jennifer was interested?

Or was she telling the truth? And, if so, had the brooch on Moses been similarly damaged? Jennifer cursed herself that she had not studied it more closely. She should have written down every detail. Perhaps Martha might remember. Her mother almost certainly would. She had an eye for such things, as Jennifer knew to her cost.

But her mother might as well be on the far side of the moon, for the filming of *Little Sinns* went on from dawn to dusk and beyond, even on Sundays, when they had the shortest possible pause for divine services. She was hardly ever in bed before midnight and was usually wakened by Cass himself at six for what he called 'storytime.' That was when he revealed which fragments of the screenplay he hoped to put 'in the box' that day. They generally set up the cameras and lights in a certain location and then shot all the bits that required that particular setting, one after the other, regardless of their position in the story. It was even more confusing than that, for they would begin with the scenes that involved all the ex-girls, then the ones that involved only some of them, then the ones that involved just Nurse English or just Lt Silk and one or other 'extra,' and, last of all, came the shots where they were alone with each other or solo.

But even that was not the end of it for the two main characters. After supper, when all the others knew they had finished for the day, Jennifer and Cardew had to go back while Cass put their 'solo responses' against that particular background in the box. These scenes were not actually part of the plot. Indeed, most of them would be thrown away after the film was finished. They were brief takes in which the hero or heroine had to appear startled, curious, amused, affronted, alarmed, pensive — the whole gamut of emotions — against that day's particular backgrounds. And not just once, either, but in lighting that also ran the gamut from bright day to dramatic gloom. They were for Cass to use if he needed to break up a longer scene, or show a particular emotion in close-up, when it came to editing the movie.

Small wonder that Jennifer usually fell asleep the moment her head settled on the pillow; she could yawn no more than a pepperminty 'G'night' to poor Faye, who slept in the only other bed in the room and who had whole *budgets* of gossip to share.

On that day when Ann Hotchkiss spoke of recognizing the brooch, however, they had been filming outdoors, so nightwork on solo responses was impossible; they would be shot at the very end of filming, when the carpenters and other hands could be gainfully employed in dismantling and packing up. So the two girls had the luxury of an early night and the chance to talk themselves hoarse. The chief topic was, of course, La Hotchkiss — to start with, anyway.

"Charlotte Morgan says she's married," Faye said. "And she should know because they were both wayward girls here at the same time."

"Ah — damn! — that reminds me. She said her old man made a brooch like mine for her once, which was why she reacted like that. And I meant to ask her — did she mean her husband or her father?"

"When they say *my* old man they usually mean husband. They call their father *the* old man. Her maiden name was Harris, by the way — when she was here."

"When was that — did Morgan tell you? Funny — my mother's maiden name was Morgan."

Faye gave a single, bleak laugh. "The stench of red herrings hereabouts is overpowering, Watson! I think it was nineteen-ten … nineteen-eleven. She said they were among the older girls here, which means they'd have been sixteen or seventeen. They kicked them out on their eighteenth birthday, didn't they?"

Jennifer nodded. "They sent them up to the workhouse then."

"And what would you say they are now? Twenty-one or -two? So that's about right. But — this is the bit where you're going to scream, Jenny — guess what she was sent here for?"

Jennifer knew it was so before she heard her own voice saying it: "She had a baby out of wedlock."

Faye reached across the space between their beds and squeezed her arm. "A baby boy."

"Oh … God!" Jennifer murmured. Then she opened her eyes and laughed — more in surprise than with amusement. "Heaven knows why I'm so interested all of a sudden. I've spent most of this past year pooh-poohing everybody's else attempts to find young Moses and now it's turning into an obsession with me, too. I suddenly feel I've just *got* to find him — but I don't know why."

"Since when?"

"Since Hotchkiss reacted in that strange manner, I suppose. I feel if I don't solve it now, once and for ever, it's going to dog me all my days. She said *her* brooch had a scratch on the queen's cheek. The infuriating thing is I can't remember if mine did, too — the one I found. Martha can't remember, either, and Crissy says the one she lost definitely wasn't damaged like that. I asked her to ask my mother tonight. She would certainly remember. She could tell you every scratch on every bit of furniture we ever had — *and* who the culprit was!"

"It could have got scratched after it was stolen from the Colletts. And if La Hotchkiss is lying about her husband making a brooch for her, then all three of these brooches could be one and the same."

Jennifer turned on her back and rubbed her eyes. "My head's spinning."

"D'you want to talk about something else?" Her tone promised amazements.

Jennifer opened her eyes, grinned, and said, "What?"

"Miss Martin?"

"Ooh yes — what about her?"

"D'you notice the way she and the Silkworm never look at each other?"

"Yes," Jennifer replied. "And I thought that was odd because you remember what I told you she said to me about him at the beginning — what a shapely little b-t-m he has?"

"That's what made me keep an eye peeled. I've been watching them pretty closely and I thought it very odd that she never looked at him, especially after her saying such things. And then, it must have been two nights ago — you were fast asleep and you looked so sweet or I'd have woken you …"

Jennifer stuck out her tongue but said nothing to hinder this exciting and scandal-promising narrative.

"Not that there'd have been anything for you to see by the time I could have got back here. Anyway, I thought I smelled burning and went out into the passage. Thank heavens my dressing gown's that dark navy-blue colour or he'd have seen me."

"The Silkworm?"

"Who else! He came out of his room, walked away from me, along the passage, stopped at the foot of the little stairs at the end, looked up and down — not seeing me, as I said — and raced up them. I mean *raced!*" She grinned as she watched her revelation take effect.

"But that only leads to ..." Jennifer's voice trailed off as she grappled with the impossible.

"Just so!" Faye said.

"But she's *sixty* if she's a day!"

"Tee hee!" Faye replied. "That's why she doesn't look at him in public. She gets an eyeful of him in private — and it's not just her eye that he fills, I'm thinking!"

"Faye!" Jennifer exclaimed, and then giggled as a further thought struck her — again prompted by something in her friend's tone of voice. "Are you just a little bit jealous, by any chance?"

"A *little* bit? I'm furious! Half my reason for leaving Medrose and coming here was to take up the Silkworm on his kind offer."

"No!" Jennifer was scandalized.

"Yes," Faye insisted. "I'm going to be married off to some boring old cad whose chin is never dry. I want to know what it's like before I start drowning in dewlap."

"But ... the Silkworm!" Jennifer pulled a sour face.

"Sibyl said he was marvellous."

"She never had the chance to ..."

"Oh yes she did! She sneaked over here after he was kicked out of Medrose. She's had quite a few men, you know — or so she *says* — and, according to her, the Silkworm was far and away the best."

Jennifer let out her breath as if she had just been hit. "Is there no such thing as respectability anywhere at all these days?"

"Among the *middle* classes, I'm sure," Faye said grandly. "But it never had much hold among us aristocrats. Nor, surely, did you demimondaines ever pay it much attention?"

"Me — a demimondaine?" Jennifer laughed.

"Of course! You're a film actress now — what else are all actresses but demimondaines? Didn't you realize?"

54 WHEN SHOOTING finished on the main body of the film, early in May, Jennifer no longer had the slightest idea what the story might be — nor, she suspected, did Cass, either. He made his movies the way quilters make quilts — collect more scraps than you'll ever need, work out some kind of overall scheme, and start stitching this bit and that bit together. All she knew for certain was that she had once been a very naughty girl, graduating from picking pockets *à la* Artful Dodger to picking them on a larger though even more sordid scale *à la* Whore with a Heart of Gold — that she had held the dying hero, Lt Silk vc, of the Tenth Royals, in her arms while he gave her a cheap but enigmatic trinket — that one week later she had kissed him passionately, two weeks later shyly, and three weeks later for the first time — that she had been reformed by a genuine demimondaine called Olga Murphy, a London actress who impersonated to perfection a genuine moral reformer like Miss Martin — and that she and the other auxiliaries had staged a marvellous pillow-fight with feathers everywhere. That, however, was the only comic relief in what, when the quilter had quilted it to perfection, would become a sombre but gripping tale of masculine and feminine heroism amidst the futilities of war.

Only the outdoor solo responses remained to go in the box. Curiously enough, Jennifer found she enjoyed these brief shots more than the longer dramatic scenes. The crew was reduced to one lighting man, a few hands, the cameraman, and Cass himself, of course. It was the sort of relaxed, intimate, yet hard-working setting that her tests with George Herbert had led her to expect.

Miss Martin seemed to enjoy them, too. After all the fuss she had made about the moral core of the movie she had taken remarkably little part in its day-to-day making. She had from time to time suggested substituting a more badly maimed soldier for one who was less scarred; and she had strengthened the wording of many of the captions that conveyed the dialogue or the scene-setting information; but that had been the limit of her contribution. She claimed she was far too busy to get more deeply involved in the business.

Now that only three days of filming were left, however — and all of them involving just Cardew Silk or Jennifer — it seemed she could find half an hour or more on each of them just to sit and watch. Jennifer took advantage of one of these sessions, when both she and Miss Martin were on the sidelines, watching the Silkworm perform, to tell her the tale about finding Moses and all the efforts she and others had made to trace him — ever since Douglas Colston-Smart had discovered that the boy had not, after all, been taken to the Helston orphanage. She concluded by telling her of Ann Hotchkiss's extraordinary reaction to the sudden appearance of what must have looked like the same bun-penny brooch on the first day of filming.

Miss Martin's face remained a basilisk mask throughout. When Jennifer had quite finished she said, "You must understand that I can give away none of the secrets my girls may have confided in me during their time here — or, indeed, since."

"So she's spoken to you since," Jennifer said at once.

"Don't be so quick, my dear."

"Sorry. Obviously, I could go to the registrar of births, marriages, and deaths and pay the appropriate fee, if there is one — I don't know — and plough through the records of births around nineteen-ten, starting with the name Harris ..."

"Ah. You know that much then?"

"Yes, I also know she was ..."

"But how d'you know the birth was registered at all?"

"Because, as I was about to say, I also know she was sent here after having a male baby out of wedlock. It's inconceivable that the authorities would do that without insisting on a proper registration, even if the baby had died in the meantime. So, in a way, the *fact* of the baby's birth, its proper name, the mother's name — and possibly the name of the father — all these *facts* are already matters of public record. They may have been given to you in confidence in the first place, but they're no longer secret. Plus the date of her admission here — if that were anywhere around the middle of June in nineteen-hundred-and-ten, which is when I found Moses ..."

"Yes? What then?"

"Well, don't you see? It would all begin to hang together."

Miss Martin was silent so long that Jennifer felt impelled to prompt her. "Or am I wasting my time pursuing yet another false trail?"

"Why d'you need to know that? You say yourself how ridiculous you thought the Colston-Smarts were in trying to trace the boy. His fate hasn't really bothered you much ever since you first ..."

"I don't know, Miss Martin. I wish I could answer you. All I can say is that ever since Ann Hotchkiss reacted in that strange way, I've been consumed with the feeling that this it *it*. This is my one chance — perhaps my one and only chance — to solve the whole riddle. But even that doesn't really explain it. I just can't."

"And if you found the boy? He'd be what now — six or seven years old? What then?"

"That would depend on the circumstances in which he's living."

"If he were living happily and comfortably in a good, loving family?"

Jennifer stared hard at her. These questions seemed to have a particular point. "Do you know something about him, then? Is that what you're hinting at by asking me such ..."

"Never you mind, young lady. Just answer my question — then I'll decide what to tell you — if anything."

Jennifer sighed. "Promise at least that you'll tell me whether or not I'm on another false trail."

"I think you already know the answer to that," Miss Martin said primly. "Now — what if you discovered that the boy were living comfortably and in a good family?"

"I'd probably just peep at him from afar and silently wish him good luck — or a continuation of the good luck he's already enjoying."

"And — to go to the other extreme — if he were living in some workhouse orphanage?"

"I'd take him out and adopt him at once."

"But you're single. It wouldn't be allowed."

"I'd get married."

"Ha! Just like that!"

"No. I know a man who'd marry me tomorrow, by special licence if necessary. My mother wouldn't withhold her consent, either."

"Ah."

There was just enough disbelief in her voice to make Jennifer add: "I'd marry Barry Moore, if you want to know. We're engaged already."

Miss Martin started at the name. "Of Ludgvan?" she asked. "Crissy Collett's nephew?"

"Yes. Of course — I forgot you'd be bound to know him."

"I'm his godmother," she said. "Not that I'm proud of the job I made of it. But ... oh dear! I think I'm going to have to break a confidence soon. Let's see how much you already know, perhaps without even realizing it."

Jennifer felt her mouth going dry. She knew something big — monstrous even — was about to happen yet she could not even guess the shape of it.

"The most important clue has been staring you in the face ever since — well, ever since you found ... let's go on calling him Moses for a little while longer. The brooch. Mrs Collett told you she lost it, remember?"

"To a kleptomaniac friend." Jennifer had sudden waves of gooseflesh up and down the backs of her arms. The monstrous truth was just beginning to take a monstrous shape; she felt a desperate urge to flee from it and never let it catch up with her.

"Which is the more likely thief?" Miss Martin went on relentlessly. "A mysterious 'kleptomaniac friend' or a member of the family? One who has already shown himself to be irresponsible to the point of amorality — if not actual immorality?"

Jennifer closed her eyes and let her head sink to her chest. "Is Moses's real name Barry? Barry junior?" she asked in a barely audible monotone.

Miss Martin exhaled a huge sigh.

The monstrous truth took shape at last. "She *knew!*" Jennifer said bitterly. "Crissy knew from the very beginning, from that very first day, that I was searching for ... Barry junior ..."

"No she didn't," Miss Martin contradicted her stoutly. "She discussed it with me. All she knew was that you were mocking the Colston-Smarts for making such a song and dance about it. You said Douglas Colston-Smart was only whipping it up so as to distract his mother from her scheme for a convalescent home. Now if you'd been searching in real earnest ... if you'd been truly conscience-stricken or anything like that ... d'you think for one moment she'd have kept the truth from you? How can you think such a thing of her?"

Jennifer felt duly chastened; it was all true, of course. In Crissy's place she'd have done exactly the same to protect a member of her own family. "Except ..." she ventured.

"What?"

"Well, I mean she knows about Barry and me. She knows I want to marry him ..."

"That's because she thinks he's sown all his wild oats and is now ready to settle down. She thinks you'll make an ideal settling-down wife for him. You must understand that where her own *family* is concerned, Crissy is ... I can't say insane, but she is certainly more unhinged than most of us would be ..."

"She once told me she thought I'd have more sense than to fall in love with Barry."

"Yes, that would be the limit of it — nothing more severe than that." She laughed mirthlessly. "A lot of lunatics are extremely plausible people, you know!"

"You don't think Barry has changed, obviously."

"No more than the leopard can change his spots."

Jennifer sank into a moody silence, which she concluded by saying, almost explosively, "Well, I shall marry him anyway."

"Of course you will, my dear," Miss Martin said in a most infuriatingly know-all tone.

Jennifer would really have exploded then if Faye had not come out onto the terrace with a face as long as she'd ever seen it. "Oh, God!" Jennifer murmured to Miss Martin the moment she saw it, "I hope her father hasn't died. I didn't think he was *that* ill."

They both rose to go to her.

At that moment Cass called out, "Now you, Rose, darling!"

"Just a moment, Cass." She continued to walk toward Faye, who was looking straight at her.

"Don't you just a moment me, my gel. We've got half an hour of good light left."

Jennifer was worried enough now by the expression on Faye's face to ignore him completely.

"D'you hear?" he shouted.

"What is it?" she asked her friend.

"Sit down, Jenny," Faye said quietly.

"Why?"

"Just *do* it!" Miss Martin grabbed her by the shoulders and made her sit on the nearest window-sill. "I never knew so perverse a young lady."

"Oi! Remember me?" Cass called out, even more angrily.

"It's Barry Moore," Faye said quietly, watching intently for Jennifer's reaction. "And it's rather bad."

"He's ... dead?" Jennifer asked in a voice she did not recognize.

"You're fined ten quid a minute," Cass shouted.

"Keep the bloody lot!" she shouted back at him.

None of the men had ever heard her use such an awful word before. It shocked them into silence until Faye had finished with her grim news.

"He's still alive," she said. "But ..." She shrugged rather than put the rest into words. "He lost a leg in France ..."

Miss Martin slipped an arm around Jennifer's shoulders; she, remembering the woman's closeness to the Colletts and Moores, did the same in return. Miss Martin gripped her even tighter.

"They had it all neatly tied back and sewn off, apparently," Faye continued. "He was shipped back to Blighty the day before yesterday, and then, yesterday, they said he'd be fit enough to travel down to Penzance — to the Royal Cornwall. That's where he is now."

"But?" Jennifer prompted. "I can hear the most dreadful *but* coming."

"But he obviously *wasn't* fit to travel. They're just so desperate for beds up around London because so many are ... you know."

"Copping a Blighty one, as they say," Jennifer said flatly, then, turning to Miss Martin, "We must go to him at once. I don't have any ... can we drive there in your car?"

"Of course, dear." She made to go, seeing that Jennifer was taking it so calmly — on the outside at least, though she did not doubt the turmoil that must be raging within.

Cass was now standing right by her. "'Ave you gawn stark, staring mad?" he asked.

"Barry's dying," she said.

"Barry?" He frowned; he was probably trying to remember a Barry in *Little Sinns*.

"Barry Moore — in real life. Crissy's nephew. My fiancé. Miss Martin's godson. *That* Barry."

"Jesus Christ!" he exclaimed and turned a full circle on one heel. Then he looked at his watch. "All right," he said magnanimously. "Fifteen minutes. We can do it all in fifteen minutes if we really ..."

"Have *you* gone stark, staring mad?" she shouted at him. "Didn't you hear what I said?"

"Perfectly," he replied coldly. "And kindly remember *whom* you are talking to. Look! See that cameraman — he's starting a new picture in Bristol tomorrow evening. He's got to pack up 'ere in 'alf an hour. That lighting man with the sun-splitter? He's on a job in Dorking this weekend. He can't stop 'ere another day. And all those people who've worked their guts out this past month to make the best movie ever — you can't let them down, darling. You're a professional now. The show must go on. You can't let everyone down like that. And what's fifteen minutes? That's all we ask. You've wasted five of them arguing like this!"

Jennifer stared hopelessly at Faye and Miss Martin, who said, "You must do what you think fit, dear. I shall drive directly to Penzance and you are welcome to come with me."

So she went with Cass, to do as he wished — not because she thought it fit but because the news had knocked all the resolve out of her and it was the line of least resistance.

"It'll be good, really," Cass said, slipping a comforting arm around her as he led the way back to the film stage. "'Cos these are all the shots where Nurse Rose has just learned about Lieutenant Silk's wounds being fatal. She knows he's only got a while to live, see." He laughed. "So you won't 'ave to act too much, eh?"

55 YET AGAIN Cass slipped an arm around Jennifer as he led her back into Little Sinns, through the great, echoing entrance hall, making for the front courtyard. "Proud of you, darling," he said. "You're my star from now on. You're a real trouper. You've got what it takes."

She walked beside him as in a dream, thinking, *I have to do these things. They are demanded of me.* The truth was, there seemed to be no *me* in there to do anything else. The necessity of acting her way through those final solo responses had kept her professional self alive while all the rest had withered and perished. "Cardew Silk ..." she began — and then forgot what she was going to say about him.

"Forget him," Cass said at once.

"But he's good. I'd like to act opposite him again." It was news to her — that is, she had not thought it out beforehand — but the moment she heard herself saying it she knew it was true.

"So you shall," he said magnanimously. "But not till after this war's over. He's safe 'ere — and that Miss Martin don't seem to mind."

She said nothing as to that.

"Well," he said as they approached the main door, "I speck this'll take a month to knock into shape and another month to print and get the distributors excited, so it'll likely be July before you'll see your name in lights in Leicester Square. What'll you do meanwhile?"

The obvious answer was that she'd stay on at Little Sinns and work as an auxiliary, as she had at Medrose — if Miss Martin would have her; but she knew better by now than to say obvious things to Cass. "I suppose I'll just wait and see what offers roll in," she replied vaguely. "I can't think clearly at the moment."

"Ah." He cleared his throat of no particular obstruction and fished in one of those ridiculous pockets. "I do 'appen to 'ave a contract 'ere, which you might care to peruse at your leisure. Let me know by tonight, 'cos I'm off to the Smoke tomorrow." He threw wide the front door and, waving a showman's hand before them, said, "Voy-la! Compliments of the company!"

A Renault.

For one wild moment she thought he was giving it to her as a present. Then the driver stepped out, tipped his cap, and said, "This the lady for Penzance, mister?"

"Fast as you can," Cass said. "Mission of mercy."

While the driver swung the starting handle Cass ushered her to the taxi. "No expense spared, darling," he said. "Compliments of Global. We look after our stars. He'll drive you all the way to Penzance. Tell 'im to wait if you want bringing back — else let 'im go. 'E's costing enough as it is."

She managed a laugh. She also managed a little kiss on his cheek. Even when doing something generous he had to pretend to be mean.

As they pulled out past Davies in his lodge she settled into the soft embrace of the upholstery and closed her eyes. The driver saw the gesture and swallowed the smalltalk he had been about to launch.

She sought within her for some remnant of a self who was not Rose English, Global star and real trouper. Finding none, she tried instead to think of Barry. Still no images came. She said the words that should evoke them: Carleen, the Flow, Gurnard's Head, Chysauster … but not even Chysauster could conjure up a picture for her comfort. She knew why, of course. Any such vision of him would mock the present reality. He wasn't dying. She would not even contemplate that. He was too tough, too hearty, too fond of life, too important for the future. But he had lost a leg and he was … well, critically ill — that much she could accept. Her mind skirted delicately round the memory that she had once, fleetingly, prayed for him to lose just one limb, so that at least he'd come home alive and never have to face another enemy bullet or shell. She tried to push the memory from her. If God had answered that prayer, she'd never forgive Him — by which she meant herself.

But it was too early to think of never forgiving herself. Barry was going to live. He was too tough, too hearty, too fond of life, too important for the future … and so her thoughts went round and round in an endless, numbing cycle. And each new revolution brought her to that comforting thought: It was too early yet to think of never forgiving herself.

"Too late, Miss Owen!" the Dragon said as soon as Jennifer appeared in the corridor.

She must have been standing there waiting.

It was a shock to Jennifer to realize, now, for the first time, that the woman must have hated her during that brief period she was in training there. Why? She wanted to stop and ask her. She almost did. She wanted to do anything that would postpone the dreadful moment which now loomed for her.

"He kept asking for you," the woman added as Jennifer walked on leaden feet toward her. "We kept assuring him you wouldn't be long."

Miss Martin appeared at that moment, standing on the threshold to one of the wards. "Enough!" she said firmly to the matron, who turned angrily on her heel and flounced away — inasmuch as anyone of her build could flounce at all.

"My dear, I'm so sorry …" Miss Martin advanced toward her.

Faye was close behind … and the Colletts … and her mother.

Jennifer ran to her mother, flung herself into her embrace, hugged her tight, and wondered why she could not weep.

Because no one called 'Action!' she thought bitterly.

Killed in action … her feelings had been killed in action.

She felt dizzy. There was a weird churning in her midriff.

"Where is he?" she whispered. "Can I …?"

"They've just taken him down to the mortuary, darling," Goronwy said. "He died even before Miss Martin and Miss Carminowe left Redruth, so you wouldn't have …"

Jennifer heard no more. She knew where the mortuary was, of course, and she was already running toward it. There were shouts behind her … voices she recognized from another world … different rules … she felt she could fly. Very dreamlike.

Pursued by voices, footsteps, anger, alarm, she flew across the back yard to the little granite outhouse in the far corner.

The door was padlocked.

She kicked it.

They were rebuilding a wall nearby. Stones in sorted heaps. Little ones. Big ones. She picked the largest she could handle and hurled it at the hasp and staple.

Gasps filled the air behind her. The strength of the insane — she knew all about that.

"If" — something, something, something — "call the police." It was the Dragon's voice but she didn't get all the words.

"Open it," she yelled. Or whispered. Said, anyway.

Something more about the police.

"Do open it." Did she say that or Miss Martin?

Miss Martin, probably.

Why couldn't she see everything as one whole scene? Why this confusing kaleidoscope of unrelated images?

She saw hands, keys, bits of uniform, polished toecaps … she even thought she saw the words, 'most irregular' painted on the door but some small bit of her brain, still clutching on to sanity, told her she had probably heard them, instead.

Darkness. Smell of carbolic. Cold. Avoid that stone.

(How did that get there?)

She drew the sheet from his face and, from that moment forth, the rest
of the world ceased to be. He was at peace — who, seeing *that,* could
doubt it? Fear no more the heat o' the sun.

His hand, dislodged by the movement of the sheet, fell from his chest.
She reached beneath the shrouds and pressed it to her belly. At once the
dizziness passed and the churning was stilled. Then, too, the images she
had striven to recall came flooding back ...

Barry, fit as a young bull, wrestling his cousin Gerald on the Flow —
golden boy with golden sun in his curly brown hair.

Barry on the front steps at Chyandour, safe, safe, safely home. "Miss
Owen, I presume?" He remembered her!

Barry in walks around the Medrose gardens, shyly talking of his poems.

Barry at Gurnard's Head, troubled eyes, gazing at the horizon, recalling
horrors no articulate words could wrap.

Barry at Chysauster, his dark head above me, against the afternoon.
Yes, I said. Now! And that ecstasy ...

She removed her hand but his remained of its own volition, or so it
seemed, pressing her belly.

"Yes," she said all over again — and then, at last, the tears began to
flow quite freely.

Kindly hands plucked her from the dark, drew her back into the light.

56 ON THE FOLLOWING Saturday morning Barry was laid to rest
beside his grandparents in Helston churchyard — the first of their
line to join them there. It was a large funeral, even by Cornish standards,
for the family that Crissy had once fought to reunite was now established
and prosperous. Even so, there was one there who probably felt herself
one too many, for she stood well back from the throng, half hidden
behind a hedge of tightly clipped yew: Ann Hotchkiss.

Two too many, in fact, for she had brought the boy as well: Barry junior.
Jennifer spotted them from the moment of their arrival, though they
tried to slip in unobserved, after the melancholy business had started. Bit
by bit she shuffled among the mourners, working her way outward to a
point where she could walk to join them.

Ann Hotchkiss saw her coming and looked for a way to escape, but it
was too late. Jennifer had anticipated that.

When she joined them she smiled at Ann, to put her at her ease, and
smiled at the boy she would always think of as 'Moses.' Then she turned

to face the ceremony once again. She saw Miss Martin whisper something to her mother, who turned and smiled sympathetically at her.

Every now and then she stole a glance at the boy. There was no doubting his parenthood, not with those rich, chestnut curls and his dark, deepset eyes. *Barry would have been proud of his son,* she told herself. Then she thought, *What am I saying! He* was *proud of the lad!*

Crissy had explained it all to her since Barry's death. Ann Harris, as she then was, a servant at the Moores' farm in Ludgvan, had at first tried to conceal the birth, but when the Moores offered to support her and the baby, she'd agreed to keep it. But then, after a year or so, she'd had the chance of marriage, had panicked and abandoned the baby ... only to come to her senses a few hours later. She'd returned to Carleen to find the baby gone, of course, but people in the village told her they'd seen Martha Walker with the boy, going toward Helston, not ten minutes since. She'd caught up with Martha and tried to get the baby back, but Martha said no, it was finders keepers. (Martha said all that was a pack of lies. Jennifer believed she had genuinely fogotten — given the damage she had done to her mind and body since then.) But Mrs Tregear, her future mother-in-law, had proved more accommodating, and so the Moores (and Ann Hotchkiss, as she now was) had got the boy back again, leaving Mrs Tregear to spin a yarn about selling him to someone called Hoskin — a name close enough to Hotchkiss to explain her 'mistake' if the need ever arose. Somewhere in all these transactions and wanderings the bun-penny brooch had genuinely been lost.

Jennifer found she lacked the courage to ask the one question that still remained to be answered: Why — knowing that Ann Hotchkiss was working as an auxiliary at Little Sinns — had Crissy chosen to give her a replica of the brooch on the day that shooting began? Did she just not think? That was hardly credible. Or did she feel guilty at having been less than frank with her about the whole business? Did she *want* her to find out about Barry's connection with 'Moses' without directly betraying it herself? Or was she just the sort of person who enjoys dropping lighted matches into powder magazines to see what happens?

Jennifer excused her cowardice in failing to ask these questions by saying that people had a right to keep some secrets to themselves. One day she'd pluck up the courage, perhaps.

After a while Barry junior — she'd better get used to naming him properly — became aware of her glances and began returning them. At first his expression was half puzzled, half apprehensive; but when he saw her smiling down at him, he relaxed and smiled back.

That smile!

It almost split her in two. It was Barry on the Flow again ... Barry at Chysauster ... Barry in her heart for ever. Tears she thought she had wept out of her all that week began to pour again.

Ann began to cry, too.

Barry junior moved between them and took a hand of each, squeezing hard, shaking them almost angrily.

When the interment was over and people began talking to drown out the repeated thud of earth on coffin, Jennifer sniffed the salt from the caverns of her nose and eyes and, squatting beside the boy, said, "He was a fine man. One of the finest. If you grow up tall and strong like him, you'll be worthy the name you bear."

Even as she spoke she thought what dreadfully trite sentiments they were. She longed to take him in her arms, to tell him she had once carried him so proudly home, that the memory of him had dogged her ever since in one way or another ... but, of course, it would be impossible. What would such words mean to a robust, outgoing little boy of seven, standing apart at the funeral of a father who only half acknowledged him? *That* was the gap he must now learn to leap. So the sentiments he would expect, and later recall, would have to do instead.

Unseen by Jennifer, Crissy turned and beckoned Ann to join them — the call of *family* overwhelming that of respectability at last, as it always would with her. Ann nudged her son's shoulder. "Go to your Aunty Crissy," she said. "Tell her I'll come directly."

His father's son, he went without a backward glance — and a swagger that once again brought a lump to Jennifer's throat. Her sinews cracked as she rose to her full height.

"I shan't let him go," Ann told her quietly.

"Of course not! The very idea!" She could not quite bring herself to say the thought had never entered her mind because, of course, it had.

"I just thought ..." Ann's tone was now turning apologetic. "You being so rich and all ..."

"Well — talking of that — I mean, I suppose you know my connection with Barry? You know we were going to announce our engagement?"

Ann nodded. Her eyes were expressionless — at least, Jennifer could read neither jealousy nor sadness there.

"Well, I'd like to help where I can — but without ever getting between you and him, you understand."

"I never told the lad about ... you know — what happened that day in Carleen and all that."

"He'll never hear a word of it from me — and I'll see that Martha never breathes as much as a whisper. But — as I was going to say — if ever there's an emergency and mere money can help ... medical bills, though God forbid, school fees ... university fees, in time ... indentures ... you know the sort of thing. As I say, if ever mere money can help, and I'm still in a position to provide it, well, I'll keep in touch with the Moores and the Colletts, and I'll only ever be as far away as the nearest telegraph office. I mean it now. I know people say these things but I really do mean it."

Ann nodded warily and licked her lips. "There is one thing, though I don't hardly like to ..." She hesitated.

"What? Just say it. If I possibly can ..."

"That brooch."

"Ah."

"If I could ... I mean, if you could ..." Her voice trailed off as she saw Jennifer shaking her head.

"Anything else but not that, please," Jennifer said. "I know it's not *the* one but it has the same origins. Besides" — she smiled — "Barry junior is long past the nappy stage, isn't he! And I rather think I shall be needing it ... in about four months' time." She put her hand to her belly in case the woman didn't take her meaning.

Ann stared at the place in disbelief.

"I know," Jennifer said. "I think we finished the movie just in time."

Ann looked her in the eye then, head on one side, smiling sympathetically as the full truth washed over her. "You too, eh?" she said.

Then, united by memories and emotions they could never have put into words the two women threw their arms around each other and wept yet again. And they continued thus until Barry junior came running back to them. He tugged at their skirts and pleaded in his piping little treble: "Please don't! Please stop! Please!"